Liberty has still a continent to live in.

HORACE WALPOLE, 1779

Marshall B. Davidson

LIFE

IN

AMERICA

BICENTENNIAL EDITION

WITH A NEW INTRODUCTION

BY THE AUTHOR

Volume I

Published in Association with
the Metropolitan Museum of Art

Houghton Mifflin Company Boston

1974

FIRST PRINTING   W

Library of Congress Cataloging in Publication Data
Davidson, Marshall B   Life in America.
"Published in association with the Metropolitan Museum of Art."
Bibliography: v. 2, p.
  1. United States—Civilization—History.   I. Title.
E169.1.D35   1974   917.3'03   74-10940

PRINTED IN THE UNITED STATES OF AMERICA

CONTENTS

INTRODUCTION

TO THE SECOND EDITION

LIFE IN AMERICA was originally published in 1951. The purpose of the two volumes was to provide a basic account of American experience from the days of the first discoverers and settlers up to the middle of the present century. To bring fresh understanding to that experience the story was presented in a blend of pictures, almost exclusively the work of contemporary eyewitnesses, and a text that complemented that graphic history with other documentary evidence from written records of the past — unalterable testimony in large part.

Such a presentation of words and illustrations in close and interdependent relationship was a pioneering venture at the time the books were first issued, as was recognized by a number of responsible critics and commentators. In a report commissioned by the Carnegie Corporation, for example, it was observed that *Life in America* was "the first successful attempt (and an ambitious one) to tell this particular story through a carefully contrived balance between pictures and text. For establishing America in the eye of the mind, there is no other volume . . . so useful as this one." As a tribute to the publisher, the books received the Carey-Thomas Award for Creative Publishing in 1951. In some important

respects, it has become increasingly clear, such a counterpoint of visual and verbal reporting offers more enlightenment than either element alone can provide, as the statement just quoted attests.

For more than two centuries after the first permanent colony was established at Jamestown, America remained on the remote fringe of Western civilization. In 1797, when John Quincy Adams arrived at the capital of Prussia to present his credentials as minister to that court, one dashing officer of the guards frankly admitted that he had never even heard of the United States of America. A brief generation ago the United States emerged victorious from a global war as the richest and most powerful nation on earth, faced with unprecedented responsibilities that came with world leadership — leadership of the free world, that is, engaged in a cold war with the totalitarian forces mustering behind the Iron Curtain.

Much has happened since then, developments that have both confirmed and challenged Americans' traditional notions about themselves and their country. Twice in that time the United States has gone to war in far places of the earth, in Korea and Indochina, where the nation's vaunted invincibility has been put to question. Or, as might better be said, any attempt to demonstrate such invincibility has implied unthinkable consequences, as was foreshadowed at Hiroshima and Nagasaki with the ending of the last world war. As Ralph Waldo Emerson long ago suggested in his essay "Compensation," if the force is there so is the limitation. His words have taken on fresh meaning for the present generation. It has become increasingly apparent that the extremes of power are indeed hedged by troubles and perils that cannot safely be ignored — in peace as in war. "The farmer imagines power and place are fine things," wrote the Sage of Concord in 1841. "But the President has paid dear for his White House. It has commonly cost him all his peace, and the best of his manly attributes." Emerson was writing in a time of intense political factionalism, but he was thinking in terms of universal principles that he considered timeless.

In recent years also, Americans have not only reached for the moon but have actually walked and driven about the lunar landscape and returned safely to earth, while the world at large watched those excursions on television screens. Although a science-fiction poet of the 1830's, a contemporary of Emerson's, related how in his "breath bag" and with "the high pressure on" he had streaked off to the moon for breakfast, any real prospect of travel through the heavens was virtually inconceivable to the ordinary layman a bare two decades ago. Yet the exploration of outer space has so quickly become commonplace that today it hardly rates headline billing.

What earthly good will come of such awesome ventures and how the results may affect the daily lives of Americans and of mankind will no doubt eventually become clear enough to the man in the street. In 1784 when ballooning was all the rage in Paris, someone asked Benjamin Franklin what was the use of this new invention. "What good is a new-born child?" Franklin retorted. However sophisticated today's space machines may be in contrast to a hot-

air balloon, the program they have been serving is still in its infancy.

Such audacious ventures into outer space would, of course, be impossible without the electronic computing devices that have become the ubiquitous tools of the current age. The "computer revolution" is confronting us with incalculable hoards of data which we are as yet not sure how best to use. It may be indeed that we have manufactured more computers than there is any present good use for. But, as Thorstein Veblen long ago pointed out, in the competitive strife of American business, once a "necessary" gadget is adopted by one firm it becomes obligatory for all rival firms to follow suit, regardless of how much it may complicate procedures in unfamiliar ways. Not to keep pace would be to lose some small advantage, or at least prestige, and thus risk losing business. The same conditions apply to personal and social affairs. When most of one's friends and neighbors have a telephone, an automobile, or a color television set, it becomes almost obligatory to own these things oneself. Not to do so is to risk isolation, to rob us of a sense of community which is vital to our human needs. Few of us can suffer loneliness with such rapture as Henry Thoreau did in his retreat at Walden Pond.

As Veblen also observed, invention is the mother of necessity. The innovations developed by such huge and fertile corporations as I.B.M., Xerox, and Polaroid, for example, have produced things and introduced practices for which there was no demand and which did not exist before World War II — things and practices to which the daily routine of American life has already become inseparably geared.

While the achievements of the past several decades have proceeded at an accelerated and sometimes bewildering pace, our traditional moral and social patterns have been altered in ways that often seem disquieting to some, liberating to others. In confrontation with a rapidly changing scene, American democracy must meet unprecedented problems that will test its flexibility and, perhaps, its viability. As we approach the two-hundredth anniversary of the Declaration of Independence, it appears that the nation may be rounding out a great, primary cycle in its historical development and entering a new phase of its destiny.

Nothing much changes on the occasion of an anniversary. The main currents of history flow along without regard for the calendar. Yet, the occasion inevitably assumes a symbolic importance; it becomes a moment of stock-taking and reckoning, a point from which to consider how the past has led us to the present and how the present may foreshadow the future.

In the end we are what the past has made us. Seen in historical perspective, the technological developments of the past several decades, for example, appear to be remarkable not so much because they have involved new principles, as because the rate of progress along such lines has been immeasurably stepped up. Despite the wonderworking nature of the novel devices and accessories that surround our daily lives, in a true sense they represent a traditional aspect of American experience. This country entered the industrial stage of development somewhat later than England and other European nations but without the hampering drag of centuries-old social and cultural habits and attitudes to impede its advances. As one consequence, the dynamics of technological progress has been more insistent and more readily acceptable here than in those older countries. It has long been apparent that nowhere on earth has a society been so profoundly modified, so richly benefited or so pitilessly tested by the advances of technology as in America. The differences between today's ways and means and those of an earlier generation are often more matters of degree than of kind.

Many years ago Henry Adams foresaw the probable outcome of the scientific developments he witnessed in his own day.

According to the "ratios and curves" he projected, man had unleashed forces moving in an unbroken sequence that was even then rapidly accelerating. They were implacable forces that could not be held in check, that would before long "tip thought upside down" and, among other dismal consequences, lead to "cosmic violence." (At some not very distant day, he mused, the human race might commit suicide by blowing up the world.) Were there to be another generation, Adams thought, a new social mind would have to evolve. His informed pessimism was expressed at a time when the nation was reaching new peaks of material prosperity and scientific achievement. He was suggesting what has long since become clearly evident, that in themselves such "advances" solved few of the fundamental problems of human existence or of American democracy as a form of government. The American dream was formed with a belief that all of the people had a right to share in the material abundance which the country was sure to produce, and had a reasonable expectancy of doing so. Technology and democracy would triumph together. Yet, in our own day we have seen confusion and distress grow from the very process that has provided material abundance.

In spite of all his pessimism, however, it seemed likely to Adams that America, more than any other country, would shape the uncertain future in the course of the twentieth century, for better or for worse. The nation was not only a youthful industrial giant, a technological prodigy of unimaginable potential, it was also a cluster of ideas and ideals that had no counterpart elsewhere in the world. In his earnest pursuit of happiness the American has often enough been accused, and not unreasonably, of crass materialism; but he has also been accused of impractical idealism, as, for example, in the person of Woodrow Wilson with his Fourteen Points, acting as a self-designated savior of the Old World.

Over the years in America faith in the

democratic process, this government "of laws, and not of men" that had a mission to the world at large, took on the fervor of a state religion. That faith was not limited to the United States. On the eve of the Civil War, the Frenchman Alexis de Tocqueville, that most perceptive of critics of America, wrote: "I earnestly hope that the great experiment in self-government which is carried out in America will not fail. If it did, it would be the end of political liberty in our world." And there were other responsible spokesmen who continued to watch the course of that crucial conflict for the same reasons and with equal concern. In our own day representative democracy is beset with other plaguing difficulties that are hardly less serious and that will not be resolved before these words appear in print. Political leaders of other lands are concerned anew over the course of American political developments, for they recognize that their nations' freedom depends heavily on the durability of American institutions, as Tocqueville had observed might be the case.

Winston Churchill once and for all described democracy as "the worst form of government except all those other forms that have been tried from time to time." As remarked in the concluding pages of these books, for all its awkwardness and, at times, its almost intolerable slowness of procedure, our democratic system has thus far served us exceptionally well. But the freedom and prosperity we have enjoyed have not been solely the triumph of political genius. During most of the formative period of our nation we enjoyed a safe isolation from the territorial rivalries and warring contentions that so often rocked Europe in that time. And we had what seemed to be illimitable resources to draw upon.

America was built on wastefulness. As Woodrow Wilson pointed out early in this century, the nation was heedless and in a hurry to be great, and must sooner or later face the consequences — count the cost of its prosperity in terms of its squandered resources. Our present day and age finds that cost almost prohibitively high; a circumstance that poses an unexpectedly severe test of the nation's ingenuity and adaptability. The earth, air, and water, which we long took for granted in their life-giving abundance, have become precious resources to be conserved and preserved.

The problems of democracy are never settled. Since these books were first published, violent protests against our extravagant and, to many, dubious military programs, along with questions dealing with civil rights, have shredded the fabric of American society. In those decades the power of central government has extended its reach over the lives of individual Americans to a degree unimaginable during the previous century and a half. For many citizens that growing dependence upon a remote and impersonal bureaucracy has robbed them of a sense of shared purposes which was so essential to the survival and development of American communities in earlier stages of our country's history; which is, indeed, still close to the concept of any livable society, and of freedom itself. One can see in the youth movements of the 1960's and in the black militancy of the same years a quest for some more immediate community of interest than can be found in the complex political framework of the time. In this same connection, in recent years, the long-professed faith in the American melting pot has been questioned by a wide variety of ethnic groups — whites, reds, and browns as well as blacks — who revert to their special group identities as a form of needed social security against what appears to be indifference on the part of government. Those in authority, to be sure, have not always been true to the high principles they have professed. There were flaws, indeed, in the idealism of our founding fathers, as the problems of integrating our present society so poignantly reminds us. Nevertheless, in formulating the declaration of Independence and the Constitution, these men had, so far as they were able — and they were exceptionally able men — re-examined the "inalienable rights" of those who must live in a governed society and had given their conclusions eloquent expression.

Changing circumstances have brought us a fresh and heightened awareness of such matters. As the late Carl Lotus Becker wrote, it is well for us to revere those men, but better to follow their example and re-examine the fundamental human rights and the economic and political institutions best suited to secure them in the light of our own times. The recent debate over the powers and privileges of the presidential office, with all their ramifications, represents such a re-examination. Arduous and painful as it may prove to be, the occasional critical review of our governmental studies is a vital function of American democracy.

However, for all that has happened since the original publication of these two volumes, most of the basic trends of life in America follow directions that were established in earlier years, as described and pictured in the following chapters. As in the century and more before the last world war, the gravitational pull of metropolitan areas continues to drain Americans off their farms and away from their small towns; and the lure of the suburbs increasingly spreads the old problems of cities — congestion, crime, traffic, and civic management — out into the neighboring countryside. The westward movement in America continues its historic trend. Between 1960 and 1970 the nation's center of population moved almost twenty-seven miles to the West. (At the latter date it lay specifically in a soybean field not far from St. Louis.) Thanks to the addition of Alaska and Hawaii to the Union in 1959, the geographical center of the country has jumped to a point close to the conjunction of Wyoming, Montana, and South Dakota — even though a vast majority of Americans clings to the seaboards of the nation.

In the past several decades, jet planes have largely superseded railroads and ocean liners for passenger travel — to such a degree that, for all the increased speed along the airways, congestion at and above airports brings diminishing rewards to the traveler, as it had begun to do well before jet planes were in service. Along the ground routes, "the final peaceful conquest of an empire by the internal combustion engine," predicted by the *New York Times* in 1947 as a newly planned country-wide system of integrated superhighways was charted, has hardly been realized. As the nation has become progressively paved over with such concrete paths and platforms, the dream that inspired them tends to become a nightmare of substantial dimensions.

In many other ways we have in recent times been rudely awakened from what has often and reverentially been referred to as "the American Dream" — the vision of a land and a people, in the words of George Washington, "peculiarly designated by Providence for the display of human greatness and felicity." On the other hand, the traditions that have developed over the centuries and that have given shape to life in America are by no means dead. Life is more complicated than it has been in the past, and its rhythms more hurried. But what is significant in contemporary American life remains deeply rooted in our experience as a people. We face a future of unavoidable change and challenge. But change and challenge as such are hardly unprecedented in American experience. Our inheritance from the past is rich in principle and in practice, and will serve us well as we choose to use it for self-understanding and confidence.

A new generation has come of age since the following chapters were written. I hope that it will find the books as worthy as earlier readers apparently did. A word should be said about the illustrations. Great stores of pictorial material have come to light in the last quarter of a century. However, it is comforting to reflect, there is little of this material that I would choose to substitute for the original selections. It should be added that some pictures originally found in private collections may have changed hands. In such instances it has not seemed feasible to trace subsequent ownership. The illustrations credited to libraries, museums, and other institutions — by far the majority — are still where they were and will no doubt remain there.

INTRODUCTION

TO THE FIRST EDITION

THIS BOOK was started five years ago when the trustees of the Metropolitan Museum of Art generously granted me a leave of absence from my duties as associate curator of the American Wing to prepare a graphic survey of American history. Several years earlier the Museum had held an exhibition of documentary paintings, also entitled *Life in America,* whose great success clearly indicated how compelling and revealing a visual account of our national history could be. It also suggested that a broader outline of pictorial resources would further clarify our understanding of the American experience. Such an outline this work purports to be.

A great mass of graphic material relating to this country's history awaits anyone who sets out to find it. Our large public museums, libraries, and historical societies abound with pictorial treasures of every variety, as the acknowledgments under the illustrations that follow clearly show. Many private collections include prints, drawings, and paintings of the greatest interest to historians, as do art stores throughout the land. In Europe, too, pictures relating to the American scene exist in quantities yet undetermined. Items occasionally turn up in unexpected places. One of the original drawings reproduced later was found in the win-

dow of a seafood restaurant in a small New Jersey town.

Yet, while good pictures often seem to be everywhere, at times they seem to be nowhere. Many important episodes of American history were witnessed only by people who had more immediate and urgent things to do than to make a sketch for posterity. In other cases a painting or drawing may constitute the most convincing record that remains of the past—at times, indeed, the only one—and it comes to light only as the result of a persistent search.

To select from such varied and scattered sources a practicable number of examples which most faithfully, expressively, and completely depict the American past has been my serious intention. I have been more concerned with social forces than with politics, personalities, and military matters. This eliminated at the start most of a large category of caricatures and cartoons, portraits, and battle scenes. For the most part I have avoided historical reconstructions by artists working long after the events they describe. At times, to be sure, such *ex post facto* depictions have a special value. Leutze's paintings of Washington crossing the Delaware, although incorrect in almost every detail, have become a symbol of an episode of great importance to Americans. In other cases purely imaginative representations, such as some of the early engravings of the New World, reflect a contemporary state of mind and feeling that is significant in itself.

However, by far the largest number of illustrations reproduce the work of eyewitnesses or of contemporaries well-enough informed to draw a scene faithfully. In more than a few instances I have been fortunate enough to locate the original drawings or paintings from which well-known prints were copied—copied sometimes with considerable license by the engraver. The fairly rare lithograph of Fort George from Captain Warre's published account of his travels to the west coast in 1846, for instance, is a loose and inaccurate copy of Warre's on-the-spot sketch which is reproduced in Chapter Two. Those to whom such matters are of special interest will recognize other examples of the same sort in the pages that follow, although they have not usually been noted in the captions or text.

A fair number of subjects, more than could be quickly listed, are illustrated here for the first time. They have been included not for that reason, however, but because they served a purpose better than any other pictures that came to hand or mind. Many others, chosen for the same reason, have previously appeared only in obscure publications and in quite different contexts. No effort was made to by-pass old favorites which in spite of their familiarity still speak more convincingly than other versions of the subject, however interesting those may be from the standpoint of rarity.

In trying to restrict the illustrations to contemporary, faithful representations I have voluntarily accepted certain limitations. One hundred years after the Revolution illustrators galore re-created the colonial scene, sometimes with scholarly care, sometimes without fear and without research. In either case such re-creations belong more to the time when they were made than to the time of their subject matter. We have all too few graphic records of very early American life drawn by men who lived at the time.

There are remarkable survivals, of course, such as the enchanting little water colors by Champlain, the skilled drawing by Le Bouteux, the primitive but forceful engravings by Paul Revere, and many others. And how fortunate that a reporter-artist was aboard the little ship *Columbia* on the epochal voyage during which she, first of ships, entered the Columbia River! But there remain gaps in the pictorial sequence that no amount of searching would close.

For the text which runs parallel to the illustrations and which in part serves to carry the narrative when they are lacking, I have relied chiefly on information to be found in standard authorities and, particularly for contemporary quotations, on the primary sources to which those helpful authorities have so conveniently directed me. All are acknowledged in the bibliography at the end of Volume Two.

George Pierce Baker, Roger Burlingame, Bernard DeVoto, Foster Rhea Dulles, J. Kenneth Galbraith, Howard Mumford Jones, Allan Nevins, Arthur M. Schlesinger, Walter M. Whitehill, and Louis B. Wright have been kind enough to read parts of the text and to offer helpful criticisms. For whatever errors remain I alone am responsible.

Those who have allowed me to use material from their collections, private and public, have done so with unfailing courtesy and friendliness. To them all I proffer sincere thanks. R. W. G. Vail, Director of the New-York Historical Society, and his staff—particularly Miss Dorothea Barck, Arthur B. Carlson, and Donald Shelley—led me to materials in that institution, so rich in resources, which I could never otherwise have found. Miss Grace Mayer, Curator of Prints at the Museum of the City of New York, has constantly helped me, with patience and with rare knowledge and understanding. Hirst Milhollen, Milton Kaplan, and Paul Vanderbilt in the Prints and Photographs Divisions of the Library of Congress gave me many valuable suggestions. Clarence S. Brigham and his associates at the American Antiquarian Society in Worcester, Lawrence

C. Wroth at the John Carter Brown Library in Providence, Lawrence W. Jenkins at the Peabody Museum of Salem, Randolph G. Adams and Colton Storm at the William L. Clements Library at Ann Arbor, Stanley Pargellis and Mrs. Pierce Butler at the Newberry Library in Chicago, Miss Anna Wells Rutledge at the Maryland Historical Society, Miss Josephine Setze at the Yale University Art Gallery, Herbert G. Kellar at the McCormick Agricultural Library in Chicago, Boies Penrose at the Pennsylvania Historical Society, Paul M. Angle and Alfred F. Hopkins at the Chicago Historical Society, Karl Kup and many of his associates at the New York Public Library—these and many others have all made it a pleasure to work at their institutions and have given much constructive aid. Mrs. J. Insley Blair, James Hazen Hyde, and the late William H. Coverdale, among others, generously allowed me to choose from their collections. Harry Shaw Newman and Edward Eberstadt have been unceasingly co-operative and helpful. My own colleagues have offered friendly encouragement and advice at every turn. To Francis Henry Taylor, Director of the Metropolitan Museum of Art, at whose specific suggestion I undertook this work, I am especially indebted. For granting me the time during which I collected much of my material I am deeply grateful to the trustees of the Museum.

The book would never have reached the stage of publication without the very considerable and valuable help I have had from Miss Katharine Bernard, Miss Helen Phillips, Craig Wylie, and Paul Brooks of Houghton Mifflin Company.

I
COLONIAL
AMERICA

COLONIAL AMERICA

INTRODUCTION

MAN will never again have the opportunity that opened to him four and a half centuries ago with the discovery of America. Then, as today, Western civilization was disillusioned by the recent past, dissatisfied with the present, and uncertain of the future. Christian Europe, divided by discordant forces, menaced by Mongol hordes at its borders, looked for a new heaven and a new earth. Within a generation it discovered both, the one through its own renascent powers, the other beyond the western ocean —an entirely new world, uncorrupted by the mistakes of civilization, remote enough to serve as a refuge from unwanted interference, large and empty enough for men to give free rein to their hopes and plans for a better life.

The discovery of that New World was an historical process rather than an event. In the centuries that followed Columbus's report long-used conventions as well as untried experiments were freighted across the Atlantic. From choice as well as from necessity ties with Europe remained firm and as constant as ocean gales would permit. Although new ways developed, almost three centuries elapsed before any group in the New World felt itself free enough to cut its leading strings from the Old. Even then the surging westward movement which gave full meaning to that freedom had hardly started. The primeval wilderness presented hazard and hardship as well as shelter and opportunity; it had retreated reluctantly during those three hundred years. Only in the recent past has it finally capitulated.

When that portion of the New World which is the subject of these volumes declared itself independent its people were confined to a thin coastal strip with little general knowledge of what lay beyond the western horizon and with less understanding of how it might influence their future. But in formulating the working principles of a new society and pledging to support them with their lives, their fortunes, and their sacred honor, they gave substance to an ancient, nostalgic dream. This people, as Turgot wrote, had become "the hope of the human race." They had defined their cause with rare eloquence; they fought, endured, and won a long war to launch their purpose. But they still had to tame a wild continent and people the solitude. And they had yet to prove that a government deriving its just powers from the consent of the governed was compatible with the highest growth of the individual and that those ideas in unison could give the world a civilization as vital and lofty as any system it boasted to supplant.

BEYOND
THE WESTERN HORIZON

EUROPEANS TRADING IN THE ORIENT.

"FOLK OF FOUL STATURE AND CURSED KIND."

THE FABULOUS DRAGONS OF CARAJAM.

Illustrations from a 14th-century *Livre de Merveilles* in the Bibliothèque Nationale de France. Reproductions from the Metropolitan Museum of Art.

Long before Columbus's landfall at San Salvador men had dreamed the truth of a New World "far out in the Western Ocean, beyond the limits of the known earth." For centuries pagan prophecies, Christian legends, and sailors' yarns kept alive that prospect of a haven in the Sea of Darkness, a refuge and a land of promise that at times was identified with Paradise itself. Long after the lands of the western hemisphere had been clearly outlined on maps of the world, earnest minds continued to search them for the substance of timeless dreams. Through the fables of the ancients, the reports of early explorers, and the letters of many later immigrants sounds the same note of credulous expectancy. Beyond the western horizon lay a world where humanity might make a fresh start.

In the later Middle Ages the common man of Latin Christendom had only a misty notion of the world beyond his own province. A century of discovery, from about 1245 to 1345, which had brought Europe back into touch with the Orient, closed when the Ottoman Turks blocked the eastward trade routes. But the tales of Marco Polo, Friar Oderic of Pordenone, and other early travelers continued to remind the western world of a fabulous East whose large and glorious cities held the most profitable markets on earth. There were cities such as Canton, wrote Oderic, "as big as three Venices and all Italy has not the amount of craft this one city hath . . . indeed it is something hard to believe when you hear of, or even see, the vast scale of shipping in these parts. . . . And as for the women, they are the most beautiful in the world."

To the untraveled mind all unseen lands are equally plausible. In the markets of

Europe there was tangible evidence that the splendor of remote Cathay was a reality. But the medieval reader had no reasonable way to tell fact from fancy in most of the tales that reached him from the world beyond his own certain knowledge. The fictions of "Sir John de Mandeville," the conjectures of the fanciful, or the more accurate reporting of Marco Polo carried equal authority. According to most accounts, Christendom was surrounded by astonishing natural wonders; by lands peopled with "folk of foul stature and of cursed kind that have no heads, and their eyes be in their shoulders," and "folk that have but one foot . . . and the foot is so large that it shadoweth all the body against the sun when they would lie and rest them." Improbable beasts such as wyverns and griffons, hippogryphs and purple unicorns, stalked distant lands; or, equally marvelous, chameleons "that changeth . . . colour oftentime," "cokodrilles . . . a manner of long serpent . . . that slay men and eat them weeping," and "gerfaunts" (giraffes) that were spotted and could look over "a great high house." Geography and hearsay, natural history and romance, were hopelessly scrambled in most men's minds.

According to similar accounts ships that ventured into certain remote waters were no match for the sea monsters that fed on hapless mariners. Long after the first bold crossings had been made the horror of the Atlantic, where "tall ships founder, and deep death waits," remained a reality that only the stoutest hearts could contemplate. What might be called an official guide to voyagers in the late sixteenth century opened with the ominous advice: "First Make thy Will."

What the Norsemen may have learned about the New World centuries earlier seems to have been forgotten or ignored by later generations of seamen and geographers alike. But in the half-century before Columbus's epic journey the improvement in ship construction and rigging and the development of better navigation aids had greatly reduced the perils and difficulties of ocean sailing. In their eminently seaworthy caravels Portuguese mariners, feeling their way down the coast of Africa, reaching around its southern tip, and stabbing westward towards the Atlantic islands, were gradually dispelling the gloomy myths that had for so long shrouded the open sea. No informed person disagreed with the ancient belief that the earth was round, although estimates of its size varied widely on both sides of the correct figure, a figure closely calculated by Eratosthenes several centuries before Christ. But few doubted that in the Western Ocean there lay islands, the legendary islands of Saint Brandan, the Seven Cities, Brasil, Antilia, Salvagio, and others including, quite possibly, the Terrestrial Paradise, which a fortunate mariner might raise on a westward voyage to the Orient. So named they

MARINE MONSTERS. From Olaus Magnus, *Historia de Gentibus Septentrionalibus*, 1555.

A FIFTEENTH-CENTURY TRADING VESSEL. A contemporary etching by an unknown artist. Unfortunately no valid representation of any ship in Columbus's fleets exists. The example depicted above is of a somewhat earlier design, more full-bodied and less effectively rigged. The difficulties of maneuvering such vessels is suggested by the galley represented in the two following illustrations. For a point-to-point passage, without regard for wind or cargo needs, rowing still provided the most dependable service.

appear on pre-Columbian maps of the world and on some later ones. St. Brandan's Island and the Island of the Seven Cities, at least, are charted on the late fifteenth-century manuscript map, now in the Bibliothèque Nationale, which may have served Columbus on his first voyage. Brasil and Antilia have left their names on lands in the western hemisphere. A century after Columbus conquistadores were still searching for the Seven Cities far inland in the deserts of the American Southwest. The rest of the legendary lands quietly dropped from the map with the discoveries of Columbus.

Along the wharves and in the taverns and warehouses frequented by sailors there was undoubtedly more current gossip and geographical information than reached most writers and mapmakers of the fifteenth century. From early in the century an occasional map showed the "fantastic islands" grouped in a manner that strongly suggests the Greater Antilles, or three of them and Florida, in approximately their correct relative positions. Outlined as improbable geometric shapes and retaining their legendary names they nevertheless indicate that the myth had married the reality, that some Iberian navigators had visited the fringe of America. "Newly Reported Islands" they were designated on a map of 1435 and in much the same standard arrangement they reappear on other maps, including the one in part illustrated below that predates Columbus's first voyage by ten years. News of their actual existence was, with little doubt, among the inciting causes of Columbus's "Enterprise of the Indies." Antilia ("the land opposite") may well have been one of his expected ports of call on his westward voyage to the East.

News of Columbus's discovery was first made public in printed copies of a letter often called "The Letter to Santangel" but

PORTUGUESE VESSELS EXPLORING THE "FANTASTIC ISLES," 1482. Detail of a manuscript map by Gratiosus Benincasa, in the University Library, Bologna. North is at the left. The western shore of Portugal appears at the top right center, Ireland at the top left. Antilia (Cuba?) appears at the lower right. Salvagio is at the lower left. *Reproduction from the American Geographical Society*

The New York Public Library
THE NATIVE AMERICANS FLEEING FROM COLUMBUS.
Illustration from Columbus's "Letter to Santangel,"
Paris edition, 1493.

The New York Public Library
BUILDING NAVIDAD. From the Basel edition, 1493, of
Columbus's letter.

actually a public announcement of his success written by the discoverer. The letter was quickly translated into several languages and issued as a small pamphlet illustrated with imaginative designs representing events described in the text. It was a modest publication for one of the most revolutionary announcements in the history of the world. With Columbus's story made known the Western Ocean had once and for all loosed "the chain of things" and revealed the huge land of Seneca's ancient prophecy.

In these offshore islands of the Orient, as he considered the West Indies, Columbus's passport and his introduction from Ferdinand and Isabella to the Great Khan were of no use. "I did not thus find any towns and villages on the seacoast," he wrote of his first landing, "save small hamlets with the people whereof I could not get speech, because they all fled away forthwith." "The people of another island," he continued, "and of all others that I have found and seen, or not seen, all go naked . . . just as their mothers bring them forth . . . they know no sect nor idolatry; save that they all believe very firmly that I with these ships and crews, came from the sky . . . others went running from house to house and to the neighboring villages, with loud cries of Come! come to see the people from Heaven! . . . for traffic with the mainland both on this side and with that over there belonging to the Great Can, where there will be great commerce and profit, I took possession of a large town which I named the city of Navidad. And I have made fortification there. . . ." "This is a land to be desired," he reported, "and once seen, never to be relinquished." Had he known that it was a barbarous wilderness half a world away from his true goal, the explorer would have died a bitterly frustrated man.

Amerigo Vespucci may have been the first to realize that South America was a continent apart from Asia. In any case his account of his travels, impressively entitled the *New World,* ran through a score of editions in a short time and at the suggestion of a German geographer, who later changed his mind, Amerigo's name was given to both western continents. One of them he never saw. Whether he or Columbus first visited the mainland of the other, South America, historians have yet to agree.

Vespucci's story provided the stage for Sir Thomas More's *Utopia.* Raphael Hythloday, the narrator in More's book, relates that he sailed with Vespucci, journeyed overland in America, and discovered Utopia in the far West. There he found a government refreshingly different from any in contemporary Europe—a co-operative society; an eight-hour working day; a system of justice which needed no lawyers; and a people who enjoyed "free liberty of mind," with education for all.

Literally Utopia means Nowhere Land. But by using Vespucci's travels for his framework, More placed it in the minds of generations to come in the New World. For a long file of flesh-and-blood pioneers who followed Raphael Hythloday across the Atlantic the utopian vision led to America.

THE ARRIVAL OF AMERIGO VESPUCCI IN THE NEW WORLD. A retrospective view. Sepia drawing by Johannes Stradanus about 1580–1585. This is probably the oldest surviving picture of American fauna and flora. Apparently the artist had genuine material, brought to him by returning voyagers, before him when he made his drawing. The anteater, the bear-like creature, the horse-like tapir, the sloth climbing a tree, and the pineapple plant at the base of the tree, each has its name beside it. The word *America* is reversed for the engraving that was subsequently made from the drawing. The likeness of Vespucci seems also to be genuine, taken from the fresco of the Vespucci family in the Church of Ognissanti in Florence, painted by Ghirlandajo during the explorer's lifetime.

Collection of James Hazen Hyde

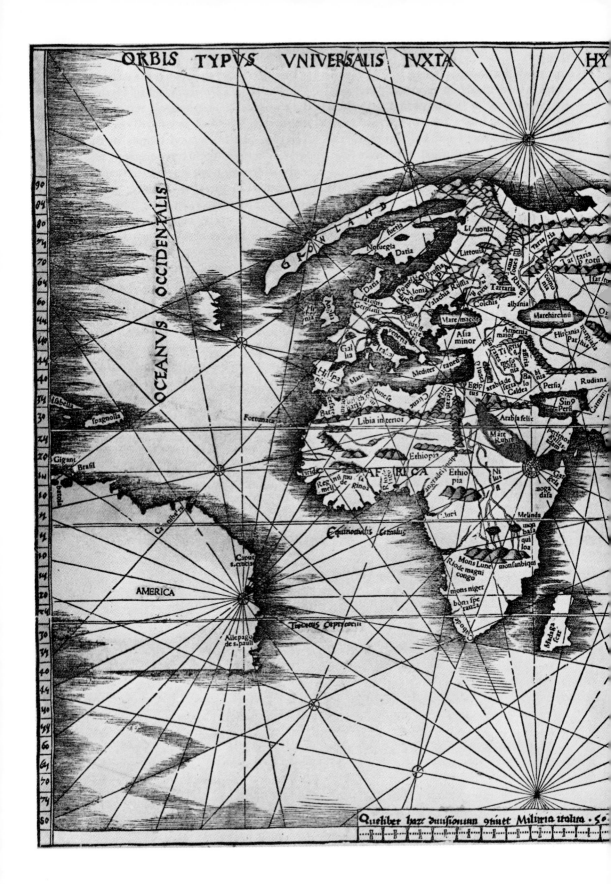

Balor regio

indei claui

Oceardo fl.

Bautifis fl.

Afmi fl. regio

Polifacus fl. fingui guin.

tholo ma puin.

Tangut p'un.

Cathaya

ASIA
Auracithis regio

facharum regio

ferica regio

Scithia intra Imau

India intra

fpiria regio

Indus fl.

Ca gangē

Quinſay ciuit

Cororou flu

Orn flu

Magi puin.

India superior

Ciamba puin.

India

Dorma fl.

gritirea

Paliandra

Murfuli regiū

Sinus magnus

Moabar regnū

Lear regnū

Iaua maior

Regnū vix

Taprobana

Mallaqua

Sin9 gam getic9

Callion cochin

anfea abafchi ande fena

Ne cuŭ

Pentā

Regnum l.ac.

Scoli

Iaua minor

10

AN EARLY APPEARANCE OF THE NAME AMERICA ON A WORLD MAP. The New World was probably first delineated on a map in 1506. In the present example, dating from about 1517, the vague little fragment of land off Greenland suggests an abiding faith in the mythical islands of the western ocean.

The John Carter Brown Library

The first reports from the West loosed a stream of discussion about the New World that broadened into a torrent in the centuries to come. Americans have never since lacked the privilege of seeing themselves as others see them. Unfortunately most of the graphic evidence of the early explorations was drawn from hearsay. Several generations passed before any artist provided authentic, eye-witness pictures of America to supplement the growing list of travel books. The very early woodcut shown below, worked by some forgotten engraver of Augsburg, borrows virtually every detail from Vespucci's description of Brazil, which he sent to Lorenzo Pietro de' Medici in 1501. "They go naked, both men and women; they have well-shaped bodies, and in color nearly red; they bore holes in their cheeks, lips, noses and ears, and stuff these holes with blue stones, crystals, marble and alabaster, very fine and beautiful. . . . They have no personal property but all things are in common. They all live together without a king and without a government, and every one is his own master . . . they eat one another. . . . In the houses salted human flesh is hung up to dry. They live to be a hundred and fifty years old, and are seldom sick."

Savage cannibals though they were, these people who lived without clothes or laws were fitted to the concept of innocent mankind, untainted by civilization, that the Old World wanted to believe in. Such strange beings were prime curiosities when they appeared on the streets of Europe. Ten red captives had returned with Columbus in 1493 and more followed in the train of later adventures, some to receive a royal welcome in the courts and palaces of Christendom.

The New York Public Library

THE INDIANS OF BRAZIL, ABOUT 1505. Wood engraving by an anonymous German artist. Although drawn from hearsay this is the first serious effort to picture native Americans. The drawings by Jacques Le Moyne, John White, and Samuel de Champlain, shown later in this chapter, are the oldest on-the-spot pictures that have survived.

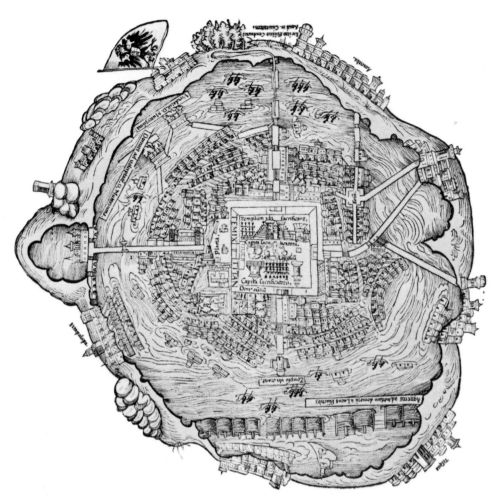

THE LAKE AND CITY OF MEXICO. From the Latin translation of Cortes, *Praeclara*, Nuremberg, 1524. The plan shows Tenochtitlan and Tlaltelolco, the two communities that composed the island city, lying in the lake filled with boats and crossed by causeways and aqueducts.

SPANISH DOMINION

Peru under the Incas, before the conquests of Pizarro, bore many resemblances to More's Utopia. When he placed his ideal commonwealth in America More may have had more real information about the Peruvian system than is generally supposed. But the notion that man had been discovered in the state of nature was as potent as any truth. "Not in vain," wrote one Spanish disciple of More, "but with much cause and reason is this called the New World, not because it is newly found, but because it is in its people and in almost everything as was the first and golden age."

Had all American Indians been the naked savages admired and envied by utopian romancers the Spanish overseas enterprise might have faded quickly enough. An easy route to the Orient, it now seemed probable, was not this way. And that America was remote from Cathay's riches had been clearly demonstrated by Magellan's round-the-

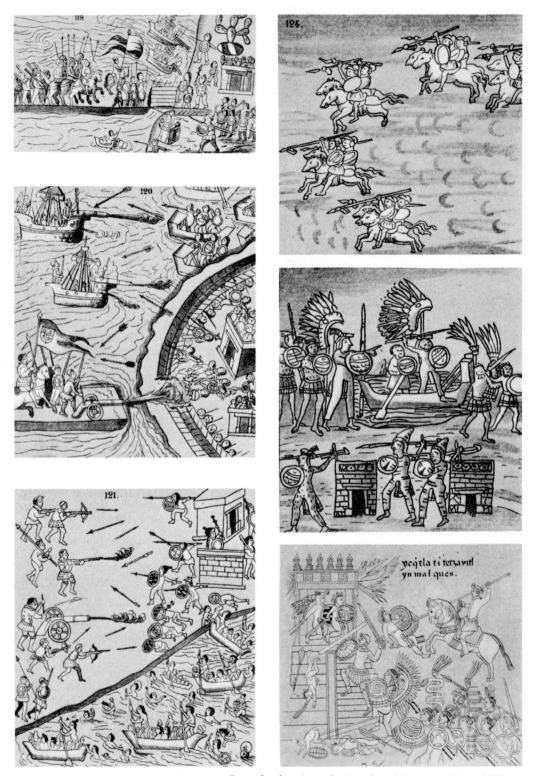

Reproductions from the American Museum of Natural History
INDIAN VERSIONS OF THE SPANISH CONQUEST. Illustrations from Indian Codices. The first five from the Codice Florentino; the last from the Lienzo de Tlaxcala; both mid-sixteenth century.

world expedition. But ten days by canoe to the west of Hispaniola were people who wore clothes and accumulated wealth in their cities. Here was a solid temptation for men of practical intentions. Cortes's conquest of these people on the plains of Teotihuacan and Pizarro's in the heights of the Andes laid open golden kingdoms that promised to outshine the legendary wealth of the Indies.

The world has rarely witnessed such triumphs as these. Mexico, the size of several Spains, Cortes took with four hundred soldiers equipped with two terrorizing agents new to the Aztecs: horses, that "swallowed the ground with fierceness and rage," and cannon, that manufactured ruinous thunder and lightning. Pizarro's men numbered only two hundred and twenty-seven. Their work was ruthless, brief, and complete.

Spain's achievements were incredible. As Germán Arciniegas has recently summarized it: "There is no phenomenon in the history of the world to compare with the conquest of America. In some, curiosity; in others, love of adventure; in nearly all, the thirst for gold and treasures moved fleets and armies with a speed that is amazing. In less than thirty years the Pacific Ocean was discovered; Mexico, Peru, Central America, Chile, the Argentine, Paraguay, Brazil, Colombia, Venezuela, were conquered; the great rivers, the Mississippi, the Amazon, the Plata, the Orinoco, the Magdalena, explored. Magellan's ships had sailed around the world; cities were founded whose names have been forever incorporated in the history of mankind: Buenos Aires, Rio de Janeiro, Mexico, Lima, Bogotá, Santiago, Quito, Panama. . . . The whole range of the Andes had been traversed and cities had been built nine, twelve thousand feet above sea-level. And all this had been done by discoverers and conquerors who came in a few little boats that did not hold fifty men each. . . . Or they hacked their way through the web of the jungles with machetes so men and horses could climb the virgin flanks of the Andes. . . . The conquistadores were this breed of men." All this, it might be added, almost one hundred years before it seriously occurred to England to colonize the New World.

The American Museum of Natural History
THE GREAT TEMPLE AT TENOCHTITLAN, THE ANCIENT MEXICO CITY. A reconstruction by Ignacio Marquina.

A European Version of the Conquest. Painting by Jan van Moestart, about 1525. Aside from the naked savages swarming about the hermit's crag from the left and the mail-clad European warriors coming to meet them from the right, Moestart's painting is a typical Flemish landscape of the period.

The Library of Congress
THE EARLIEST PICTURE OF THE AMERICAN BISON. From
Gómara, *Historia General de las Indias*, 1554.

The Spanish empire endured long after England had lost a good share of the colonies it founded so much later in America. Even after Spain's power in Europe seriously declined New Spain grew on, reaching up into the regions of the present United States. From the North came tall tales of "wild hunch back cows" that were the very substance of life for the natives and whose incredible numbers blackened the illimitable prairies far beyond reach of the eye.

Less improbable seemed rumors of the Seven Cities of Cibola, famed for immense wealth. Coronado's search in the New Mexico, where Montezuma's treasure was said to be equaled in yet undiscovered hoardings,

SAN MIGUEL IN SANTA FÉ. As it was before the earthquake of 1872. The church had been rebuilt in 1710.
Collection of Philip Medicus

revealed only humble pueblos. But years later Spaniards were still hoping for riches and empire north of the Rio Grande. La Vida Real de la Santa Fé de San Francisco—Santa Fé, in short—was grafted on an Indian pueblo as a frontier outpost about 1609. Had the expected wealth been there Santa Fé would have become a new center of Spanish power for a vast inland region. As it was, the little village survived the feuds of civil and ecclesiastical powers, Indian uprisings from within, and Apache raids from without, to become eventually one of the oldest cities of the United States.

The frontiersmen of New Spain were not the independent, mobile, and equalitarian types who later opened our own western borderland. With paternal legislation, insistence upon caste, and impressment of unwilling Indian and Negro labor by Church and military alike, the Spanish frontier was never a happy place for the common man as it was in the United States. Samuel de Champlain, the real herald of French empire in America, observed the scene in New Spain while sailing with a Spanish fleet at the turn of the fifteenth century. "At the commencement of his [the Spanish King's] conquests," wrote Champlain, "he had established the Inquisition among them [the Indians], and enslaved them or put them cruelly to death in such great numbers, that the mere account of it arouses compassion for them. . . .

"The system now adopted is that in every *estancia,* which are like villages, there is a priest who regularly instructs them . . . in the priest's presence, they are asked the reason why they did not come to divine services, for which they allege some excuse, if they can find any; and if the excuses are not found true and reasonable the said priest orders the Indian proctor to give the defaulters thirty or forty blows with a stick, outside the church, before all the people. . . . All these Indians are of a very melancholy disposition."

Champlain was amazed by the magnificence of the City of Mexico with its "fine temples, palaces, and houses, and the streets so well laid out, with fine big shops, full of all sorts of very rich merchandize." Like many others before him he suggested that a canal might be cut through the Isthmus of Panama.

"ALL THESE INDIANS ARE OF A VERY MELANCHOLY DISPOSITION."

The John Carter Brown Library

THE INQUISITION IN NEW SPAIN, 1599–1601.

Both illustrations are reproduced from water colors in Samuel de Champlain's manuscript journal of his first voyage to America.

Along the far-flung borders of the land it claimed in America Spain felt an increasing pressure from nations who had learned from Spain herself the promise of New World empire. France was making stupendous conflicting claims. On April 9, 1682, La Salle, after the prodigious effort that had taken him down the Mississippi to its mouth, announced the claims of France to the great American West.

"The Frenchmen were mustered under arms," wrote Francis Parkman, "and while the New England Indians and their squaws looked on in wondering silence, they chanted the *Te Deum*, the *Exaudiat* and the *Domine salvum fac Regem*. Then, amid volleys of musketry and shouts of *Vive le Roi*, La Salle planted the column in its place, and, standing near it, recited a long proclamation of possession in a loud voice.

"On that day the realm of France received

THE ARRIVAL OF LA SALLE AT MATAGORDA BAY, TEXAS. 1684. Engraving by J. van Vianen from Father Louis Hennepin, *Nouveau Voyage d'un Pais Plus Grand que l'Europe*, 1698.

on parchment a stupendous accession. The fertile plains of Texas; the vast basin of the Mississippi from its frozen northern springs to the sultry borders of the Gulf; from the woody ridges of the Alleghanies to the bare peaks of the Rocky Mountains—a region of savannas and forests, sun-cracked deserts and grassy prairies, watered by a thousand rivers, ranged by a thousand war-like tribes, passed beneath the scepter of the Sultan of Versailles; and all by virtue of a feeble voice, inaudible a half a mile."

Two years later, in a vain effort to reach that historic spot by sea, La Salle arrived at Matagorda Bay in what is now Texas. After weeks of futile searching he fell victim to a shot from one of his own disgruntled followers. With his death the New World lost one of its most inspired pioneers.

At San Antonio in Texas the Spaniards established a border outpost in 1718 to guard the western region Spanish enterprise had first discovered. Five struggling missions and a presidial garrison of forty-three men were posted as a bastion at that remote edge of empire. But the church and the military were ever at odds over the exploitation of the natives and the Indians were unresponsive to the conflicting demands of civilization. In 1730 the Viceroy imported fifteen families from the Canary Islands in the hope of invigorating the colony. Careful and ingenious plans were laid for its successful growth and, though the villa did not flourish mightily, a picturesque civilization combining Spanish and Indian cultures was maintained until a day when it would be infused with fresh admixtures of people—American frontiersmen, Davy Crockett with his famous rifle "Betsy," Jim Bowie and his equally famous knife, and others who made history at the Alamo. Then German immigrants, ranchers, businessmen, tuberculosis patients, soldiers of the United States Army, and winter vacationists. Yet San Antonio today has more Mexicans than all but four cities within Mexico itself. In 1940 it was reported that 36 percent of its population was of "Mexican blood."

THE MISSION SAN JOSE Y SAN MIGUEL DE AGUAYO, SAN ANTONIO, TEXAS, BUILT 1720–31.

THE MISSION OF SAN CARLOS, NEAR MONTEREY, CALIFORNIA, IN 1792. Water color by William Alexander. Worked up from an on-the-spot drawing made by a member of George Vancouver's crew.

A new threat to Spain's extended claims came from Alta California where Russian, English, and American vessels were appearing ever more frequently. Short of cash, Spain wielded her most effective instrument of defense, her Sword of the Spirit. Under the inspired direction of Junípero Serra, a chain of twenty-one red-tiled adobe missions was stretched up the coastal valleys at intervals of a day's march, with four modest presidios for their aid.

PART OF THE CITY OF LOS ANGELES, 1847. Drawing by William Rich Hutton.

Less than two hundred men set out for Monterey to launch the project. Half of them marched up what was to become the Camino Real—a tiny expedition of leather-armored *soldados,* sandaled Franciscans, and Christian Indians from Lower California. The other half, including the commandant Gaspar de Portolá and Father Serra, sailed up the coast in two tiny packets and on June 3, 1770, with impressive ceremonies, the shores of Monterey were consecrated and the royal standard planted. The Mission of San Carlos and the presidio of Monterey had been founded. Shortly after, the mission was moved about a league to the south, near Point Pinos, and the little settlement, built by the Indians, baptized with the name of Mission de San Carlos del Rio Carmel.

The other missions were built in the years that followed. Near the Mission of San Gabriel, in 1791, the tiny pueblo of Los Angeles came to life. The sketch shown opposite is one of the earliest views of the inchoate metropolis. In the foreground is the Church of Our Lady the Queen of the Angels, erected in 1818–22, remodeled in 1861, and still standing within the modern city.

The Library of Congress
THE SAN FRANCISCO PRESIDIO, 1816. From Louis Choris, *Voyage Pittoresque autour du Monde*, Paris, 1822.

In 1775, as other men far across the continent were stirring in rebellion against European rule, Juan de Ayala took the first ship through the Golden Gate to survey the great untenanted bay within. Portolá had already been there by land six years before, but had thought little of it. Cabrillo, Drake, and others had missed the port completely in their excursions up and down the California coast.

"Indeed, although in my travels I saw very good sites and beautiful country," wrote Father Pedro Font the next year, "I saw none which pleased me so much as this. And I think that if it could be well settled like Europe there would not be anything more beautiful in all the world, for it has best advantages for founding in it a most beautiful city with all the conveniences desired, by land as well as by sea, with that harbor so remarkable and so spacious, in which may be established shipyards, docks, and anything that might be wished." So, too, thought Richard Henry Dana, Jr., sixty years later when he visited the still all-but-empty landscape.

The presidio of San Francisco was dedi-cated and the Mission Dolores, two leagues to the southeast, was consecrated in the summer of 1776, the unhappy year that saw Washington beating a retreat before the British army. The shot heard 'round the world hardly sounded in the pastoral region along the west coast. Moreover, little was changed by Mexico's revolt from Spain in 1822. In the 1840's there were hardly ten thousand white people in all California to await annexation to the United States.

The John Carter Brown Library
A PART OF SAN FRANCISCO BAY, 1776. Map from the manuscript journal of Father Pedro Font. The first delineation of the famous bay.

23

FRANCE STAKES A CLAIM

A century and a half before La Salle made his formidable pronouncement at the mouth of the Mississippi, France had made an earlier bid for empire in the West. French and Portuguese fishing vessels were constant visitors to the Great Banks throughout the fifteenth century. It is even claimed, plausibly but with no proof, that Basque and Breton fishermen were familiar with the North Atlantic American coasts long before Columbus hove to at Watling's Island in 1492. Cabot and Verrazano had surveyed those coasts a generation before Jacques Cartier in 1534 planted a cross at Gaspé in the name of his majesty Francis I (see pp. 26-7). It

was, Cartier confidently thought, a way point on the high road to Cathay.

A year later the explorer was back. With the feeble aid of two impressed Indian guides he forced a perilous passage down the St. Lawrence. Eight hundred miles from the sea, beside the majestic cliffs which Quebec would one day crown, he was treated to an incomprehensible harangue by the greasy ruler of the local Indians, while a group of jubilant squaws, knee-deep in the water, sang and danced a continuous noisy welcome. Farther up the river he paused at a Huron village of oblong huts that clustered below the Mont Réal. From there Cartier

Collection of James Hazen Hyde

LAUDONNIERE AND THE FLORIDA INDIANS, 1564. The earliest known eye-witness depiction of American Indians *in situ*. Drawing by Jacques Le Moyne de Morgues

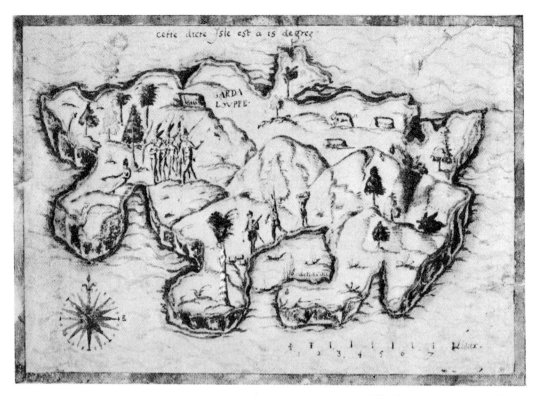

GUADELOUPE, 1599–1601. From Champlain's manuscript journal.

saw the end of his dreams in the narrows which blocked his way to China and which he humorously dubbed Lachine Rapids.

For a lifetime following those voyages official France, busied by civil commotions, fratricidal wars, and international animosities on the continent, paid scant heed to the lands of the West. An effort to settle Huguenot colonies in Brazil and Florida was checked by Portuguese and Spanish countermeasures and by natural difficulties. The first Florida colony was starved. Two years later, in 1564, René de Laudonnière returned to the site of settlement to find a column that had been erected there "wreathed from top to bottom with flowers of all sorts, and bough of trees esteemed choicest" by the local Indians in honor of the departed whites. It was a minor episode in the great play for empire, but it provided as a by-product the oldest surviving eye-witness drawing of an Indian on his native ground.

On his first voyage with the Spanish Champlain visited Guadeloupe, which he found "peopled by savages . . . who fled away into the mountains without it being in our power to overtake a single one of them, they being more nimble in running than all our men who tried to follow them." He made note of, and sketched, a number of good harbors into one of which his ship sailed to take on water. In the eighteenth century Guadeloupe was to become, as a French possession, the most profitable colonial holding in the world.

On this voyage Champlain saw with his own eyes the enormous, fully organized colonial empire upon which rested, in the words of Francis Bacon, "the ticklish and brittle state of the greatness of Spain." And he previsioned a New World empire, no less great and more humanely administered, under the rule of France.

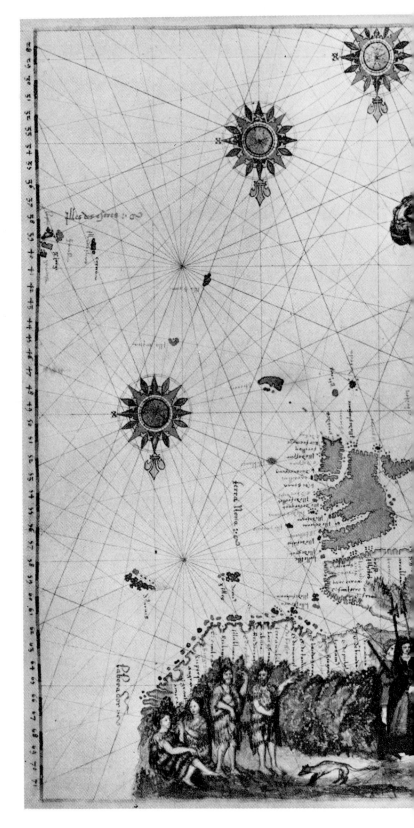

THE LANDING OF CARTIER IN CAN-
ADA, 1534. From a manuscript
chart. North is at the bottom of
the chart; Newfoundland is shown
as a large island in the gulf into
which empties the St. Lawrence.
Cartier, in the center of the
group imaginatively drawn in the
foreground, wears a short cloak.
That the natives are all generously clad in furs offers a fair indication that the staple wealth
of the northern forest was already recognized.

CHAMPLAIN'S HABITATION AT QUEBEC, 1608. From Champlain, *Voyages*, Paris, 1613.

In 1608, on his fourth voyage to America, Champlain laid the foundations of Quebec on the site earlier visited by Cartier. "I had the work on our quarters continued," he wrote, "which was composed of three buildings of two stories. . . . I had a gallery made all around our buildings, on the outside, at the second story, which proved very convenient. There were also ditches, fifteen feet wide and six deep. On the outer side of the ditches, I constructed several spurs, which enclosed a part of the dwelling, at the points where we placed our cannon. . . . Surrounding the habitation are very good gardens."

There Champlain and his small crew weathered the first bitter winter at Quebec. As the snow lay four and five feet deep about the Habitation thirteen of the twenty-two men died of scurvy and dysentery. About them the survivors, ill themselves, saw the improvident Indians in their hunger wolf down shreds of long-dead carrion, the distant stench of which gagged the whites.

It was the fate of both French and English to become involved in Indian hostilities and to breed new ones in their own interest. Eager as he was to forge friendships with the natives, Champlain took arms against the Iroquois to appease the Algonquins. At Ticonderoga, beside the lake which bears his name, he first met the foe. With the first shot of his arquebus, loaded with four bullets, Champlain relates, he killed two In-

CHAMPLAIN VS. THE IROQUOIS AT LAKE CHAMPLAIN, 1609. The Algonquins are fighting with the French. From Champlain, *Voyages*, Paris, 1613.

MARTYRDOM OF THE JESUITS OF NEW FRANCE, 1656(?). A composite portrayal of several different incidents. From P. Francisco Creuxius, *Historiae Canadensis*, Paris, 1664.

dians and mortally wounded a third. When one of his two companions fired from the woods, the astonished Indians, "seeing their chiefs dead . . . lost courage and took to flight, abandoning their field and their fort, and fleeing into the depths of the forest."

With that one paltry battle the French won the fierce, lasting enmity of the Five Nations. Champlain, despite his earnest intentions to the contrary, had antagonized the most murderous tribes of the northern forests. For a century and a half to come the Iroquois neither forgot nor forgave the first shot fired in their wilderness domain.

At the spearheads of French advance into the New World labored the Jesuit priests. Conversion of the savage ranked as high as fur-trading among the motives of French enterprise. In the terse, conscientious *Relations*

of their work the Jesuits left a record of dauntless heroism and physical and spiritual adventure that hardly has an equal. The black-robed fathers illumined the American wilderness with an apostolic flame, ignoring the constant threat of horrible death, suffering unremitting hardship, and finding God's wonder in all they saw.

"Men steeped in antique learning, pale with the close breath of the cloister, here spent the noon and evening of their lives, ruled savage hordes with a mild, parental sway and stood serene before the direst shapes of death. Men of courtly nurture, heirs to the polish of a far-reaching ancestry, here, with their dauntless hardihood, put to shame the boldest sons of toil." So wrote the eloquent Francis Parkman of the conquerors of New France.

THE EARLIEST PUBLISHED VIEW OF NIAGARA FALLS. Engraving by J. van Vianen from Father Louis Hennepin, *Nouvelle Découverte d'un Très Grand Pays*, 1697.

In their explorations of inland America, Frenchmen, priests and laymen alike, clarified the geography of the enormous back country of the continent, replacing the shadowy legends of earlier romance with some real knowledge of the land.

At the start of their epic journey to the Mississippi the young priest Jacques Marquette and his companion Louis Jolliet were grimly warned that they would meet "nations who never show mercy to strangers, but break their heads open without cause." But the salvation of souls could not wait. The little group pressed on to discover "prairies extending further than the eye can see," covered by a sea of grass spangled with myriad flowers—a land, as one of them wrote, "that somewhat resembles an earthly Paradise in beauty." So to the wondering eyes of those early pious adventurers seemed the American Midwest at first glimpse.

In that great Midland, wrote the Recollet friar Louis Hennepin, "situate between the Frozen Sea and New Mexico," there was nothing wanting "to lay the Foundation of one of the Greatest Empires in the World." While preparing for his voyage with La Salle down the Mississippi Hennepin earned immortal fame by finding the imperial cataract of Niagara. There is something singularly fitting that those almost incredibly majestic falls should have first been reported by a man with a developed flair for tall tales, which Hennepin truly had. Here was, he wrote, "a vast, prodigious Cadence of Water which falls down after a surprising and astonishing manner, insomuch that the Universe does not afford its Parallel." Even so Niagara was not tall enough for his tale and Hennepin wrote in the first edition of his book that it was five hundred feet high, about three times the actual height. In the next edition he raised the figure to six hundred. The restless friar's book ran to thirty-five editions in four languages before it went out of print, proof enough that it was read by a wide public.

French travel literature concerning the American West included some of the most popular books of the seventeenth century. The French, it has been said, were the real discoverers of America. It is true in the sense that in this flow of best sellers about the western wilds the French found a new world of ideas, ideas that were explored to their farthest consequences. The picture of the red savage of the forest who was free of the follies that had corrupted civilization and naturally wise in his freedom, was easy to draw from the stories, accurate and inaccurate, that emanated from America. One of the most influential books of early travel, by the talented young Baron de Lahontan, made a Huron chieftain the mouthpiece of the author's own cynical thoughts about European society. Lahontan had roamed over a large part of the American wilderness and developed an admiration for the Indians that, in reflection, he exaggerated into a fierce purpose. "Really, you weary me with your talk of gentlemen, merchants, and priests!" remarks the rhetorical savage Adario. "Would you see such a thing were there neither *thine* nor *mine*? You would all be equal, as the Hurons are . . . those who are only fit to drink, eat, sleep, and amuse themselves would languish and die; but their descendants would live like us." It was revolutionary talk. Adario was the natural man of Rousseau's *Social Contract*.

The New York Public Library

BARON DE LAHONTAN'S CONVERSATION WITH ADARIO, THE HURON CHIEFTAIN. From Lahontan, *Suite du Voyage de l'Amérique*, 1704.

ONE OF THE MISSISSIPPI BUBBLES; JOHN LAW'S CONCESSION AT NEW BILOXI (BILOXI, MISSISSIPPI), 1720. Wash drawing by Jean Baptiste Michel Le Bouteux.

Practical aims mingled with religious fervor and a spirit of adventure to promote French enterprise in America. The vague regions La Salle had called Louisiana must be had, it was urged, as a base of attack upon Mexico, as a depot for furs and ore from the interior, and as a bulwark against English expansion. A great monopolistic trading company, *La Compagnie des Indes,* was formed to settle the territory. John Law, a Scotch promoter who was also Comptroller-

General of France, bent his genius to attract money and people to the Mississippi Valley, describing "the almost incredible advantages" of the landed concessions that he peddled throughout Europe. New Biloxi, now Biloxi, Mississippi, was to serve as a transshipping point for vast, inland developments that would secure the prosperity of French empire. The artist of the accompanying drawing, Le Bouteux, who pictures himself in a boat in the foreground, was *sous-direc-*

VEUE DU CAMP DE LA CONCESSION DE MONSEIGNEUR LAW. AU NOUVEAU BILOXY. COSTE DE LA LOUISIANNE

The Newberry Library, E. E. Ayer Collection

teur of Law's concession and an eye witness of the scene he depicts.

"We commenced our work," wrote one of the settlers, "with large wooden buildings to serve as barracks. Each one made his own. After everyone was under cover we worked on the Director's dwelling. A storehouse was built to store the provisions that had been unloaded on the beach. The work was begun with great ardour. All the workmen, then, animated with the same spirit, willingly un-

dertook the founding of a new city. Nothing, in truth, was lacking for their encouragement.... At the start all was well...."

Europe responded to Law's scheme in a frenzy of real-estate speculation. Law was idolized and his "Mississippi Bubble" blown up to immense proportions. In December, 1720, the month in which the drawing on these two pages was made, the bubble burst. Paper fortunes proved worthless and Law and all his schemes were castigated in a fresh burst of illustrated literature that spared no invective. At Biloxi half the colonists had died and the rest sat at the shore watching for ships that it seemed would never come.

Out of the great excitement of the times the Crescent City of New Orleans was founded in 1718 by one of the first acts of the Directors of Law's company. Four years later the little town was made the capital of Louisiana Colony. "The plan as arranged is handsome," wrote a witness at that time, "the streets are perfectly aligned, and of convenient width. In the centre of the town, facing the square are all the public buildings; at the end is the church, with the Director's house on one side and the stores on the other. The architecture of all the buildings is of the same model, very simple. There is only one storey, raised a foot above the ground, resting on carefully placed foundations and covered with bark or boards [they were soon mostly half-timbered]. Each block or *ile* is divided into five parts, so that each private citizen may be comfortably lodged and may have a yard or a garden."

The French thrust into the interior and down the length of the Mississippi to distant New Orleans was brilliant strategy in the duel for empire. From her rocky eminence in the North, Quebec looked down over a vast inland arena where France would battle with England for a rich continent. The military and political issue was finally settled on the Plains of Abraham. But French experience on American soil enriched both countries in incalculable ways. Even today, three hundred years later, a strong Gallic spirit still flourishes in and about the ancient capitals of Quebec and New Orleans.

A DUTCH SATIRE ON LAW'S "MISSISSIPPI BUBBLE." *der Dwaasheid*, Amsterdam, 1720. Folly drives pectuses. True Commerce is crushed under the wheels as the whole group progress to the doors of hospitals for the mad, the ill and the destitute.

The New York Public Library
Engraving by B. Picart from *Het Groote Tafereel* the chariot from which Chance scatters pros-

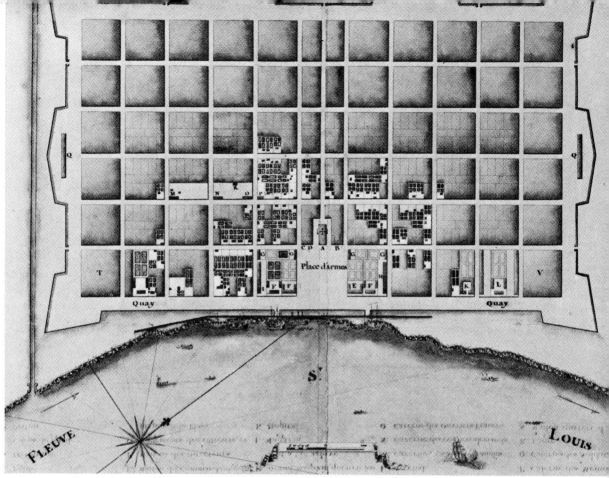

PLAN OF NEW ORLEANS, JANUARY, 1723. Manuscript.

HÔTEL DIEU, QUEBEC, ABOUT 1830. Water color by Major General James Pattison Cockburn.

HOLLAND'S BRIEF TENANCY

The Dutch claim to empire in America was brief and modest. The West India Company of Amsterdam, founded with the tacit purpose of distracting and looting Spanish shipping in the western Atlantic, did just that so well that within a few years 545 ships with cargoes valued at ninety million florins had been captured. When, in 1628, Admiral Piet Hein with a few small ships captured a Spanish fleet loaded with precious metals, pearls, spices, and drugs, twelve million florins worth in all, the brightest dream of the Company had come real. Spain's lifeline had taken a deep cut and as Spain bled, other countries could more easily and safely fatten on their overseas projects.

"Having about that time come into possession of Pieter Heyn's booty," wrote an early chronicler, the directors "bestowed not a thought upon their best trading post . . . whether people were making farms there or not . . . [but] would rather see booty arrive than speak of their colonies." The "best trading post" was, of course, New Amsterdam at the mouth of Hudson's River. Two years before the memorable sea battle the island of Manhattan had been purchased from the Indians for the value of sixty guilders.

Even if silver fleets were not captured every day Holland in the seventeenth century enjoyed immense prosperity. In their contentment Dutch farmers and tradesmen were not easily tempted to colonize the New World, for all the stories of beautiful rivers, bubbling fountains, agreeable fruits, and tasty venison that came from America. In any case tales of Dutch gains in silks, tea, and spices from the Orient had more appeal to a trading nation than bargaining with greasy natives for furs.

New Amsterdam, planted as a trading post

PIET HEIN'S CAPTURE OF THE SPANISH SILVER FLEET OFF HAVANA, 1628. Engraving by D. V. Bremden. The Dutch West India Company gained twelve million florins by this action. The Spanish commander, Torres, was executed as soon as he reached Spain.

The National Maritime Museum, Greenwich, Macpherson Collection

The New-York Historical Society

NEW AMSTERDAM, ABOUT 1650. Wash drawing by Laurens Block.

on what was to become the wealthiest small area on earth, rose to little importance under Dutch rule. In 1646, Father Isaac Jogues, the heroic Jesuit missionary, spoke of the fort at the tip of Manhattan as "the commencement of a town" not yet realized. Trade in furs promised quick profits and early won the interest of the Company. But, as France in Canada could testify, fur traders were not ideal settlers. They just didn't "settle," and the Company's small post at New Amsterdam remained for years a traders' and sailors' town. "Nearest ye Westerside . . . stands a Windmill," it was reported, "and a Fort four square. . . . In this Fort is ye Church, ye Gouerner's house, and houses for soldiers, ammunition, etc. . . . The town . . . hath good air, and is healthy, inhabited with severall sorts of Trades-men and merchants and mariners, whereby it has much trade, of beaver—otter, musk—and other skins from ye Indians. . . ."

Almost everywhere the Dutch paused in their world commerce they left tidy reminders of their prosperous homeland (see pp. 38–9). Small as it was, hemmed in on its island tip by a protective wall, New Amsterdam developed into a miniature replica of a typical Dutch trading city—of Amsterdam, Leiden, or Hoorn. Its "gutte" or canal running through the heart of the community, "whereby at high water boats goe into ye towne"; its curving streets and its neat

gardens and orchards; its nestling houses of particolored brick and tile, stepped gable ends facing the street; its battery, pointed fort, and windmill; its polyglot, free-spending, cosmopolitan population—all seemed exotic and curious to visitors from other American colonies.

The General Government Archives of the Netherlands

LOWER MANHATTAN FROM THE EAST RIVER, 1650–53. Water color by an anonymous artist. A detail from the so-called Prototype View, showing the Church in the fort and the Governor's house in the background. In the foreground the "gallows," crane, and houses of the settlers. Photograph courtesy of The Museum of the City of New York.

REDRAFT
of
THE CASTELLO PLAN
NEW AMSTERDAM
in
1660

AN AERIAL VIEW OF NEW AMSTER-
DAM, 1660. Redraft of the Castello
Plan. The most important of the
drawings copied from West India
Co. originals for Cosimo de' Medici. The plan shows about three
hundred dwellings in addition to
other buildings. Just inside the
Wall (Wall St.) the West India
Co. garden was laid out with formal Dutch flower beds and fruit
trees. Broadway runs from the
Fort beyond the wall into the
country. On Broadway in front
of the Fort was the square later
known as Bowling Green. The
canal or Graft bisected the present Broad Street.

The Rijksmuseum, Amsterdam

THE MORNING TOILET, ABOUT 1660. Painting by Pieter de Hooch.

The New-York Historical Society
GOVERNOR PETER STUYVESANT. Painting by an unidentified artist, 1660–70.

Almost every material trace of New Amsterdam has long since vanished. But from the few physical survivals and, principally, from the documents of that day, feature after feature of the early city and the domestic scene can be likened to those depicted in the luminous paintings of the Dutch Little Masters of the seventeenth century. Jan Steen, de Hooch, Vermeer, Terborch, and others painted such interiors as any New Netherlander would have found familiar. Early visitors described the plastered walls, the woodwork "kept very white scowr'd," the closet-beds, the jambless fireplace, "the hearths . . . laid with the finest tile . . . and the stair cases laid all with white tile which is ever clean, and so are the walls of the Kitchen"—all in the image of old Holland.

As early as 1643 Father Jogues described the babble of eighteen different languages in and about the short streets of New Amsterdam. For many reasons the English were attracted to Dutch territory in relatively large numbers. "Doe not forbeare to . . . crowd on," the Governor of Connecticut was advised in 1642, "crowding the Dutch out of those places where they have occupied, but without hostility or any act of violence." The crowding was already well under way. When the little English fleet arrived to take over New Amsterdam formally in 1664 there were numerous Englishmen among the fifteen hundred inhabitants who watched the city become New York "without a blow or a tear." Governor Stuyvesant stamped his wooden leg in protest but the burghers preferred peaceful surrender to bloodshed and plundering. Dutch colonial policy in America, counter attractions within the Dutch empire, and the tide of history all had provided England with the next opportunity along the broad and tranquil Hudson.

The most lasting memorials to Dutch tenure are the legends and genially satirical histories of Washington Irving. As an important and entertaining part of our early national literature those stories have created an enduring caricature of the typical New Netherlander as a slow-witted, fat, pipe-smoking tippler. Few of his contemporaries, familiar with the shrewd, bustling trader of Manhattan and Albany, would have recognized that portrait by Irving. In their forty years of occupation the Dutch contributed little that determined the later growth of the country. But it was Dutch enterprise and Dutch conquests, energy, and valor, that did so much to weaken Spain to the point where others could fan out in the New World at Spain's expense.

The Return of Rip Van Winkle. Painting by John Quidor, 1829.

The National Gallery of Art

CAPTURE OF A SPANISH TREASURE GALLEON BY THE ENGLISH OFF PERU, 1628. Engraving.

ENGLAND
SECURES A FOOTHOLD

England, too, found the Spanish carracks, gorged "with rubies, carbuncles, and sapphires," fair game on the open sea. Thomas Cavendish sailing up the Thames after capturing a Manila galleon, his ships rigged with sails of silk-grass and his sailors bedecked with pure golden chains; Francis Drake arriving home in the *Golden Hind* to be knighted after spreading terror over both coasts of Spain's American lands, after rifling, among others, the great treasure ship *Nuestra Señora de la Concepción*, "the chiefest glory of the whole South Sea," and entertaining its amazed and defeated admiral with violin music and "all possible kinds of delicacies" served on silver plate; Sir Richard Grenville in his single "mad little craft," the *Revenge*, standing up to a fleet of fifty-three Spanish vessels—"God of battles, was ever a battle like this in the world before?" —such was the way Elizabethan England opened a right of way to American empire. "My very good Lord," wrote Drake to Lord Burleigh, "there is now a very great gap opened, very little to the liking of the King of Spain."

While Drake and his fellow Sea Dogs were "singeing the King of Spain's beard" Sir Walter Raleigh started moving colonists through the "very great gap" that opened into the New World. "I shall yet live to see it an Inglishe Nation," he wrote Sir Robert Cecil. He did not; but he did launch England's colonizing effort. Raleigh's first expedition, an exploring party, reached North Carolina in July, 1584. The following year he dispatched "the first colonie of Virginia" in seven ships under the command of Sir Richard Grenville, the hero of the "one and the fifty-three" immortalized by Tennyson in *The Revenge*. Grenville left the group on Roanoke Island and returned to England, promising to return the next year with supplies.

Early reports from the American coast fired Michael Drayton to rhapsodize of "*Virginia*, Earth's only paradise." It was a "delicious land" of "luscious smells" where cedars reached to kiss the sky. But the first small group of colonists gratefully quitted their paradise when Drake, homeward bound from a buccaneering voyage, offered them

AN° DÑI · 1571·
ÆTATIS · SVÆ
· 29 ·

Sir Richard Granville, killed
in a sea-fight near the Azores.
1591

SIR RICHARD GRENVILLE. Painting by an unidentified artist, 1571.

CIVITAS S. Dominici sita
in Hispaniola Indica Angliae mag:
nitudine fere aequalis, ipsa vrbs elegan:
ter ab Hispanis extructa, et omnibus
circumiacens insulis nitro dat

DRAKE'S FLEET ATTACKING SANTO
DOMINGO, 1585. From *Expeditio
Francisci Draki*, etc., Leyden,
1588.

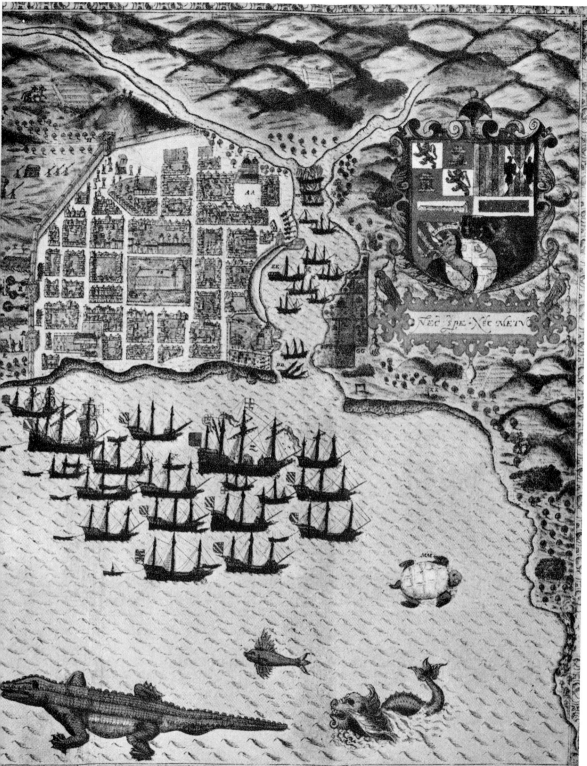

The British Museum

THE VIRGINIA COAST, 1585–87. Contemporary water color map by John White. Photograph courtesy of the Harvard College Library.

passage back to England. Within a few years Roanoake was re-colonized but the prospective Americans utterly disappeared before the visits of a relief ship.

With Grenville's expedition went one John White, artist, whose capable water colors, now in the British Museum, provide the most precious surviving record of sixteenth-century America. With the expedition also was Thomas Hariot who, after his return to England, reported to Raleigh: "The sea coasts of Virginia arre full of Ilāds, wehrby the entrance into the mayne lād is hard to finde. For although they bee separated with divers and sundrie large Division, which seeme to yeeld convenient entrance, yet to our great perill we proved that they wear shallowe, and full of dangerous flatts, and could never perce opp into the mayne lād,

untill wee made trialls in many places with or small pinness. At lengthe wee fownd an entrance uppon our mens diligent serche therof. Affter that wee had passed opp, and sayled ther in for a short space we discovered a migthye river fallnige downe in to the sownde over against those ilands, which nevertheless wee could not saile opp any thinge far by Reason of the shallewnes, the mouth therof beinge annoyed with sands driven in with the tyde therfore saylinge further, wee came unto a Good bigg yland, the Inhabitante therof as soone as they saw us began to make a great an horrible crye, as people which never befoer had seene men apparelled like us, and camme a way mak inge out crys like wild beasts or men out of their wyts. But beenge gentlye called backe, wee offred the[m] of our wares, as glasses, knives, babies [dolls], and other trifles, which wee thougt they deligted in. Soe they stood still, and percevinge our Good will and courtesie came fawninge upon us, and bade us welcome. Then they brougt us to their village in the iland called, Roanoac, and unto their Weroans or Prince, which entertained us with Reasonable curtesie, althoug the[y] wear amased at the first sight of us. Suche was our arrivall into the parte of the world, which we call Virginia, the stature of bodee of wich people, theyr attire, and maneer of lyvinge, their feasts, and blanketts, I will particullerlye declare unto yow."

Even to this day the American Indian remains something of a prodigy to many Europeans, a creature of innumerable contrasting legends, curiously resembling the uncanny, savage hunter of the early tales by James Fenimore Cooper, the incredibly chaste and virtuous Atala of Chateaubriand, or the bloodthirsty scalp-hunter of the movie thrill-ers. The first visiting Englishmen were for very good reasons intensely interested in the natives whose land they would usurp.

In the arts of living the Indians had little to teach the English. But to gain a foothold in the wilderness the white man had to learn from the red man methods of cultivation and harvesting adapted to American soil and to those plants that would flourish in it. (Arthur M. Schlesinger points out that in the four and a half centuries since Columbus Americans have not developed a single indigenous staple beyond those he learned of from the Indians.) Until that necessary adaptation was made the colonist was in constant danger of starving in the midst of a possible plenty. He had to learn the red man's eternal vigilance as the price of survival. The first adjustments to American life were violent; adaptability became a condition of life.

But by European standards Indian housing, community life, and domestic arts

THE ARRIVAL OF THE ENGLISH AT ROANOKE, VIRGINIA, 1585. From Thomas Hariot, *A Briefe and True Report . . . of Virginia*, Manchester, Eng., 1888. The whereabouts of White's original of this scene is not known.
The New York Public Library

Labels within the illustration:

Their rype corne.

Their greene corne

Corne newly sprong

Their sitting at meate

The place of solemne prayer

The house wherin the Tombe of their Herounds standeth

·SECOTON·

A Ceremony in their prayers w
strange gestures and songs dansing
abowt posts carued on the topps
lyke mens faces .

THE INDIAN TOWN OF SECOTON (NOW BEAUFORD COUNTY, NORTH CAROLINA), 1585–87. Water color by John White.

The manner of their fishing.

"THE MANNER OF THEIR FISHING IN VIRGINIA," 1585–87. Water color by John White.

offered nothing to emulate. The mat- and bark-covered shelters, "without windowes, and . . . noe lighte but by the doore," towns frequently on the move with the season, with the hunt, or before the enemy, and a culture that lacked iron or steel tools, were no models for men with a bent to improve their lot and witness the more wonderful works of God.

England was almost the last of the great colonizing powers of Europe to swing into action. Her first colorful efforts were born in the martial spirit of her gentlemen adventurers, the Elizabethan sea dogs who swept the oceans of the world before the colonists' advance. But by the dawn of the seventeenth century the exploitation of America had become a matter of commercial speculation. To succeed, it had been learned,

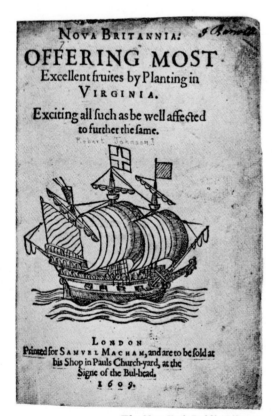

The New York Public Library
THE TITLE PAGE OF AN EMIGRATION TRACT BY ROBERT JOHNSON, 1609.

colonization needed the pooled resources of many investors. Chartered corporations were organized to tap the public purse, however they could, for ventures in the New World. Pamphlets, ballads, and sermons carried the word to the hopeful of every class with money to gamble for "sure" profits.

At the very moment when the pitiful survivors of the first Jamestown settlement were eating their horses, the snakes of the woods, their leather boots, and ultimately, the carcasses of their dead comrades, the Virginia Company of London was cheerfully promoting the advantages of life overseas with the sort of gush that would shame the most irresponsible modern advertiser. Virginia, wrote the author of *Nova Britannia* during Jamestown's "starving time," abounded in delights and resources of every description— "aire and clymate most sweete and wholesome," "fish, both scale and shell," "land and water fowles," "Deere, Coneys, and Hares, with many fruits and rootes good for meate," and "mountains making a sensible proffer of hidden treasure." The Indians, he added, were "generally very loving and gentle, and doe entertaine and relieve our people with great kindnesse. . . ."

In 1622 after the "loving and gentle," but inconstant, savages had all but annihilated the Jamestown settlers, John Donne, poet and dean of St. Paul's, was persuaded to preach a sermon, afterwards published, boosting the colony in the name of God and King. For his blurb he received a parcel of stock in the company. But for all its blandishments the company had "to take any that could be got on any terms." As one contemporary Englishman observed: "We are knowne too well to the worlde to love the smoake of our owne chimneyes so well that hopes of great advantages are not likely to draw many of us from home."

Three factors altered the destiny of Virginia: the discovery of a method of curing tobacco assured the colony of a staple, profitable commodity; the abolition of a communistic economy in 1616 and the offering of private property stimulated individual en-

THE INCONVENIENCIES

THAT HAVE HAPPENED TO SOME PERSONS WHICH HAVE TRANSPORTED THEMSELVES

from *England* to *Virginia*, vvithout prouisions necessary to sustaine themselues, hath greatly hindred the *Progresse* of that noble *Plantation*: For preuention of the like disorders heereafter, that no man suffer, either through ignorance or misinformation; it is thought requisite to publish this short declaration: wherein is contained a particular of such necessaries, as either priuate families or single persons shall haue cause to furnish themselues with, for their better support at their first landing in Virginia; whereby also greater numbers may receiue in part, directions how to prouide themselues.

Apparrell.

Apparrell for one man, and so after the rate for more.

	li.	s.	d.
One Monmouth Cap	00	01	10
Three falling bands	—	01	03
Three shirts	—	07	06
One waste-coate	—	02	02
One suite of Canuase	—	07	06
One suite of Frize	—	10	00
One suite of Cloth	—	15	00
Three paire of Irish stockins	—	04	—
Foure paire of shooes	—	08	08
One paire of garters	—	00	10
One doozen of points	—	00	03
One paire of Canuase sheets	—	08	00
Seuen ells of Canuase, to make a bed and boulster, to be filled in *Virginia* 8.s.			
One Rug for a bed 8.s. which with the bed seruing for two men, halfe is	08	00	
Fiue ells coorse Canuase, to make a bed at Sea for two men, to be filled with straw, iiij.s.			
One coorse Rug at Sea for two men, will cost vj.s. is for one	05	00	
	04	00	00

Victuall.

For a whole yeere for one man, and so for more after the rate.

	li.	s.	d.
Eight bushels of Meale	02	00	00
Two bushels of pease at 3.s.	—	06	00
Two bushels of Oatemeale 4.s. 6.d.	—	09	00
One gallon of *Aquanita*	—	02	06
One gallon of Oyle	—	03	06
Two gallons of Vineger 1.s.	—	02	00
	03	03	00

Armes.

For one man, but if halfe of your men haue armour it is sufficient so that all haue Peeces and swords.

	li.	s.	d.
One Armour compleat, light	—	17	00
One long Peece, fiue foot or fiue and a halfe, neere Musket bore	01	02	—
One sword	—	05	—
One belt	—	01	—
One bandaleere	—	01	06
Twenty pound of powder	—	18	00
Sixty pound of shot or lead, Pistoll and Goose shot	—	05	00
	03	09	06

Tooles.

For a family of 6. persons and so after the rate for more.

	li.	s.	d.
Fiue broad howes at 2.s. a piece	—	10	—
Fiue narrow howes at 16.d. a piece	—	06	08
Two broad Axes at 3.s. 8.d. a piece	—	07	04
Fiue felling Axes at 18.d. a piece	—	07	06
Two steele hand sawes at 16.d. a piece	—	02	08
Two two-hand-sawes at 5.s. a piece	—	10	—
One whip-saw, set and filed with box, file, and wrest	—	10	—
Two hammers 12.d. a piece	—	02	00
Three shouels 18.d. a piece	—	04	06
Two spades at 18.d. a piece	—	03	—
Two augers 6.d. a piece	—	01	00
Sixe chissels 6.d. a piece	—	03	00
Two percers stocked 4.d. a piece	—	00	08
Three gimlets 2.d. a piece	—	00	06
Two hatchets 21.d. a piece	—	03	06
Two froues to cleaue pale 18.d.	—	03	00
Two hand-bills 20. a piece	—	03	04
One grindlestone 4.s.	—	04	00
Nailes of all sorts to the value of	02	00	—
Two Pickaxes	—	03	—
	06	02	08

Houshold Implements.

For a family of 6. persons, and so for more or lesse after the rate.

	li.	s.	d.
One Iron Pot	—	07	—
One kettle	—	06	—
One large frying-pan	—	02	06
One gridiron	—	01	06
Two skillets	—	05	—
One spit	—	02	—
Platters, dishes, spoones of wood	—	04	—
	01	08	00

For Suger, Spice, and fruit, and at Sea for 6. men — 00 | 12 | 06

So the full charge of Apparrell, Victuall, Armes, Tooles, and houshold stuffe, and after this rate for each person, will amount vnto about the summe of — 12 | 10 | 00

The passage of each man is — 06 | 00 | 00

The fraight of these prouisions for a man, will bee about halfe a Tun, which is — 01 | 10 | 00

So the whole charge will amount to about — 20 | 00 | 00

Nets, hookes, lines, and a tent must be added, if the number of people be greater, as also some kine.

And this is the vsuall proportion that the Virginia Company doe bestow vpon their Tenants which they send.

Whosoeuer transports himselfe or any other at his owne charge vnto *Virginia*, shall for each person so transported before Midsummer 1625. haue to him and his heires for euer fifty Acres of Land vpon a first, and fifty Acres vpon a second diuision.

Imprinted at London by FELIX KYNGSTON. 1622.

The John Carter Brown Library

ADVICE TO PROSPECTIVE SETTLERS IN JAMESTOWN, VIRGINIA, 1622.

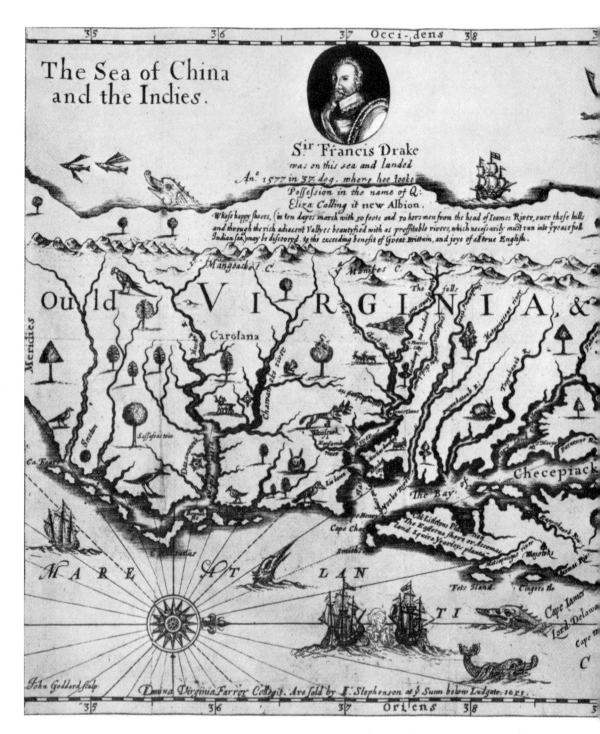

VIRGINIA AND ITS SURROUNDINGS. From Edward Williams, *Virginia*, London, 1651.

The map bears the following inscriptions:

Scala Miliárum

A mapp of Virginia discouered to y Falls, and in it's Latt: From 35. deg: & ½ neer Florida, to 41. deg: bounds of new England.

Noua Francia

new.

LAND

Swee ds Plant at Planted

Noua Albion

Rarritis

Richnek woods

Hudsons

Cape Codd

terprise; and the calling together of a representative assembly in 1619, the first in the New World, gave a practical character to the laws of the province. By 1634 the inhabitants of Virginia, occupying eight shires, numbered upwards of seventy-five hundred whites and several hundred Negroes.

In spite of all the ecstatic reports that issued from the presses—often just because of them—few Englishmen were reliably informed about the geography of the New World, or the real condition of life there, for scores of years to come. America was a continent "of a huge and unknown greatness" and the truthful reports about it, which were partial at best, were barely distinguishable from stories that were utterly false. Early instructions from the royal council to at least one set of adventurers in America emphatically enjoined them to settle along the river reaching farthest inland, or its branch that "bendeth most towards the northwest." "For that way," they were advised, "you shall soonest find the other sea," that is, the Pacific, pictured in the map at the left as being "ten dayes march ... from the head of the James River." It was only when the Lewis and Clark expedition returned East in 1806, after more than two years of traveling, that Americans began to understand all that lay between sea and sea.

One French traveler, a Huguenot who had briefly visited Virginia in the late seventeenth century and who wrote to urge others of his conviction to cross the seas for sanctuary, reported that he had traveled fifty leagues into the country. "From there," he wrote, "one sees mountains as great as the Alps, always covered with snow [any mountains he saw were visible from Chesapeake Bay]. Beyond, in the southern part of America, are Peru with rich mines of gold, Brazil, and all those beautiful islands that the Spaniards and Portuguese possess. It is from there that flow the handsome rivers that water Virginia." Such misinformation along with the truth played its full part in attracting colonists.

The Library of Congress
SAINT LUKE'S CHURCH, ISLE OF WIGHT COUNTY, VIRGINIA. Built in 1682(?).

Colonists always tend to recreate the world they leave behind. Those that settled in America in the seventeenth century were no exception. They brought to the "howling desart" that received them a way of life rooted in old habits. The habits had to be reshaped to meet new conditions but the world new-founded was, for a while and in some ways, less new than the one abandoned. The manner of living of the first colonists, the houses that sheltered them, and the equipment that served them, revealed an archaic strain which the handicaps of the frontier preserved before they modified. In the villages and along the byways of the New World the waning traditions of the Middle Ages lingered long after they had been damned as unfashionable in the courts and capitals of Europe. St. Luke's Church in Isle of Wight County, Virginia, built many years after near-by Jamestown was founded, with its pointed arch windows and brick tracery, its buttressed walls, and its steep-pitched roof, is a picturesque survival of the Gothic style. Elsewhere in Tidewater Virginia, buildings still stand whose plan

and style reflect on a modest scale the fashions of Jacobean England. Such enduring and handsome structures, erected so soon after the first strains of settlement, remain symbols of the vitality and the sense of a continuous tradition that went into England's colonizing effort.

Unlike some of the French to the north and many of the Spanish to the south the English did not intermarry with the natives, save in special instances and, later, along the ragged edge of the frontier. John Rolfe was a notable exception. He fell "in love with one whose education hath bin rude, her manners barbarous, her generation accursed." He took to wife, he wrote, "an unbeleeving creature, namely Pokohuntas. To whom my hartie and best thoughts are, and have a long time bin so intangled, and enthralled in so intricate a laborinth, that I was even awearied to unwinde my selfe thereout." The Indian Princess was received at the English court and, according to Ben Jonson, she occasionally disappeared through London tavern doors. The famous marriage was followed by few others of the sort, although two centuries later Patrick Henry almost carried a bill through Congress providing sizeable bonuses for intermarriage of whites with Indians.

The National Gallery
POCOHONTAS. Painting, British School, 1616.

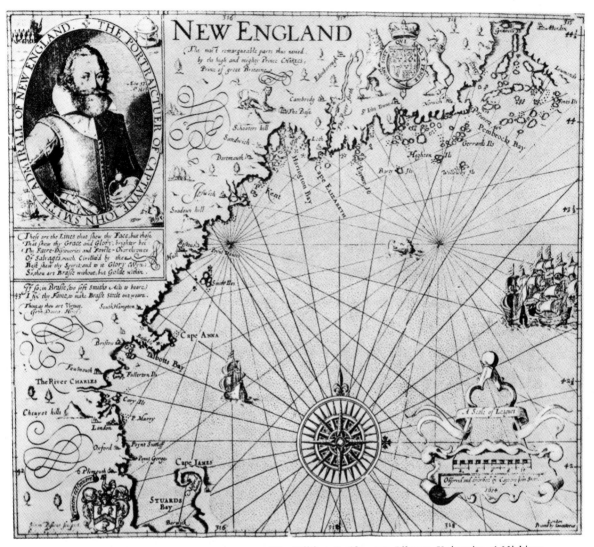

The William L. Clements Library, University of Michigan
CAPTAIN JOHN SMITH AND HIS MAP OF NEW ENGLAND. From Smith, *Description of New England*, 1616. The map shows Plymouth named after Smith's voyage of 1614, six years before the Pilgrims arrived there.

Captain John Smith's story of his rescue from death by Pocahontas was one of the first tall stories in a land where tall stories flourish. "Two great stones were brought before *Powatan*," he wrote, "then as many as could lay hand on him, dragged him to them, and thereupon laid his head, and being ready with their clubs, to beat out his brains, Pocahontas, the King's daughter, when no entreaty could prevaile, got his head

in her arms, and laid her owne upon it to save him from death." So it may have happened. But Smith's Virginia exploits have overshadowed his vital career as a "founder" of New England which he explored, mapped, named, and described. To save charges, wrote Smith, the Pilgrims, when the time for their own journey arrived, declined his services, "saying my books and maps were much better cheape to teach them, than myselfe."

Halliday Historic Photograph Co.

THE "SCOTCH"-BOARDMAN HOUSE, SAUGUS, MASSACHUSETTS. Built in 1651.

New England, too, is dotted with houses that were built during the first hundred years after the earliest settlements were established—small but sturdy monuments to the continuous traditions that lived on so lustily in the New World. Hope of owning such a home, and the land to build it on, was an outstanding cause for colonization. The breakdown of the medieval system of landholding brought widespread discontent to seventeenth-century England. Enclosure of open fields and the transfer of tillable land to sheep-farming disturbed an ages-old relation of men to the soil; both the landless and the land poor felt an inexorable pinch.

"Why then," asked John Winthrop, "should we stand striving here [in England] for places of habitation, etc, (many men spending as much labour & coste to recover or keepe sometimes an acre or twoe of Land, as would procure them many, & as good or better in another Countrie) and in the

The John Carter Brown Library

DETAIL FROM A MAP OF NEW ENGLAND BY JOHN SELLERS, 1612.

mean time suffer a whole Continent as fruit-full & convenient for the use of men to lie waste without any improvement?"

Why indeed, when America offered also the opportunity to worship God in one's own way? Land, as Roger Williams scornfully pointed out, was one of the gods of New England. But among the many and mixed motives that brought settlers overseas, the claims of religious conviction bulked large, and never larger than in seventeenth-century New England. The men and women who crossed the Atlantic at the demand of their conscience to settle a more godly plantation in Massachusetts were people of strong fiber, capable of real self-sacrifice. "They are too delicate and unfitte to begine new planta-tions and collonies," wrote William Brad-ford, "that cannot enduer the biting of a muskeeto; we would wish such to keepe at home till at least they be muskeeto proofe." Perched on the rim of an unknown world whose resources were but dimly understood and whose climate was unexpectedly severe,

at the end of a tenuous supply line and faced by generally hostile natives, those earnest souls needed their rugged virtues.

Their morals were high but arbitrary. Yet against the forbidding black and white ef-figies of the Mathers, Winthrops, and the rest, known to all school children, we must balance the bright, even gaudy, color of Captain Savage's trappings—the gold fringe, his sash, lace, and red breeches, and gold-topped cane. To generations brought up on *Twice-Told Tales* and *The Scarlet Letter* a Puritan in such a garb is almost a paradox. But if Hester Prynne had a scarlet letter for her shame, Governor Bellingham had a scar-let cloak as a mantle of respectability and authority, and the records tell of green doub-lets, blue stockings, red waistcoats with silver buttons, and similar Puritan finery. And even in "Mount Sion in the Wildernesse," wrote one candid reporter, there was a human share of ineptitude and frailty. "As to truth and godliness," he warned, "you must not expect more of them than of others."

The Massachusetts Historical Society
INCREASE MATHER, 1688. Painting by Jan Vander-spriet. Statesman, theologian, college president, and author, Increase was the most influential member of the famed "Mather dynasty."

Collection of Henry L. Shattuck
THOMAS SAVAGE, CAPTAIN OF THE ANCIENT AND HON-ORABLE ARTILLERY COMPANY. The Company, Beacon Hill, and Boston Harbor are in the background. Painting by an unknown artist.

North and south, the battle for a foothold in the "howling wildernesse" was won long before the seventeenth century ran out, and the promise for the future was secure. Nothing short of confident optimism, earnestness of purpose, and a faith in inherited values, could have prompted the founding of two colleges, Harvard and William and Mary, at such an early date.

"After God had carried us safe to *New England*," reads an anonymous pamphlet of 1643, "and wee had builded our houses, provided necessaries for our liveli-hood, rear'd convenient places for Gods worship, and settled the Civill Government; One of the next things we longed for, and looked after was to advance *Learning,* and perpetuate it to Posterity, dreading to leave an illiterate Ministry to the Churches, when our present Ministers shall lie in the dust . . . it pleased God to stir up the heart of one Mr. Harvard . . . to give the one halfe of his Estate . . . towards the erecting of a College, and all his Library."

The southern colonists were hardly less eager, for a seat of higher learning at home. Two earlier attempts, one as early as 1619,

The Society for the Preservation of New England Antiquities
A CONJECTURAL RESTORATION OF THE "OLD COLLEGE" (1638–1679) AT HARVARD. Drawing by H. R. Shurtleff.

were made before William and Mary College was chartered and its endowment started in 1693. Just half a dozen years later a new capital for the colony, to be named Williamsburg, was surveyed and laid out on land adjoining the college. It was one of the most deliberate accomplishments in city planning in colonial history, as today's restoration so dramatically reveals.

Colonial Williamsburg, Inc.
WILLIAM AND MARY COLLEGE (upper). The Capitol (lower left), and the Governor's palace (lower right), at Williamsburg, about 1740. Engraving possibly after a drawing by John Bartram. (The so-called "Bodleian Plate.")

58

A WORLD OF DIFFERENCES

By the end of the seventeenth century English colonies had been planted or acquired practically everywhere along the American coast, from the St. Croix River in the North to the Ashley in the South. During the early years of the following century Georgia and Nova Scotia, the thirteenth and the fourteenth colonies, were added at either end of the stretch as buffers for the others against the French, Spanish, and Indians.

Close to a third of a million people had already come to claim their futures under British rule in the western continent by 1700. They were a trifling few set against the vast wilderness of North America, still unimagined in its immensity. But for a time yet they clustered along the tidal and coastal waters, within reach of a lifeline from Europe. From the beginning they were a mixed breed with mixed convictions and intentions. Columbus had brought with him Irishmen, Jews, and Italians as well as Spaniards in his tiny crew, and most subsequent English ventures attracted no less a mixture. As Thomas Paine pointed out, Europe, not England, was the parent country of America.

Differences between colonies, and differences within colonies, were too many and too great for any pat summary of conditions. "Fire and Water are not more heterogeneous than the different colonies in North America," concluded one traveler after an extensive tour. No two people reporting on the colonial scene saw it the same. Franklin, who understood the situation better than anybody else, pointed out that each colony had "peculiar expressions, familiar to its own people, but strange and unintelligible to others." Some expressions were intelligible enough all around, as when the Virginian William Byrd complained to a friend of the "Banditti" from Massachusetts who anchored near his estate to traffic with his slaves, "from whom," he remarked, "they are sure to have good Pennyworths." Or, as

when Gerardus Beekman, a New York merchant, described Connecticut as "that dam'd country."

There was enough room on North America to prevent any serious friction between the differing groups of colonists, enough profitable work to do so that few could honestly feel dispossessed, and enough adaptability in most of those who made a go of colonial life, to enable people to get along together. But there was also enough centrifugal force in local and sectional differences to spin the various political and economic groups off along the tangents of their particular interests.

In the late seventeenth century while Indians, egged on by the French, were laying waste the New England frontier, Boston and New York merchants made capital by providing the enemy with munitions and supplies. In the next century colonists who had ventured into the interior were already looking back at an effete East whose money-changers were selfishly exploiting western interests. Everywhere, from the savannahs of the South to the "Arctic braced" forests that bordered hostile Canada, widely different climates and physical surroundings promoted different regional rivalries.

A few years before the Revolution it seemed to some a sadly disjointed empire. Left to themselves, it was said, the colonies would soon engage in civil warfare. Even if they might "get along" with a semblance of amity, it seemed too unlikely to hope that they would ever form an enduring union for their common benefit. "Everybody cries, a union is absolutely necessary," said Franklin in 1758, "but when it comes to the manner and form of the union their weak noodles are perfectly distracted."

From south to north, each colony presented a unique situation and history, and yet, as we shall see, there were bonds which were ultimately to prove irresistible.

Georgia

Georgia, last and southernmost of the thirteen original colonies, was projected in a true utopian spirit. James Edward Oglethorpe, a young, public-minded Englishman, witnessing the miseries of London's debtors' prison, envisaged a colony where such victims of social injustice could make a new start in life—a "calm retreat of undeserved distress." In the benevolent economy he planned there was to be no slavery, no liquor, no land monopoly. The trustees he enlisted to help with the colony were men of wealth and influence who provided means for most of the first settlers to sail away to the useful, happy lives promised to them overseas. Oglethorpe himself went as governor with the first batch of hopefuls in 1733.

Efforts were made to exclude undesirables who might disrupt the idealistic program of the colony. On the other hand, well-directed advertising pictured the advantages of emigration under the liberal arrangements provided by the trustees, appealing to those of good character everywhere, regardless of their condition and, for the most part, their beliefs. Europe as well as England was tapped for promising colonists. In 1734 a group of Lutheran exiles who had been driven to England from their homes by their ruler, the Archbishop of Salzburg, were equipped and sent off as new settlers. "At the Place of our Landing," wrote one of them, "almost all the Inhabitants of . . . *Savannah* were gather'd together; they fired off some Cannons, and cried Huzzah! . . . A *Jew* invited our *Salzburgers,* and treated them with a good Rice-Soup for Breakfast. . . . The *Jews* . . . of which there are 12 Fami-

JAMES OGLETHORPE WITH A COMMITTEE OF THE HOUSE OF COMMONS INVESTIGATING CONDITIONS AT FLEET PRISON, LONDON, 1729. Painting by William Hogarth.

National Portrait Gallery, London

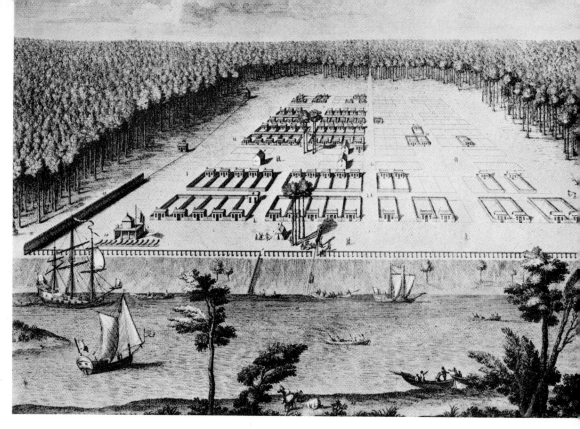

SAVANNAH, MARCH 29, 1734. Engraving by P. Fourdrinier after a drawing by Peter Gordon.

THE SALZBURGERS LEAVING THEIR HOMES. Engraving by David Ulrich Böcklin in The Salzburger Collection of Tracts, 1732.

OGLETHORPE PRESENTING TOMO-CHI-CHI AND THE INDIANS TO THE LORD TRUSTEES OF THE COLONY OF GEORGIA, 1734. Painting by William Verelst.

lies here, come to Church, and seem to be very devout: They understand the *German* tongue."

Baron von Reck, leader of the Salzburgers, described the rising town of Savannah in 1734. "The Town is regularly laid out," he wrote, "divided into four Wards, in each of which is left a spacious Square for holding of Markets and other publick Uses. The Streets are all straight, and the Houses are all of the same Model and Dimensions, and well contrived for Conveniency. For the Time it has been built it is very populous, and its Inhabitants are all White People. And indeed the Blessing of God seems to have gone along with this Undertaking; for here we see Industry honored and Justice strictly executed, and Luxury and Idleness banished from this happy Place where Plenty and Brotherly Love seem to make their Abode, and where the good Order of a Nightly Watch restrains the Disorderly and makes the Inhabitants sleep secure in the midst of a Wilderness."

Georgia, it was hoped, would serve as a buffer against the Spanish and French along the southern frontier, and as a friendly link with the Lower Creek and Choctaw Indians. As a buffer against the Spaniards the Georgians did their work well at the Battle of Bloody Marsh in 1742. With the Indians Oglethorpe established and maintained friendly relations throughout his sojourn in the colony. "Mr. Oglethorpe," wrote a

Salzburger minister in 1734, ". . . being very sollicitous that the poor Indians should be brought to the Knowledge of God, has desired us to learn their Language; and we, with the Blessing of God, will joyfully undertake the Task. . . ." That same year Oglethorpe took Tomo-chi-chi, Chief of the Yamacraw Indians, with his wife, nephew, and several tribesmen back to London with him for a four months' visit. The natives were received by George II at Kensington Palace and by the Archbishop of Canterbury at Lambeth Palace. Interest caused by their visit won valuable patronage for the colony.

At his death in 1785 Oglethorpe had long outlived the dream he had projected in Georgia. The colony grew and in fair measure prospered; Savannah's squares and streets still recall in their symmetry the careful plans of the founder. But Oglethorpe's vision of a commonwealth of small self-supporting, abstemious landholders never did materialize. Nor did elaborate plans to foster silk growing, encouraged as they were by law and by special inducements, ever result in commercial success.

By the middle of the century, when the Crown took over Georgia from the trustees, most of the benevolently intended restrictions that gave the colony its unique beginnings had been abandoned as impracticable. As Carolina just to the north was clearly demonstrating, conditions in the southern colonies encouraged large-scale operations of land that inevitably concentrated in the hands of relatively few owners. Only by following suit could Georgia compete with its prosperous neighbors in the South.

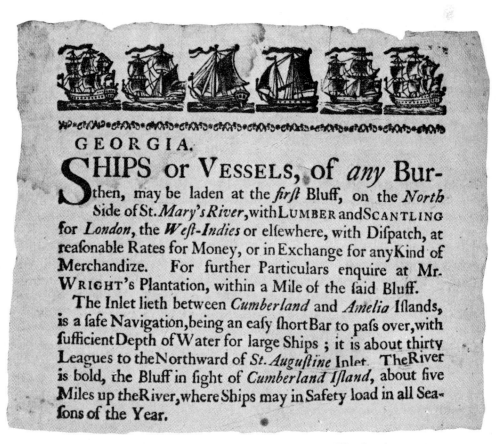

AN EIGHTEENTH CENTURY BROADSIDE.

The American Antiquarian Society

SOUTH CAROLINA RICE FIELDS. Engraving after a drawing by Basil Hall, 1828.

Carolina

At each point of settlement separate circumstances conditioned life in a different manner. At few points did the reality of New World experience jibe with preconceived notions of life in America that most colonists brought with them. The climate, the topography, the soil, and the native savages all posed novel problems that varied from one latitude to the next. To choose the wrong season or the wrong point of arrival could have tragic consequences. To recognize the limitations and possibilities of a new environment, to adapt habits and hopes to the unexpected, was necessary to a decent prosperity, if not to bare survival.

Georgia's neighbors had passed the awkward stage of settlement long before Oglethorpe launched his experiment in philanthropy. From Maryland south a plantation economy had developed based principally on the production of cash crops and featured by large, land holdings operated by slave labor. Carolina, just to the north of Georgia, prospered abundantly by concentrating first on rice and later on indigo, two exotic staples precisely answering the demands of England's mercantile policy. To prepare and cultivate the malarial fields where rice

flourished and where white freemen could not and would not work, large numbers of black slaves were imported. Standing "ankle and even mid-leg deep in water which floats an ouzy mud, and exposed all the while to a burning sun . . ." wrote one reporter, "these poor wretches work in a furnace of stinking putrid effluvia." Even among slaves the death rate was high. But more ships brought more slaves and took away increasing piles of rice. As early as 1700 the governor and council of the colony reported to England: "Your Lordships' Country hath made more rice the last Crop than we have ships to Transport." As the eighteenth century progressed South Carolina became the greatest slaveholding colony in North America, and one of the most prosperous ornaments of the British Empire.

About the middle of the century, at a time when there was grave concern over decreasing profits from rice, the development of indigo gave a fresh spurt to the colony's prosperity. "It must be apparent, at first sight," wrote the author of *American Husbandry*, "that no husbandry in Europe can equal this of Carolina; we have no agriculture in England—where larger fortunes are made by it than in any other country—that will pay any thing like this . . . plenty of good land free from taxes, cheapness of labour, and dearness of product sold, [together] with cheapness of that consumed—are, united, sufficient to explain the causes of a Carolina planter having such vastly superior opportunities of making a fortune than a British farmer can possibly enjoy . . . liberty reigns in perfection; taxes are too inconsiderable to be mentioned; no military service; no oppressions to enslave the planter and rob him of the fruits of his industry. When all these great and manifest advantages are considered, I think it must appear surprising that more emigrants from different parts of Europe are not constantly moving from thence to America. . . ."

The colony did indeed prosper beyond the fondest dreams of its founders, but in its own independent fashion. According to the original plan Carolina was to have been a feudal colony. For the Proprietors the philosopher John Locke drew up the Fundamental Constitutions of Carolina, a remarkable document of one hundred and twenty articles composed in the quiet of an Oxford study and designed to regulate the degrees of nobility and dependency that would be observed in the forests of the New World. It was a fantastic blueprint for life in America.

The romantic titles of baron, cacique, and landgrave never stuck to the large landholders who acquired them. Serfs and leetmen did not rush to take their place at the bottom of the social heap. The absentee proprietors, repeatedly opposed by colonists who were intent on shaping their own destiny and who "so disrespectfully refused our Excellent Constitutions," gladly relinquished their claims to the King early in the eighteenth century.

An aristocracy quite as impressive as any envisioned by Locke did develop in South Carolina. But it grew out of the raw, primeval swamps and the hot seasons of the lowlands, not out of temperate, storied Oxford; it was built on rice and "black gold," not on theory. The productive lowlands where the grain flourished and the Negro survived his work did, thanks in part to large proprietary grants, find their way into the hands of a relatively small group of landholders. But this oligarchy was composed of active, resident planters, not of distant peers of the realm. As the colony demonstrated in 1776 and the state in 1861, the fundamental constitution of South Carolina was an insistent, spirited faith in home rule.

Throughout the colonial period the city of Charleston was the social, cultural, and business center of the Carolina low country.

INDIGO CULTURE IN SOUTH CAROLINA. From a Map of the Parish of St. Stephén in Craven County, etc., after a drawing by Henry Mouzon. The scene supposedly depicts Mulberry, a plantation on the Cooper River.
The Charleston Library Society

CHARLESTON BEFORE 1739. Engraving after a painting by B. Roberts. The most important view of early Charleston.

From its beginnings it attracted no less a mixture of peoples than New York and Philadelphia — Barbadians, French Calvinists, English dissenters, Scotch Covenanters, Dutchmen from Holland and New York, New England Baptists, Quakers, Irish Catholics, and Jews among others. In that benign, subtropical climate those diverse faiths and traditions fused into a unique civilization—leisurely, cosmopolitan, and aristocratic.

Even before the growth of its rice trade

Historic American Buildings Survey,
The Library of Congress
MEDWAY, NEAR CHARLESTON. Built in 1682.

Charleston was an active shipping port for products of the forest. Hardy fur traders, who were gathering pelts in the remote inland regions claimed by La Salle in perpetuity for Louis XIV, also used the city as an entrepôt. Within a generation it had gained "ye reputation of a wealthy place," and, until they were chased away, Blackbeard and others of his trade waited on the swarm of richly laden vessels plying in and out of the port. "It will perhaps surprize your Lordships," reported Governor Glen in 1749, "to be informed there is annually imported a considerable quantity of fine laces of Flanders, the finest Dutch linnens, and French cambrick, chintz, Hyson Tea, and other East India goods, silk, gold and silver laces, etc." In their extravagant manner of living, he went on to warn, Carolinians were going the way of ancient Romans. Just before the Revolution, Josiah Quincy, Jr., found that in "grandeur, splendour of buildings, decorations, equipages, numbers, commerce, shipping, and indeed in almost everything" Charleston surpassed all he had seen or hoped to see in America.

Charleston was never large but it was

distinctive among colonial cities. It was far more intimately related to its surrounding countryside than any other city in the colonies. Virtually every family of importance— and that importance was relatively greater than elsewhere in America — maintained houses in both country and city. Seasonally the rice aristocrats retreated from the unwholesome heat of their swamps to occupy their houses in town and to join in a round of urban diversions. To Quincy, fresh from staid Boston, the gaiety and hospitality of Charlestonians during that social season had a disturbing warmth and excitement. But for most others Charleston, in season and according to the canons of the eighteenth century, was the most cultivated and civilized center in the New World.

It must have been difficult to remember, at times, how new and raw that world really was in which Charleston sparkled so brightly. Two of the men in the group, pictured in the sketch at the right, guests at the table of Peter Manigault, graduate of the Inner Temple and one of the most accomplished and best equipped of Charleston hosts, were later killed by Indians on the near-by frontier.

Captain Demeré, sitting directly in front of the fireplace, survived Braddock's expedition but was slain at Fort Luden a few years later. Ensign Coytmore, sitting at the lower right in the sketch, with his hand on a decanter, lost his life at the hands of the Cherokees at Fort Prince George. Manigault, also holding a decanter, sits opposite Coytmore. The artist is at Manigault's right.

Collection of Dr. Hawkins Jenkins
MR. PETER MANIGAULT AND HIS FRIENDS AT A SUPPER PARTY AT MANIGAULT'S HOUSE, ABOUT 1754. Drawing by George Roupell.

A VIRGINIA TOBACCO WHARF. From a Map of . . . Virginia, etc., drawn by Joshua Fry and Peter Jefferson, 1775.

The Tobacco Kingdom

Although tobacco was well known to and appreciated by Englishmen long before Virginia was settled, growing the "divine herb" was not in the original plans for that colony. However, as soon as cultivating it proved feasible and profitable the Virginia colonists concentrated on tobacco in earnest. Indeed, their single-minded devotion to the main cash crop at the expense of subsistence farming endangered the very life of the colony in its early days. But that crisis past, tobacco became the staple commodity that dictated the economic, social, and political order of a wide region.

Before the seventeenth century ended Virginia's history was being shaped by a relatively few planters whose holdings were large and whose slaves were many. As early as 1653 Captain Adam Thoroughgood had acquired 5350 acres of land, holdings that were dwarfed by the 300,000 acres amassed by "King" Carter before his death in 1732.

Tobacco could be profitably raised by unskilled hands and the encouragement of slavery was almost automatic. When the leaf was ripe, explained an early reporter, it was carried "in bunches by the negroes to a building called the tobacco house, where every plant is hung up separate to dry, which takes a month or five weeks. . . ." The cured leaves were then stripped from the stalks and

prized, or compressed, for carriage to the warehouse. "Upon all the rivers and bays . . . at the distance of about twelve or fourteen miles from each other, are erected warehouses, to which all the tobacco in the country must be brought . . . inspectors are appointed to examine all the tobacco brought in, receive such as is good and merchantable, condemn and burn what appears damnified or insufficient. . . . The inspectors give notes of receipt for the tobacco, and the merchants take them in payment of their goods, passing current indeed over the whole colonies; a most admirable invention. . . ."

Gradually the tobacco country of colonial America spread over most of eastern Maryland, almost all of tidewater and Piedmont Virginia, and the northern counties of North Carolina. It was a rich, widely populated area of tremendous value to England. The wharves of the early tidewater plantations were within easy reach of the ocean-going vessels of the day. But tobacco is a soil-exhausting crop and, as the search for fresh lands widened, transportation to deep water became a vital maneuver. Fastening two canoes together to secure a heavy cargo against the pitchings of a downstream journey became a common practice during the years before the Revolution.

King James complained that smoking was

STAGES IN THE CULTURE AND MARKETING OF TOBACCO: *(a)* A Common Tobacco House *(b)* Hanging the Leaf on a Scaffold *(c)* Prizing *(d)* Tobacco Hanging to Cure It *(e)* Public Warehouse *(f)* Inspecting Tobacco in the Warehouse *(g)* Conveying Tobacco by a Double Canoe. From William Tatham, *An Historical and Practical Essay, etc.*, London, 1800.

ENGLISH TRADE CARD ADVERTISING VIRGINIA TOBACCO.
From the George Arents Collection. About 1750.

"a custome lothsome to the eye, hatefull to the Nose, harmefull to the braine, dangerous to the Lungs, and in the blacke stinking fume thereof, neerest resembling the horrible Stigian smoke of the pit that is bottomelesse." But he spoke not for a great mass of his countrymen. The air of London coffee shops grew ever blacker with the smoke of Virginia tobacco brought in constantly growing fleets from the Old Dominion. About 2500 pounds were exported to England in 1616. Two years later, the figure had risen to 50,000 pounds, and by the eve of the Revolution it had climbed to over 100,000,000 pounds.

The baronial estates of the tobacco kingdom that grew on the profits of that trade housed a group of wealthy aristocrats whose influence was out of all proportion to their numbers. This untitled nobility owed its prominence more to its own efforts than to its pedigrees. Despite the abiding legends of Virginia Cavaliers whose ancestry was rooted

STRATFORD, WESTMORELAND COUNTY, VIRGINIA. Built by Thomas Lee about 1725. Photograph by C. O. Greene from the Historic Buildings Survey.

in the battlefield of Hastings, the British gentry were only rarely represented among the early emigrants to Virginia. "It is known," wrote one reporter in 1656, "such preferment hath this country rewarded the industrious with, that some, from being wool-hoppers and of as mean or meaner employment in England, have there grown great merchants and attained to the most eminent advances the country afforded." Capital for buying land and slaves gave those who came with it a head-start in the race for fortune, but the F.F.V.'s became the first families *in* Virginia.

Those who made this goal, reported the author of *American Husbandry,* "live more like country gentlemen of fortune than any other settlers in America; all of them are spread about the country, their labour being mostly by slaves, who are left to overseers; and the masters live in a state of emulation with one another in buildings (many of their houses would make no slight figure in the English counties), furniture, wines, dress, diversions, and this to such a degree, that it is rather amazing they should be able to go on with their plantations at all. . . . In most articles of life, a great Virginia planter makes a greater show and lives more luxuriously than a country gentleman in England, on an estate of three or four thousand pounds a year." That they were often in debt to their English agents, it was explained, was the fault of extravagance, not of any lack of returns from their estates. At Stratford, birthplace of two signers of the Declaration of Independence and of Robert E. Lee; at Westover, ancestral seat of the Byrds; at Carter's Grove, where Rebecca Burwell refused to marry Thomas Jefferson—at these and other historic homes the rich, landed aristocrats set a pattern of life that had no parallel in the colonies. It was by no means a life abandoned to diversions. These leaders of the colony took their leadership seriously and exercised their influence with re-

THE ENTRANCE SALON AT CARTER'S GROVE, JAMES CITY COUNTY, VIRGINIA. Built by Carter Burwell between 1751 and 1753.

Photograph by Tebbs

THE END OF THE FOX HUNT. Painting by an unidentified American artist, about 1780.

markable results. At Westover, as an outstanding example of the more serious aspect of Virginia life, William Byrd owned a hardworked library of 3600 volumes that was equaled in America only by that of Cotton Mather, his New England contemporary. At his death in 1744, William Byrd II left a princely estate of 179,000 acres—a fortune that had its origins, in some part at least, in shrewd trading in trinkets, rum, and furs with Indians along the frontier.

By the very nature of things Virginia's was almost exclusively a rural society. "Such a country life as they lead," wrote one traveler, "in the midst of a profusion of rural sports and diversions, with little to do themselves, and in a climate that seems to create rather than check pleasure, must almost naturally have a strong effect in bringing them to be just such planters as foxhunters in England make farmers." That was a partial view of Virginia life. Without earnest and industrious care by the planter and his wife no estate could flourish. During at least one

week of his life, in 1769, George Washington rode to hounds on six successive days, in English-made riding frocks and handsome buckskin breeches. But he was also tirelessly in the saddle paying serious and loving attention to his estate at Mount Vernon.

In many respects Virginia seemed less like the threshold of the New World than the back garden of the old. As in the Carolina low country people of substance turned to England for the luxuries, and many of the necessities, of life, as well as for their cultural guidance. Writing in 1724 the Reverend Hugh Jones observed, "The habits, life, customs, computations, etc. of the Virginians are much the same as about London, which they esteem their home; and for the most part have contemptible notions of England, and wrong sentiments of Bristol, and the other out-ports, which they entertain from seeing and hearing the common dealers, sailors, and servants that come from those towns, and the country places in England and Scotland, whose language and manners are strange to them; for the planters, and even the native negroes generally talk good English without idiom or tone, and can discourse handsomely upon most common subjects; and conversing with persons belonging to trade and navigation from London, for the most part they are much civilized, and wear the best of clothes according to their station; nay, sometimes too good for their circumstances, being for the generality comely handsome persons of good features and fine complexions (if they take care), of good manners and address."

At Williamsburg, the capital of the Old Dominion until 1780 and almost the only "urban" retreat in the colony, Jones found that the population "behave themselves exactly as the gentry in London, most families of any note having a coach, chariot, berlin, or chaise." Architecturally the little city was the most impressive community in America at the time of Jones's visit. The Capitol, the Governor's Palace, William and Mary College, and other "modern" buildings that looked over Duke of Gloucester Street—all so well known to tourists of the present—embodied the most advanced and fashionable styles of their day.

The first professional theatrical performance in the colonies—a series of "comedies, drolls and other kinds of stage plays"—was

The Harvard College Library, Theater Collection
MRS. HALLAM AS "MARIANNE" IN "THE DRAMATIST." Engraving by C. Tiebout.

given at Williamsburg. In 1752 Sarah Hallam, of England, "the queen of the colonial stage," gave her first performances. According to notices in the *Virginia Gazette* the audience was assured of "being entertained in as polite a Manner as at the Theatre in London." At the theatre, as at the hunt, Washington lent his enthusiastic presence.

Life immediately north of the Potomac in Maryland differed little from that in Virginia. The colonial traveler noted, in general, the same scattering of plantations about a countryside largely given over to tobacco-growing.

In both colonies small landholders far outnumbered those with big estates and worked more total acreage; and tobacco was by no means the only crop. "A man may be a farmer for corn and provisions," reported the author of *American Husbandry*, "and yet employ a few hands on tobacco, according as his land or manure will allow him.

Colonial Williamsburg
THE CAPITOL AT WILLIAMSBURG. Photograph by Thomas L. Williams.

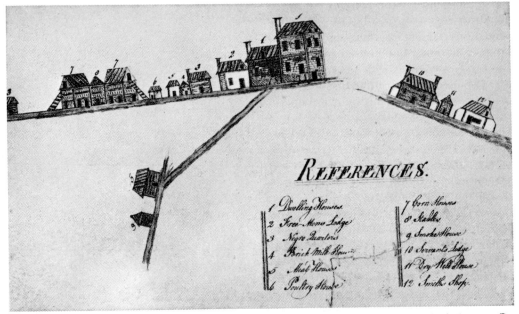

REFERENCES.

1 Dwelling Houses
2 Free-House Lodge
3 Negro Quarters
4 Brick Milk House
5 Meat House
6 Poultry House

7 Corn Houses
8 Stables
9 Smoke House
10 Servants Lodge
11 Dry Well House
12 Smiths Shop

Collection of Miss Elizabeth Forsman Day

TAYLOR'S MOUNT, BALTIMORE COUNTY, MARYLAND. Drawing by its owner, Edward Day, 1779. Photograph courtesy of The Maryland Historical Society.

The Library of Congress

ENTRANCE OF THE HAMMOND-HARWOOD HOUSE, ANNAPOLIS, MARYLAND. Built in 1768. Photograph by Charles E. Peterson (1942) from the Historic American Buildings Survey.

This makes a small business very profitable, and at the same time easy to be attained, nor is anything more common throughout Maryland and Virgina."

In a region with few towns the plantations, or manors, were the principal community centers. With the "dwellinghouse in the center, with kitchens, smoke-house, and out-houses detached, and from the various buildings, each plantation has the appearance of a small village . . ." wrote one visitor early in the eighteenth century. "All the Drudgeries of Cookery, Washing, Daries, &c. are perform'd in offices detacht from the Dwelling-Houses, which by this means are kept more cool and Sweet." Situated at the head of Gunpowder River Taylor's Mount, shown above, was a typical home of a moderately well-to-do planter, "[with] every necessary and convenient building for the reception and accomodation of a genteel family."

Originally called Providence by the Puritan exiles from Virginia who founded it in 1649, Annapolis long remained the only town of any size in Maryland. The settlement flourished and with the eighteenth century became the social center, not only of Maryland, but of neighboring regions of Virginia as well. In response to the needs of its elegant, handsomely housed society one domestic advertised that he was ready "to wait at table, curry horses, clean knives, boots and shoes, lay a table, shave and dress wigs, carry a lanthorn, and talk French." He was, said the advertisement, "as honest as the times will admit and as sober as can be."

The Tuesday Club of Annapolis, whose ceremonial antics are illustrated, was but one of innumerable convivial societies which sprang up in all the leading colonial towns during the eighteenth century. Members of such groups, usually including the more prominent local personalities, gathered periodically for divers serious and frivolous reasons—political and literary discussion, music, the pleasures of wining and dining, and a wide variety of high jinx. They were, explained one contemporary, "Knots of men rightly sorted."

Baltimore was not founded until 1729 and by mid-century contained only twenty-five houses and some two hundred people. Its site, however, beside a spacious harbor and with water power from the local river, Jones Falls, made it a natural market for the Susquehanna watershed. Milling wheat from the productive Pennsylvania-German farms

The Johns Hopkins University Library
"THE GRAND REHEARSAL OF THE ANNIVERSARY ODE OF THE TUESDAY CLUB," Annapolis, Maryland, about 1746. Wash drawing by Dr. Alexander Hamilton (?), a member of the club.

of the hinterland and exporting flour, largely to the West Indies, developed into a thriving business in the years preceding the Revolution. In 1754 Governor Sharpe considered that Baltimore already had "the Appearance of the most Increasing Town in the Province." As the century wore on the town outstripped Annapolis in size and commercial importance if not in social distinction.

The Maryland Historical Society
BALTIMORE TOWN, 1752. Drawing by John Moale, Jr. Photograph courtesy of the Frick Art Reference Library.

WILLIAM PENN'S TREATY WITH THE INDIANS, 1682. Idealized painting by Benjamin West, about 1771. Actually Penn made several treaties with the Indians.

Pennsylvania

In 1763–67 two English surveyors, Mason and Dixon, drew a line across the eastern seaboard to settle the long-disputed boundaries between Maryland and Delaware to the south and Pennsylvania to the north. To this day that line represents the boundary between southern and northern sentiment in the United States. Long before it was drawn the slave-operated plantations of the South gave way at approximately this point to the commercial and farming settlements of the North.

The land immediately to the north was already sparsely occupied by a modest number of Swedes, Finns, and Dutchmen when, in 1682, William Penn founded there one of the largest colonies on the continent. Here he offered a haven to those "schismati-cal factious people" the Quakers, and to any others who would share their plan to live together in a spirit of brotherly love. "When the Purchase [of Pennsylvania] was agreed," wrote Penn in 1682, "great Promises past between us of Kindness and good Neighborhood, and that the Indians and English must live in Love, as long as the Sun gave light." Penn's allusion to his colony as "The Holy Experiment" was made in deep sincerity and the history of Pennsylvania in the years to come gave real meaning to the phrase. The laws Penn made, wrote Voltaire years later, "were very wise and have remained unchanged. The first is, to mistreat no one because of his religious belief, and to regard all those who believe in God as brothers. . . ." Penn's treaty with the Indians, he observed, was "the only treaty between these peoples and the Christians which was not sworn to and which has not been broken." Here, at last, Voltaire concluded, was proof that men of many beliefs and races could lead the good life side by side without need of autocratic restraints.

Penn's land of freedom had been widely advertised abroad and Philadelphia became a port of entry for great swarms of immigrants. The promise of a new start in life appealed particularly to the discontented German peasantry; in 1738 alone some nine thousand immigrants from the Rhineland landed at the city. "It has not been necessary to force people to come and settle here," wrote Peter Kalm, the Swedish scientist; "on the contrary, foreigners of different languages have left their country, houses, property and relations and ventured over wide and stormy seas in order to come hither . . .

Pennsylvania . . . has received hosts of people which other countries, to their infinite loss, have either neglected, belittled or expelled." Many of the newcomers had no sentimental loyalty to the English government, nor to any other than that which promised some practical arrangement for living among neighbors of varying convictions.

The Reverend Andrew Burnaby, a genial English clergyman who toured the "Middle Settlements" in 1759–60, found the Pennsylvanians "a frugal and industrious . . . [and] by far the most enterprising people on the continent. As they consist of several nations and talk several languages, they are aliens in some respect to Great Britain: nor can it be expected that they should have the same filial attachment to her which her own immediate offspring have."

"They are great republicans," he added, "and have fallen into the same errors of in-

The Metropolitan Museum of Art

THE STATE HOUSE (INDEPENDENCE HALL), PHILADELPHIA, BUILT IN 1735. Engraving from the *Columbian Magazine*, 1778, after a drawing by Charles Willson Peale.

The Metropolitan Museum of Art
DETAIL FROM A PENNSYLVANIA-GERMAN BIRTH CERTIFICATE, 1789.

American shores as the eighteenth century progressed. The Moravians with their missionary zeal, gentle demeanor, and peculiar devotions were welcome newcomers. In 1741 they settled the back-country town of Bethlehem and it quickly flourished in a manner that made it one of the show-places of America, visited by a file of curious and interested travelers. Practicing a sort of agrarian communism, enriching the land they occupied, and maintaining a vigorous cultural life according to their particular lights they, like the Mennonites, Dunkers, and other German sectarians, added immeasurably to the colony's growing importance.

dependency as most of the other colonies have." In its State House Pennsylvanians had already built the shrine in which those "errors" would be consecrated a few years later.

The German Pietist groups who were attracted by the promise of peace and tolerance in the land Penn had opened formed one current in the tide of non-English emigrants that beat with increasing force on

No colony was more heterogeneous than Pennsylvania in its population. The Secretary of the Province complained in 1729 that all Ireland seemed to be moving into the colony. "The common fear is," he wrote, "that if they continue to come they will make themselves proprietors of the province." In 1753 Benjamin Franklin thought the Germans might assume control. "I re-

The New York Public Library
MORAVIANS BAPTISING AMERICAN INDIANS. Engraving from Kurze, *Zuvelassige Nachricht,* 1762.

BETHLEHEM, PENNSYLVANIA, 1742. Water color drawing.

member," he said, "when they modestly declined intermeddling in our elections, but now they come in droves and carry all before them." Baptists, vigorous champions of equality among the "plain people," were also rapidly making Philadelphia the principal base of that denomination in America.

But all in all, Burnaby concluded after witnessing the accomplishment of Pennsylvania, "can the mind have a greater pleasure than . . . in perceiving a rich and opulent state arising out of a small settlement or colony? This pleasure every one must feel who considers Pennsylvania." Yet where peo-

BAPTISMAL CEREMONY BESIDE THE SCHUYLKILL. Engraving by Henry Dawkins (?) from Morgan Edwards, *Material towards a History of the Baptists in Pennsylvania*, Philadelphia, 1770.

ple of every persuasion rubbed elbows they sometimes generated friction and heat.

Many observers of the colonial scene felt that differing interests in America would bring about serious civil conflicts before any common cause for union might be found. Not only were the individual colonies disparate and separate in their interests but groups within each colony were at odds with one another. In Pennsylvania, as elsewhere, class and sectional differences caused grave tensions that occasionally broke the peace. "Those from the westward," wrote Charles Biddle of that colony, "look upon the people in any of the commercial towns as little better than swindlers, while those of the east consider the western members a pack of savages." Infuriated by eastern indifference to their claims for adequate frontier defenses a group of rangers from the town of Paxton—"the Paxton Boys"—murdered a band of Indians in retaliation for raids by other redskins. The following year, 1764, six hundred armed "back inhabitants" marched on Philadelphia to force their claims. Armed resistance was planned in the East but Benjamin Franklin's diplomacy averted open conflict. He rode to Germantown to greet the invading force and convinced them to turn back. "The fighting force we put on," wrote Franklin, "and the reasonings we used with the insurgents, having turned them back and restored quiet to the city, I became less a man than ever; for I had by this transaction, made myself many enemies among the populace."

In the Pennsylvania election of that same year sectional and economic grievances were aggravated by religious and racial differences. It was managed, wrote Franklin, "with more decency and good manners than would have been expected from such irritated partisans. . . . The Dutch Calvinists and the Presbyterians of both Houses . . . assisted the new ticket. The Church were divided and so were the Dutch Lutherans. The Moravians and most of the Quakers were the grand supporters of the old; the McClenaghanites

The New York Public Library

PREPARING FOR THE PAXTON EXPEDITION AGAINST PHILADELPHIA, 1764. Engraving by Henry Dawkins. A satirical account of an affair which typified the strained relations between the back country and the "effete," monied East which existed in most of the colonies. The engraving is also interesting as the earliest known interior view of Philadelphia, showing the Old Court House on Second Street and the buildings about it.

THE ELECTION OF 1764. Anonymous engraving.

The American Antiquarian Society

were divided, though chiefly of the old side. The poll was opened about 9 in the morning . . . and the steps so crowded till between 11 and 12 at night, that at no time a person could get up in less than a quarter of an hour. . . . About 3 in the morning, the advocates for the new ticket moved for a close, but . . . the old hands kept it open . . . til 3 in the [next] afternoon. . . . A number of squibs, quarters, and half sheets were thrown among the population on the day of the election." Franklin, as usual in the dead center of controversy, lost his seat in the Assembly by twenty-five votes out of nearly four thousand.

Despite such controversies and differences of opinion, perhaps because of them, Philadelphia evolved into the most progressive and the largest city in the colonies. Even omitting the incomparable Franklin, the list of its distinguished inhabitants—artists, scientists, humanitarians, and scholars—was second to that of no city in the British empire except London and despite the sobering influence of the Quakers no colonial city enjoyed a more consistently active and brilliant social life.

The Historical Society of Pennsylvania
FRANCIS HOPKINSON CONVERSING WITH A LADY (POSSIBLY ELIZABETH GRAEME). From Benjamin West's sketchbook.

81

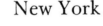

THE SKYLINE OF "YE FLOURISHING CITY OF NEW YORK," 1716–1718. Engraving after a drawing by William Burgis. Photograph courtesy of The Metropolitan Museum of Art. When the view was drawn New York,

New York

THE TIP OF MANHATTAN ISLAND, 1716–1718. A detail from the Burgis View (above). At the extreme left, next to the houses with "their gavell ends fronting the street," a portion of the ruins of Governor Stuyvesant's Great House at Whitehall. The British flag flies from the Fort which houses the Chapel just to the right.

England's ready-made colony, reaching up along the Hudson River to Canada, was little altered by the change from Dutch administration in 1664. It remained a mixture of races and religions and for years was divided in its interests and torn by internal disputes. "Our chiefest unhappyness here," complained one early resident, "is too great a mixture."

Then as now the port of New York served as gateway to the New World for infinite varieties of people; and it had early acquired, according to one witness, the arrogance and the sounds of Babel. Above the clatter from the city streets one might have heard, in the late seventeenth century, polite conversation in an easy medley of French, Dutch, and English at Governor Lovelace's club. On the streets and in the taverns the talk, more or less polite, might have been in still different languages. The city's population has always been polyglot, at every level; and it has always been a sailors' town.

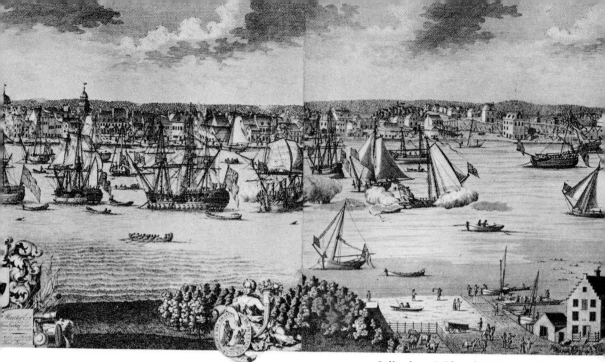

Collection of Edward W. C. Arnold

with a population of about 6500, was the third largest city in the colonies. It shows the East River front, as seen from Brooklyn Heights, from the tip of Manhattan island to a point just north of Catherine Street.

In 1704 when Sarah Knight, the sprightly Boston matron, traveled to New York on horseback, she found that the budding metropolis still retained much of its Dutch flavor. "The Bricks in some of the Houses," she wrote, "are of divers Coulers and laid in Checkers, being glazed look very agreeable. The inside of them are neat to admiration" . . . as one might expect of Dutch houses.

Forty years later colonial America's most witty and urbane traveler, Dr. Alexander Hamilton of Maryland (he whose sketch of the Tuesday Club is illustrated several pages back), found the city "less in extent but, by the stirr and frequency upon the streets, more populous than Philadelphia; I saw more shipping in the harbour; the houses are . . . in generall, higher built, most of them after the Dutch modell with their gavell ends fronting the street. . . . It is a very rich place, but it is not so cheap living here as at Philadelphia. . . ."

"At Albany," wrote Hamilton, ". . . they

The Metropolitan Museum of Art
THE NEW DUTCH CHURCH AT NASSAU AND CROWN STS., NEW YORK, 1731. Engraving after a drawing by William Burgis. The earliest view of the interior of the city.

NORTH PEARL AND STATE STREETS, ALBANY, ABOUT 1805. Sketch by James Eights. The sketch, one of a series of Albany views by Eights, is a careful retrospective study drawn in good part from memory.

are entirely Dutch, and have a method of living something differing from the English . . . [they] keep their homes very neat and clean, both without and within. Their chamber floors are generally laid with rough plank, which in time, by constant rubbing and scrubbing, becomes as smooth as if it had been planed. Their chambers and rooms are large and handsome. They have beds generally in alcoves, so that you may go thro' all the rooms of a great house and see never a bed. They affect pictures much, particularly scripture history, with which they adorn their rooms. They set out their cabinets and *buffets* much with china. Their kitchens are likewise very clean, and they hang earthen or delft plates and dishes all around the walls, in manner of pictures, having a hole drilled thro' the edge of the plate or dish, and a loop of ribbon put into it to hang it by; . . . They live in their houses . . .

as if it were in prison, all their doors and windows being perpetually shut. . . . The young men here call their sweethearts *luffees,* and a young fellow of eighteen is reckoned a simpleton if he has not a *luffee;* but their women are so homely that a man must never have seen any other *luffees* else they will never entrap him."

The colony of New York stood as a main bulwark against the French and Indian menace from the North and West. At an early date New England had sensed the strategic position of Albany standing on the high road between French Canada and the English settlements. The city, it was pointed out in 1690, "is a strong & well fashioned Curb for o^r Enemies, which if it be broken they would run at a prodigious Rate. Albany is the Dam, wch should it through neglect be broken down by ye weight of ye Enemy, we dread to think of the Inundation of Calamities yt would quickly follow thereupon."

During most of the colonial period Albany remained a main English trading center for furs and, as such, was also close to the focus of irritation between the two colonial powers. As trappers and traders advanced ever farther into the wilderness to reap the fabulous harvest of pelts, expenses mounted and large interests became involved that were often at odds with British colonial policy. All along the western frontier, from West Florida to Maine, France and England, dueling for empire, touched points where the French *coureurs de bois* and the colonial borderers matched wits — and frequently their own hides, in addition—to secure "the vast inland trade of furs and skins." The Indians became hopelessly involved in the bitter rivalry of the whites, were dragged into a vicious cycle of trade and strife, and were corrupted endlessly by a competitive traffic

that usually recognized few if any scruples.

To hold the Five Nations, most powerful of the Indian forces, to the English cause, Colonel Peter Schuyler of New York took five Iroquois sachems to London early in the eighteenth century, hoping to impress them with the might and majesty of Queen Anne. The friendly savages attracted enormous attention, were reported constantly in the press, and had their portraits painted. "Four Indian sachems [one had died en route] . . . lately arrived here," remarked a contemporary Londoner, "offering their services to assist her majestie against all her enemies in those parts . . . had yesterday an audience with the queen, and accepted very gratiously: her majestie ordered them presents, the lord chamberlain to entertain them at her charge, and that they be shewn what is remarkable here: 'tis said they'll goe over and have a view of our army in Flanders."

The New York Public Library
A FRENCH CANADIAN, 1778. From an extra-illustrated copy of Max von Eelking, *Memoirs and Letters and Journals of Major General Riedesel*, Albany, 1868.

The New-York Historical Society
TEE YEE HO GA ROW. ONE OF THE INDIAN "KINGS" WHO VISITED ENGLAND IN 1709–1710. Engraving by I. Simon after a painting by I. Verelst.

If the savages were impressed by the sights they saw in Europe, England was apparently impressed by the sight of the savages; at least their visit seemed to dramatize the situation in the distant colonies. From Columbus' day to the present Indians from the forests and plains of America have always had a peculiar fascination for Europeans.

Sir William Johnson, Superintendent of Indian Affairs, was for many years previous to the Revolution a powerful factor in keeping the Iroquois along the New York frontier at peace with the English. The testimonials and honorary commissions which accompanied his gifts of medals and silver gorgets to the more important chiefs added to the solemnity of the peace councils and, incidentally, preserve for those of a later day a contemporary representation of such ceremonies, as shown below.

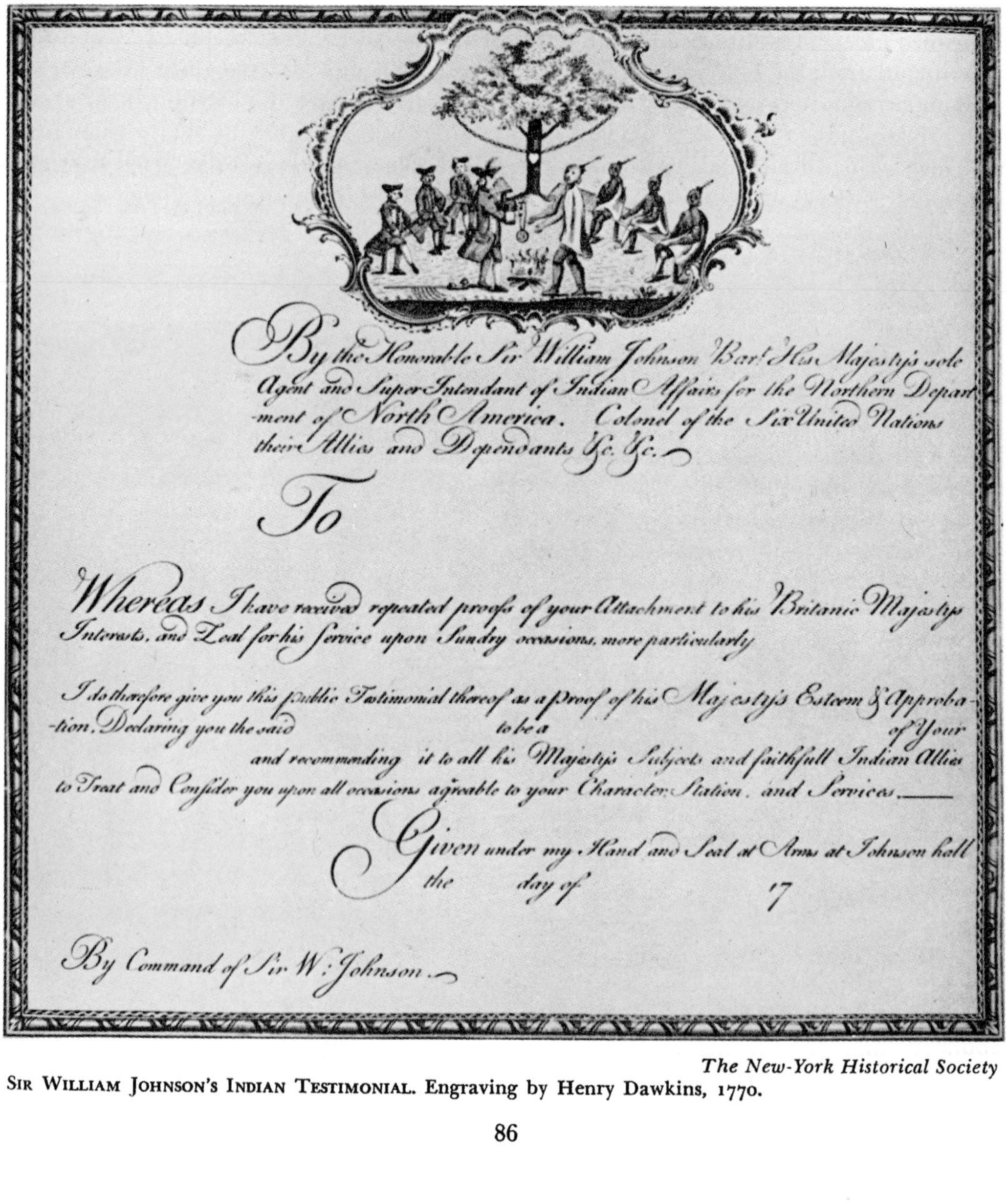

By the Honorable Sir William Johnson Bar.t His Majestys sole Agent and Super Intendant of Indian Affairs for the Northern Depart-ment of North America. Colonel of the Six United Nations their Allies and Dependants &c. &c.

To

Whereas I have received repeated proofs of your Attachment to his Britanic Majestys Interests, and Zeal for his Service upon Sundry occasions, more particularly

I do therefore give you this Public Testimonial thereof as a Proof of his Majestys Esteem & Approba-tion, Declaring you the said to be a of Your and recommending it to all his Majestys Subjects and faithfull Indian Allies to Treat and Consider you upon all occasions agreable to your Character, Station, and Services.

Given under my Hand and Seal at Arms at Johnson hall the day of 17

By Command of Sir W: Johnson

The New-York Historical Society

SIR WILLIAM JOHNSON'S INDIAN TESTIMONIAL. Engraving by Henry Dawkins, 1770.

THE PHILIPSE MANOR AT YONKERS, NEW YORK, 1784. Water color by D. R. Photograph courtesy of the Frick Art Reference Library. The Philipse Manor covered a great triangular tract of land with its base running along the Harlem River from the Hudson to the Bronx Rivers and its apex at the junction of the Croton and Hudson Rivers.

The land of what seemed an unbounded continent was a strong temptation to men of various motives. Everywhere in the colonies it opened the way to rapid fortune for those who stood in well with the dispensing powers and could amass vast holdings. Everywhere, too, it suggested to common men an escape from landlordism by moving ever beyond the surveys, or beyond reach of any land agents.

In New York the patroon system of the Dutch and the extravagant handouts of England's royal governors brought enormous estates into the hands of certain colonial families, the Livingstons, Schuylers, Rensselaers, Philipses, and others. Such land monopolization had a lasting effect on the development of the colony. Together with the presence of the Iroquois in the Mohawk Valley and the mountain barrier of the Catskills and Adirondacks, it long discouraged abundant immigration such as fed the hinterland of Pennsylvania.

THE RAPALJE CHILDREN—GARRET, GEORGE, ANNA, AND JAMES. Painting by John Durand, about 1768. The Rapaljes, originally a Huguenot family, bought their land in Brooklyn directly from the Indians.

87

THE RURAL SCENE. Engraving in the *Pennsylvania Town and Country-Man's Almanack,* printed by John Tobler, Germantown, Pa., 1756.

New England

In the innumerable settlements that dotted New England the pattern of life was set by a separate order of natural conditions. At best agriculture succeeded on hardly more than a subsistence level. At worst, wrote one Jeremiah, "the air of the country is sharp, the rocks many, the trees innumerable, the wolves at midnight howling." New England youths who were "verie Sharp and early Ripe in their Capacities" according to Cotton Mather, looked rather to the sea for their fortunes. The ocean was their plantation and their hunting ground; the cod and its scaly cousins were their staple crop.

The fishing banks and trade routes of the Atlantic were fields of plenty but they were not always on the direct road to salvation. The devil and the deep blue sea often went together. In port, lamented Governor Bradford, seamen "spente and scattered a great deale of money among the people, and yet more sin . . . than money." As time passed a little less faith and a little more debit and credit, proportionately, crept into the daily transactions of New England life; the ledger gained on the Bible.

Just before the Revolution Captain William Owen, himself a seafaring man in port

THE LURE OF THE SEA AND THE COUNTING HOUSE. Engraving by Nathaniel Hurd from a table of weights and measures, 1750–1775.

The William L. Clements Library, University of Michigan
NEW ENGLAND PSALM SINGERS. Engraving by Paul Revere from *The New England Psalm-Singer or Chorister*, composed by William Billings, 1770.

at Boston, observed: "The character of the Inhabitants of this Province is very much improved, in comparison to what it was: but puritanism and a spirit of persecution is not yet totally extinguished." Nor would it be for time to come. Through the centuries New England remains the legendary home of the primitive American conscience. In 1945 a whimsical Massachusetts senate refused to reverse the action by which the General Court banished Anne Hutchinson in 1637 for her religious beliefs.

The restriction of others, which has been called the essence of Puritanism, had some practical explanations now all but forgotten. Young men were forbidden to fish or loiter in the woods, not to spoil their fun, but to prevent their falling into the hands of the Indians who might seize their guns to use against other settlers. Cooking on the Sabbath was forbidden so that during the long hours a family was at church the house might not catch fire and endanger the rest of the settlement. Smoking was limited to remove the temptation to plant tobacco when corn was so much needed.

Boston was ever the hub of New England activity and "the principal mart of trade in North America." When Dr. Hamilton visited the city in 1744 he found over one hundred ships in the harbor besides a great number of smaller craft even though the times were "very dead" because of the war—King George's War or the War of the Austrian Succession. He also saw at least one privateer abuilding on the stocks and a French prize laden with wine, brandy, and other booty that had been brought into port shortly before by the brigantine *Hawk*.

Armed merchantmen bearing letters of marque and reprisal provided ample employment and excitement for New England fishermen during colonial wars. In 1748 the *Bethel*, Portsmouth-built and manned by thirty-eight men, successfully bluffed and captured a Spanish treasure ship of twenty-four guns and one hundred and ten men. The easy step from privateering, in wartime, to piracy in peacetime—the tricks were very

much the same in both trades—led more than one New England seaman to wealth, or the gibbet, according to his luck. In peace, in war, and in every season, the sea was the cradle of New England's fortune. The fisheries, the ocean lanes, and the trading ports of the Atlantic area swarmed with Yankees.

Boston, like every other major community in English America, was a city of mixed peoples. French, Irish, Scotch, German, Dutch, and Welsh—as well as English—contributed distinguished names to the city's early history and blue blood to the Yankee strain. When Captain Francis Goelet, a convivial New York merchant, visited Boston in 1750 he described it as "The largest Town upon the Contenant, Haveing about Three Thousand Houses in it, about two Thirds of them Wooden Framed Clap Boarded &c. and some of them Very Spacious Buildings which togeather with their Gardens about them Cover a Great deal Ground. . . . The Streets are very Erregular the Main Streets

TWO VIEWS OF THE LETTER OF MARQUE SHIP "BETHEL" OF BOSTON, 14 GUNS, 1748. The *Bethel* was owned by Josiah Quincy and Edward Jackson. Painting by an unidentified artist. Photograph courtesy of the Massachusetts Historical Society.

The Peabody Museum of Salem

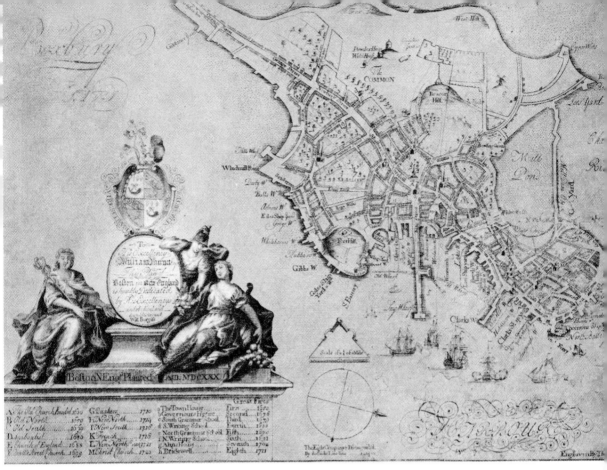

A PLAN OF BOSTON, ABOUT 1728. Engraving by Thomas Johnston.

are Broad and Paved with Stone the Cross Streets are but Narrow mostly Paved Except towards the Outskirts the Towne. The Towne Extends ab^t two Miles in Lenght North and South and is in some places ½ mile and Others ¾ mile Broad has One Main Street Rung the whole Length The Towne from North to South and Tolerable broad the Situation is Vastly Pleasant being on a Neck Land. . . . In Boston they are very Strict Observers of the Sabath day and in Service times no Persons are allow'd the Streets but Doctors if you are found upon the Streets and the Constables meet you they Compell you to go either to Curch or Meeton as you Chuse, also in Sweareing if you are Catcht you must Pay a Crown Old Tenor for Every Oath being Convicted thereof without farther dispute the ¾ths of the Inhabitants art Strict Presbyterians."

THE STATE HOUSE, BOSTON, BUILT IN 1748. Engraving from the *Massachusetts Magazine*, July, 1793.

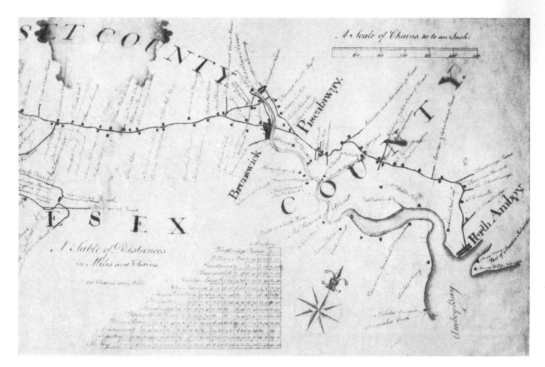

PORTION OF THE ROAD FROM TRENTON TO AMBOY, N. J., 1762. Manuscript map. The location and ownership of the original are unknown.

E PLURIBUS UNUM?

Intercolonial Traffic

In terms of time required for travel and communication between its various parts colonial America was immensely larger than the full-grown nation is today. Colonial society was more varied than American society is in the twentieth century. To weave such separate and disparate elements into a seamless fabric—or even a tightly joined patchwork—seemed beyond reasonable expectation.

Yet, in many respects the differences between colonies were frequently more obvious than profound. Throughout the eighteenth century a web of common and mutual interests—economic, political, and cultural—was spinning over and about the diversities of colonial experience. Perhaps, as some observers reported, a new and recognizable

American strain was developing in the "free aire of the New Worlde," up and down the coast from the southern rice fields to the northern shipyards. At the conclusion of his 1624-mile journey in 1744, Doctor Alexander Hamilton concluded: "I found but little difference in the manners and character of the people in the different Provinces I passed thro'. . . . As to politeness and humanity they are much alike, except in the great towns, where the inhabitants are more civilized, especially at Boston."

A generation later in 1776, it had become, as Thomas Paine expressed it, only common sense to recognize the single, free destiny that loomed larger than all apparent differences between Americans. It was "the seedtime of Continental union," a union that would involve one of the crucial experiments in the history of government.

Along the eastern seaboard an incessant and increasing passage of men and goods between the colonies gradually developed new, interlocking interests. Roads through the wilderness only slowly became reasonably passable and, despite the uncertainties of wind and weather, travel and transport by water usually offered more advantages. Myriad small vessels plied the coastal routes between the larger settlements and searched out markets far up the rivers of the tidewater. Boston built the first colonial lighthouse ("a high stone building in form of a sugar loaf, upon the top of which every night they burn oil to direct and guide the vessels att sea into the harbour") in 1716 to help protect the heavy traffic of its port. By 1728 a regular packet service was established between New York and Charleston to handle the provision trade between these two points.

On land, too, intercolonial traffic, growing in volume, gradually beat the Indian trails into roads that could be recognized as such. Madam Knight's lively account of her horseback trip from Boston to New York, through a "thickly" settled portion of the colonies recounts overland travel as it was at the dawn of the eighteenth century. "Jogging on with an easy pace," her guide warning her "it was dangero's to Ride hard in the Night," or "riding very hard" with another guide, she sometimes found it thirty miles between houses. At times the road was little more than a trace, the trees and bushes scratching her from either side. After swimming one river on her horse she emerged "like a holy Sister Just come out of a Spiritual Bath in dripping Garments," and after five days of travel managed to reach New Haven. However, country roads constantly

THE BOSTON LIGHTHOUSE AND AN ARMED SLOOP, ABOUT 1729. Engraving by Will Burgis. A unique copy.
The U.S. Bureau of Lighthouses

Collection of Edward W. C. Arnold

THE NEW YORK LONG ISLAND FERRY AND FERRY HOUSE WITH CATTLE FOR THE NEW YORK MARKET, 1716–18. Detail from the Burgis view of New York. Photograph courtesy of The Metropolitan Museum of Art.

became wider rather than deeper. In 1732 America's first road guide was issued, presumably in response to some need and demand. It listed among other things the locations and dates of the principal fairs held in the northern colonies. Better roads in New Jersey made possible regular weekly stage service from Amboy to Trenton and Philadelphia after 1730. Milestones marked the main roads and taverns increased along the roadside. In 1748 Peter Kalm reported that the inhabitants of New Brunswick got "a considerable profit from the travellers who every hour pass on the high road."

Accommodations en route might vary from a lousy bed shared with other travelers, and all but inedible fare, to "large and lofty Apartments with a noble Prospect" and a bountiful variety of good food and drink. At one Mother Stack's in 1750 James Birket "with great Intreaty and fair words" managed to obtain a candle to find his way into her tavern—and when he got there the cup-

board was bare. About the same time George Fisher, on the other hand, was ushered into a tavern room in Maryland that was elegantly outfitted with mahogany furniture "and so stuft with fine large glaized Copper Plate Prints" that he almost fancied himself in a fine London print shop.

In some seasons some roads were probably very good by the standards of the day, but the best of them were smoother with the winter's snow that sleighs could glide over. Ferries served the traveling public at all important points where rivers and bays crossed the road. Madam Knight ferried across the river at Providence in a cranky canoe, "not daring so much as to lodg my tongue a hair's breadth more on one side of my mouth than tother, nor so much as think on Lott's wife, for a wry thought would have oversett our wherey." However, ferries slightly later and at other points were quite up to carrying wheeled vehicles. As early as 1723 the ferry at the Schuylkill River offered to cross with a coach or chariot for one shilling, a loaded cart for the same, and a sled, loaded or unloaded, for one penny.

English travelers were relieved that traveling by night or day was safe since there were "no highway robbers to interrupt them" as so often there were at home. Regular, periodic stage service on heavily traveled routes had progressed far enough by 1771 to support a "Flying Machine" that advertised a New York to Philadelphia run in a day and a half for twenty shillings plus food and lodging. That same year the artist Copley, journeying from Boston to New York, reported "you scarcely lose sight of a house" on the way. Before the Revolution the intercolonial arterial system permitted a brisk, if undependable and not always easy, circulation. A false report of British troop movements "flew like Lightning" through the country; "In . . . five or six days the Alarm spread thro' above half a Million of People." On the other hand it took news of the Declaration of Independence twenty-nine days to reach Charleston from Philadelphia.

Collection of Morgan B. Brainard
TAVERN SIGN, 1773, probably from the Yellow House, Rocky Hill, Connecticut.

The American Antiquarian Society
THE GREEN DRAGON TAVERN, ON UNION STREET NEAR HAYMARKET SQUARE, BOSTON. Drawing by John Johnston, 1773. Under the original drawing appears the inscription: "Where we met to Plan the Consignment of a few Shiploads of Tea." It was here that patriots, including Paul Revere, held their meetings in the months preceding the Revolution, to watch over British designs.

A Common Threat

The need of co-operation between the colonies was most poignantly felt in matters of war. More than one Parliament had tried to awaken the colonies to their common cause of self-protection but, as one report stated, found them "stuffed with commonwealth notions" and "of a sour temper in opposition to government." The threat of French competition for empire, for land and furs and fish, menaced the whole length of colonial America in various degrees. Franklin, not usually an alarmist, warned his countrymen in lurid fashion of their peril from French and Indian attacks. "On the first alarm," he wrote, "terror will spread over all: and, as no man can with certainty know that another will stand by him, beyond doubt very many will seek safety by a speedy flight. . . . Sacking the city will be the first, and burning it, in all probability, the last act of the enemy. This, I believe, will be the case, if you have timely notice. But what must be your condition, if suddenly surprised, without previous alarm, perhaps in the night!" The danger was real enough, as many frontier settlements could testify. Out of the fear and the determination it bred, if not from any theory of union, the colonists learned a few lessons in the value of common effort.

Governor Shirley's "mad scheme" to protect New England's trade and fisheries by reducing the French fortress at Louisbourg on Cape Breton launched a dramatic joint effort in 1745. Connecticut, Massachusetts, and New Hampshire raised men, New York supplied cannon, Pennsylvania and New Jersey sent provisions. The entire army was American, recruited from farmers, fishermen, shopkeepers, artisans, and others little disciplined in military matters. "Pepperrell's Yokels" they have been called, after the Kit-

LANDING OF THE NEW ENGLAND FORCES AGAINST CAPE BRETON, 1745. Engraving by Brooks after a painting by J. Stevens.

Yale University Art Gallery, Mabel Brady Garvan Collection

tery merchant who, though completely inexperienced in leading troops into battle, was chosen by Shirley as commander. He was, at least, no less experienced than anybody else in military matters and he, like the other officers who were appointed, had a popularity indispensable in attracting volunteers for the expedition.

"The News of our Government's Raising an army," wrote one volunteer," (Together with the Help of the other Neighbouring Governments) In order to the Reduction of Cape Breton (Viz) Louisbourg, which was Like to prove Detremental if not Destroying to our Country. So affected the minds of many (together with The Expectation of Seeing Great things, etc.) —As to Incline many, yea, Very Many to Venture themselves and Enlist into the Service Among whom, I was one, which was the, 14th of March 1745. I And having had the Consent of my friends, (and asking their Prayers), Which was A great Comfort to me. Even all the Time of my being Asent. I set out for Boston, Tuesday March 19th."

A fleet of ninety transports escorted by a few provincial cruisers sailed from Nantasket Roads on March 24, 1745. The landsmen were miserable on the high seas. "Sick, day and night, so bad that I have not words to set it forth," wrote one of them, a Northampton gunsmith. By the end of April the motley fleet, now buttressed by three British ships of war, had assembled at their destination. "A Party of our Men landing under the Fire of some of our smaller Cruizers, row'd on Shore very briskly in their Whale Boats," reported the New York press weeks later, "and so resolutely march'd up and attacked the Enemy, that they kill'd 8 on the Spot, wounded several others, and took ten Prisoners. . . . This was done without the Loss of one Man on our side, and in this their first Action our Men took so good Aim, that one of the Slain was found with five Balls lodg'd in his Breast." Actually surf and rocks had been more formidable than the enemy at that point; but it was a skillful, critical landing. According to Parkman the

The Metropolitan Museum of Art
SIR WILLIAM PEPPERRELL, COMMANDER IN CHIEF OF THE AMERICAN FORCES AT LOUISBOURG. Engraving by Peter Pelham, 1747, after a painting by John Smibert. Pepperrell, the son of an immigrant Welshman, was one of the chief merchants of New England as well as a successful land speculator. After his extraordinary command at Louisbourg he was made a baronet and commissioned colonel in the British Army.

ragged Yankee militia, barefoot and tattered as they quickly became in the campaign, "toiled on with indomitable pluck and cheerfulness, doing the work which oxen could not do, with no comfort but their daily dram of New England rum as they plodded through the marsh and over rocks, dragging their ponderous guns through fog and darkness" towards their objective. Like true Puritans and self-appointed champions of the gospel, Parkman explained, they were pleased to be teaching their duty to others, in this case the idolators of Catholic France. After a forty-nine-day siege the "Canadian Gibraltar" fell to the colonists. "Never was a place more mal'd [mauled] with cannon and shells," Pepperrell wrote to Shirley after he had entered Louisbourg, "neither have I red in History of any troops behaving with greater courage."

THE WAGGONER AND HERCULES. From *Plain Truth,* written and published by Benjamin Franklin, 1747.

Visiting Boston in 1746 Benjamin Franklin found the city in a military ferment following the successful Cape Breton expedition. He caught the martial spirit and returning to Philadelphia aroused the citizens to preparedness in the little pamphlet already quoted from. On the inside cover an engraving, possibly designed by Franklin himself, depicted Hercules on a cloud, leaning on his club, while three horses struggle in the foreground to pull a wagon through the mud. The waggoner prays to the gods for help. The sketch apparently recalls the an-

FRANKLIN'S HISTORIC SLOGAN. From the *Pennsylvania Gazette,* May 9, 1754. Published by Benjamin Franklin in Philadelphia.

cient fable in which Hercules remarks: "Heaven helps only those who help themselves."

"Join or Die," pleaded Franklin in a slogan that was reproduced frequently in the colonial press. As part of a European peace settlement Louisbourg had been restored to the French in 1748, the bloody French and Indian Wars were starting, and in 1754 Franklin called for a necessary union among the colonies at the Albany Congress.

Almost at the same moment of Franklin's plea young George Washington was surrendering Fort Necessity on the western frontier. The Christmas before, Washington had carried a note from Governor Dinwiddie at Williamsburg to the French commander at Fort Le Boeuf expressing astonishment that he was occupying territory "so notoriously known to be the property of the Crown of Great Britain."

The note was rebuffed with Gallic courtesy. A year later Washington was back on the frontier in command of an improvised militia to insist upon English claims. The French, determined to garrison the passes to the Western country, and seal the colonists forever within their narrow coastal strip, had already built Fort Duquesne on the site now occupied by Pittsburgh and, following a brief but important skirmish at Great Meadows, Washington was forced, on July 4, to surrender the meager defenses of Fort Necessity. Of that skirmish Voltaire wrote, "Such was the complication of political interests that a cannon shot fired in America could give the signal that set Europe in a blaze." Thus was started the Seven Years War, the fourth of the nine world wars in which America has been involved.

A year still later almost to the day found Washington the only unwounded officer of Braddock's staff to survive in another bitter retreat before the enemy near Fort Duquesne. Before his ultimate triumph at Yorktown Washington was well schooled in defeat. The fight, a French witness reported, "was obstinate on both sides . . . but the enemy at last gave way. Efforts were made, in vain, to introduce some sort of order in their retreat. The whoop of the Indians, which echoed through the forest, struck terror into the hearts of the entire enemy. The rout was complete. . . . Some deserters, who have come in since, have told us that we had been engaged with only 2000 men, the remainder of the army being four leagues further off. Those same deserters have informed us that the enemy were retreating to Virginia . . . the thousand men who were not engaged, had been equally panic-stricken and abandoned both provisions and ammunition on the way. . . . The enemy have left more than 1000 men on the field of battle. They have lost a great portion of their artillery and ammunition, provisions, as also their General, whose name was Mr. Braddock, and almost all their officers. . . . We have had 3 officers killed; 2 officers and 2 cadets wounded."

Grim as it was, Braddock's defeat was ultimately less important than the fact that the British then, and again a few years later, hacked a route through the wilderness from the Potomac to the Ohio. It was soon to become a highway for a vast movement of people to the West.

Washington and Lee University
COLONEL GEORGE WASHINGTON OF THE VIRGINIA MILITIA. Painting by Charles Willson Peale, 1772. "Inclination having yielded to importunity, I am now contrary to all expectations," wrote Washington, "under the hands of Mr. Peale; but in so grave—so sullen a mood—and now and then under the influence of Morpheus, when some critical strokes are making, that I fancy the skill of this Gentleman's Pencil will be put to it, in describing to the World what manner of man I am."

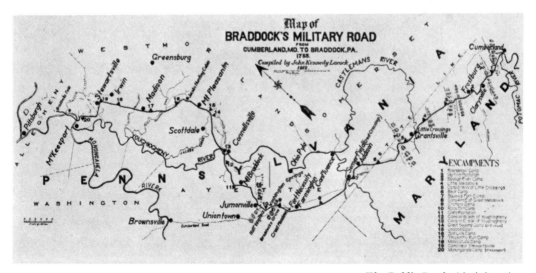

The Public Roads Administration
BRADDOCK'S ROUTE. A modern map, drawn by John Kennedy Lacock, 1912.

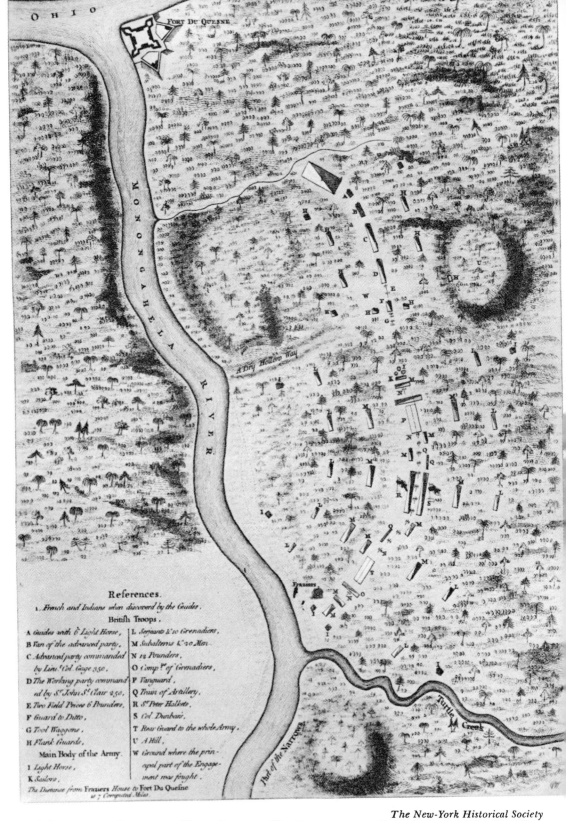

A PLAN OF THE BATTLEFIELD WHERE BRADDOCK WAS DEFEATED, 1755. Engraving printed for T. Jeffery, London, 1758.

Lakes George and Champlain lay along a natural trading route, and just as naturally a great route for war parties, between Canada and the British Colonies. Two months after Braddock's defeat another highly miscellaneous American expeditionary force, drawn in good part from the farmers of the New Hampshire, Connecticut, Massachusetts, Rhode Island, and the New York countryside, launched an attack on the French position at Crown Point. They never made their objective but at Lake George, on September 5, 1755, they scored an incidental victory that helped to temper the provincial soldiery. "Perhaps," wrote Seth Pomeroy, he who had been seasick en route to Louisbourg ten years before, "the hailstones from heaven were never much thicker than their bullets came; but, blessed be God! that did not in the least daunt or disturb us." After the battle the wounded and captured French commander remarked that the provincials had fought like good boys in the morning, like men about noon, and like devils in the afternoon.

Commanding the way between Lake George and Lake Champlain, Fort Ticonderoga, which was to become such a historic landmark on the American scene, was begun by the French as an outpost in 1755–56. Here was fought, on July 8, 1758, one of the bloodiest battles in British military history. The British forces, which included 9034 provincials, lost in killed, wounded, and missing, almost 2000 men in this wilderness encounter. Montcalm, the victorious French defender, exultantly wrote to a friend: "The army, the too-small army of the King, has beaten the enemy. What a day for France! If I had had two hundred Indians to send out at the head of a thousand picked men . . . not many would have escaped. Ah, my dear Doreil, what soldiers are ours! I never saw the like." Lord Jeffrey Amherst took Ticonderoga the next year, Ethan Allen and Benedict Arnold took it from the British in 1775, and Burgoyne took it back again in 1777.

America was by now critically involved in a war that had quickly spread from the dark forests about Fort Necessity to the distant Philippines—here called the French and Indian War. The opening years of conflict were not unlike the more recent days that followed Pearl Harbor. England seemed to be not quite "muddling through" and, as Franklin's dire warnings indicated, her colonies were faced with the consequences.

The tide turned with William Pitt's determination to take the three main French strongholds, Quebec, Ticonderoga, and Fort Duquesne, the Key to the Great West, clearing the way, once and for all, for a great expansion of the English people.

William H. Coverdale Collection

A VIEW OF TICONDEROGA (IN 1788). Water color by Henry Rudyerd, Captain of the Royal Engineers.

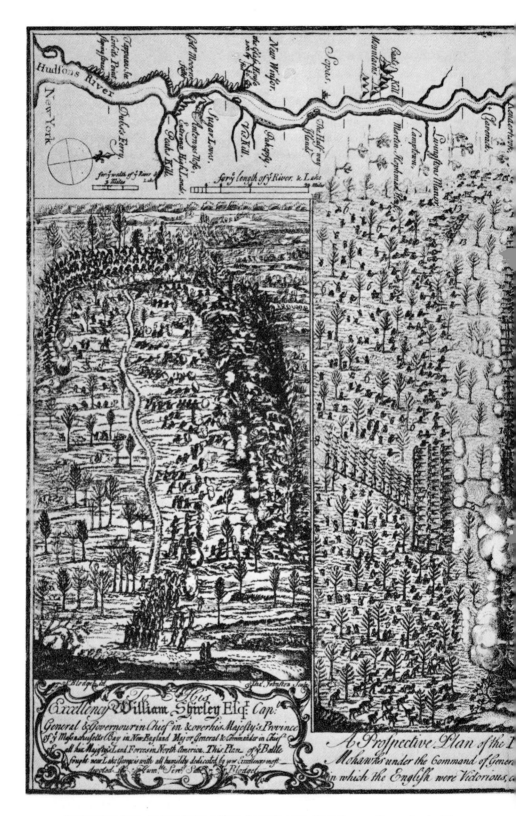

PERSPECTIVE PLAN OF THE BATTLE NEAR LAKE GEORGE, SEPT. 8, 1755. Engraving by Thomas
Johnston after a drawing by Samuel Blodget. A map of the Hudson River from New York
City to the Great Carrying Place is shown at the top; in the left inset, an advance British

detachment, the "bloody morning scout," is shown with the head of the column broken and surrounded by the French in ambush; and in the center the French regulars are receiving the fire of four provincial field pieces.

PLAN OF LOUISBOURG ON CAPE BRETON, JULY 26, 1758. Part of a manuscript figurative map showing the situation shortly before the French surrender. Remnants of the French fleet lie above the town: the British to

The culmination of this program was the attack on Quebec, the heart of French American empire, but to conquer Quebec, Louisbourg, greatly strengthened since its return to France at the Peace of Aix-la-Chapelle, must first be taken all over again. On June 2, 1758, a great armada of British ships fanned out before the Canadian citadel. British naval power, during the century past, had risen greatly and here, at the edge of the New World, it overpowered the defenses of France's greatest bastion in the West. On July 26, 1758, Louisbourg fell and the path

to Quebec lay open. But the French had fought well and the season was too late for the English to advance farther in Canada.

On November 24, however, a force of British, Americans and Indians, after a two months' arduous advance from Virginia, took Fort Duquesne.

William Pitt's decision to concentrate on America as the decisive theater of a European war was paying handsome dividends both to the homeland and her colonies. It was also revealing serious differences between British and colonial opinion. Lord

the left. The large building above the French ships is the Grande Batterie, ignominiously deserted by the French both in 1745 and 1758, the town being thus exposed to a strong fire.

Jeffrey Amherst complained bitterly of the sloth of the provincials in meeting their share of the bargain. Elsewhere it was reported by British critics that the colonial levies were "an extreme bad collection of inn-keepers, horse jockeys and Indian traders . . . a gathering from the scum of the worst people . . . who have wrought themselves up into a panic at the very name of Indians." On the other hand the colonists were often little better pleased by the exacting demands and arrogant manners of their red-coated saviors. Just whose country was being saved and for whom was a question that could open a serious argument.

The spring of 1759 opened with a dual threat to Quebec with Amherst advancing by way of Lake Champlain and Wolfe, with a strong force, both naval and military, appearing in the St. Lawrence. This danger led the French to withdraw from Ticonderoga which was possessed by Amherst in June. Pitt's second objective was gained.

The British came up before Quebec, in the late summer of 1759 under the command of James Wolfe. "Here he could see, in part,"

Yale University Art Gallery, Mabel Brady Garvan Collection

THE TAKING OF QUEBEC, 1759. Engraving printed for R. Sayer and J. Bennett, London. The engraving, following an ages-old practice in graphic representation, shows in one scene a sequence of events: the British barges are seen rowing up the river looking for their landing place; the advance patrol is shown scaling the cliffs and engaging the French defenders in the darkness; and the two main armies, with the French already beginning to break their ranks, are represented as they fought the climactic battle the next day on the Plains of Abraham.

wrote Parkman, "the desperate nature of the task he had undertaken. Before him, three or four miles away, Quebec sat perched upon her rock, a congregation of stone houses, churches, palaces, convents and hospitals; the green trees of the seminary garden and the spires of the cathedral, the Ursulines, the Recollets and the Jesuits. Beyond rose the loftier height of Cape Diamond, edged with palisades and capped with redoubt and parapet. Batteries frowned everywhere; the Chateau battery, the Clergy battery, the Hospital battery on the rock above and the Royal, Dauphin's and Queen's batteries on the strand, where the dwellings and warehouses of the lower town clustered beneath the cliff.

"Full in sight lay the far-extended camp of Montcalm, stretching from the St. Charles beneath the city walls to the chasm and cataract of Montmorenci. From the cataract to the river of Beauport its front was covered by earthworks along the brink of abrupt and lofty heights; and from the river of Beauport to the St. Charles, by broad flats of mud swept by the fire of redoubts, intrenchments, a floating battery and the city itself."

Week after long week of patient probing and thinking passed before the final sudden assault was attempted. "We debarked," wrote a naval officer, in "thirty flat-bottomed boats, containing about sixteen hundred men. This was a great surprise to the enemy, who, from the natural strength of the place, did not suspect . . . so bold an attempt. The chain of centries, which they had posted along the summit of the heights, galled us a little, and picked off several men, and some officers, before our light infantry got up to dislodge them. This grand enterprise was conducted, and executed with great good order and discretion; as fast as we landed, the boats put off for reinforcements, and the troops formed with much regularity. . . . We lost no time here, but clambered up one of the steepest precipices that can be conceived, being almost perpendicular, and of an incredible height. As soon as we gained the summit, all was quiet, and not a shot was heard, owing to the excellent conduct of the light infantry under Colonel Howe. . . . About six o'clock the enemy first made their appearance upon the heights, between us and the town; whereupon we halted, and wheeled to the right, thereby forming the line of battle. . . . "

Both commanders, Wolfe of the British and Montcalm of the French, lost their lives in the brief action on the Plains of Abraham next day. Quebec, the keystone of French America, had fallen before General Wolfe died in peace, praising God for victory. With the mopping up that followed the British colonies for the first time in generations felt free of an awful menace.

In his *History of the English People* Green wrote that it was "no exaggeration to say that three of the many victories of the Seven Years War determined for ages to come the destinies of mankind. With that of Rossbach began the re-creation of Germany; with that of Plassey the influence of Europe told for the first time since the days of Alexander on the nations of the East; with the triumph of Wolfe on the Heights of Abraham began the history of the United States."

Wolfe was the victim of his own enterprise for it was he who had proposed the tragic project to Pitt. It was well for the prospects of those future states that he did not survive to guide the British armies in the next war on American soil. England has not had many more capable and gallant generals.

The triumph at Quebec tossed England from one horn of a dilemma to another. Now, with France in America crushed, would the colonies shake off their dependence on the mother country as the French

THE DEATH OF WOLFE, 1759. Painting by Benjamin West, 1776.

The National Gallery of Canada

COLONEL BOUQUET'S CONFERENCE WITH THE INDIANS, 1764. Engraving by Henry Dawkins from William Smith, *An Historical Account of the Expedition . . . under the Command of Henry Bouquet*, Philadelphia, 1765.

foreign minister warned? Whether England should return Canada to the French was seriously deliberated before the peace treaty was finally signed. Benjamin Franklin contributed to the pamphlet warfare that worried the question, pointing out that if the colonies of their own accord had not united against the French and the Indians there was small chance they would do so against their parent country—without, he cannily added, "the most grievous tyranny and oppression. . . . *The waves do not rise but when the winds blow.*"

The fall of Canada meant little to many colonists unless it also meant that the way to the West was cleared. Even before French power was broken many hundreds of American families, besides traders and land speculators, had crossed the mountains into the upper valley of the Ohio. To thousands of others the peace treaty that ended the Seven Years War was a signal to swarm West. As

Lord Dunmore remarked, Americans "do and will remove as their avidity and restlessness incite them."

However, the Indians who had themselves so often by timely alliance, now one way, now another, tipped the scales in the white man's struggle for empire, were not willingly dispossessed of their primeval home. With tragic bitterness and despair they witnessed every new intrusion. "We are not well used with respect to the Lands still unsold by us. Your People daily settle on those Lands and spoil our Hunting. . . . It is customary with us to make a Present of Skins, whenever we renew our Treaties. We are ashamed to offer our Brethern so few, but your Horses and Cows have eat the Grass our Deer used to feed on." So in the garbled reports of interpreters and transcribers read their piteous objections.

To the white man's lust for land the Indian returned a savage resentment that reached one furious climax, traditionally under the leadership of Pontiac, although his part in the uprising has probably been exaggerated. From Virginia to Niagara, the red avengers ravaged the back country. Every western fort except Detroit and Pittsburgh fell to the savages.

The bloody business was settled when Colonel Henry Bouquet, in command of the Royal Americans and Scottish forces, annihilated a howling mass of Indians at Bushy Run in 1763, called his foe to council the next year, and laid down the white man's law. In a "bower" erected for the ceremony near the Muskingum River, Kiyashuta, chief of the Senecas, Custaloga and Beaver, chiefs of the Wolf and Turkey tribes of the Delawares, and Kiessinautchtha, a chief of the Shawanese with their warriors accepted their fate. Redcoats, not Americans, had quieted the storm.

The trans-Appalachian region was still a "dark and bloody ground" for years to come. But with the organized "Conspiracy," as Pontiac's defense of the wilderness preserves was called, quelled, with Pittsburgh, Detroit, and other stations of the West in English hands, and with the population of the East rising at a phenomenal rate neither British edict nor the remaining uncertainties of life along the frontier could stay the country's "Drang nach Westen." Speculator, adventurer, and homeseeker moved to take over what, with sublime arrogance, they considered the negligible claims of the red natives. Daniel Boone, blazing the Wilderness Trail through and beyond the Cumberland Gap in 1775 as agent for The Transylvania Company — a large-scale land speculation — was the embodiment of most of the motives that carried men and women West along the course of Empire.

DANIEL BOONE ESCORTING A BAND OF PIONEERS INTO THE WESTERN COUNTRY IN 1775. Painting by George Caleb Bingham, about 1851. Bingham's painting is, of course, the product of artistic imagination, but like Leutze's equally fanciful painting of Washington Crossing the Delaware, it has acquired a symbolic importance.
Washington University

The House of Employment, Alms-House, Pennsylvania Hospital, and Part of the City of Philadel-phia. Engraving by J. Hulett after a drawing by Nicholas Garrison, about 1767. The House of Employment and Almshouse, shown at the left of the view, were opened in October, 1767. The justly famed hospital,

Urban Similarities

At five points along the major routes of travel—at Boston, Newport, New York, Philadelphia, and Charleston—little, but full-fledged, cities had risen out of earlier village settlements by mid-eighteenth century. Old World visitors were often startled by the urban character of these "Cities in the Wilderness." In 1748 Peter Kalm remarked on the "grandeur and perfection" of Philadelphia which, he added, were "by no means inferior to those of any, even of the most ancient towns of Europe." He also remarked on "its fine appearance, good regulations . . . natural advantages, trade, riches, and power. . . ."

The growth of Philadelphia was phenomenal. Before 1700 it was already as large as New York and by 1720, with its ten thousand inhabitants, it was close to Boston's twelve thousand and had outstripped New York. Enough of the great influx of immigrants that used the city as a threshold to America stayed right there to swell the size and aggravate the problems of the fast-growing town. More moved out into the rich surrounding lands and poured their bounty back into the city's trade. By the time of the Revolution Philadelphia had bloomed into the first city of the colonies and the second

appearing at the right center, was opened to patients in 1756 thanks, in good part, to the helpful activity of Benjamin Franklin.

city in population of the British Empire.

City status brought city problems, problems of public concern beyond reach of individual effort, problems that bred certain fundamental attitudes in city dwellers of whatever region. The relief of the poor, the sick, and the unfortunate generally was handled by public and private agencies in a manner that reflected civic pride and interest in the general welfare above the usual standards set in Europe. Visitors from abroad commented on the lack of poverty and unemployment in the New World. A beggar in America, it was said, was as rare as a horse on the streets of Venice. But native city dwellers were aware of an increasing problem in the poor and in those who, in a generally hard-working society, "misspent"

their time and needed care at public expense. Sickness was another problem common to all the growing cities. Thanks to the humanitarian and scientific spirit that flourished in Philadelphia, that city attracted medical students from all parts of the continent. The Pennsylvania Hospital, founded in 1755, was well known to most visitors to America. Its cornerstone bore the inscription: "In the year of Christ MDCCLV, George the second happily reigning, (For he sought the happiness of his people) Philadelphia flourishing, (For its inhabitants were public-spirited) This building By the bounty of the government And of many private persons, Was piously founded For the relief of the sick and the miserable. May the God of Mercies bless the undertaking."

FIGHTING A FIRE IN NEW YORK CITY. Engraving by Abraham Godwin, from a fireman's certificate, about 1787.

The constant menace of fire grew with the size and density of cities. Purchased either with private funds or with money provided by public authorities, fire engines were early on the scene. Boston had up-to-date apparatus twenty years before Paris had its first fire engine. Long before the Revolution all towns of any size possessed modern equip-

THE UNION FIRE ENGINE, SALEM, ABOUT 1748. Anonymous painting. Photograph courtesy of the Smithsonian Institution.

ment and organizations of eager volunteer firemen to combat conflagration.

The disaster of fire so often experienced in colonial cities sometimes laid bare the community of interest that reached beyond boundary lines. In 1760 when Boston was swept by fire the New York legislature voted £2500 for the relief of victims since they were their "own Countrymen and members of the same Polity."

Crime and punishment gave urban societies mounting concern as people crowded together in larger, tighter masses. The humanitarian feelings that swept through the nineteenth century were only budding in the eighteenth. Branding, whipping, and sometimes mutilation, as well as fines, imprisonment, and compulsory labor, punished breaches of moral and criminal codes that varied from colony to colony. Except in Pennsylvania the death penalty was imposed for numerous offenses considered less heinous today. In earlier days dispensing justice was simplified by the general feeling that lawyers were an evil unnecessary in the New

World, a condition of social innocence outlined by Thomas More for his utopian commonwealth several centuries earlier. However, punishment became less brutal more quickly in America than in Europe. In later years Tocqueville believed that the equalizing tendencies in American society had softened customs and generated a mutual compassion among those who considered themselves alike in privilege as well as in responsibility.

The New-York Historical Society
A HANGING IN CAMBRIDGE, MASS., 1755.

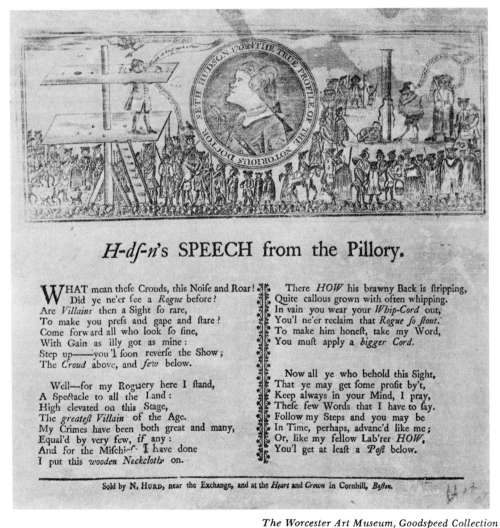

H-df-n's SPEECH from the Pillory.

WHAT mean thefe Crouds, this Noife and Roar!
Did ye ne'er fee a *Rogue* before?
Are *Villains* then a Sight fo rare,
To make you prefs and gape and ftare?
Come forward all who look fo fine,
With Gain as illy got as mine:
Step up——you 'l foon reverfe the Show;
The *Croud* above, and *few* below.

Well—for my Roguery here I ftand,
A Speĉacle to all the Land:
High elevated on this Stage,
The *greateft Villain* of the Age.
My Crimes have been both great and many,
Equal'd by very few, *if* any:
And for the Mifchief I have done
I put this *wooden Neckcloth* on.

There *HOW* his brawny Back is ftripping,
Quite callous grown with often whipping.
In vain you wear your *Whip-Cord* out,
You'l ne'er reclaim that *Rogue fo ftout.*
To make him honeft, take my Word,
You muft apply a *bigger Cord.*

Now all ye who behold this Sight,
That ye may get fome profit by't,
Keep always in your Mind, I pray,
Thefe few Words that I have to fay.
Follow my Steps and you may be
In Time, perhaps, advanc'd like me;
Or, like my fellow Lab'rer *HOW,*
You'l get at leaft a *Poft* below.

Sold by N. HURD, near the Exchange, and at the *Heart* and *Crown* in Cornhill, *Bofton.*

The Worcester Art Museum, Goodspeed Collection
SETH HUDSON'S SPEECH FROM THE PILLORY. Engraving by Nathaniel Hurd, 1762. The self-styled "Doctor" Hudson, posing as a wealthy Dutchman, was finally convicted of counterfeiting. He and his accomplice (shown at the whipping post at right) were punished before a large, exultant crowd of more proper Bostonians.

113

Commercial Ties

Colonial merchants, both by competing with merchants of other colonies and by co-operating with them in ventures of joint interest, helped break down provincial barriers to understanding and unity between different parts of the country. Small ships, constantly weaving in and out of eastern seaports, exchanged ideas along with commodities. Quaker, Yankee, Knickerbocker, and Newport skippers vied with one another to supply the markets of southern colonies where concentration on staple crops made it necessary to import foodstuffs. New York flour was sold in Charleston to provide credit for Dutch merchants to buy rice for Europe. Charleston packets, on the other hand, carried freight to Savannah. And hawkers swarmed overland everywhere beyond colony boundaries to peddle their wares. To convert the currency of any colony into standard Sterling became a common arithmetical problem taught in school and text as a preparation for normal business practice. A knowledge of the customs and habits in different colonies became the indispensable adjunct of a successful merchant.

By land as well as by sea the net of common, interdependent interests was drawing Americans together. More than five hundred letters remaining unclaimed in the Philadelphia post office in 1759 suggest the amount of intercommunication that was developing in pre-Revolutionary years, granting they were only a fraction of the letters successfully delivered. When Benjamin Franklin, as Postmaster General, reduced the rates a few years later the increased use of the mails kept the revenue of his office as high as ever.

The Bella C. Landauer Collection in the New-York Historical Society
A MERCHANT'S COUNTING HOUSE. Engraving by Alexander Lawson, late 18th century.

JAMES TILLEY, NEW ENGLAND MERCHANT. Painting by John Singleton Copley, 1757.

SEA CAPTAINS CAROUSING AT SURINAM, 1757–8(?). Painting by John Greenwood. The artist depicts himself passing out of, and very nearly at, the door; Mr. Jones Wanton of Newport, asleep and being baptised; Capt. Ambrose Page, next to Wanton, quite as sick as the artist; Capt. Nicholas Cook (later Governor of Rhode

Such enterprisers as Thomas Hancock of Boston, uncle of John the bold Signer, had agents in London, Bristol, Lisbon, Bilbao, Amsterdam, and St. Eustacius, as well as in Nova Scotia, Cape Breton, New Brunswick, and a half-dozen New England ports. Smuggling contraband tea from Holland and transshipping condemned, vermin-ridden provisions from army stations in Canada for the use of French prisoners of war were only two items in a long list of more respectable commercial ventures by which he amassed one of the largest fortunes yet recorded in Massachusetts.

As their paths crossed in the ceaseless search for profitable markets colonial sea cap-

Island) with a broad hat and a long pipe, talking at the table with Capt. Esek Hopkins (later Commander of the Continental Navy) who wears a cocked hat and holds a wine glass; Mr. Godfrey Malbone of Newport being instructed in a dance by Capt. Nicholas Powers. There are two Dutchmen among the carousers.

tains had occasional rendezvous in places far beyond the reach of local conventions. The artist John Greenwood was present at such a gathering in Surinam probably in the late 1750's and pictured himself among the convivial seafarers—mostly Rhode Island men of some prominence. Cotton Mather had once written a tract, the *Sailours Com-* *panion and Counsellour*, about just such goings-on. "It is a matter of saddest complaint," he solemnly but vainly observed, "that there should be no more *Serious Piety* in the *Sea-faring Tribe.* Old *Ambrose* called the Sea, *The School of Vertue.* It afflicts all the vertuous here, that the *Mariners* of our Dayes do no more make it so."

The John Carter Brown Library
COLONIAL TRADE CARD. Engraving by Nathaniel Hurd, 1750–1775. The extent of the colonial market for whale oil is indicated by the fact that this advertisement was printed in French, Spanish, German, and Italian, as well as in English.

The whale fishery also brought together on distant seas and in distant markets ships from many colonial ports. Up to less than a century ago whale oil was a vital commodity and competition for the precious stuff was keen. To control the intense rivalry and to assure a satisfactory distribution of profits a group of New Englanders, in 1761, formed the "United Company of Spermaceti Candlers." Through price-fixing and monopolistic regulation of the market, " by all fair and honourable means," they operated what amounted to an intercolonial trust company

whose interests covered most of America.

The sounds, the sights, and the smells of the shipyard were familiar to every inhabitant of every coastal and river town in colonial America. According to one contemporary report, more than 700 vessels were built in New England alone in the year 1723. Five years before, at least ten shipyards were kept busy in Philadelphia. And in varying degrees, so it was up and down the seaboard. As Edmund Burke pointed out in 1757, shipbuilding was a "very considerable business" in America. "Ships are sometimes built here on commision," he wrote, "but frequently the merchants of New England have them constructed on their own account, and loading them with the produce of the colony, — naval stores, fish and fish-oil principally, — they send them out upon a trading voyage to Spain, Portugal, or the Mediterranean; where having disposed of their cargo, they make what advantage they can by freight, until such time as they can sell the vessel herself to advantage, which they seldom fail to do in a reasonable time. They receive the value of the vessel, as well as of the freight of the goods which from time to time they carried, and of the cargo with which they sailed originally, in bills of exchange upon London."

In 1774 shipbuilders along the Thames complained that American competition was

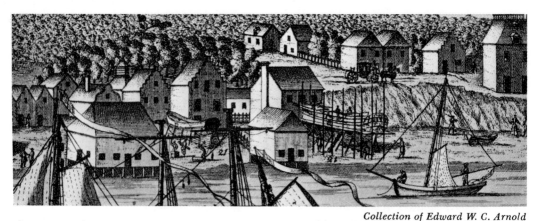

Collection of Edward W. C. Arnold
SHIPBUILDING ALONG THE EAST RIVER, NEW YORK, 1716–18. Detail from the Burgis view of New York. Photograph courtesy of the Metropolitan Museum of Art.

ruining their business. But construction costs were lower in the colonies, wood was everywhere, and England needed ships. On the eve of the Revolution almost a third of the vessels in the English merchant marine were American-made.

Colonial manufactories, modest as they were, sought markets for their products up and down the coast. Benjamin Franklin's "Pennsylvanian Fire-Places" and "Baron" Stiegel's varied assortment of glassware were frequently advertised in the newspapers of several cities where they successfully competed with imported goods for the local trade. Such native products were at times exported to foreign countries. The growing abundance and variety of articles from home and abroad that were channeled through the larger seaports increased the complexities of merchandising. Well before the Revolution retail and specialty shops throughout the colonies were supplementing the auctions, markets, and "Publick Vendues" that served urban communities. The middleman was emerging as an important factor in the distribution of goods and he, along with the artisan and the direct trader, called attention to his wares ever more insistently in a growing number of newspapers. Modern advertising was a-borning and the colonist might, in the "big" cities, shop for excitement as well as market for necessities.

The long battle between sales appeal and sales resistance was fairly joined before the close of the century. Sophisticated New York ladies might go to Mrs. Edward's in 1736 for such frivolous items as a "Beautifying Wash" that would make their skin "soft, smooth and plump," and take away "Redness, Freckles, Sun-Burnings, or Pimples . . . cure Postules, Itchings, Ring-worms, Tetters: Scurf, Morphew, and other like Deformities of the Face and Skin. . . ." They were also becoming more dependent on imports from other colonies and the back country of their own localities for such necessities as rice, spermaceti candles, flour, fish, firewood, and a host of other items. More than 6000 packs of playing cards were disposed of in Boston in 1772.

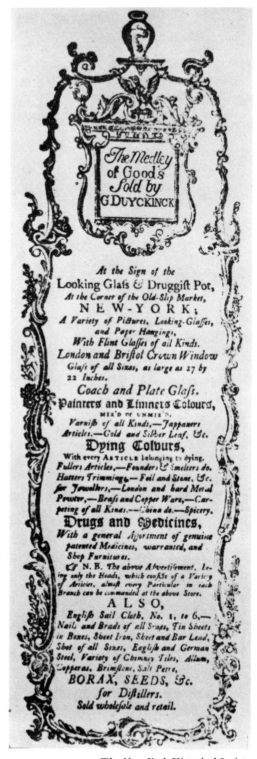

The New-York Historical Society
NEWSPAPER ADVERTISEMENT, 1769. From the *New-York Gazette,* and the *Weekly Post-Boy.*

BENJAMIN FRANKLIN WITH HIS LIGHTNING DETECTOR WHICH SOUNDED WHEN THE AIR WAS CHARGED. Engraving by Edward Fisher after a portrait by Mason Chamberlain, London, 1762.

A Common Culture

Whatever their origin, wherever they settled, colonists in British America were inevitably influenced by English patterns of thought and culture. The very document by which the colonists declared their independence reveals a heavy debt to the political thinking of Locke, Sidney, Harrington, and other English writers. In other ways the separate colonies were sometimes closer to the mother country than they were to one another. For all of them London set a common standard in matters of dress, literature, art, architecture, and home furnishings. Even the most alien strains in the American melting pot felt, in greater or less degree, the solidifying influence and the authority of the parent civilization.

No one encouraged a general community of interests among the separate colonies more repeatedly than Benjamin Franklin. The range of his own interests — human, scientific, business, family, and political — was widely intercolonial. His proposal in 1743 to his learned friends in most of the other colonies, suggesting they form an American Philosophical Society, which they did, was typical of the way he ignored provincial barriers to understanding. He was but one of many colonial scientists who reached out to colleagues throughout the country and, indeed, throughout Europe, in a large communion of intelligent minds seeking common ends. But above all others Franklin caught the world's attention. The self-made republican, the tallow chandler's son, the printer, the many-sided tradesman, moving with ease and honor among the powdered heads of Europe and quipping with royalty, became to a large section of the world an indivisible symbol of America.

The maxims of Poor Richard, Franklin's most popular brain-child, were immediately and repeatedly republished in the colonial press from Boston to Charleston. They were translated at least three times into French. A Russian edition was published at St. Petersburg in 1784. They had currency everywhere. In the trying times of the Revolution such disparate personalities as Abigail Adams and John Paul Jones found inspiration in quoting one or another of the maxims. Throughout the colonies, to the man in the street, such lines as "Keep thy shop, and thy shop will keep thee," "God heals, the doctor takes the fee," "Experience keeps a dear school, yet fools will learn in no other," constituted something of a common primer for more than a generation before 1776.

Yale University Art Gallery, Mabel Brady Garvan Collection
POOR RICHARD ILLUSTRATED. Engravings from *Bowles Moral Pictures*, London, late 18th century.

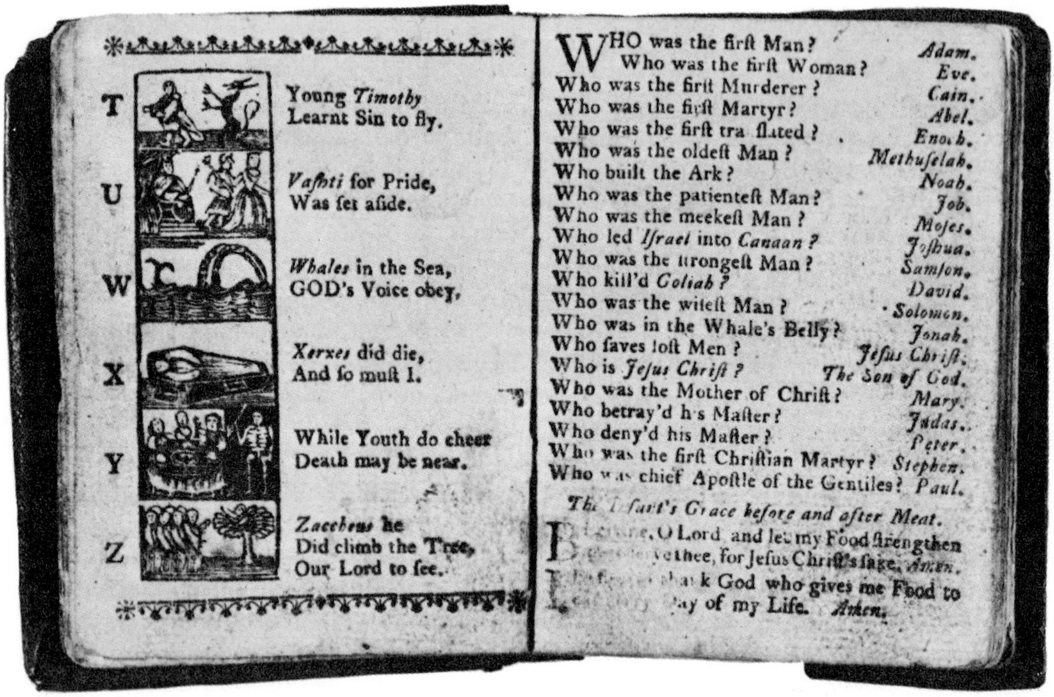

The alphabet illustrations (left page):

T — Young *Timothy* Learnt Sin to fly.

U — *Vashti* for Pride, Was set aside.

W — *Whales* in the Sea, GOD's Voice obey,

X — *Xerxes* did die, And so must I.

Y — While Youth do cheer Death may be near.

Z — *Zaccheus* he Did climb the Tree, Our Lord to see.

Catechism (right page):

WHO was the first Man? *Adam.*
Who was the first Woman? *Eve.*
Who was the first Murderer? *Cain.*
Who was the first Martyr? *Abel.*
Who was the first tra fluted? *Enoch.*
Who was the oldest Man? *Methufelah.*
Who built the Ark? *Noah.*
Who was the patientest Man? *Job.*
Who was the meekest Man? *Mofes.*
Who led *Israel* into *Canaan?* *Joshua.*
Who was the strongest Man? *Samfon.*
Who kill'd *Goliah?* *David.*
Who was the wifest Man? *Solomon.*
Who was in the Whale's Belly? *Jonah.*
Who faves loft Men? *Jefus Chrift.*
Who is *Jefus Chrift?* The *Son of God.*
Who was the Mother of Chrift? *Mary.*
Who betray'd his Mafter? *Judas.*
Who deny'd his Mafter? *Peter.*
Who was the first Chriftian Martyr? *Stephen.*
Who was chief Apoftle of the Gentiles? *Paul.*

The Infant's Grace before and after Meat.

PAGES FROM *The New England Primer*. From the Boston edition, 1767.

The *New England Primer* was another collection of knowledge that, long before Poor Richard, had tended to indoctrinate the young of all the colonies with a common point of view. For a century and a half, from its first appearance in about 1690, more than three million copies of this "Little Bible of New England" saw service in school and home. The blurred little pictures alphabetically representing biblical incidents from

In Adam's fall
We sinned all.

to

Zaccheus he
Did climb the Tree
Our Lord to see

became a common heritage the country over.

It might be more exact to say that the little book enjoyed such widespread favor because the colonists, in spite of the feeling that sometimes ran high between different denominations, were overwhelmingly Protestant. Even the Catholic haven of Maryland had a Protestant majority. Moreover, all denominations were intercolonial in their constituency and many supported a movement for ecclesiastical unity that would ignore provincial boundaries. Many of the minor and formal differences between religions were completely washed away by the great wave of evangelism that swept over the colonies in the middle years of the eighteenth century.

Probably no other private colonial libraries could match Cotton Mather's and William Byrd's with their three or four thousand titles. But in every colony there were collections of respectable size and variety representing the common heritage of the world's learning; and even before the seventeenth century was out, several public libraries had opened in various colonies to supplement the restricted collections. One remarkable effort in that century to get books to the people over all handicaps was made by Doctor

Thomas Bray, an Anglican cleric. "Standing Libraries," he wrote, "will signifie little in the Country, where persons must ride miles to look into a Book; such journeys being too expensive of Time and Money: But Lending Libraries which come home to 'em without Charge, may tolerably well supply the Vacancies in their own Studies." As a result of his determination Maryland, Virginia, and the Carolinas were for a brief time well peppered with reading matter freely available to the public. By the middle of the eighteenth century, locally organized subscription libraries were forming at the rate of at least one a year throughout the colonies. Most notable of all was the Library Company of Philadelphia founded by Benjamin Franklin in 1731. "Reading became fashionable," Franklin wrote in later years, "and our people having no public amusements to divert their attention from study, became better acquainted with books, and in a few years were observed by strangers, to be better instructed and more intelligent than people of the same rank generally are in other countries."

To serve its reading public Boston had a "Bookebynder" as early as 1637 and ten years later a bookshop. In the century that followed, all the larger communities supported shops where imported and American-made

The Brookline Historical Society
THE REVEREND EBENEZER DEVOTION IN HIS LIBRARY. Painting by Winthrop Chandler, 1770. The subject was graduated from Yale in 1732, later became pastor of The Third Church in Windham (now Scotland), Conn., and died leaving a large library. Many volumes identified in this painting still exist.

The American Antiquarian Society
TRADE CARD. Engraving by Thomas Johnston, middle of the 18th century.

books could be had in wide variety. Wandering hawkers supplied the back country with literature. In April, 1705, the *Boston News-Letter* reported the death of one James Gray, "That used to go up and down the Country selling of Books, who left a considerable Estate behind him"—an achievement not common among his twentieth-century counterparts.

By 1723 the library at Cambridge had grown from John Harvard's original gift of two hundred and sixty books to a collection of thirty-two hundred titles. At New Haven, reported a traveler a quarter of a century later, Yale (the third colonial college, founded in 1701) had "a very pretty Library And well kept, their Books are many of 'em Much Later date and better Choose than those at Cambridge . . . they have also Some Curiositys in this Library And Some Aparatus for Natural and Experimental Philosophy." The

HARVARD COLLEGE (HARVARD, STOUGHTON, AND MASSACHUSETTS HALLS). Engraving after a drawing by William Burgis, 1725–26.

NASSAU-HALL, PRINCETON, NEW JERSEY. Engraving by Henry Dawkins after a drawing by W. Tennant, 1763.

college, he added, "brings many People here from different parts of the Country."

Princeton was founded in 1746 as a descendant, with variations, of Yale, as Yale had been of Harvard. Here, too, the opportunities for learning attracted young men from widely separated areas and dispersed them upon graduation with certain common notions and viewpoints. "The building is extremely convenient, airy, and spacious," wrote Andrew Burnaby who visited the college in 1759, ". . . Two students are in each set of apartments which consists of a large bed-room with a fire-place, and two studies. There is a small collection of books, a few instruments, and some natural curiosities." Nassau Hall, the main college building, was indeed so "convenient" that it later served as model for Brown's University Hall, Dartmouth Hall, and other colonial buildings. At Princeton, wrote Philip Fithian, a student there in 1772, "I have an Oppertunity . . . of acquainting myself with Mankind, by observing the Conduct & Temper of the Students in this Seminary . . . filled with Young-Men . . . from almost every Province, in this Continent . . . also many from the *West Indies,* & some few from Europe." So it was at the other institutions of higher learning, five more of which had opened their doors before the Revolution. As ever, college chums looked one another up in later years to secure the ties they had formed in undergraduate days. That intercolonial fraternity of letters and sentiment stretched from Maine to Georgia.

Regardless of the advantages of higher education, conditions in colonial America did not favor intensive specialization along any line of study or work. With so much to be done in a country of untold resources, and with relatively so few hands to do it, America typically developed Jacks-of-all-trades. The practice of medicine, as a single example, only slowly broke away from the old tradition of family remedies and the curious formulas of barber-surgeons and grocer-apothecaries, to become a special science. As a cure for the ague John Winthrop, Jr., advised par-

ing the patient's nails into a little bag of fine linen and tying it about a live eel's neck in a tub of water. The eel would die and the patient recover. At that, Winthrop was one of the first Fellows of the Royal Society and, as indicated by the library of one thousand volumes in more than half a dozen languages that he brought to Massachusetts in 1631, had one of the best-informed scientific minds in the colonies. But he was also a magistrate, farmer, soldier, pioneer, prospector, industrialist, and statesman.

By the 1760's, however, two reputable medical schools had been founded in Philadelphia and New York, their graduates, along with colonial graduates of European schools, had greatly improved professional standards, and by the time of the Revolution a reasonably competent medical personnel was prepared to serve the Continental forces.

Tinkers, artisans, and artists sought and found an intercolonial market for their wares. The silverwork of John Coney of Boston was known in New York. Stiegel's Pennsylvania glass was familiar ware throughout

Campus Martius Museum, Marietta, Ohio
DR. WILLIAM GLYSSON. Painting by Winthrop Chandler, about 1780. The subject was a physician of Dudley, Mass., who served with the Revolutionary Army.

SAMUEL VERPLANCK OF NEW YORK. Painting by John Singleton Copley, about 1771. Verplanck was typical of the "Gentry of this place" (New York) who, Copley remarked, knew so well what they wanted in the way of a painted portrait that the artist could afford to "slight nothing" in his work. Verplanck was a member of the first class to graduate from King's College (Columbia), in 1758, and went to Amsterdam for banking and mercantile training with his uncle's firm before returning to his home on Wall Street.

the colonies. A Boston carpenter built Yale's early building. A Philadelphian designed Nassau Hall in New Jersey. Robert Feke, Joseph Blackburn, Benjamin West, John Singleton Copley, and other painters all accepted commissions for portraits in various cities.

Up and down the east coast the "gentry" were gradually uniting and consolidating their interests through intercolonial business deals, intermarriages, college friendships, and vacation trips — and were having their portraits painted by the leading artists. Copley, a Bostonian and the foremost colonial artist, managed to record a surprising number of them. In his progress from one city to another he complained that his commissions were so many he hardly had time to eat his victuals. America had no titled aristocracy, but a family portrait by Copley has come to be virtually the American equivalent of an ancient coat of arms. Just before the Revolution he was doing some of the best work of his career. Native talent had come to a fair flower even in "so remote a corner of the Globe as New England," to borrow Copley's own words. But he, like many of his countrymen, was dissatisfied with provincial standards and expectations and he went abroad for richer opportunity. There he stayed and joined the Pennsylvania-born · Benjamin West in the ranks of the leading painters of Great Britain.

Like other American artists before and after him Copley gravitated to the London studio of West, who ruled British art for more than half a century. To them all West gave guidance, help, and shelter as needed. The painting below presumably shows West, on the extreme left, correcting a drawing held by his fellow American, Matthew Pratt, while other colonial students look on.

THE AMERICAN SCHOOL. Painting by Matthew Pratt, 1765.

The Metropolitan Museum of Art

The Metropolitan Museum of Art
DESIGN FOR A MANTEL FROM ABRAHAM SWAN'S *British Architect*, London, 1754.

Photograph by Frank Cousins
MANTELPIECE AFTER SWAN'S DESIGN IN THE JEREMIAH LEE HOUSE, MARBLEHEAD, MASS., BUILT 1768.

Large numbers of colonists were returning "home" to Britain, to read law at the Inns of Court, to take orders in the Anglican Church, to study painting with West or medicine at the universities, and to sample the gracious ways of life abroad. Quite a few gentlemen of leisure went on to make the grand tour of the Continent, occasionally gaining interviews with the Pope and royalty en route. The flow of students and tourists from America did not stop with independence. "I hardly know how to think myself out of my own country," wrote Abigail Adams from London shortly after the Revolution, "I see so many Americans about me."

During the quarter-century preceding the Revolution, more than ever before or since perhaps, America depended heavily on England for cultural guidance. The rise of English prestige was one of the strong historical currents of the eighteenth century and it reached just then a high level. Though the tide of their own separate future was rapidly

gaining force, the American colonists in large measure conceded the pre-eminence of English models. The patriot John Adams was not immune to what one contemporary resentfully termed that "evil Itch of over-valuing Foreign parts." While attending the Continental Congress he paused in his labors for political independence and economic freedom to write his wife that Bostonians' manners were superior to Philadelphians' because they were "purer English." Even Franklin with his sure instinct for what was valid in his country's civilization advised his wife to follow the latest London fashions in home furnishings and decoration.

Colonial craftsman in all media were turning out superb work, much of it bearing an unmistakable native touch. But particularly in the generation before the Revolution they generously borrowed from pattern books by Swan, Gibbs, Chippendale, Manwaring and other English designers. Almost every outstanding colonial house of the period, from Mount Vernon on down a long list, shows clearly the reliance on English models. While Washington was fighting for independence on the battlefield his workmen at home were using English design books for reference in renovating Mount Vernon. In 1765 when Samuel Powel of Philadelphia announced his intention of returning from his European tour with a shipment of foreign furniture for his home his uncle warned him of a strong local feeling against such importations. And, he added, "household goods may be had here as cheap and as well made from English patterns." Each sample figure in the trade card shown below, advertising the accomplishments of Benjamin Randolph, master craftsman of Philadelphia, can be traced to some English design book.

The Library Company of Philadelphia

TRADE CARD, PHILADELPHIA. Engraving by James Smithers, about 1770.

AN ENGLISH SATIRE ON THE REPEAL OF THE STAMP ACT. Engraving printed for C. Bowles, London, 1766.

A Spirit of Independence

The ties of a common tongue and, by and large, a common culture were not enough to hold America within the British empire. Nor were the policies of George III nor the armies he could put in the distant battlefields. The ultimate cause of separation, as Burke pointed out to Parliament, lay "deep in the natural constitution of things" — in three thousand miles of ocean, among other things.

Those who crossed the ocean demonstrated by that act a degree of independence that found ample encouragement in their new home. More than a century before the Revolution a British sea captain remarked that Bostonians were already looking "upon themselves as a free State" and in succeeding years similar observations about the colonists as a whole were repeatedly made. Royal officials frequently complained of town meetings where, as Governor Shirley bitterly remarked, "the meanest inhabitants" could and did voice their protests against the imperial government.

The ultimate dispute between England and the colonies was seen by a large number of Englishmen, not as a revolt of America against the parent country, but as a civil war being enacted across the Atlantic. It was not, explained a London paper in 1775, "Great Britain against America, but the Ministry against both." Graphic proof of that feeling appeared in a huge number of comic satires which were published in England and which were almost invariably hostile to government policy. The prints were not subsidized propaganda but commercial publishing ventures whose success depended upon a wide popular appeal. For the funeral of the Stamp Act, reported the London *Chronicle,* "there being great rejoicing and ringing of bells throughout the town this evening, it was judged proper to perform the ceremony in the dead of night."

To defend the king's officials and pro-British merchants and to compel obedience to unpopular measures British troops were stationed in Boston. There had been long and heated discussion about the support of a standing army of British soldiers to serve as a protection for England's colonial empire. In 1768 they came as a police force. Paul Revere depicted the arrival of ships of war and transport, "their Cannon loaded . . . as for a regular Siege. At noon on Saturday, October the 1st the fourteenth and twenty-ninth Regiments, a detachment from the 59th Reg^t and Train of Artillery, with two pieces of Cannon, landed on the Long Wharf; there Formed and Marched with insolent Parade, Drums beating, Fifes playing, and Colours flying up King Street, Each

The New York Public Library
A New England Town Meeting. Engraving from John Trumbull, *M'Fingal*, 1795.

The New York Public Library, Stokes Collection
British Ships of War Landing their Troops at Boston, 1768. Engraving by Paul Revere. The Long Wharf is prominently shown in the foreground. At its shore end stands the Town House. Christ Church is the second spire from the right and the "Old Brick Church" at the extreme left. This is one of Revere's most important prints.

131

The Metropolitan Museum of Art

"THE BLOODY MASSACRE" AT BOSTON, MARCH 5TH, 1770. Engraving by Paul Revere after a drawing by Henry Pelham. The night of the "bloody work in King Street" every man, colonist and soldier, fought for himself, according to Miss Esther Forbes. Revere, however, shows British Captain Prescott, with an evil grin and a wave of the sword, directing a concerted volley against what appear to be helplessly innocent Bostonians. Actually Prescott risked his life to prevent bloodshed. Revere's intention to produce quickly a hair-raising bit of propaganda is clearly shown by the sign "Butcher's Hall" which he has engraved over the custom house. How well he succeeded is indicated by the fact that Josiah Quincy especially warned the jury which tried the British soldiers against "the prints exhibited in our houses" which had added "wings to fancy."

Soldier having received 16 rounds of Powder and Ball." This engraving, like others by Revere, was not a purely patriotic gesture. It was a commercial publishing venture aimed at a buying public.

From the earliest beginnings of the country America had looked askance at a standing army, even one organized among its own people. The presence of the ill-paid, unsympathetic British troops in Boston was doubly offensive and opened the door to trouble. Bloody trouble came on March 5, 1770, when a snowballing affair turned into a "horrid Massacre" in which the redcoats killed four townsmen. The ugly incident, to which Paul Revere gave such wide and Whiggish publicity with his engraving, did not start the war. The soldiers were at once removed from the town and, across the ocean, on the day of the slaughter, all the duties of the Townshend Acts were removed excepting that on tea.

It almost seemed the quarrel between mother and child were composed. Tea, after all, could be smuggled in from Holland or the small duty forgot. Tea was cheaper in America than in London in either case. But when Parliament permitted the East India Company to dump its stored-up teas on the colonial market, to provide it with a monopoly and save it from bankruptcy, trouble burst out anew. New York and Philadelphia returned the shipment of tea sent to those ports. Boston, however, held a Tea Party. "They say the actors were *Indians* from Narragansett," wrote one witness. "Whether they were or not, to a transient observer they appear'd as *such*, being cloath'd in Blankets with the heads muffled, and copper color'd countenances, being each armed with a hatchet or axe, and pair of pistols, nor was their dialect different from what I conceive these geniusses to *speak*, as their jargon was unintelligible to all but themselves. Not the least insult was offer'd to any person," save to one person who tried to sneak some of the tea ashore; "and nothing but their utter aversion to make *any* disturbance prevented his being tar'd and feather'd."

The Metropolitan Museum of Art
THE BOSTON TEA PARTY, DECEMBER 16, 1773. Engraving by Daniel N. Chodowiecki from *Calender für 1784*, Berlin.

Parliament felt that its authority had been flouted and, among other corrective measures, closed Boston's harbor to commerce and planned to quarter His Majesty's troops on the town's inhabitants. And with this even conservative colonists began "to snuff the approach of tyranny" in the tainted breezes from across the Atlantic.

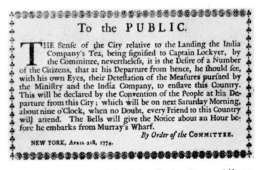

To the PUBLIC.

THE Sense of the City relative to the Landing the India Company's Tea, being signified to Captain Lockyer, by the Committee, nevertheless, it is the Desire of a Number of the Citizens, that at his Departure from hence, he should see, with his own Eyes, their Detestation of the Measures pursued by the Ministry and the India Company, to enslave this Country. This will be declared by the Convention of the People at his Departure from this City; which will be on next Saturday Morning, about nine o'Clock, when no Doubt, every Friend to this Country will attend. The Bells will give the Notice about an Hour before he embarks from Murray's Wharf.
By Order of the COMMITTEE.

NEW YORK, APRIL 31ſt, 1774.

The John Carter Brown Library
BROADSIDE, 1774.

The patriotic resolution of the ladies of Edenton to drink no more tea until justice were done in America was only one episode in America's indignant response, one that received immediate publicity in London broadsides. Several colonial newspapers carried the poem, "A lady's Adieu to her Tea-Table," reading in part:

> Farewell the Teaboard with your gaudy attire,
> Ye cups and saucers that I did admire;
> To my cream pot and tongs I now bid adieu;
> That pleasure's all fled that I once found
>   in you . . .
> No more shall my teapot so generous be
> In filling the cups with this pernicious tea,
> For I'll fill it with water and drink out
>   the same,
> Before I'll lose Liberty that dearest name. . . .
> Before she shall part I will die in the cause,
> For I'll never be govern'd by tyranny's laws.

The "Intolerable Acts" which Parliament passed to punish Boston had brought England's colonial troubles into a white light, and Europe, as well as the immediate participants, looked on with fervent interest. The French engraving shown below bears the caption: "Father Time shows with his magic lantern, to the four corners of the earth, that the storm the English have excited (with the tea tax) will smite themselves and will give America the means of seizing the Liberty cap." A congress of delegates from twelve colonies met in Philadelphia in September, 1774, "to consult upon the present unhappy State of the Colonies." It was the nearest America had yet come to unified action.

In spite of the marching events and the mounting feelings that led to the first skirmishes at Lexington and Concord, there was very little violence during pre-Revolutionary days. Compared to the French, Russian, and Nazi revolutions, the restraint and temperance on both sides of the growing disagreement in America were amazing.

A FRENCH COMMENTARY ON THE TEA CONTROVERSY. Engraving published in Paris, about 1775.
The Metropolitan Museum of Art

We the Lady's of Edenton do hereby Solemnly Engage not to Conform to that Pernicious Custom of Drinking Tea, or that we the aforesaid Lady's will not promote ye wear of any Manufacture from England untill such time that all Acts which tend to Enslave this our Native Country shall be Repealed

The Metropolitan Museum of Art

A SOCIETY OF PATRIOTIC LADIES, AT EDENTON IN NORTH CAROLINA, PLEDGING TO DRINK NO MORE TEA, 1775.
Engraving by Philip Dawe (?) published by R. Sayer and J. Bennett, London.

WAR, PEACE, AND UNION

What happened in America during the next few years is to Americans the most familiar part of their country's history. How Paul Revere's steed, "flying fearless and fleet," struck a spark with his hoof that kindled the countryside into flame, has since passed into legend with the events that followed.

At Lexington on April 19, 1775, reported the Salem *Gazette* the following week, "a company of Militia, of about one hundred men, mustered near the Meeting-House; the Troops came in sight of them just before sunrise . . . the Commanding Officer accosted the Militia in words to this effect: 'Disperse, you rebels — damn you, throw down your arms and disperse'; upon which the Troops huzzaed . . . then there seemed to be a general discharge from the whole body: eight of our men were killed and nine wounded."

According to official reports from White-hall the British troops at Lexington "found a body of the country people under arms, on a green close to the road; and upon the King's Troops marching up to them, in order to inquire the reason of their being so assembled, they went off in great confusion, and several guns were fired upon the King's Troops from behind a stone wall, and also from the meeting-house and other houses, by which one man was killed, and Major Pitcairn's horse shot in two places. In consequence of this attack by the rebels, the troops returned the fire and killed several of them."

The minutemen were coming over the hills in swarms. Farther along at Concord, according to one of them, "We was all

The Battle of Concord, April 19, 1775. Engraving by Amos Doolittle after a painting by Ralph Earle.
The New York Public Library

ordered to load and had stricked orders not to fire firs, then to fire as fast as we could." The London *Gazette,* in a slight variant of the embattled farmers theme, reported that as the British troops returned from Concord, "they were very much annoyed, and had several men killed and wounded by the rebels firing from behind walls, ditches, trees, and other ambushes ... they kept up in that manner a scattering fire during the whole of their march of fifteen miles ... such was the cruelty and barbarity of the rebels that they scalped and cut off the ears of some of the wounded men. ..."

In England two brash Londoners went to jail for suggesting a subscription be taken up for the widows and orphans of "our BELOVED American Fellow Subjects, who FAITHFUL to

The Metropolitan Museum of Art
THE BATTLE OF LEXINGTON, APRIL 19, 1775. Wash drawing by Johann Heinrich Ramberg, about 1783. Ramberg, a German, lived in London from 1781 to 1788, where he was a friend of Benjamin West, the famous American expatriate. In West's circle he must have met both American and English veterans of the Revolution, among them John Trumbull, who could have supplied him with documentation for this and the other sketches, later reproduced, illustrating the American scene.

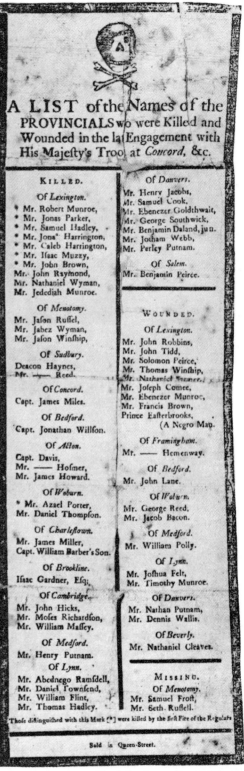

A LIST of the Names of the PROVINCIALS who were Killed and Wounded in the late Engagement with His Majesty's Troops at *Concord,* &c.

KILLED.

Of *Lexington.*
* Mr. Robert Munroe,
* Mr. Jonas Parker,
* Mr. Samuel Hadley,
* Mr. Jonas Harrington,
* Mr. Caleb Harrington,
* Mr. Isaac Muzzy,
* Mr. John Brown,
Mr. John Raymond,
Mr. Nathaniel Wyman,
Mr. Jedediah Munroe.

Of *Menotomy.*
Mr. Jason Russel,
Mr. Jabez Wyman,
Mr. Jason Winship.

Of *Sudbury.*
Deacon Haynes,
Mr. —— Reed.

Of *Concord.*
Capt. James Miles.

Of *Bedford.*
Capt. Jonathan Willson.

Of *Acton.*
Capt. Davis,
Mr. —— Hosmer,
Mr. James Howard.

Of *Woburn.*
* Mr. Azael Porter,
Mr. Daniel Thompson.

Of *Charlestown.*
Mr. James Miller,
Capt. William Barber's Son.

Of *Brookline.*
Isaac Gardner, Esq;

Of *Cambridge.*
Mr. John Hicks,
Mr. Moses Richardson,
Mr. William Massey.

Of *Medford.*
Mr. Henry Putnam.

Of *Lynn.*
Mr. Abednego Ramsdell,
Mr. Daniel Townsend,
Mr. William Flint,
Mr. Thomas Hadley.

Of *Danvers.*
Mr. Henry Jacobs,
Mr. Samuel Cook,
Mr. Ebenezer Goldthwait,
Mr. George Southwick,
Mr. Benjamin Daland, jun.
Mr. Jotham Webb,
Mr. Perley Putnam.

Of *Salem.*
Mr. Benjamin Peirce.

WOUNDED.

Of *Lexington.*
Mr. John Robbins,
Mr. John Tidd,
Mr. Solomon Peirce,
Mr. Thomas Winship,
Mr. Nathaniel Farmer,
Mr. Joseph Comee,
Mr. Ebenezer Munroe,
Mr. Francis Brown,
Prince Easterbrooks,
(A Negro Man.

Of *Framingham.*
Mr. —— Hemenway.

Of *Bedford.*
Mr. John Lane.

Of *Woburn.*
Mr. George Reed,
Mr. Jacob Bacon.

Of *Medford.*
Mr. William Polly.

Of *Lynn.*
Mr. Joshua Felt,
Mr. Timothy Munroe.

Of *Danvers.*
Mr. Nathan Putnam,
Mr. Dennis Wallis.

Of *Beverly.*
Mr. Nathaniel Cleaves.

MISSING.
Of *Menotomy.*
Mr. Samuel Frost,
Mr. Seth Russell.

Those distinguished with this Mark [*] were killed by the first Fire of the Regulars

Sold in Queen-Street.

The John Carter Brown Library

The Metropolitan Museum of Art
THE BATTLE OF BUNKER HILL, 1775. Wash drawing by Ramberg, 1786.

Enemy within, and the Danger, to which they are exposed from an Assault of the Militia without."

Two months later of a summer's night Colonel William Prescott with a fair-sized provincial force threw up an earth-and-wood redoubt on Breed's Hill, just down the Charlestown peninsula from Bunker Hill (the ensuing battle took its name from the wrong hill) as an advance post against the British army besieged in Boston. General Gates immediately countered with a series of frontal assaults with about three and a half thousand well-armed troops. Twice the redcoats were so close to victory the defenders could see the whites of their eyes, but the charges were turned back. On the third try the "rebels" with their ammunition gone used clubbed guns and rocks in a last futile stand. Charlestown peninsula went to the British but as the colonists retired, almost one third of the total enemy force awaited burial. "The trial we have had," concluded General Gage in a report to England, "show the rebels are not the despicable rabble too many have supposed them to be."

The companies of backwoodsmen from Virginia, Pennsylvania, and Maryland who had hiked up to Cambridge to support Washington there were among the best-armed and most expert marksmen in the world. "The worst of them," the Pennsylvania press warned the English, "will put a ball into a man's head at the distance of 150 or 200 yards, therefore advise your officers who shall hereafter come out to America to settle their affairs in England before their departure."

Washington urged the Continental Congress to manufacture at least ten thousand hunting shirts of the type worn by the frontiersmen. "I know nothing in a speculative view more trivial, yet which, if put into practice, would have a happier tendency to unite the men, and abolish those provincial distinctions that lead to jealousy and dissatisfaction," wrote the General. It would have the further advantage of carrying "no small terror to the enemy who think

the Character of Englishmen, preferring Death to Slavery, were for that reason only inhumanly murdered by the KINGS Troops." From America one of the King's Troops was reported to have written: "I am still here with the Forces under General Gage, but have no reason to boast either of our Situation or our Spirits; the contrary is too true, as you will naturally imagine from our Repulse by the Provincials on the 19th instant. The Action (in which we lost near 100 men) is likely to cost us very dear, for the whole Country is now in Arms, and irritated beyond Expression. . . . Boston! the famous and once flourishing Town of Boston, is now reduced to the wretched State of a Garrison . . . the distressed Inhabitants, who would be glad to leave the Town, their Houses, their Furniture, their Employments, all they possess in the World, to retire into the Country, and avoid the Insults and Menaces of the

CONTEMPORARY REPRESENTATIONS OF SOLDIERS OF THE CONTINENTAL ARMY. (1 and 2, from an extra-illustrated copy of Max von Eelking, *Memoires and Letters and Journals of Major General Riedesel,* Albany, 1868, in the New York Public Library; 3 and 4, Engravings by Chodowiecki from *Calender für 1784,* Berlin, Metropolitan Museum of Art; 5, an anonymous engraving in The Metropolitan Museum of Art.)

ENGLISH RECRUITS FOR AMERICA. Engraving by Watson & Dickinson after a drawing by W. H. Banbury, London, 1780.

every such person a complete marksman."

When stories of these "shirt-tail men, with their cursed twisted [rifled] guns" reached England, it is said, enlistments in the British army fell off sharply.

A report on the progress of recruiting in England for the Army and Navy was printed in the London press in 1776. "A gentleman just arrived from Somersetshire," it read, "says that, the Accounts given of the Success of the Recruiting Parties . . . are absolutely false. . . . It is true, indeed, they have picked up some recruits, but not a stout, hearty, young man among them; the whole consisting of elderly Men, and mere Boys, some of the latter being even under twelve Years of Age and most of them less than fifteen!"

Such observations might have seemed more entertaining on the other side of the Atlantic if recruiting efforts in the colonies had been any better. In the hopeful summer of 1776 Washington's army reached a peak of about eighteen thousand men. But before the year was over more than two thirds of them had quit to return to their homes. The colonial army, for all Thomas Paine's talk of "summer soldiers and sunshine patriots," never again numbered many more than five thousand soldiers.

Meanwhile, however, Washington had a stranglehold on Boston with its British garrison, although the occupation was hard on the inhabitants. "Their beef all spent," wrote Abigail Adams to her husband John, in Congress at Philadelphia, "their malt and cider all gone. All the fresh provisions they can procure they are obliged to give to the sick and wounded. . . . No man dared now to be seen talking to his friend in the street. They were obliged to be within, every evening, at ten o'clock, according to martial law; nor could any inhabitant walk any street in town after that time, without a pass from Gage . . . not one pin to be purchased for love or money."

The artist of the sketch reproduced below, a besieged officer, described one of the British forays into the outskirts of their position on January 14, 1776: "At 4 o'clock in the morning 6 Companies of Light Infantry and 6 of Grenadiers went across the ice to Foster's hill on dorchester neck; in all about 400 men. At the same time the 64th Regiment landed on the Neck from Castle William. The whole amounting to about 800 men. They went over the whole ground on the Neck, met with no opposition, did not fire a shot, took 6 Rebels prisoners, Burnt 6 or 8 Empty uninhabitable houses and barns, and return'd about ½ after 6 o'clock."

That same month Washington's officers' mess, as liberty-loving Englishmen, still toasted the king's health. That same month appeared Thomas Paine's *Common Sense*. Two months later Washington planted on Dorchester Heights cannon that had been hauled by oxen over the snows from Ticonderoga. The British, evacuating an untenable position, left Boston to reappear at New York the following summer.

Abigail Adams again wrote her husband: "I am charmed with the sentiments of 'Common Sense,' and wonder how an honest heart, one who wishes the welfare of his country and the happiness of posterity, can

THE BURNING OF THE HOUSES ON DORCHESTER NECK, MASS., JANUARY 14, 1776. Wash drawing by Archibald Robertson, a British officer.

The New York Public Library, Spencer Collection

hesitate one moment at adopting them. I want to know how these sentiments are received in Congress. I dare say there would be no difficulty in procuring a vote and instructions from all the Assemblies in New England for Independency."

Franklin had long since written his famous letter to William Strahan. "You are a Member of Parliament," he had said, "and one of that Majority which has doomed my Country to Destruction. You have begun to burn our Towns, and murder our People,—Look upon your Hands!—They are stained with the Blood of your Relations!—You and I were long Friends:—You are now my Enemy,—and I am, Yours, B. Franklin."

The cause of the colonists seemed just; union among them might now be managed, and the resources and spirit of the country were great enough to meet the issue squarely. The United Colonies, it was resolved by unanimous vote on July second and pro-

claimed to the world on July 4, 1776, were and of right ought to be free and independent states.

America had acted like a free nation—and was, in fact, free—before the declaration of its independence. A free America was, indeed, in the natural constitution of things and had been frequently predicted for fifty years and more past. But that brief, lucid declaration went far beyond announcing a separate polity. That all men were created free and equal; that governments, deriving their just powers from the consent of the governed, were instituted to secure the inalienable rights of life, liberty, and the pursuit of happiness; and, when that security was not preserved, that the people had the right to overthrow their government — such tenets challenged the fundamental traditions of society. Even to many Americans eager for independence it seemed to commit the struggling, infant nation to nothing short of

CONGRESS VOTING INDEPENDENCE, JULY, 1776. Painting by Robert Edge Pine, 1788; completed by Edward Savage.

The Historical Society of Pennsylvania

THE BRITISH FLEET FORCING THE HUDSON RIVER PASSAGE, 1776. Painting by Dominic Serres, the elder.

everlasting revolution. "Our most wise and sensible citizens," wrote one patriot on the eve of the Declaration, "dread the anarchy and confusion that must ensue."

Practically no one mentioned the word democracy, an epithet reserved for the extreme radical viewpoint. But, exulted John Adams, "the decree has gone forth, and cannot now be recalled, that a more equal liberty than has prevailed in other parts of the earth, must be established in America." At the moment no radical could have asked for a larger promise.

Then came the times that tried men's souls. Washington reached New York from his success at Boston to confront the most formidable military and naval force that the colonial world had yet seen. Inevitably Howe took the city whose Loyalist population, during the course of the war, supplied more troops to George III than to George Washington. The British fleet forced the Hudson River passage and compelled Washington to retreat across New Jersey into Pennsylvania with less than three thousand

troops fit for duty. Congress, meanwhile, packed up its papers and fled to Baltimore.

"We are in a very disaffected part of the Province," wrote Washington to his brother from his halt across the Delaware, "and between you and me, I think our affairs are in a very bad situation; not so much from the apprehension of General Howe's army, as from the defection of New York, Jerseys, and Pennsylvania. . . . "

Six months after the Declaration of Independence the heroic commander had to write: "I think the game is pretty near up, owing in great measure, to the insidious acts of the Enemy, and disaffection of the colonies . . . but principally to the accursed policy of short enlistments." To the President of Congress he wrote: "No person ever had a greater choice of difficulties to contend with than I have. . . . It may be thought that I am going a good deal out of the line of my duty . . . to advise thus freely. A character to lose, an estate to forfeit, the inestimable blessing of liberty at stake, and a life devoted, must be my excuse."

Washington's inspired maneuvers in re-crossing the Delaware on Christmas night, 1776, capturing a host of Hessians, and subsequently moving onto the British army's flank at Morristown Heights, won the praise of Cornwallis and Frederick the Great. "Over the river we went in a flat-bottomed scow," wrote one participant in that bitterly cold crossing, "and as I was the first that crossed, we had to wait for the rest and so began to pull down the fences and make fires to warm ourselves, for the storm was increasing rapidly. After a while it rained, hailed, snowed and froze, and at the same time blew a perfect hurricane. . . . As we had been in the storm all night we were not only wet through ourselves, but our guns and powder were wet also so that I do not believe one would go off, and I saw none fired by our party. When we were all ready we advanced, and, although there was not more than one bayonet to five men, orders were given to 'Charge bayonets and rush on!' and rush on we did. Within pistol-shot they again fired point-blank at us; we dodged and they did not hit a man, while before they had time to reload we were within three feet of them, when they broke in an instant and ran like so many frightened devils into the town, which was at a short distance, and we after them pell-mell. . . .

"The next day, being two days after our time was out, we received three months' pay —and glad was I. We were offered twenty-six dollars to stay six weeks longer, but as I did not enlist for the purpose of remaining in the army, but only through necessity, as I could not get to my parents in Boston, I was determined to quit as soon as my time was out. . . . I told my lieutenant that I was going home, 'My God!' says he, 'you are not, I hope, going to leave us, for you are the life and soul of us and are to be promoted to be an ensign.' I told him I would not stay to be a Colonel." And off he walked, 350 miles home to Boston.

Without his unwilling recruit Washington defeated a force of British at Princeton and continued on to a temporary headquarters at Morristown.

Ten months later, at Saratoga, under General Gates, America won its first important victory. Burgoyne, intent on closing the gap between Canada and New York along the Hudson River and sealing New England off from the southern colonies, started south from Canada with seven thousand men. Between John Stark's Green Mountain Boys

"WASHINGTON CROSSING THE DELAWARE," DECEMBER 25, 1776. Painting by Emanuel Leutze, about 1850. A study for the famous painting in The Metropolitan Museum of Art, which, although false in almost every detail, has become the accepted symbol of the event.

Collection of Hall Park McCullough

THE BATTLE OF PRINCETON. Oil painting by William Mercer. Photograph through the courtesy of the Princeton University Library.

and Herkimer's German-Americans from the Mohawk Valley, Burgoyne's plans were badly upset and on October 16, 1777, he surrendered his entire army.

Not one of the Americans, wrote a Hessian captive, "was regularly equipped. Each one had on the clothes he was accustomed to wear in the field, the tavern, the church and in everyday life. No fault, however, could be found in their military appearance, for they stood in an erect and a soldierly attitude. They remained so perfectly quiet that we were utterly astounded. Not one of them made any attempt to speak to the man at his side; and all the men who stood in array before us were so slender, fine-looking and sinewy, that it was a pleasure to look at them.... The determination which caused them to grasp a musket and powder-horn can be seen in their faces, as well as that they are not to be fooled with, especially in skirmishes in the woods. . . ."

"I went into the British Camp that Eve," wrote Daniel Granger, a fifteen-year-old Yankee campaigner, "& became acquainted with several young Lads of about my Age,

The Metropolitan Museum of Art

THE DEFEAT OF BURGOYNE'S ARMY AT SARATOGA. OCTOBER 16, 1777. Wash drawing by Ramberg, about 1785.

The Metropolitan Museum of Art

VALLEY FORGE, 1777–8. From a bank-note vignette, 19th century.

The Historical Society of York County, Pa.
WASHINGTON CALLED THE FATHER OF HIS COUNTRY
FOR THE FIRST TIME IN PRINT. Engraving from *Der
Gantz Neue Verbesserte Nord-Americanische Calen-
dar*, 1779.

pleased with them, and they seemed to be pleased with me, & said that we were no longer Enemies. I traded with them."

The following winter Washington spent the grimmest season of the war at Valley Forge with his tag-end of an Army. A French volunteer described his impressions at sight of the encampment: "My imagination had pictured an Army with uniforms, the glitter of arms, standards, etc., in short, military pomp of all sorts. Instead . . . I saw, grouped together or standing alone, a few militiamen, poorly clad, and for the most part without shoes. . . . I also noticed soldiers wearing cotton nightcaps under their hats, and some having for cloaks or greatcoats coarse woolen blankets, exactly like those provided for the patients in our French hospitals. I learned afterwards that these were the officers and generals."

During his hour of trial Washington was toasted in at least one English home as the greatest man on earth. "No man," declared a London newspaper, "ever united in his own character a more perfect alliance of the virtues of the philosopher with the talents of a general." In America the affectionate title "Father of His Country" appeared in print for the first time on the cover page of a Pennsylvania-German almanac (on the opposite page) published in Lancaster by Francis Bailey in 1779.

America's little navy was no match for Britain's great fleet on the high seas. Yet, as Washington clearly realized, the great advantages of the war could be won along the seaways. American privateers captured or destroyed about six hundred English vessels and sent shipping insurance rates in London up out of sight. But neither privateering nor the occasional successes of the American navy vitally changed the situation at sea. John Paul Jones's celebrated victory over the *Serapis* in his rotten and riddled ship, the *Bonhomme Richard*, was, nevertheless, one of the most brilliant individual exploits in American naval history. "A person must have been an eye witness," wrote

The Metropolitan Museum of Art
CAPTAIN JOHN PAUL JONES SHOOTING A SAILOR WHO HAD ATTEMPTED TO STRIKE HIS COLORS. Anonymous engraving.

THE *Bonhomme Richard* AND THE *Serapis*, SEPTEMBER 23, 1779. Engraving by J. Boydell.
The Harry Shaw Newman Gallery

THE FRENCH FLEET AT SEA EN ROUTE TO AMERICA, 1778. Wash drawing from Pierre Ozanne's *Collection of Drawings Relative to the War of Independence of the United States and to the Sending by France of a Squadron Commanded by Count d'Estaing.*

Jones of the conclusion of the battle, "to form a just idea of the tremendous scene of carnage, wreck, and ruin which everywhere appeared. Humanity cannot but recoil from the prospect of such finished horror, and lament that war should be capable of producing such fatal consequences."

When Franklin, in France, was told of the British capture of Philadelphia he replied, "You are mistaken; it is not the British army that has taken Philadelphia, but Philadelphia that has taken the British army." While Washington sweated it out at Valley Forge, the British gave themselves up to a round of entertainments, capped by a fabulous medieval pageant, called the Mischianza, in honor of General Howe. Washington's troops emerged from their winter's trial better disciplined than they had ever been. The British were enervated by their easy pleasures and withdrew to New York.

News of Saratoga brought first France, eager for revenge, into the war, then other European nations. As Washington well realized, naval power would play a decisive part in the conflict. After several years the excellent French fleet did swing the tide of war to victory. When the treaty with France was concluded in 1778, Franklin wrote: "Several of the American ships, with stores for Congress, are now about sailing under the convoy of a French Squadron. England is in great consternation, and the minister . . . confessing that all his measures had been wrong and that peace was necessary, proposed two bills for quieting America, but they are full of artifice and deceit, and will, I am confident, be treated accordingly by our country." At Valley Forge, in a scene of near famine, Washington dined in public, it is said, to celebrate the alliance. The French fleet of twelve ships of the line and five frigates sailed from Toulon in April, 1778, with instructions to perform "some action advantageous to the Americans, glorious for the arms of the King, and fitted to show the

A FRENCH INTERPRETATION OF THE SURRENDER OF CORNWALLIS. A bit of pure fantasy intended to emphasize the important part played by the French fleet in the final capitulation of the English army at Yorktown. The two following versions are somewhat more realistic.

protection which his Majesty extends to his allies."

When Washington heard of the arrival of De Grasse's naval squadron at the commencement of the siege of Yorktown it is said that he "acted like a child whose every wish had been gratified." The French fleet did make possible the great victory that followed and the French artist who depicted his country's ships almost on the field of surrender (above) must be forgiven his faulty geography. As the British laid down their arms their band played "The World Turned Upside Down" while the French in fresh new uniforms looked on. The Americans, wrote one of them, were "but part in uniform, and all in garments much the worse for wear, yet with a spirited, soldier-like air, not the worse in the eyes of their country-men for bearing the marks of hard service and great privations." The war was not yet over but it was ending, George the Third to the contrary notwithstanding.

THE SURRENDER OF CORNWALLIS, 1781. Wash drawing by Ramberg, about 1785.

THE BRITISH SURRENDER AT YORKTOWN, OCTOBER 17, 1781. Contemporary copy of a painting by Van Blaren-
berghe executed for the Marquis de Rochambeau. Rochambeau wrote Washington that the painting followed
"an excellent design by the young Berthier, who was deputed quartermaster at the siege" and that he

planned to hang it in his study beside his portrait of Washington. Presumably the painting still hangs there. The reproduction is from a photograph generously provided by the State Street Trust Co. of Boston.

With the signing of the treaty of peace in 1783, America faced one of the most critical periods in its history. The country embarked upon a novel and portentous experiment in state-building with few of the familiar props that government had traditionally relied upon. Monarchy had been discarded over the protests of some important American monarchists. No titled aristocracy exercised its privilege in the interest of an ordered, stable society. No established church lent its cohesive force. Even political unity among the independent states was largely lacking.

"A long time, and much prudence, will be necessary," wrote David Ramsay, "to reproduce a spirit of union and . . . reverence for government. . . . The right of the people to resist their rulers, when invading their liberties, forms the cornerstone of the American republics. This principle, though just in itself, is not favorable to the tranquillity of present establishments. The maxims and measures, which in the years 1774 and 1775 were successfully inculcated and adopted by American patriots, for oversetting the established government, will answer a similar purpose when recurrence is had to them by factious demagogues, for disturbing the freest governments that were ever devised." The first good evidence that the United States would succeed, over all disagreements and difficulties, in remaining an independent republic firmly united within a federal system, came with the adoption of the Constitution and the inauguration of Washington as President.

JOHN JAY, JOHN ADAMS, BENJAMIN FRANKLIN, HENRY LAURENS, AND WILLIAM TEMPLE FRANKLIN AT THE CONFERENCE OF THE TREATY OF PEACE WITH ENGLAND, 1783. Unfinished painting by Benjamin West.
Collection of Henry F. du Pont

THE INAUGURATION OF GEORGE WASHINGTON, APRIL 30, 1789. Engraving by Amos Doolittle, 1790, after a drawing by Peter Lacour. New York's old (second) City Hall, on Wall at the end of Broad St., had been especially modernized by Charles Pierre L'Enfant, a French veteran of the Revolution, to accommodate the national government should the city be selected as the capital. When Washington's inaugural was scheduled for there in 1789 people from all over converged on the city. "The windows and roofs of the houses were crowded," wrote one witness, "and in the streets the throng was so dense that it seemed as if one might literally walk on the heads of the people. . . . All eyes were fixed on the balcony where, at the appointed hour, Washington entered, accompanied by the Chancellor. To the great body of people he had never been seen except as a military hero. The first in war now to be the first in peace."

When the capital was moved, in 1790, it was predicted that New York would be deserted "and become a wilderness, peopled with wolves, its old inhabitants."

II
EAST
GOES WEST

EAST GOES WEST

INTRODUCTION

WHEN THE PEOPLE of Newtown, Massachusetts, wanted to move westward into Connecticut in the seventeenth century they gave as one of their reasons "the strong bent of their spirits to remove thither." Nothing else so concisely explains the steady westward migration of Americans. Greener pastures, blacker soil, more golden hills, gave express purpose to those who looked for one. But the "bent" was ingrained. If hell lay to the West, ran a proverb, Americans would cross heaven to reach it. Time and again nature and legislators threw up obstacles which were overcome or ignored by people hell-bent to follow the sun.

"How beautiful," Carlyle wrote to Emerson in 1849, "to think of lean tough Yankee settlers, tough as gutta-percha, with most *occult* unsubduable fire in their belly, steering over the Western Mountains to annihilate the jungle, and bring bacon and corn out of it for the Posterity of Adam.—There is no *Myth* of Athene or Herakles equal to this *fact*." So it was. Nothing in history could match this epic migration of people—not all Yankees by any means—in volume, pace, or character. This was not a wandering of tribes nor the settlement of compact colonies. Individuals, families, and small groups, on their own initiative, found their way through a wilderness to new homes and new adventures. Great masses of them moved West, often improvising their means of travel as they went, sticking to the rivers where they could, embarking on the plains with a "mule as a shallop" and a covered wagon as a prairie schooner, or simply walking their way towards a new future.

The land seemed illimitable. As one Kentuckian said, the West was bounded only by the Day of Judgment. And it all seemed as free as air and sunshine. To people who remembered Europe's cramped and taxed acres it was hardly credible. "Those animals called in your country excisemen," one immigrant wrote home from his western settlement, "are not known in this country, so that we boil soap, make candles, gather hops, and many other things, without fear, which *you must not do*." The fact was indeed better than any myth, by most reports, and a human host raced to realize it.

The pace of migration was terrific. Year after year what had been a West became an East with bewildering speed. Even Franklin, our major prophet and apostle of expansion, miscalculated that it would take ages to fill the western continent, perhaps because until a much later date no one was sure just what did lie to the west. From the East it looked at first like an interminable, dense, and dreary forest that the most expert axmen might never be able to clear to let the sunlight in. But beyond that were the prairies and plains, "a world of unexplored deserts and thickets," wrote Volney at the time of the Louisiana Purchase; and beyond that the Rockies, standing "like a Chinese Wall," as a Congressman thought in 1828.

And it was all over in a few generations. In 1890 the Superintendent of the Census reported that to all intents the old frontier was closed. Geronimo had only just been captured, a few straggling buffalo remained on the Plains, and several territories still awaited statehood. But the good free land to the west was all staked out. The "interminable" forests were well on their way to destruction. (The first reserves were created the next year in an effort to save what was left.) For the generations of Americans to come, the Land of Promise would no longer be beyond the horizon but underfoot, in familiar neighborhoods.

The nation was born with vast holdings of open land as a special birthright. Within two generations gigantic chunks were added —the Louisiana Territory, Texas, California, New Mexico—any one of them as large as a good-sized European country. Within forty years the West drew to it more people than all the original colonies had accumulated in a century. It seemed impossible that a country could expand so fast and so violently without tearing the social fabric to bits. The older sections did appear to be breaking up and moving westward, exclaimed one witness in 1817. How to make it all hang together, old and new, posed a large problem for statesmen.

The frontier was always outdistancing the lawmakers. It made its own laws when the need became imperative. "It is really an incredible thing," wrote Tocqueville, "how this people keeps itself in order through the single conviction that its only safeguard against itself lies in itself." On the far western border people passed their lives with little regard for remote authority. Nothing decreed in London had dissuaded the colonists from breaching the boundary along the crest of the Appalachians set by Parliament while it pondered how best to handle the western lands. After all, Burke told that body, you could not station garrisons in every part of the wilderness—"those deserts," he called it. The land was abundant, the people used it wastefully, and they *would* move on to fresh fields. Nothing said in Washington deterred citizens of the new Republic from pressing on down the Ohio, beyond the Mississippi, across the Plains, and over the Rockies to the Pacific. The frontier set its own pace, invading lands "forever" set aside for the Indians, crossing lands that were "impassable," and opening for settlement land that was "uninhabitable."

Other countries have had frontiers—Russia, Australia, Canada, Argentina. But nowhere has the borderland population been so free to control its own development as in our West. Squatters and adventurers vied with speculators and architects of empire to dispossess the Indians, clear the forests, and people the land. The man out in front, the true frontiersman, caught the imagination of the world. These were "America's peculiar sons, known to no other land," said Scott. Daniel Boone, singing alone in the wilderness, as one report described him, became the symbol of man in his most glorious freedom. The West came to seem like a clean slate where a man could begin anew the record of his life. Restless Easterners and Europeans burning with "America fever" went west to try their fortune in the wake of the frontiersmen.

Not all of them found cause for singing. Even in the middle border, women went mad with loneliness and despair. The outer border left many defeated spirits who could not accept the terms the wilderness imposed. "When this home-building and land-clearing is accomplished," wrote one pioneer in sober reflection, "a faithful picture would reveal not only changes that have been wrought, but a host of prematurely brokedown men and women, besides an undue proportion resting peacefully in country graveyards." Most of their stories have been lost in the tall tales of accomplishment, the boasts of conquerors of a continent, and the sheer optimism that kept so many people forever moving on.

Before it was over, pioneering had become the common experience of an untold number of Americans. People had learned self-reliance and resourcefulness the hard way, from close contact with raw adversity. They also learned the need of common effort in the face of problems too big for any individual. "It is a universal rule here," wrote one frontiersman, "to help one another, each one keeping an eye single to his own business." Out in the West people from all corners of the earth met and mingled, once the American had cleared the way. For the borderlands were as truly a melting pot as the seaboard cities, vastly thinned out, but cosmopolitan in character. The boom towns of the mining fields were even more of the same. San Francisco attracted "one of the most heterogeneous masses that ever existed since the building of the tower of Babel," wrote a forty-niner. Among them, according to another witness, were more well-informed and

clever men than might be found in any other community of its size. "A graduate of Yale considers it no disgrace to sell peanuts on the *Plaza*," wrote Frank Marryat of those boom days, "a disciple of Coke and Blackstone to drive a mule-team, nor a New York poet to sell the New York *Tribune* at fifty cents a copy."

In the woods, on the Plains, or at the diggings, Mrs. Grundy arrived late. Until she came, social lines were only faintly drawn. Life in the raw made one man as good as another—and often a damned sight better, as the saying went—although it may have pulled more down than it raised up. "Emigration to the extreme limits of this western America," said Morris Birkbeck, an early English traveler, "will not repair a bad character"; and to be sure it did not. Bad characters flourished in the West. So did the good. People of every sort had free play in all directions to act out their particular dreams. While the great immigration into the wild West lasted they staged a drama unlike anything the world had seen. It left the country with an imperishable legend.

MOUNT-VERNON, *April* 2, 1784.

THE Subscriber would lease about 30,000 acres of land on the Ohio and Great Kanhawa, for which he has had patents ten or twelve years: Ten thousand of these, in three tracts, lie upon the Ohio, between the mouths of the two Kanhawas, having a front upon the river of fifteen miles, and beautifully bordered by the——The remaining 20,000 acres, in four other s̶u̶r̶v̶e̶y̶s̶ lie upon the Great Kanhawa, from the mouth, or near it, upwards.—These four tracts, together, have a margin upon that river, by which i̶s̶ ̶b̶o̶u̶n̶d̶e̶d̶, of more than 40 miles.

After having said thus much of the land, it is almost superfluous to add that the whole of it is river low grounds, of the first quality—but it is essential to remark that a great deal of it may be converted into the finest mowing ground imaginable, with little or no labour, nature, and the water-stops which have been made by the bever, having done *more in* effect this, than years of hard labour in most other rich soils; and that the land back of these bottoms, must for ever render the latter uncommonly profitable for stock, on account of the extensiveness of the range, as it is of a nature, being extremely broken, not to be seated or cultivated.

These lands m̶a̶y̶ ̶b̶e̶ ̶h̶a̶d̶ on three tenures—First, until January 1795, ̶a̶n̶d̶ ̶t̶h̶e̶ ̶l̶o̶n̶g̶e̶r̶—Second, until January 1795, renewable ever̶y̶ ̶t̶e̶n̶ ̶y̶e̶a̶r̶s̶ for ever.—Third, for nine hundred and ninety-nine years.

The RENTS, CONDITIONS, and PRIVILEGES, are as follow:

FIRST, An exemption from rent three years, upon condition, that five acres for every hundred, and proportionally for a greater or lesser quantity, contained in the lease, shall, within that space be cleared and tilled, or in order for the latter; and a house fit for the comfortable accommodation of the tenant erected on the premises.

Second, That before the expiration of the term of the leases of the first tenure, or the first ten years of those of the second and third, a dwelling-house of brick, or stone, or of framed work, with a stone or brick chimney, and a good barn, suited to the size of the tenement, shall be built thereon; an orchard of good fruit, to consist of as many trees as there are acres specified in the lease planted and inclosed; and five acres for every hundred, and proportionbly for a greater or lesser quantity, improved into meadow, which, or the like quantity, shall always be retained for mowing.

Third, The land to be accurately measured to each grantee, who will be allowed to take (in regular form with an extension back proportioned to the front of the river) as much as his inclination and ability may require, which quantity shall be secured to him and his heirs, by a lease in the usual form, with proper clauses, binding on landlord and tenant, for performance of covenants.

Fourth, A Spanish milled dollar of the present coin, shall pass in payment for six shillings, and other gold and silver in that proportion.

Fifth, The staple commodity, or other article of produce (for the greater ease and convenience of the tenant) may be substituted in lieu of money-rent in the leases, if the parties, at or before the first rent shall become due, can agree upon a medium value for it.

Sixth, If the exigency or policy of the State in which these lands lie, should at any time impose a tax upon them, or their appendages, such tax is to be borne by the tenant.

Seventh, These conditions, &c. being common to the leases of the three different tenures, the rent of the first will be *Four Pounds* per annum, for every hundred acres contained in the lease, and proportionally for a greater or lesser quantity.—Of the second, O̶n̶e̶ for e̶v̶e̶r̶y̶ acre contained in the lease, t̶h̶e̶ ̶f̶i̶r̶s̶t̶ year t̶o̶ ̶b̶e̶ *One Shilling and Sixpence* for th̶e̶ ̶l̶i̶k̶e̶ quantity a̶f̶t̶e̶r̶wards, until the year 1805—*Two Shillings* a̶f̶t̶e̶r̶wards, till the year 1̶8̶15—and the like increase per acre for every ten years, until the rent amounts to and shall have remained at *Five Shillings* for the ten years next ensuing—after which it is to encrease *Three-pence* per acre every t̶e̶n̶ years for ever.—Of the Third, *Two Shillings* for every acre therein contained, at which it will stand for 999 years, the term for which it is granted.

The situation of these lands are not only pleasant, but in any point of view, in which they can be considered, must be exceedingly advantageous; for if the produce of the country according to the ideas of some, should go down the Mississippi, they are nearly as conv̶e̶n̶i̶e̶n̶t̶ for that transportation, having tho̶s̶e̶ ̶w̶i̶t̶h̶o̶u̶t̶ obstruction in it to descend, as t̶h̶o̶s̶e̶ ̶w̶h̶i̶c̶h̶ are now settling about the Falls of the Ohio, and upon Kentucky—to the choice of which, among other reasons, people were *driven* by the grants to the officers and soldiers, of which these are part in the upper country, and from the impracticability of obtaining lands in extensive bodies elsewhere.—If it should come by way of Fort-Pitt to Potomack (which is the most natural) or to the Susquehanna—by the Great Kanhawa to James-River—or by the Lakes Erie and Ontario to New-York, they are infinitely more so—being, according to Hutchins's table of distances, 4̶0̶0̶ miles (all of which is against the stream) nearer to those markets than the settlements last mentioned:—And what in the present situation of things, is a matter of no trifling consideration, no other claims can interfere with these, patents having been long granted for the land, and the property of it well known; —and besides, by lying on the south east side of the Ohio, can give no jealousy to the Indians—the proprietors of it therefore may cultivate their farms in peace, and fish, fowl, and hunt, without fear or molestation.

Although I do not lay any stress upon it, the presumption being that the Indians, during the late war, have laid all *in ruins*—yet it is on record in the courts of Botetourt and Fincastle (in which counties the land did lie) that buildings, meadows, and other improvements, which were made thereon in the years 1774 and 1775, designedly for the accommodation of tenants, cost the Subscriber, as appears by the oaths of sworn appraisers (conformably to the directions of an act of the Assembly of Virginia, for seating and cultivating new lands) £. 1568 18s. 7¼, equal to £. 1961 3s. 8d. Maryland, Pennsylvania, or Jersey currency.

These lands being peculiarly well adapted for small societies, who may incline to be detached and retired—Any such applying in a body, or by their pastors or agents, shall have every assistance and encouragement, which can with convenience and propriety be given, by

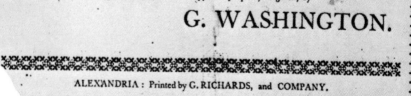

G. WASHINGTON.

ALEXANDRIA: Printed by G. RICHARDS, and COMPANY.

BREACHING
THE APPALACHIANS

During America's early colonial days the British Government had never been able to establish a satisfactory policy for dealing with colonization of the land beyond the Alleghenies. After Wolfe's victory at Quebec and the French withdrawal from the great inland area some practical system of imperial organization and some plausible method of dealing with the Indians were imperative. In 1763, as a stopgap, King George did "strictly forbid, on pain of our displeasure, all our loving subjects from making any purchases or settlements in that region," until some plan for orderly expansion could be devised. That proclamation was re-affirmed by the Quebec Act in 1774. Thus, it was hoped in London, might the fur trade be preserved, the Indians kept reasonably quiet, and trouble at the border generally minimized.

It was a large problem, one on which America's destiny would hinge in the years to come, but it couldn't wait until Parliament made up its mind. As Lord Dartmouth admitted a decade later, no authority on earth could effectively restrain "that dangerous spirit of unlicensed emigration" which had already carried the first pioneers over the mountains. George Washington, as told earlier, had been over the crest on the King's business many years before. Good husbandman that he was, and with his eye for land promotion, the urgency of his official business did not blind the young Virginia colonel to the "exceedingly beautiful and agreeable" land he passed through, nor to the numerous advantages it offered settlers. Twenty years later, during the grim winter at Valley Forge, Washington must have remembered that land when, it is said, he vowed that "sooner than surrender to the enemy upon any probable terms, he would retire beyond the mountains, and establish another base in the Ohio Valley."

Most Americans had but little knowledge of what lay beyond the Alleghenies at the close of the Revolution, but early fur traders and colonial land speculators knew the richness of the western country. Speculation in the "wild lands" had built more than one colonial fortune. It had also led to serious intercolonial disputes, Indian wars, and land-jobbery of the most scandalous sort.

But the first emigrants crossed the mountains with little accurate information to guide them. In 1784 John Filson published the first history of Kentucky, "incredible as it may appear to some . . . not . . . from lucrative motives, but solely to inform the world of the happy climate, and plentiful soil of this favoured region." With the book he published a map (see pp. 162–3) showing "the foundations of cities, laid that, in all probability, will rival the glory of the greatest upon earth." It was inscribed to "his Excell^y. George Washington," a man whose interest in the West was second to none.

That same year Washington rode west, past Braddock's grave and Fort Necessity, to visit his own property beyond the mountains. His western lands were not vast compared with those of contemporary capitalists like Robert Morris and William Bingham. In the spring of 1796, however, he felt it was time to get out of the market. "Distant property in land," he concluded, was "more pregnant of perplexities than profit." Robert Morris, the greatest speculator of them all, he who had supplied the money for Washington's campaigns of Trenton and Princeton, he who had been Washington's chief reliance in every emergency during the Revolution, was caught in the crash that followed and went to debtor's prison.

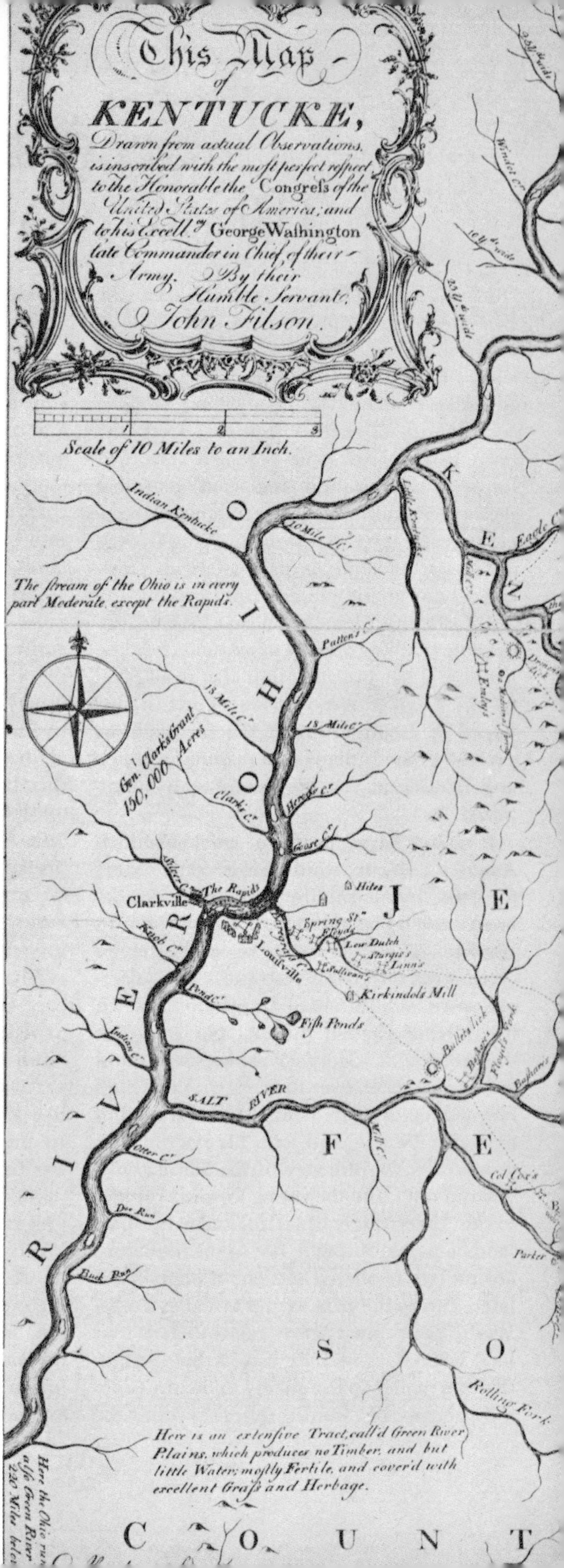

This Map of
KENTUCKE,
Drawn from actual Observations, is inscribed with the most perfect respect to the Honorable the Congress of the United States of America; and to his Excell.y George Washington late Commander in Chief of their Army. By their Humble Servant, John Filson.

Scale of 10 Miles to an Inch.

Indian Kentucke

The stream of the Ohio is in every part Moderate, except the Rapids.

O H I O

Gen.l Clark'sGrant 190,000 Acres

18 Mile C.

18 Mile C.

Patten's C.

Beargrass C.

The Rapids

Clarkville

Hites

Spring St

Floyds

Low Dutch

Sturgis's

Lann's

Sullivans

Louisville

Kirkindols Mill

Beech C.

Ponde

Fish Ponds

Bullitts lick

Floyds Fork

SALT RIVER

Otter C.

Doe Run

Col Coxe's

Parler C.

Black Br.

R I V E R

Here is an extensive Tract, call'd Green River Plains, which produces no Timber, and but little Water; mostly Fertile, and cover'd with excellent Grass and Herbage.

Rolling Fork

Eagle C.

Wimbs C.

Eagle C.

C O U N T

The Library of Congress

JOHN FILSON'S MAP OF KENTUCKY, 1784. Engraving by Henry D. Purcell. "Col. Boon's" house is shown just to the right and below dead center. Louisville is represented by ten buildings. Other notations are worth close examination. The map was printed twenty-three times between 1784 and 1929. The second state, shown here, is apparently a unique copy.

The Missouri Historical Society
DANIEL BOONE. Engraving by J. O. Lewis. Apparently a unique example of the print made from Chester Harding's portrait painted in 1819 and said to be the only authentic likeness of Boone. Only the upper portion of the original painting still exists. Lewis engraved the print because, he said, "to transmit to the posterity of a country the actions and features of those who fought and bled in her cause is a duty too sacred to neglect." It is the earliest print known to have been made west of the Mississippi.

new-found Eden. Heaven itself, as a native later put it reverently enough, was a very Kentuck of a place.

In that boundless paradise Boone was completely at home. "I asked him one day, just after a description of one of his long hunts," wrote Harding, who painted his portrait, "if he never got lost, having no compass. 'No,' said he, 'I can't say as ever I was lost, but I was *bewildered* once for three days.'" Another time, as the legend goes, Boone chipped away the bark from an ash tree to reveal a spot on the trunk where thirty years before in the depths of the forest he had gashed a sapling with his tomahawk. Walking a hundred and sixty miles, with only one stop, snuffing a candle with a shot from his Kentucky rifle, miraculously escaping from bands of murderous, cunning savages—these were only a few more of his exploits retold across the mountains.

The legend of the backwoodsmen grew with time, the truth hopelessly mixed with fiction. Writers, European as well as American, picked up the theme and embroidered it according to their need and fancy. In the eighth canto of *Don Juan,* Byron interrupts his description of the siege of the Moslems long enough to praise Boone and make him a popular figure wherever the poet is read.

The General Boone, back-woodsman of
    Kentucky,
Was happiest among mortals anywhere;
For killing nothing but a bear or
    buck, he
Enjoy'd the lonely, vigorous, harmless
    days
Of his old age in wilds of deepest maze.

Crime came not near him—she is not
    the child
Of solitude; Health shrank not from
    him—for
Her home is in the rarely-trodden wild.

The most appealing feature of Filson's book was its account of Daniel Boone, written as though Boone himself were the narrator. The little volume was translated into several foreign languages and widely circulated abroad. It introduced the heroic legend of the American frontiersman, a novel story that enchanted a world weary of its twice-told tales. Boone, a backwoods Adam, became the living symbol of unspoiled man. One day, it was reported, he was discovered lying on his back in the forest, singing in sheer delight at being alone and free in this

For generations past, utopians abroad had pictured the land beyond the Alleghenies as a retreat where white men might start life over, guided in their fresh beginning by un-

164

contaminated, redskinned children of nature. Until the Indians were pushed back a safe distance Americans contributed little to the notion of noble savages. However, in 1790 Mrs. Sarah Wentworth Morton, "the American Sappho," snug in Boston, wrote her romantic epic *Ouâbi; or the Virtues of Nature* in which she described a West where whites and reds mingled and married in peaceful goodfellowship. Here the refugee from civilization, "tired of scenes, where crimes beguile, fond of virtue's honest smile," could find a dusky bride to share his pursuit of the good life.

But for some years to come Indian relations in old "Kaintuck" were no fit subject for rhapsody. Boone, with other intrepid backwoodsmen, had fairly neutralized the Red Terror south of the Ohio, but the price had been stiff. Of the two hundred and fifty-six men who in 1780 drew up the first government in what was to become Tennessee, hardly a dozen were living in 1790, and only one had died a natural death. The Indians had never intended men, white or red, to settle in their hunting grounds—the "Dark and Bloody Ground," as Chief Dragging Canoe called it. In Filson's book Boone reflected, "My footsteps have often been marked with blood, and therefore I can truly subscribe to its original name."

The New-York Historical Society
"ON THESE FAR-EXTENDED PLAINS, TRUTH AND GOD-LIKE JUSTICE REIGNS!" Engraving by S. Hill. A vision of good fellowship among the Indians and whites of the West, as seen from a sedate Boston parlor. Frontispiece from Mrs. Morton's *Ouâbi*, after a drawing by Christian Gullager, a Danish-born, Paris-trained artist who, like the author, very obviously had only a remote knowledge of the American West.

"ATTACK OF THE INDIANS UPON DAN'L. AND SQUIRE BOONE & JOHN STEWART THE LAST OF WHOM WAS KILLED AND SCALPED." Engraving by G. Murray. Frontispiece from Humphrey Marshall, *History of Kentucky,* 1812.
The Library of Congress

SCENES ON THE ROAD TO THE WEST IN THE EARLY 19TH CENTURY. Drawings by Joshua Shaw. Drawn by an observer who was apparently on the spot.

"Shelter" in the Wilderness. Anonymous drawing. A pen sketch from a manuscript diary, 1808.

Thousands of families had already crossed the ridge into the new West before peace with England was concluded in 1783. With the Indian menace reduced, fresh hordes sweated and strained and chopped their way over the mountains and through virgin forests. "Come to a turable mountain that tired us all almost to death to git over it and we lodge this night . . . under a granite mountain . . ." wrote one of those indomitable pilgrims in his diary. "Met a good many peopel turned back for fear of the indians but our Company goes on Still with good courage we came to a very ugly Creek with steep Banks and have to cross it several times. . . ."

Chief Justice Robertson of Kentucky remembered his parents saying that "thousands of men, women, and children came in successive caravans, forming continuous streams of human beings, horses, cattle and other domestic animals, all moving onward along a lonely and houseless path to a wild and cheerless land . . . driving stock and leading packhorses, and the women, some walking with pails on their heads, others riding with children in their laps, and other children swung in baskets on horses, fastened to the tails of others going before."

A journal of one early trek concludes: "Wednesday 26th [April 1775]—We Begin Building us a house and a plaise of Defense to Keep the indians off   this day we begin to live wthout bread. Saturday 29th—We git

our house kivered with Bark and move our things into it at Night and Begin housekeeping. . . ." Such huts, wrote an English traveler who hiked through western New York a generation later and who drew the accompanying sketch, often could keep out neither wind nor rain.

But, as the late Carl Becker once wrote, to venture into the wilderness one must see it not as it is, but as it will be. The American frontier was a promised land to be entered only by those with faith in tomorrow. For many emigrants who pressed on behind the first settlers, that tomorrow arrived day after day. "We were worth nothing when we landed at this place," wrote John Watson from Indiana in 1823 to friends in England, "and now we have 1 yoke of oxen, 1 cow, 9 hogs. . . . Whilst this letter is writing, my wife is eating preserved peaches and bread, and washing them down with good whiskey and water."

Such letters, and others that told of disaster and disenchantment beyond the mountains, many of them trumped-up to promote or discourage interest in the western road, made emigration a lively subject of debate. After the War of 1812 English newspapers teemed with accounts of popular meetings held to discuss the possible advantages of emigration to America and, as well, with editorials lamenting the departure for an alien land of so many valuable citizens.

To emigrants from the settled regions of Europe and the American seaboard, the back country, north of the Cumberland River, seemed at first an unending, dark forest. (Someone judged that squirrels might have hopped for a thousand miles without touching the ground and scarcely seeing the sunlight.) To travel days on end through a thick gloom among trees a hundred feet high was oppressing beyond the imagination of people who had not experienced it. One eighteenth-century traveler observed that the American had developed "an unconquerable aversion" to the trees that hemmed him in at every turn. He cut away all before him without mercy, even without need. But making a clearing out of such solid woods for a log house and a corn patch was only the necessary beginning of life in the wilderness.

The easiest method to increase a clearing was to girdle the trees and burn the dead timber. It was wasteful but there were forests to burn and much to be done. Basil Hall, an English visitor, looked with horror at the vast number of magnificent trees, "standing around him with their throats cut, the very Banquos of the murdered forest! The process of girdling is this": he reported, "a circular cut or ring, two or three inches deep, is made with an axe quite around the tree at about five feet from the ground. This, of course, puts an end to vegetable life, and the destruction of the tree being accelerated by the action of fire, these wretched trunks in a year or two present the most miserable objects of decrepitude that can be conceived. The purpose, however, is gained and that is all the American settler can be expected to look to. His corn crop is no longer overshadowed by the leaves of these unhappy trees, which, in the process of time, are cut down and split into railings, or sawed into billets of firewood,—and their misery is at an end. Even in the cultivated fields, the top of the stumps were seen poking their black snouts above the young grain, like a shoal of seals."

A ROAD THROUGH THE FORESTS IN THE ALLEGHENY MOUNTAINS, 1833. Aquatint after a drawing by Charles Bodmer. An illustration from the *Atlas* accompanying Maximilian, Prince of Wied, *Travels in the Interior of North America*. This and all the following illustrations after Bodmer are from the same volume.
The New York Public Library

BURNING FALLEN TREES IN A GIRDLED CLEARING, ABOUT 1840. Aquatint by W. J. Bennett. After a water color by George Harvey, an English artist; one of a series of forty *Atmospheric Landscapes* in which Harvey hoped to capture the peculiar character of the American scene.

The Museum of Science and Industry, Chicago
PIONEER AXMEN, ABOUT 1820. Drawing by Joshua
Shaw.

The ax was no tool for a novice, as Captain John Smith had pointed out two centuries earlier. At Jamestown, he said, every third chop was drowned out by the oath of some bungler. Many later European emigrants turned back from the frontiersman's task content to let the more experienced American make the clearings. "At *cutting down* trees or *cutting them up*," observed a critical English editor early in the nineteenth century, the Americans "will do *ten times* as much in a day as any other men I ever saw. Let one of these men on upon a wood of timber trees, and his slaughter will astonish you."

The typical frontier hut was built as it was in order to save time and money, and was often completed in a day with the help of the nearest neighbors. At worst it was, in the words of one Indiana pioneer, "a barbarous rectangle of unhewed and unbarked logs, bound together by a gigantic dove-tailing called notching." At best it could not be compared with the painstakingly contrived log houses built by the early Swedish and German settlers in the East.

Tocqueville thought he had seen a few odd volumes of Shakespeare in almost every pioneer's hut he visited, however rude and hastily improvised it might be. He himself

AN AMERICAN LOG-HOUSE, 1796. Engraving after a drawing by Victor Collot. Illustration from Collot, *Voyage dans L'Amérique Septentrionale.*

The New York Public Library

The New-York Historical Society
"THE TRAPPERS RETURN." Engraving by G. Murray. This engraving, published in *The Portfolio* in 1810, was taken from a sketch by Alexander Wilson, a Scotch poet, ornithologist, and amateur musician, who knew the backwoods, its people, and its birds quite as intimately as Audubon.

read *Henry V* for the first time in a backwoods log house. Like John James Audubon, who roamed the forests with all the freedom of the wild things he painted so lovingly, Tocqueville found a hearty welcome in all the wilderness homes he entered. Audubon wrote of having stumbled into such a hut one stormy night, wet, weary, and hungry:

"Our host returned, and we already began to feel the comforts of hospitality . . . 'I have no whisky in the house,' he said, 'but father has some capital cider, and I'll go over and bring a keg of it.' I asked how far off his father lived. 'Only three miles, Sir, and I'll be back before Eliza has cooked your supper.' . . . The cabin was new. The logs of which it was formed were all of the tulip-tree, and were nicely pared. Every part was beautifully clean. Even the coarse slabs of wood that formed the floor looked as if newly washed and dried. . . . A large spinning-wheel, with rolls of wool and cotton, occupied one corner. In another was a small cupboard, containing the little stock of new dishes, cups, plates and tin pans. The table was small also, but quite new, and as bright as polished walnut could be. The only bed that I saw was of domestic manufacture, and the counterpane proved how expert the young wife was at spinnning and weaving. A fine rifle ornamented the chimney-piece."

Audubon, to be sure, was welcome anywhere he went. The lithe and handsome "woodsman from America" had a great gift of friendliness and innumerable talents. His inexhaustible and lyrical tales of the American back country were the delight of British society when he crossed the Atlantic to show his pictures. To such circles he strongly resembled the "natural man" rhapsodized by their romantic poets come to real life. He was fêted and feasted until, as he wrote home, he hoped they would not make "a conceited fool of Mr. Audubon at last."

Although the Revolutionary War campaign of George Rogers Clark had won the land north of Kentucky for the United States, it remained hostile Indian ground for a decade more. In 1785, to exercise some control over the savages, Fort Harmar was built at the confluence of the Ohio and Muskingum Rivers by a handful of Congress troops. Three years later General Rufus Putnam with a group of pilgrims sailed down the Ohio in a latter-day *Mayflower* to settle the point of land opposite the fort in the name of the Ohio Associates. At the risk of their scalps thousands of emigrants were already floating on beyond the town site— the future Marietta—in search of new homes.

In 1789, in the little council house shown at the left in the picture below, General St. Clair signed a treaty with the Miamis, the Shawnees, the Delawares, and other tribes in which they granted the American claims to the territory north of the Beautiful River. But the Indians did not share the white man's notion of land cession. To them the wilderness was common property to be freely used for hunting. They were ceding that same usage to others, not delivering absolute title. Many natives not signatory to the pact felt no compulsion to respect it in any sense. Others, encouraged by British fur traders of the Northwest, were urged to rid their preserves of the interlopers with their all-conquering plowshares.

Time and again military patrols sent out to protect the advancing frontier and awe the resistance were routed by aroused redmen. General Harmar's expedition of 1790 was thrown back in disorder and sought the protection of the nearest fort. A winter of terror followed. The next year General Arthur St. Clair, in the field at Washington's order, was worried back to his headquarters by Little Turtle's warring tribes. The issue was settled only in 1794 when Anthony Wayne (anything but "Mad Anthony," for he took elaborate precautions) sallied from

FORT HARMAR IN 1790. Lithograph after a drawing by Joseph Gilman. Illustration from *The American Pioneer*, 1842. An early copy of Gilman's original drawing, showing the Ohio River at the right, the Muskingum at the left, and the site of Marietta on the farther shore.

The New-York Historical Society

SIGNING THE TREATY OF GREENVILLE, AUGUST 3, 1795. Anonymous painting. Reputedly painted by a member of Wayne's staff.

Fort Defiance with carefully schooled troops and, fighting through the timber felled by a tornado, broke the resistance. Wayne destroyed the Indians' cornfields and their villages and Little Turtle finally came to terms. With pipe-smoking and drinking a treaty of peace was concluded the following summer at Greenville. This one "took" and with that frontier quiet at last, more people streamed West in ever growing numbers.

Within another few years square-rigged vessels were sailing out of Marietta and neighboring towns for eastern and European ports. New Englanders with salt water in their blood had settled in the Northwest. Surrounded by abundant cheap timber, close to more fertile country than they had ever seen, and with a broad river at their door, they might hope to develop a trade in low-priced farm produce, carried by locally built vessels, that would rival the enterprise of Boston or Philadelphia. In 1801 when the Marietta-built brig *St. Clair*, 104 tons burden and laden with pork and flour, set sail from the home port to do a profitable business at Philadelphia by way of Havana, the town flocked to the river's edge to cheer it on. Commodore Whipple, the commander, thought it was a greater event than his escape out of Newport with dispatches from Congress through a blockade of seven British ships during the Revolution. For the six or eight years that followed Marietta was a thriving shipbuilding town.

The American Antiquarian Society
THE ROAD TO THE WEST, ABOUT 1820. After a drawing by Charles A. Lesueur, a French naturalist whose travels during twenty-one years in America (1816–37), sketching tools in hand, took him over a wide area of the United States of that time.

Most of the early traffic from Virginia and Pennsylvania to the West followed the old army roads Braddock and Forbes had hacked out in their campaign against Fort Duquesne (Pittsburgh). As those were improved and others were built, wagons replaced pack trains on the routes. On the wide, graded surface of the Great Cumberland, or National, Road, completed as far as Wheeling by 1818, vehicles streamed westward in what seemed like a continuous parade.

"Old America seems to be breaking up and moving westward," wrote one British traveler. "We are seldom out of sight, as we travel on this grand track [the Cumberland Road] towards the Ohio, of family groups, behind and before us, some with a view to a particular spot, close to a brother, perhaps, or a friend who has gone before and reported well of the country. . . . They are great travellers, and in general, better acquainted with the vast expanse of country spreading over their eighteen states . . . than the English with their little island. They are also a migrating people and even when in prosperous circumstances can contemplate a change of situation which, under our old establishments and fixed habits, none but the most enterprising would venture upon when urged by adversity."

Tocqueville pointed out that the restless disposition, the unbounded desire for wealth, and the excessive independence which spurred Americans westward, would in Europe, be considered propensities dangerous to society. In America, on the contrary, they seemed an assurance of prosperity for the future. "For such is the present good fortune of the New World," he wrote, "that the vices of its inhabitants are scarcely less

NAVIGATING THE MOHAWK RIVER, 1807–8. Engraving by P. Maverick. Illustration from Christian Schultz, *Travels on an Inland Voyage*, 1810.

The New-York Historical Society

favorable to society than their virtues."

He also observed that the American migrated so fast and moved so frequently that the wilderness often closed in behind him as he pushed on to new goals. In western New York State where the deep silence of the forests was broken "only by the monotonous cooing of the wood-pigeons and the tapping of the woodpecker on the bark of the trees," where the woods seemed primeval, the young Frenchman stumbled on the abandoned ruins of a settler's hut, its logs sprouting anew and its props entwined by growing vines. Nature, for the moment, had silently resumed her sway, the wild beast returned to its old haunts, until the next hopeful broke a fresh path to the West.

A break in the Appalachian Mountains north of the Catskills gave New York the only level route to the West. It was a natural funnel for emigration. In 1791 Elkanah Watson had already noticed that people were swarming into this fertile region "in shoals." The series of locks, built in 1796, made the Mohawk River navigable for small boats 110 miles inland to Rome, and that added inducement to travel quickened the western fever. Real-estate advertisements suggested that emigrants "might reasonably stop in the Genesee Country without taking so long a journey as many of their countrymen have

heretofore done." Many did stop, as will be shown in Chapter IV, long enough to make a huge granary of the Genesee Valley.

En route to Niagara Falls in 1808 an English tourist passed "waggons loaded with tea, coffee, groceries, crates of earthen-ware which were going more than 200 miles back into the country. . . . Utica," he found, "has had a very rapid increase, for in the year 1794 it contained only two houses, there are now in the place upwards of 2000 inhabitants; it is a great emporium of European and other foreign goods with which the traders here supply a considerable portion of the country to the westward." New Englanders, he added, "have already given to this [country], by their industry, very much the appearance of that which they have left; many of their houses are neat framed ones, handsomely painted white or stone colour with green Venetian blind shutters and piazzas." A generation later James Fenimore Cooper wrote with misgiving about the Yankee invasion that had almost converted western New York into "an eastern colony." Those "locusts of the West," he called the Yankees.

In Daniel Webster's opinion no law in history produced more beneficent and lasting results than the Northwest Ordinance of 1787. Its enlightened provisions banned slavery, assured religious freedom, and ac-

UTICA IN 1807. One of a series of water color views by the French émigrée, Baroness Hyde de Neuville, whose husband had been banished for alleged royalist intrigue against Napoleon.

The New York Public Library, Stokes Collection

THE NORTHWEST TERRITORY, 1783. From *An Accurate Map of the United States of America, According to the Treaty of Peace of 1783.* Drawn and engraved by Rupel.

From a photostat in the American Antiquarian Society
"SALE OF THE SCIOTO DESERTS BY THE ANGLO-AMERICANS: (1790)...better to ensnare dupes, they draw up geographical maps, convert the rocky wastes into fertile plains, show roads cut through impassable cliffs, and offer shares in lands which do not belong to them." Engraving published in Paris.

tively encouraged education in the land north of the Ohio River. It denied once and for all the ancient contention that colonial territories were subordinate to the mother country in their political and social interests. The five future states from that area were to enter the Union "on an equal footing with the original states, in all respects whatever." It announced, in brief, a new, organic concept of empire.

Unfortunately the passage of the Ordinance was attended by a disgraceful piece of land-jobbery. Constructive as the measure was it had been pushed through the waning Continental Congress by a group of private land companies. One of these, the Scioto Associates, including "many of the principal characters of America," sold to a large group of hopeful Frenchmen land it never really owned. Congress tried to make amends for the fraud, Gallipolis, the town first settled by the disillusioned immigrants in 1790, still survives, but the affair had bitter repercussions at home and abroad. It was the worst

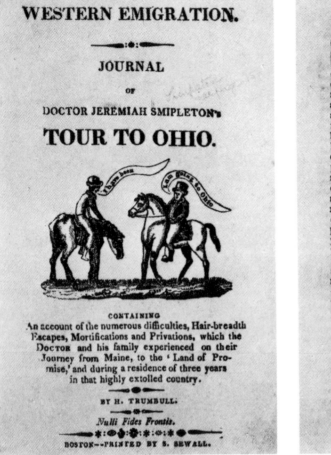

WESTERN EMIGRATION.

JOURNAL

OF

DOCTOR JEREMIAH SIMPLETON's

TOUR TO OHIO.

CONTAINING

An account of the numerous difficulties, Hair-breadth Escapes, Mortifications and Privations, which the Doctor and his family experienced on their Journey from Maine, to the 'Land of Promise,' and during a residence of three years in that highly extolled country.

BY H. TRUMBULL.

Nulli Fides Frontis.

BOSTON---PRINTED BY S. SEWALL.

---36---

rents---that provisions abound in such profusion, that geese, turkeys, oppossums, bears, raccoons and rabbits may be seen running in the woods in droves, ready cooked, with knives and forks stuck in their flanks, crying out to the newly arrived emigrant, come eat me.'---The reverse of this, friend Scruple, is the case, as you may perceive by my account of the mishaps and disasters that I met with. You will, on your arrival there, be obliged to sleep in a hollow tree, or build yourself a log hut, for here are no carpenters---kill and dress your own game, for here are no butchers---clothe yourself in skins, when your stock of apparel is worn out, for here are no factories, shoemakers, tailors, hatters or tanners---and pound your own corn, for you may travel in this wild wilderness fifty miles, without discovering the sign of a mill---in short, nothing an be obtained here without costing more for the transportation than the original price of any article you may want. As to *society*, if you wish to converse in any human language out of your family, you must go twenty or thirty miles to your next door neigbor, with your axe instead of staff---for you must cut your way thither, for want of roads---and perhaps, after all, find him almost as hoggish as the 'swines in your pens' or the more numerous class of the inhabitants of Ohio, the wild-cat, panther, &c. who frequently associate with our tame animals to their sorrow, and sometimes with young children to *our* mourning ;---And fags I'd rather be a hog-reeve in good New-England, than hold any office in this back woods country, where the inhabitants walk on all fours, with the exception of a few double headed fools. Take my advice, therefore, Scruple, and put off your journey, till you think a little further on the subject.

FINIS.

The American Antiquarian Society

AN ANTI-EMIGRATION TRACT. Published in Boston, 1819.

example yet of the speculative frenzy with which Americans "promoted" their country. But no passing scandal could stop the rush to new lands.

Long-established families of the eastern seaboard paced the rush to the West until it seemed that the exodus might depopulate the older regions. "Our dwellings, our schoolhouses, and churches will have mouldered to ruins," wailed Timothy Flint, a Harvard missionary, "our graveyards will be overrun with shrub-oak, and but here and there a wretched hermit, true to his paternal soil, to tell the tale of other times." The Virginia legislature echoed his lament as it viewed the wasted fields of the Old Dominion that had been abandoned for the fresh soil farther inland. "The fathers of the land," a committee reported, "are gone where another outlet to the ocean turns their thoughts from the place of their nativity."

Propagandists tried to stem the flow with all the discouragements they could improvise. In the interest of "truth" a Connecticut newspaper published "A Farmers Song" in 1817, advising potential emigrants:

Let the idle complain
And ramble in vain,
An Eden to find in the West.
They're grossly deceiv'd

Their hearts sorely griev'd
They'll sigh to return to the East.

But Eden, as ever, lay somewhere to the West. In Ohio, it was said, the earth needed "only to be tickled with the hoe to laugh with the harvest," and despite efforts to discourage them, people from everywhere poured into the region by path and waterway, pressed on down the Beautiful River in boatloads to new sites, and spread over the land in such numbers that Ohio became a state in 1803. It became, moreover, a mixing bowl within the Melting Pot, to stretch an image. Here Puritan mingled with "foreigners" from Virginia and Pennsylvania—themselves of many extractions—and with first generation Americans from European countries to breed a typical New World civilization.

Enough of the westward drift settled at Cincinnati (see illustration on following pages) to build it in short order into a shining ornament of the new country. In 1835 Chevalier found it "a large and beautiful town, charmingly situated in one of those bends which the Ohio makes, as if unwilling to leave the spot." From the neighboring hills, he wrote, the eye took in the windings of the river with its busy parade of steamboats, the warehouses, the factories, and the numerous church spires that proclaimed an abundant and peaceful prosperity. "On all sides the view is terminated by ranges of hills, forming an amphitheatre yet covered with the vigorous growth of the primitive forest. This rich verdure is here and there interrupted by country houses surrounded by colonnades, which are furnished by the forest. The population which occupies this amphitheatre, lives in the midst of plenty; it is industrious, sober, frugal, thirsting after knowledge, and if, with very few exceptions, it is entirely a stranger to the delicate pleasures and elegant manners of the refined society of our European capitals, it is equally ignorant of its vices, dissipation, and follies."

THE PASSING SCENE ON THE OHIO RIVER IN 1821. Water color by Félix-Achille Beaupoil de Saint-Aulaire, dedicated to Mme. Razon. The artist pictured himself in the foreground on the north bank of the river looking across to Guyandotte, West Virginia, and recording flatboats (to the left) and a keelboat (right center) working downstream, and a very early western steamboat chugging against the current. This is just about the earliest known eye-witness depiction of both a keelboat and a western steamer.

Collection of Herman P. Dean

An Early View of Cincinnati, 1830-40. Painting by Johann Casper Wild, a Swiss artist whose views of Philadelphia, St. Louis, and the Mississippi Valley provide important references to the history of those parts.

FLATBOAT. Drawing by Charles A. Lesueur.

THE RIVERMEN

Even after a few "roads" had threaded the wilderness, their pitiful inadequacy, from an early date, led Americans to prefer the natural waterways for travel and communication. Until the railroads were built America seemed almost to be a nation of river folk. The Ohio and its tributaries opened a glistening highway that wound for more than a thousand miles through the lands of the farther West and that led, via the Mississippi and Missouri, on to New Orleans in one direction and out to the Great Plains in the other. At terminal points of the routes from the East—at Radstone, Pittsburgh, Wheeling, and Olean (Hamilton, New York)—the riverbank swarmed with emigrants awaiting passage downstream. "It is estimated," wrote one of them from Hamilton in 1818, "that there are now in this village and its vicinity, three hundred families, besides single travellers, amounting in all to fifteen hundred souls, waiting for a rise of the water to em-

bark for the promised land. I have just returned from taking a view of this *inland flotilla,* as they lie hauled up along the shore."

Craft of all description were built in almost every creek of the Ohio valley. Some were so shallow "a heavy dew" sufficed to float them. Others were over one hundred feet in length with a three- or four-foot draft. Packet-boat service had started on the Ohio in the eighteenth century. In 1794 the proprietor of one packet advertised that, "being influenced by love of philanthropy, and a desire of being serviceable to the public, [he] has taken great pains to render the accomodations on board the boats as agreeable and convenient as they could possibly be made. No danger need be apprehended from the enemy, as every person on board will be under cover made proof to rifle balls, and convenient port holes for firing out. Each of the boats is armed with six pieces, carrying a

182

pound ball; also a good number of muskets, and amply supplied with ammunition, strongly manned with choice men, and the master of approved knowledge."

Flatboats carried most of the migrant families downstream. Built of square timbers, rising fortress-like above the water line, partly roofed over, they often traveled in fleets for mutual protection and guidance. Sometimes they reached out of sight along the river. "I could not conceive what such large square boxes could be, which seemed abandoned to the current," wrote a French traveler on the Mississippi, "presenting alternately their ends, their sides, and even their angles. As they advanced I heard a confused noise, without distinguishing anything, on account of the height of the sides. On ascending the banks of the river I perceived in these boats several families, bringing with them their horses, cows, fowl, carts, ploughs, harness, beds, instruments of husbandry; in short, all the furniture requisite for housekeeping, agriculture, and the management of a farm."

To drift with the current from Pittsburgh to New Orleans took flatboats about five or six weeks. Whatever their destination, since

The Museum of Science and Industry, Chicago
TRAVELERS ON A FLATBOAT, 1810-1820. Drawing by Joshua Shaw.

they were too clumsy to propel upstream, they were broken up at the journey's end for house timber. Between 1806 and 1823 over twelve thousand of them, among other craft, landed at New Orleans from upriver. At one time as they unloaded their miscellaneous cargoes at that city, their decks provided a mile-long promenade at the riverbank.

The New-York Historical Society
A PROMENADE OF FLATBOATS AT NEW ORLEANS, 1828. Etching after a drawing by Basil Hall. Captain Hall's original drawings, from which this and other etchings were made, are owned by the University of Indiana.

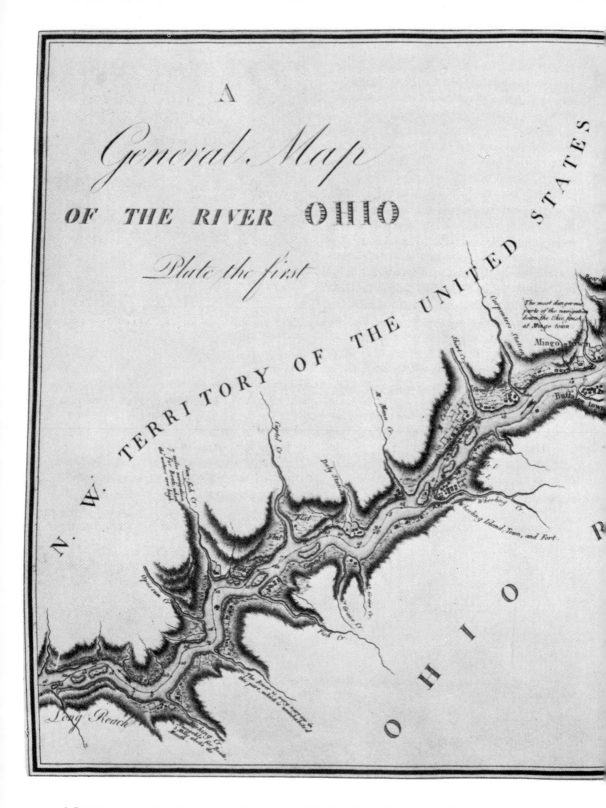

A PORTION OF THE OHIO RIVER, 1796. Engraving by Tardieu *l'aîné*. From a map drawn by General Victor Collot and published in his *Voyage dans l'Amérique Septentrionale*. Collot, a French officer who served in the Revolutionary War, was commissioned by the French minister to the United States to supply "a minute detail of the political, commercial and military state of the western part" of the United States and of the

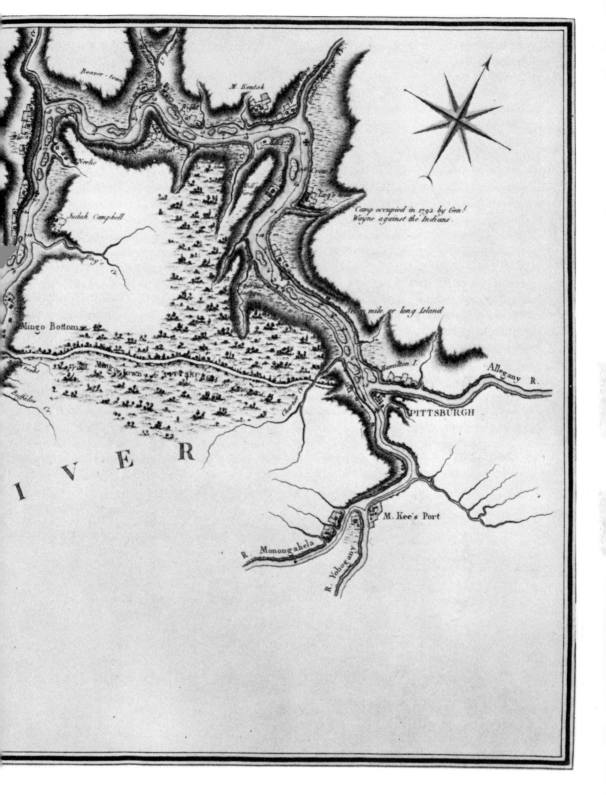

Ohio and Mississippi Valleys. The Directory, apparently, had every intention of containing the United States within its bounds by taking over Louisiana, the Floridas, and Canada. For that purpose Collot's handsome work was invaluable reconnaissance. It was not published until 1826.

Keelboats were the speediest and most easily managed of the pre-steamboat inland trading vessels. Longer and narrower than flatboats, double-ended and with a shallow keel for protection and stability, they could be rowed when small enough, sailed where feasible, or poled through the water, upstream as well as down. They attracted the most valuable freight and the most competent crews.

A round trip between Pittsburgh and New Orleans took almost six months. The difficulty of propelling the boat against the current is obvious, and this leg of the journey took at least four months. The most common method was to "walk" the craft against the water, with men apparently transfixed by the long poles they pushed against as they crept along the sides of the vessel.

At Maysville, Kentucky, in 1817, the English traveler John Palmer witnessed the arrival of a keelboat from New Orleans that had been poled by its crew of sixteen hands most of the 1730 miles "fernenst," as they said, the current. The boat was a hundred-ton affair equipped with two masts and it carried a valuable cargo of West Indies produce. The exuberant and relieved merchants of Maysville saluted the safe return of the craft after an absence of many months with repeated salutes from a cannon. Without another thought the crew raced to the nearest tavern to celebrate the halt to their back-breaking work and to liquidate their earnings in true riverman fashion.

Until the advent of the steamboat, and even for some years after, keelboats carried a large share of the trade between the East, the South, and Europe to the upper Mississippi and Ohio River towns. That a steamboat could survive the perils and difficulties of such heroic navigation—that the newfangled machines could ascend Horsetail Ripple or Letart's Falls without the help of "good setting poles" or cordelles—was a ludicrous notion to the men who manned keelboats. "It could not be done nohow." For, as one of their songs ran, "No one can do as the boatman can, The boatman dance and the boatman sing, The boatman is up to everything." (The cordelle was a towline from several hundred to a thousand feet long by which the crew pulled a boat upstream where setting poles could not be used.) By

The New-York Historical Society

A KEELBOAT USING SAILS AND OARS. Illustration from *The Davy Crockett Almanac*, 1838. Compare this with the water color view (page 179) showing a keelboat, flatboats, and an early steamboat on the Ohio River.

The New-York Historical Society

A KEELBOAT WORKING UPSTREAM. Illustration from *Harper's Magazine,* 1855.

INTERIOR OF A KEELBOAT. Drawing by Lesueur.

Photograph from The American Antiquarian Society

The St. Louis Mercantile Library Association
A WESTERN RIVERMAN. Drawing by George Caleb
Bingham. A study for one of his paintings.

whatever method the craft was maneuvered upstream, fifteen miles was a fair limit to a day's progress, although twice as much might be traveled under good conditions. The shortest run on record from New Orleans to Cincinnati was made in seventy-eight days.

In the heyday of the barge and keelboat the professional boatmen were a special breed of men. They were rough and hardy, said Mark Twain, "rude, uneducated, brave, suffering terrific hardships with sailor-like stoicism; heavy drinkers, coarse frolickers in moral sties like the Natchez-under-the-hill of that day, heavy fighters, reckless fellows, everyone, elephantinely jolly, foul-witted, profane, prodigal of their money, bankrupt at the end of the trip, fond of barbaric finery, prodigious braggarts, yet, in the main, honest, trustworthy, faithful to promises and duty, and often picturesquely magnanimous."

Mike Fink, the "ginewine article," was by

RAFTSMEN PLAYING CARDS, 1851. Painting by Bingham. Much of the work of this Missouri artist was devoted to portraying the vanishing race of western rivermen at work and play. His drawings and paintings provide a unique record.

The City Art Museum, St. Louis

his own boast the greatest of them all, a very Jason of a fellow who could "out-run, out-jump, out-shoot, out-brag, out-drink, an out-fight, rough-an'-tumble, no holts barred, ary man on both sides the river from Pittsburgh to New Orleans an' back ag'in to St. Louiee." As an infant Mike refused his mother's milk for a bottle of whisky; as a man, every lick he made in the woods let in an acre of sunshine. His legendary self-portrait was drawn to a Gargantuan scale, big and bold enough to fit the enormous Mississippi world that framed the boatman's life. When he and his ilk descended upon New Orleans that city of genteel traditions took on a new dimension.

Until more and better roads were built between the East and the West, and before the railroads altogether rerouted the nation's traffic, it seemed likely that New Orleans would become the great trading center for the whole interior of America. It seemed

Crockett Almanac '38

Mike Fink, the Ohio Boatman.

The New-York Historical Society

New Orleans in 1840. Aquatint by W. J. Bennett. One of a series of superb views of American cities undertaken by Bennett. A number of others (Detroit, Buffalo, etc.) are reproduced elsewhere in this volume.
The Yale University Art Gallery, Mabel Brady Garvan Collection

The Museum of Fine Arts, Boston, M. & M. Karolik Collection

VOYAGEURS. Painting by Charles Deas.

particularly likely when steamboats (to the bitter despair of old-time rivermen) solved the upstream difficulties on the Mississippi.

In the Northwest, tributaries of the parent river stretched out over the wilderness like a giant net, spread to catch a yearly harvest of furs and drag it in to the principal trading posts. It was far easier to float the pelts downstream than to take them by lake, river, stream, and portage cross country to Montreal, the popular trade route of pre-Revolutionary days. With the Louisiana Purchase the Missouri, "that savage river . . .", as Parkman described it, "descending from its mad career through a vast unknown of barbarism," became the mainstream of the traffic. Each spring when the waters were at flood, the winter's catch, combed out of the wilderness and collected at remote outposts, came hurtling down a hundred smaller streams that joined the muddy torrent of the Missouri.

Until the advent of the steamboat, and after that in the shallower reaches, the precious freight was carried in pirogues, dugouts, canoes, Mackinaw boats, and keelboats, manned by northern rivermen whose lives and fortune were staked on getting their haul to market.

Of all the international proletariat that trapped the back country the most picturesque were the French-Canadian and halfbreed *voyageurs* whose gaudy dress and gay song, whose endless stamina and expert zeal were a never-ceasing wonder. "To conquer distance and labor, at the same time, with a song, has occurred to no other people," wrote Schoolcraft after he had come to know these extraordinary people. "They are short, thick set, and active, and never tire," wrote Thomas L. M'Kenney, in 1827. It was the despair of Canadian youth to grow as tall as five feet ten or eleven inches, he added. "There is no room for the legs of such people in these canoes. But if he should stop growing at about five feet four inches, and be gifted with a good voice, and lungs that never tire, he is considered as having been born under a most favorable circumstance."

In holiday garb the *voyageur* wore colored fringe on cap and shirt, with bells and beads clinking on sleeves and leggings. A bright turban or plumed hat topped his outfit. In 1851 the fur trade of the Upper Missouri had passed its peak. But one visitor to the Red River then found there "the descendants of the 'voyageurs'. . . . How different their manner, appearance & attitude from the 'Americans' around them. They have the vivacity, merry jest & . . . expressive . . . gesture of old france. . . . Most of them have Indian or half-breed wives which gives rise to another branch in the population of Minnesota. The scarf sash, pipe, & mocassins are the only remnants of the old voyageurs dress to be seen among them."

1. HENRY BELLAND, VOYAGEUR. "Cap of blue cloth with wolf tail crest, fur border & ribbons." 2. "Winter dress of Red river half-breeds   a coat of buff lappels embroidered on light color'd doe skin—red sash or belt embr^ed   Buff trousers fringed & garnished—mocassins—fur collar & trimmings." 3. (Rear view) "Buffalo Skin coat—dark buff." The artist's notations are quoted. All three drawings were made in 1851 by Frank Blackwell Mayer and are in the E. E. Ayer Collection at the Newberry Library. 4. MISSOURI FUR TRADER. Study by Bingham for the well-known painting in the Metropolitan Museum of Art. From the St. Louis Mercantile Library Association.

1

2

3

4

"St. Louis (from the River Below, in 1836), a Town on the Mississippi, with 2,500 Inhabitants." Painting by George Catlin. With the Steamboat *Yellowstone* in the Foreground. Catlin, the artist, first journeyed up the Missouri in the *Yellowstone* in 1832. He went as far as Fort Union and descended the river in a dugout.

PLAINSMEN
AND MOUNTAIN MEN

St. Louis was the "Montreal of the Mississippi," the depot of the Missouri River traffic and the heart of the western fur trade. The town had been born as a fur-trading post in 1764 when Pierre Laclède Liguest and a company of followers operating from that site obtained a monopoly of the Indian trade. Long after the Louisiana Purchase the streets of St. Louis swarmed with the hunters and rivermen who made up the bulk of the population. "Most of their days are passed beyond the borders of the wild buffalo plains at the base of the Rocky Mountains," wrote a visitor in 1838. "Most of them

are trappers, hunters, traders to the distant post of Santa Fé, or *engagés* of the American Fur Company."

It was at St. Louis that, inspired by reports from the farther West brought back by Lewis and Clark in 1806, Manuel Lisa, Pierre Chouteau, Andrew Henry, and Governor William Clark formed the Missouri Fur Company. From here, too, John Jacob Astor hoped to win complete control over the fur trade, planning at first a chain of posts up the Missouri and down the Columbia to his remote factory at the mouth of the latter river. Failing that, his American

Fur Company took over the Missouri Fur Company and in 1822 started to work the upper Missouri valley. Nine years later the company sent the first steamboat, the *Yellowstone,* up the Missouri to a point beyond Council Bluffs and, in the following year, to Fort Union near the mouth of the Yellowstone River.

Following the War of 1812 the War Department set up a series of garrisons along the frontier to guard the extreme limits of the farmer's advance into the West. The forts became a natural gathering place for fur traders, red and white. For a score of years after its inception in 1819, Fort Snelling, at the head of navigation on the Mississippi, dominated the northwestern wilderness. "Fort Snelling is about a mile from the [American Fur Company] factory, and is situated on a steep promontory, in a commanding position," wrote Captain Marryat in 1839; "it is built of stone, and may be considered as impregnable to any attempt which the Indians might make, provided that it has a sufficient garrison. Behind it is a splendid prairie, running back for many miles. . . . The band of warriors attached to Monsieur Rainville have set up their war-tent close to the factory, and have entertained us with a variety of dances. Their dresses are very beautiful. . . ." Close by that remote outpost of civilization St. Paul and Minneapolis grew up in another generation. By then the farmers had advanced far beyond.

A View of Fort Snelling, about 1838. Anonymous Painting. The painting has been attributed to Seth Eastman, sometime commandant at the fort.

The Minneapolis Institute of Arts

Bureau of American Ethnology,
The Smithsonian Institution
INTERIOR OF FORT UNION(?), 1852. Drawing by Rudolph Friederich Kurz.

Fort Union, three miles above the mouth of the Yellowstone River and many miles northwest of Fort Snelling, was built by Astor's company in 1829 as a permanent frontier trading post and as a depot for posts still farther out in the wilderness. It was the Company's greatest fort and to it were attracted a curious variety of visitors, from savages—both white and red—a bare cut

above the wild beasts they hunted to kill, to postgraduates of Europe's salons and studios eager for adventure and study. The German artist, Rudolph Friederich Kurz, arrived there one day in 1851 just as "the sun went down and a golden shimmering light spread over the landscape. Soon the stockade was visible and the white bastions, over which appeared the top of the tall flagstaff, that stood within the courtyard."

He found the fort a "Babylonian confusion of languages," with Assiniboin, Crow, Hidatsa, Cree, Mandan, and Blackfoot Indians mingling their various dialects with the English, French, Spanish, and German of the whites and blacks. Trading was done through a trap window in a doubly fortified store where the savages could be covered from loopholes. Attracted by their own desire to trade, or by the efforts of roving "salesmen," by cajolery, gifts and strong drink, the Indians came to the fort to swap their furs for tobacco, vermilion, and the white man's firearms, hardware, fabrics, and trinkets. All the fripperies and necessities of life beyond the frontier changed hands in a perpetual bazaar.

"Men in charge of trading posts like to

FORT UNION, 1833. Aquatint after Bodmer.

The New York Public Library

marry into prominent Indian families when they are able to do so," wrote Kurz; "by such a connection they increase their adherents, their patronage is extended, and they make correspondingly larger profits. Their Indian relatives remain loyal and trade with no other company. They have the further advantage of being constantly informed through their association with the former as to the demands of the trade and the village or even the tent where they can immediately find buffalo robes stored away."

The trading fort was the social center of a wide neighborhood. The food supply was usually plentiful and varied, not excluding such exotic dainties as white bread, fresh dairy products from the post's herds, and smuggled potables of different vintages. The value of the trade goods in stock was normally close to a hundred thousand dollars, and the Indian wives of the factors bedecked themselves in the latest fashions that had reached St. Louis from New York and Europe. Periodic balls brought a colorful variety of celebrants in from the surrounding prairie, visitors who usually traveled on horseback. With squaws dancing the cotillion, halfbreed girls peddling kisses, and an

Bureau of American Ethnology, The Smithsonian Institution
"RETURNING FROM THE DOBIE BALL AT FORT UNION." 1852. Drawing by Kurz.

orchestra, brought together as might be, thumping and scraping out the tunes, the party usually lasted through till broad daylight and frequently ended in disorder. Kurz described the "ballroom" at Fort Union decorated with mirrors, candles, precious fur skins, and Indian ornaments. "As I do not dance myself," he concluded resignedly, "I beat the tattoo on the drum."

INDIANS APPROACHING FORT BENTON, 1859. Painting by Charles Wimar. Fort Benton stood at the head of steam navigation on the Missouri River, over a month's journey from St. Louis.

The Washington University, St. Louis

SCENE AT FORT MACKENZIE, AUGUST 28, 1833. Aquatint after Bodmer.

BELLEVUE, MR. DOUGHERTY'S AGENCY, 1833. Aquatint after Bodmer.

At all times trading with the Indian was a highly explosive business in which any or every incident might play the torch. At Fort Mackenzie a few hundred miles up the Missouri from Fort Union, Maximilian, Prince of Wied-Neuwied, on a tour of the West in 1833, witnessed an assault by prairie Indians. "About 18 or 20 Blackfoot tents, pitched near the fort," he wrote, "the inmates of which had been singing and drinking the whole night, and fallen into a deep sleep toward morning, had been surprised by 600 Assinboins and Crees.... The fort was seen to be surrounded on every side by the enemy, who had approached very near. They had cut up the tents of the Blackfoot with knives, discharged their guns and arrows at them, killed or wounded many of the inmates, roused from their sleep by this unexpected attack. The men ... had partly fired their guns at the enemy, and then fled to the gates of the fort, where they were admitted. They immediately hastened to the roof, and began a well-supported fire on the Assinboins."

That particular mêlée was just another intertribal affair. As often as not it was the whites who were at the other end of the gunfire. The point of contact between white and red was almost always sore throughout our history. In their attack on the animal kingdom the hunters and fur companies were relentlessly dispossessing the Indian of his diminishing empire and stripping it of its natural wealth. Traders, agents, the military, and tourists appeased the natives for intruding on their lands and bribed them for their favor and trade with looking glasses, needles, combs, pins, baubles, blankets, tobacco, guns, liquor—with any type of inducement that could profitably be used. It was cutthroat competition, in several senses of the term. It was a war of extermination, also in several senses, waged on an international scale. As an ally or enemy, a competitor or hired helper, the Indian was inexorably drawn into the white man's struggle for dominion over the red man's own wilderness home.

To reduce friction and corruption on both sides, government agents were appointed to supervise relations along the borderlands. All too often the agency became an additional irritation through maladministration. Occasionally it was a focus of civilization far beyond the main line. When the artist George Catlin entered Major John Dougherty's model agency at Bellevue near the mouth of the Platte River in what is now a suburb of Omaha, he said, "It is a pleasure to see again, in this great wilderness, a civilized habitation; and still more pleasant to find it surrounded by corn-fields, potatoes, with numerous fruit-trees bending under the weight of their fruit—with pigs and poultry and kine." A few years later a school for Pawnee children was conducted at Bellevue. Dougherty could speak more than a dozen native dialects and he kept up an incessant struggle to protect the Indians from corruption by the fur traders.

The Walters Art Gallery
PRESENTS FOR THE SNAKE INDIANS, 1837. Painting by Alfred J. Miller. This and the several other paintings by Miller that are reproduced on the following pages are worked-up versions of field sketches made by the artist. Miller's spot-news pictures of the early West were made on his trip across the Plains with Captain William Drummond Stewart, an English adventurer who hired Miller's services for the purpose.

AMERICAN FUR COMPANY CARAVAN EN ROUTE TO WYOMING, 1837. Painting by Miller.

White trappers, unwilling to leave the fur harvest in Indian hands, reached farther into the back country on their own account, along the river courses and later, forsaking the waterways, directly across the Plains to the mountains. Although white men had earlier gone overland to the Rockies, and even on to the Pacific, it was the trappers under General William Ashley who, in the 1820's, established a route overland from the Missouri to the Green River valley beyond the Rocky Mountains and from there to the Pacific. In time that route would serve the missionaries and emigrants to Oregon, the Mormons, the forty-niners, and, ultimately, the Union Pacific Railroad. But when Ashley's men opened the "road" it lay through utter wilderness. Over it, tapping a land as large as European Russia, they trundled back to civilization their season's catch of furs—otter, silver fox, mink, marten, buffalo, and, most important, beaver.

"On Tuesday last," reported the *Missouri Intelligencer* at Columbia on October 9, 1830, "a large company of trappers and traders from the Rocky Mountains passed through this place, with Furs and Mules valued at *one hundred and fifty thousand dollars....* A considerable number of large and substantial waggons, laden with the fruits of their toils, accompanied them, exclusive of the pack horses and mules, of which there were a considerable number." By that time Ashley had sold out to a group of other entrepreneurs who, in turn, sold out to the Rocky Mountain Fur Company. All fought with Astor's American Fur Company and, at times, with the Hudson's Bay Company, for control of the wilderness resources. With their agents, white and red, the companies that exploited the uncharted West waged a fierce international contest for monopoly. Pelts from the American forests were sold from Leipzig to Canton, and manufactures from such unlikely places were bought to peddle for pelts on the plains and in the valleys of the West—little bells and mirrors from Leipzig, clay pipes from Cologne, beads from Italy, calicoes from France, blankets and guns from England, and various oddments from anywhere in the wide world. In its scope and in its intense rivalry it was Big

SCENE AT THE GREEN RIVER RENDEZVOUS OF 1837. Painting by Miller. Kit Carson, Jim Bridger, and other famous mountain men were present, as were representatives of the Hudson's Bay Company.

Business a half-century before its time.

To gather the trappers, Indian and white, to a common trading ground an annual rendezvous was held in the late spring of the year. At Pierre's Hole, the Green River valley, Powder River, and other places where forage and game were plentiful, company supply caravans and purchasing agents met the roving hunters—sometimes the gathering numbered in the thousands—in what usually became a trapper's circus. News was swapped or fabricated in prodigal style—helpful reports from all over the wilderness and tall tales piled one on another to fantastic heights. Pelts were exchanged for supplies and wilderness luxuries — sugar, coffee, liquor, and tobacco. But that took less time than the revelry of mobs of lonely men. Riding, running, and jumping contests were held, squaws bedecked with tinkling bells were bargained for with calicoes and other treasures. Gambling, brawling, shooting—both harmless and fatal—and drinking were carried on with saturnalian extravagance. The Indians put on a spectacular show of their own, bucks and squaws in their sepa-rate fashions. "Every freak of prodigality was indulged to its fullest extent," wrote Washington Irving, "and in a little while most of the trappers, having squandered away all their wages and perhaps run knee-deep in debt, were ready for another hard campaign in the wilderness." The company pack trains left for home base weighted down with all the beaver the mules could carry or cart.

Back in St. Louis the arrival of a fur-laden caravan from the West was one of the climaxes of the season. "It is impossible to describe my feelings at the sight of all that beaver," wrote one French-born Baltimore-an, "all those mountain men unloading their mules, in their strange mountain costume—most of their garments of buckskin and buffalo hide, but all so well greased and worn that it took close observation to tell what they were made of. To see the mules rolling and dusting was most interesting and shocking at the same time; most of them having carried their burdens of two hundred pounds weight about 2000 miles, return with scarcely any skin on their backs; they are peeled from withers to tail. . . ."

LONG JAKES, MOUNTAIN MAN. Engraving by W. G. Jackman after a lost painting by Charles Deas. Illustration from the *New York Illustrated Magazine,* 1846. The same engraving served to represent more than one western character to be publicized in eastern papers.

The State Historical Society of Colorado
JIM BAKER, MOUNTAIN MAN (right), with Charles
Stobie, the pioneer artist-scout, and Major D. C.
Oakes whom disgruntled Pikes Peak. gold seekers
hanged in effigy after they failed to find gold in 1859.
They erected a sign reading: "Here lies the body of
D. C. Oakes, Hung for starting this damn Pikes
Peak hoax." Photograph taken about 1867.

faced challenges unknown to the foresters,
rivermen, and earlier heroes of the frontier.
They had moved out into the "biggest clearing on the Almighty's footstool" and combed
the mountains on the far side. When their
heyday was over, the land had yielded both
its furs and its geographical secrets and lay
ready for the invasion of immigrants that followed. For all the glory he showered on the
mountain men it was the total scale of their
exploitation, the success of the huge speculation, that most appealed to Washington
Irving. His real hero was the businessman
who pulled the strings of the world-wide
drama from a city office. Jim Bridger was

The Colorado State Museum
A THOROUGHLY DRESSED-UP PORTRAIT OF JIM BAKER
WEARING A COSTUME MADE BY A SIOUX SQUAW. Painting by Waldo Love. Baker's "hand to hand" fight
with two young grizzlies both of which he killed was
a well-known story in the mountains.

In the stories that came out of the West
the mountain men seemed like figures mold-
ed a bit larger than life. But they were flesh
and blood and the best of them—Andrew
Henry, Jedediah Smith, Kit Carson, Jim
Bridger, Joe Meek, and the rest—could, by
eye-witness account, outdo most of the prodigies ascribed to Leatherstocking, that symbol
of all frontiersmen who spent his own later
days in the prairie country. They knew the
wilderness by heart, in all its moods and
complex patterns. They knew it more keenly
and sensitively than the native savages and
wild beasts which they had to outwit if they
were to live and to make a living.

"Across the wide Missouri" the hunters

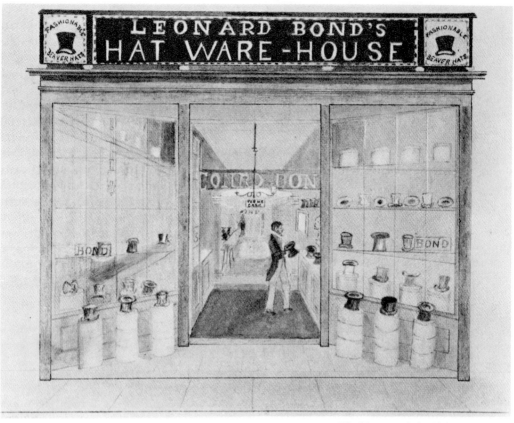

LEONARD BOND'S HAT STORE ON CHATHAM STREET, NEW YORK, 1828. Water color drawing by Alexander Jackson Davis. The artist was one of the best known architects of his day.

just one of the keen tools with which the master craftsman, John Jacob Astor, carved out a profitable empire.

The free trappers, the men who got along by themselves or with their own small group of companions beyond the control of the big fur companies, were the aristocrats of their trade, "the cavaliers of the mountains." There were enough of them to constitute the vital balance of power between the competing organizations and their skill in every phase of frontier life was legendary even in their own day. According to one storyteller of the early West, Jim Bridger would not swallow the tales of Baron Munchausen; but he had to acknowledge that his own exploits among the Blackfeet would seem quite as marvelous "ef writ down in a book."

Washington Irving spent only a month on the Plains but he had talked with Astor and Captain Bonneville—he had all the latter's notes and maps—and he knew what had been said of the West. For him there was "no class of men on the face of the earth who lead a life of more continued exertion, peril, and excitement, and who are more enamoured of their occupations, than the free trappers of the West. No toil, no danger, no privation can turn the trapper from his pursuit. His passionate excitement at times resembles a mania. In vain may the most vigilant and cruel savages beset his path; in vain may rocks, and precipices, and wintry torrents oppose his progress; let but a single track of beaver meet his eye and he forgets all dangers and defies all difficulties. At times he may be seen with his traps on his shoulder, buffeting his way across rapid streams, amidst floating blocks of ice: at other times, he is to be found with his traps swung on his back clambering the most rugged mountains, scaling or descending the most frightful precipices, searching, by routes inaccessible to the horse, and never before trodden by white man, for springs and lakes unknown to his comrades, and where he may meet with his favorite game. Such is the mountaineer, the hardy trapper of the West; and such . . . is the wild, Robin Hood kind of life, with all its strange and motley populace, now existing in full vigor among the Rocky Mountains."

At the end of the trapper's trail was the hapless little beaver whose pelt, by a decree of London fashion, was the prize of a continent. Improvident men gambled their lives to earn the four dollars or more a pound which, in good years, the fur companies would pay for pelts—and which, in turn, the trappers would lose or spend in one rollicking night at a rendezvous. The end of the trail for the beaver, in turn, was usually the hat stores of remote markets. America was the home of the beaver and, as one delighted immigrant reported from New York, "a first-rate beaver hat, which cannot be surpassed by anything of French or English manufacture, can be obtained for Five Dollars." Actually the chief market for beaver was in foreign lands. American beaver pelts were a prime commodity at the annual Easter and Michaelmas Fairs at Leipzig.

By 1840 the mode was waning, and as silk hats moved into fashion for men, the beaver trade passed its peak. In 1842 the old beaver headdress worn in the British Army was replaced by a new kind of cap and the demand for beaver pelts dropped even lower. Those changes came in good time to save the little "varmint" from extermination.

The Metropolitan Museum of Art
THE END OF THE BEAVER. An advertisement from
Joshua Shaw, *United States Directory*, 1822.

THE CAPTIVE CHARGER. Painting by Charles F. Wimar, 1854. Although the picture was painted in Düsseldorf, Germany, and clearly shows the influences of that center of academic art, Wimar learned his calling in St. Louis. The artist spent fifteen of his thirty-four years in America where the study of the Indian was his absorbing interest. He died in St. Louis in 1862.

INDIANS ON HORSEBACK

The first miners, homeseekers, and farmers who followed the trappers out onto the Plains and across the mountains faced a world still uncharted save by word of mouth. Between them and their manifest destiny to invest the whole breadth of the continent stood the Plains Indians—Arapaho, Blackfoot, Crow, Comanche, Apache, Sioux, and a half-dozen other tribes. Mounted on wild little horses, those roving tribes constituted the toughest adversary the white man had yet faced in his western march.

The introduction and spread of horses over the Plains and prairies in the past several centuries had revolutionized the life of the Indian. From a plodding, earthbound pedestrian he had become a swift-traveling nomad. Horses were his source of wealth, his means of transportation, his pride, and, if need be, his supply of food. "The only property of these people," explained Captain Randolph B. Marcy, "with the exception of a few articles belonging to their domestic economy, consists entirely in horses and mules, of which they possess great numbers. ... The most successful horse thieves among them own from fifty to two hundred animals." In Indian life a successful horse thief enjoyed, roughly speaking, the same prestige and prosperity that a smart exchange broker would enjoy in white circles. One chief remarked that his four sons were a great comfort to him in his old age: they could steal more horses than any other young men of their tribe. Colonel Richard I. Dodge, an experienced Westerner, reported that a Comanche could crawl into a bivouac where a dozen men were sleeping, each with his horse tied to his wrist by the lariat, cut the rope within six feet of the sleeper's person, and get away with the horse without waking anyone.

Of the animals owned by the Comanches, the best horsemen of the Plains, Catlin wrote: "The wild horse of these regions is a small, but very powerful animal; with an exceedingly prominent eye, sharp nose, high nostril, small foot and delicate leg." Good judges of thoroughbred horses were often deceived by the unkempt little beasts. In later years Colonel Dodge wrote of "a miserable sheep" of an Indian pony, with legs like churns and a three-inch-thick coat of shaggy hair, a patient and helpless-looking creature mounted by an overweight buck, which outraced the best blooded horses the cavalry at a Texas fort could muster. The Comanche jockey finished the scrape sitting face to the tail of his steed and, with every taunt of a varied vocabulary, urging the Kentucky pureblood to hurry along. Different horses were trained for the hunt, war, cartage, and other purposes. His war or buffalo horse was the Indian's greatest security in a hazardous life, his most cherished possession, and his pride made manifest. "I can imagine nothing more perfectly graceful than a Blackfoot Indian in his war costume," wrote Captain Henry James Warre, an English traveler who crossed the continent in the 1840's, "decorated with paint and feathers floating wildly in the wind, as he caracoles on his small, but wonderfully active barb, in the full confidence of his glorious liberty. War, his occupation; and the scarcely less hazardous and exciting chase of the buffalo, his amusement." Catlin's slight little sketch, shown below, drawn from memory when he was peddling his diminishing talents in London, catches the spirit of Warre's remark but somewhat overdramatizes the details. At his best Catlin was one of the most faithful artists of the Indian's West.

Speaking of the Comanches of the south-

The New York Public Library
"A CROW CHIEF making a display of his magnificent dress and horsemanship with scalps attached to his bridle reins and his hair over eight feet long floating in the wind." Sketch by Catlin. From Catlin's *Souvenirs of the North American Indians*, 1850.

Bureau of American Ethnology,
The Smithsonian Institution
A BLACKFOOT PONY, 1852. Drawing by Kurz. A life study of a characteristic Indian horse: in all probability a descendant of the animals stolen by the Indians from Spanish ranches.

The New York Public Library

"COMANCHEE MODE OF PASSING THEIR ENEMY ON HORSEBACK." Sketch by Catlin. Illustration from Catlin, *Souvenirs of the North American Indians*, 1850.

BALL-PLAY OF THE CHOCTAWS, 1832. Painting by Catlin. A lacrosse game in full swing.

Division of Ethnology, The United States National Museum

ern Plains, Catlin wrote: "Amongst their feats of riding, there is one that has astonished me more than anything of the kind I have ever seen, or expect to see, in my life:— a stratagem of war, learned and practiced by every young man in the tribe; by which he is able to drop his body upon the side of his horse at the instant he is passing, effectually screened from his enemies' weapons as he [lies] in a horizontal position behind the body of his horse, with his heel hanging over the horse's back; by which he has the power of throwing himself up again, and changing to the other side of his horse if necessary. In this wonderful condition, he will hang whilst his horse is at fullest speed, carrying with him his bow and his shield, and also his long lance of fourteen feet in length, all or either of which he will wield upon his enemy as he passes; rising and throwing his arrows over the horse's back, or with ease and equal success under the horse's neck. . . ."

In his games and ceremonies as in his strife the Indian's stamina was the measure of his virtue. Along the eastern fringe of the Plains country where lacrosse was played, white spectators watched games that lasted, with only slight intermissions, the entire day. According to the young Baltimore artist Frank Blackwell Mayer, who witnessed "le jeu de la crosse" near the Traverse des Sioux treaty grounds in what is now Minnesota, the contestants sometimes ran as much as forty or fifty miles before the play was over. "One can have no idea of the physical powers of this race," Mayer wrote, "until he has witnessed this display. They sally forth with wild whoops of defiance to their opponents. The neat and airy head dress, brilliant in color and not subject to derangement from motion, but contributing to the grace of their swift movements, as their long hair and pendant 'tails'. . . stream upon the wind, their feathers & crests tossing, their bodies turning with serpentine ease & deerlike swiftness, they run, vault & spring into the air, & course from one end to the other of the lawn-like prairie, like so many Mercuries, the brilliant colors of dress & paint, &

The Newberry Library, E. E. Ayer Collection
INDIAN LACROSSE PLAYERS. Drawings from the journal of Frank Blackwell Mayer.

the flashing armlets & diadems, & varied position leading the eye thro' an exciting & luxuriant chase."

Probably the most famous lacrosse game in history was staged outside Fort Michilimackinac between groups of Sac and Chippewa Indians in 1763, the fateful year of Pontiac's conspiracy. Inviting the whites to witness the sport, to be played for a high wager, the red men threw the post's garrison off its guard and, once the gates of the fort were open and unprotected, turned from their game to slaughter every Englishman in sight. Alexander Henry, a native of New Jersey and a well-known fur trader of the eighteenth century, was one of the few survivors left to tell the tale, which he did in his autobiography.

But it was on horseback that the savage of the Plains showed his prowess. In the buffalo chase the Indian and his horse were a single, lithe organism (see illustrations on next pages). For the red man, hunting bison was not the spoiling sport it became for the white man; the animal was food, shelter, fuel, and clothing for the savages of the Plains. Captain Marryat, another early visitor to the West, observed that "a Sioux, when on horseback chasing the buffalo, will drive his arrow which is about eighteen inches long, with such force that the barb shall appear on the opposite side of the animal. And one of their

207

INDIANS HUNTING BISON, 1833. Aquatint after Bodmer.

greatest chiefs, *Wanataw,* has been known to kill two buffaloes with one arrow, it having passed through the first of the animals, and mortally wounded the second on the other side of it." Marryat apparently didn't realize quite what a long bow the Indian *could* draw. Most seasoned campaigners in the West testified that such a feat was impossible, though an arrow could be shot clear through a buffalo. As Benjamin Franklin pointed out during the Revolution when he urged colonial troops to adopt the bow and arrow, Indian weapons had certain obvious advantages over the white man's gun. Even if the wound inflicted by an arrow were not a serious one, the barb had to be removed before the victim was free to fight effectively again. No flash of powder betrayed a hidden adversary. A flight of arrows, visible in the air, was a very disconcerting sight to the human targets. What was more important, arrows could be shot in quick succession. According to reliable eye-witnesses an Indian could hold up to ten arrows in his left hand and discharge them so rapidly with his right that they would all be in the air at the same time, all propelled with force enough to wound a man seriously, and all delivered while the savage was riding at top speed.

At least some U.S. Army veterans of the border wars believed that the Indian youth was the hardest-riding natural fighter in the world by the time he was twelve or fifteen years of age. One officer remarked that given the training and discipline of such recruits he could whip an equal number of any cavalry in the world.

Colonel R. B. Marcy, who spent thirty years of his military career on the western border, described the special conditions of Indian warfare that made the standard books on the art of war useless on the Plains. "To act against an enemy who is here to-day and there to-morrow," he wrote, "who at one time stampedes a herd of mules upon the head waters of the Arkansas, and when next heard from is in the very heart of the populated districts of Mexico, laying waste haciendas, and carrying devastation, rapine, and murder in his steps; who is every where without being any where; who assembles at the moment of combat, and vanishes whenever fortune turns against him; who leaves his women and children far distant from the theatre of hostilities, and who has neither towns or magazines to defend, nor lines of retreat to cover; who derives his commissariat from the country he operates in, and is not encumbered with baggage-wagons or pack-trains; who comes into action only when it suits his purpose, and never without the advantage of numbers or position—with such an enemy the strategic science of civilized nations loses much of its importance, and finds but rarely and only in peculiar localities, an opportunity to be put into practise."

For two centuries the western Indian held out against the combined forces of gunpowder, lead, whisky, disease, and missionaries. In *The Great Plains,* from which much of the material in this section has been taken, Walter Prescott Webb describes Colt's revolver as the first radical adaptation to the conditions of the Plains that enabled the whites to crush native resistance. With the Colt the white horseman could for the first time match the firing speed of the Indian with his bow and arrows. Traditionally the savage drew the fire of the white men by devious tactics and then turned quickly to the attack before they could reload their single-shooting weapons. At a battle in Nueces Cañon in 1844 the Texas Rangers, armed with revolvers, charged a group of unsuspecting, marauding Comanches. "Never," recalled an old Indian-fighter, "was a band of Indians more surprised than at this charge. They expected the Rangers to remain on the defensive, and to finally wear them out and exhaust their ammunition. . . . In vain the Comanches tried to turn their horses and make a stand, but such was the wild confusion of running horses, popping pistols, and yelling Rangers that they abandoned the idea of a rally and sought safety in flight." As one undersized outlaw later put it, the Colt made all men equal.

ADVERTISEMENT, ABOUT 1855. The pictorial designs are reproduced from the cylinders of presentation Colt revolvers.

A VIEW OF NOOTKA SOUND, VANCOUVER ISLAND (1783). Painting by John Webber, the official artist of Captain Cook's last expedition. Webber's view, showing the coast, some Indians, and one of Cook's landing parties in 1778, is the earliest known depiction of this part of the world. A landing canoe is dimly visible in the lower left foreground. Nootka Sound became a major rendezvous for fur traders on the northwest Pacific coast in the years that followed.

THE EDGE OF EMPIRE

Beyond the range of the Plains Indians lay the wastes of the Pacific Northwest, "the continuous woods where rolls the Oregon, and hears no sound save its own dashing." The first Englishmen to make a landfall in that shadowy region at the other end of the fabulous Northwest Passage were the crews of the *Resolution* and the *Discovery* under Captain James Cook. It was the famous explorer's last, tragic voyage. With him were William Bligh who later captained the *Bounty*, George Vancouver who later also made history on his own, and John Webber, the first artist to depict the northwest coast.

Also with Captain Cook was young John Ledyard of Connecticut who had joined the expedition just before the Declaration of Independence was issued. In March, 1778, Ledyard and his companions landed at Nootka Sound in what was to become Vancouver Island. The sight of the American coast, although it was "more than 2000 miles distant from the nearest part of New England," left the young corporal of marines "painfully afflicted" with nostalgia.

From there on his story developed into a historic saga. He noted that although the Indians of the region had never before seen white men they carried European-made bracelets and knives. "No part of America," he concluded, "is without some sort of commercial intercourse, immediate or remote." He had all but found the true northwest passage. He learned, also, that the pelts of the sea otters that sported in great numbers along those shores could be picked up from the natives for a few pence worth of iron and sold at an enormous profit in the Orient.

Escaping murder at Cook's side in the Sandwich Islands, Ledyard returned to England, then went on to America where he jumped ship and where, at the end of the Revolution, he set about his plans to return to the Northwest. His own fortune and his country's glory were involved in his project to open the fur trade of those distant parts both by land and by sea, setting a pattern for Astor's efforts in later years.

Unable to find backers in America Ledyard went to Europe where he talked over his plans with John Paul Jones, Benjamin Franklin, Thomas Jefferson, and others. It was just about at this point of time that Jefferson wrote to George Rogers Clark suggesting an overland expedition to the northwest coast but wondering if among Americans there was "enough of that kind of spirit to raise the money." Ledyard alone had spirit enough without the money and, encouraged by Jefferson, he started to walk his way to his objective by way of Siberia and Kamchatka. From there he would find a ship to Nootka Sound; from Nootka Sound he confidently intended to hike overland to the east coast.

"I had a letter from Ledyard lately, dated at St. Petersburg," wrote Jefferson in 1787. "He had but two shirts, and yet more shirts than shillings. Still he was determined to obtain the palm of being the first circumambulator of the earth. He says, that having no money, they will kick him from place to place, and thus he expects to be kicked around the globe." Ledyard did earnestly believe that the efforts of an honest man could triumph over any season and any hardship. But at Yakutch in distant Siberia, with "but two long frozen stages" between him and his first main objective, Catherine of Russia dropped an iron curtain before his march. The most heroic hike in history had been halted and the penniless visionary was kicked back over all the long, dreary miles he had covered.

Still insisting he would one day find his way again to the Northwest, John Ledyard died in Cairo the next year, his restless life quieted, his dream transferred to other men.

The Newberry Library, E. E. Ayer Collection
FRIENDLY COVE, NOOTKA SOUND, 1792. Water color by William Alexander. The original sketch of this scene was "taken on the spot by H. Humphries," a member of Captain George Vancouver's crew. This finished view, worked up by Alexander, first curator of prints and drawings in the British Museum, was followed for an illustration in Vancouver's *A Voyage of Discovery*.

His own account of Cook's last voyage had been printed in America before he left there but it had not excited immediate interest in the Pacific fur trade. With the publication of Cook's account of his voyages in 1784, which was peddled by no less a character than Parson Weems and was, as well, reprinted in the Pennsylvania *Packet,* Ledyard's dreams came back to life. While Ledyard himself was still struggling over the frozen crust of Siberia the ship *Columbia* and the sloop *Lady Washington,* purchased and outfitted at a cost of $50,000 by a group of Boston merchants, were despatched around the Horn to the Northwest to trade oddments for furs with the Indians, and fur for tea with the Chinese at Canton.

The two vessels, the sloop first, arrived at their rendezvous in Nootka Sound and in good time the *Columbia*, Captain Gray, set sail for Boston via Hawaii and China with skins bartered for a chisel apiece. "They do not seem to covet usefull things," wrote Gray's clerk, "but anything that looks pleasing to the eye, or what they call riches." The

Lady Washington remained in Pacific waters plying between the Northwest and Canton and, en route, developing a lively trade in sandalwood in the eastern islands. Attended by a Hawaiian "prince" decked out in a glittering, feathered helmet and a plumed coat, Captain Robert Gray brought the *Columbia* back into Boston harbor in the summer of 1790. He was the first American sea captain to sail around the world.

Commercially, the voyage was not much of a success. But it proved that the United States could find on its own other shore the commodity it needed to trade with the Chinese, and that trade was vital to the economic life of the young nation.

The *Columbia* was off the Pacific coast again in 1791. Ships of six other nations were already cruising those newly important waters. Captain Gray was charged to offer no insult to foreigners, nor to receive any without showing the becoming "spirit of a free, independent American." After swapping for pelts and pausing to build the sloop *Adventure* Gray returned down the coast, hailing

Captain George Vancouver on the way up. Vancouver had been commissioned to reclaim territory seized earlier by the Spanish and to make an accurate survey of the coast. On May 11, 1792, two days after Vancouver had advised Gray that nothing important was to be observed to the South, the crew of the *Columbia*, as a mate's journal recorded it, "saw an appearance of a spacious harbor abrest the Ship, haul'd our wind for itt, observ'd two sand bars making off, with a passage between them to a fine river . . . we directed our course up this noble *river* in search of a Village. . . . Capt. Gray named this river *Columbia's*, and the North entrance Cape Hancock, and the South Point, *Adams*. This River in my opinion, wou'd be a fine place for to sett up a *Factory*. . . ."

To all intents the ancient riddle of the Northwest Passage was finally solved by the little ship from Boston. Gray had discovered the great River of the West that for centuries had troubled the dreams of the world's most hopeful adventurers. It was no anticlimax that its waters did not reach back to the eastern ocean. Gray had planted the flag of empire and opened a world-wide dominion for American trade. The Russians, who had originally monopolized affairs along the northwest coast, were steadily forced off the scene. The British, in turn, were for a while outsmarted and outsailed by Yankee traders who flocked to the northwest coast in the wake of the *Columbia*. By the turn of the century the sea-otter trade had become an almost exclusively Boston business. In 1801 fourteen thousand pelts were sold in China at an average of thirty dollars apiece.

Collection of Dr. Gray Huntington Twombly

"CAPTAIN GRAY GIVING ORDERS CONCERNING THE BUILDING OF THE SHIP," 1792. (From an old inscription on the backing of the original sketch.) Drawing by George Davidson. The "ship" was the sloop *Adventure*, Mr. Yendell, the "Carpentar," is receiving the orders, and Clayoquot Sound, Vancouver Island, was the site of the operation. Davidson, the artist of this sketch, shipped as "painter" on the *Columbia* for its historic voyage. Others of his drawings are illustrated in Chapter III.

"CAPT'N LEWIS SHOOTING AN INDIAN"

"CAPT'NS LEWIS & CLARK HOLDING A COUNCIL WITH THE INDIANS"

"CAPT. CLARK & HIS MEN BUILDING A LINE OF HUTS"

"A CANOE STRIKING A TREE"

These fanciful recreations are from illustrations in Patrick Gass, *A Journal of the Voyages and Travels of a Corps of Discovery, under the Command of Capt. Lewis & Capt. Clark,* 1811, the first journals from the expedition to be published. From a copy in the New York Public Library.

Before the trappers, Ashley's men and their successors, had found their different ways to the Pacific coast, others had made the overland journey successfully. As early as 1793 Alexander Mackenzie, an agent for the Hudson's Bay Company, had crossed Canada to its western shore. A decade later a congressional grant gave Thomas Jefferson money and authority to launch his own long-cherished project of an overland expedition to the Northwest. He chose as leader Meriwether Lewis, his sometime secretary and a veteran of the frontier wars. Lewis, in turn, shared his command with William Clark, "a youth of solid and promising parts, and as brave as Caesar," brother of George Rogers Clark. Together, in the spring of 1804, the two explorers led a band of thirty-two men out of St. Louis and up the Missouri.

The last outpost the expedition passed was the tiny village of La Charette where Daniel Boone was magistrate. From there on the route lay through lands of unimag-

inable wilderness, so little known that Jefferson had posted the party to look for mastadons and mammoths. A six months' struggle upstream brought the expedition to the Mandan villages, where it wintered and where it learned how profitable the fur trade was for Great Britain. The Hudson's Bay Company and its rivals were doing a lively trade with Montreal and making a killing at both ends of their traffic.

After a month and a half's travel the next spring, the band caught sight of the Rockies late in May, "several ranges [of] which rise above each other till the most distant mingles with the clouds." Very few white men had seen that sight before. It was far more impressive than the solid rock-salt mountain, only one hundred eighty miles long and forty-five miles wide, that Jefferson had told Congress the year before might be found a thousand miles up the Missouri. After a long trek across the Great Divide and then once more by boat down the tributaries of the Columbia, the expedition, in November, 1805, "saw the waves like small mountains" rolling out of the Pacific.

Twenty-eight months after they had left St. Louis, Lewis and Clark were back with the first official report of the nation's new West. The men who made the journey were not schooled reporters, but at Jefferson's insistence they had kept their separate journals. The vivid descriptions of what they saw contained none of the scientific revelations that Jefferson might have hoped for, but a note of enchantment runs through every passage. They had traveled through a greater variety of natural wonders than any eastbound imagination could have foreseen. Theirs was a project made for greatness and their stories, when ultimately pieced together, became our national epic of exploration.

It was the stories they brought back that inspired Manuel Lisa, Ashley, and other early fur traders to penetrate the farther West. A few years later John Jacob Astor, following Ledyard's early design, launched his plan to drain the northwest fur country from both ends. The divide was to be from a post on the Columbia River, sea otters going west into the China Trade, beaver and other furs going to the American and European markets. In May, 1811, slipping in before Russia or England could lay prior claims to the spot, Astor's agents completed a stockaded fort between the mouth of the Columbia River and Young's Bay. In the autumn of 1813 the English took it over, practically at the point of a frigate's guns, changing the name from Fort Astoria to Fort George.

To most Americans that was too remote a matter to worry over. As one representative derisively asked Congress as late as 1828, "What can lead any adventurer to seek the unhospitable regions of Oregon unless, indeed, he wishes to be a savage...."

The American Antiquarian Society

FORT GEORGE, FORMERLY FORT ASTORIA, 1846. Drawing by Henry James Warre. This and the illustration of the American Village on p. 231 are the original drawings made by Capt. Warre on his trip across the continent in 1846. The lithograph used to illustrate Warre's published report distorts the details of this original.

217

VIEW OF SANTA FE, 1849. Lithograph by P. S. Duval. Illustration from R. H. Kern, *Lt. Simpson's Report on the Arkansas Route.*

Another lure beyond the unbroken plains lay far to the southeast where Santa Fe in New Mexico, a town as old as Jamestown or Quebec, slumbered quietly at the dead end of a thin, 1500-mile-long trail from Vera Cruz and 1000 trackless miles from St. Louis. Official Spain was inhospitable to foreign visitors as Zebulon Pike learned in 1806 when, reaching the Rio Grande after an exploratory trip of indescribable hardships, he was arrested for trespassing on Spanish soil. But Pike reported a market there if it could be reached in any practical manner and, when Mexico claimed its independence in 1821, a flood of Yankee traders found their way to Santa Fe with unerring direction. The lazy little town was hardly the golden city Coronado had hopefully looked for two hundred years before. But the first northern salesmen found all the trading prospects Pike had visualized. In short order they opened a highly profitable traffic in furs, mules, calicoes, ribbons, scissors, tacks, and all manner of "notions" which were common to New England store shelves but which no one would have dreamed of carting up from Vera Cruz.

"The inland trade between the United States and Mexico," reported the *Missouri Intelligencer* in 1830, "is increasing rapidly. This is perhaps the most curious species of foreign intercourse which the ingenuity and enterprise of American traders ever originated. The extent of country which the caravans traverse, the long journeys they have to make, the rivers and morasses to cross, the prairies, the forests, the all but African deserts to penetrate, require the most steel-formed constitutions and the most energetic minds. The accounts of these inland expeditions remind one of the caravans of the East."

The trip to Santa Fe by horse and mule train, and later by caravan through barren, torrid country harassed by savages, was indeed an ordeal, though a lesser one than that

INDEPENDENCE, MISSOURI. Engraving after Hermann J. Meyer. Illustration from Charles A. Dana, *United States Illustrated*, 1853.

of the Oregon Trail. The end of a journey was hailed with equal delight by the Amercans who survived it and the Mexicans who waited, wondering if they would. "I doubt . . ." wrote the principal chronicler of the trail, "whether the first sight of the walls of Jerusalem were beheld by the crusaders with much more tumultuous and soul-enrapting joy" than filled the caravans when they first spotted the adobe town. Runners forewarned the town of a caravan's arrival and the natives celebrated its entry with holiday gusto.

As Oregon, Santa Fe, and, later, California became the distant goals of an increasing swarm of westering people, the settlement at Independence, Missouri, developed from a small trading post into the busiest town west of St. Louis. It had become within a few short years the jumping-off place to the farther West. Travelers avoided several hundred miles of bad roads by taking the Missouri River as far as the new town. Parkman

tells of a river steamboat in 1846, "loaded until the water broke alternately over her guards. Her upper deck was covered with large wagons of a peculiar form, for the Santa Fe trade, and her hold was crammed with goods for the same destination. There were also the equipments and provisions of a party of Oregon emigrants, a band of mules and horses, piles of saddles and harness, and a multitude of nondescript articles, indispensable on the prairies"—all directed towards the common rendezvous at Independence. The town itself he found jammed with men, horses, mules, and wagons; noisy with the "incessant hammering and banging of a dozen blacksmith's sheds, where the heavy wagons were being repaired, and the horses and oxen shod"; and busy with endless preparations for travel. Traders, hunters, Indians, emigrants, invalids, and desperadoes from every state in the union and a half dozen foreign countries used the booming town as the gateway to points beyond.

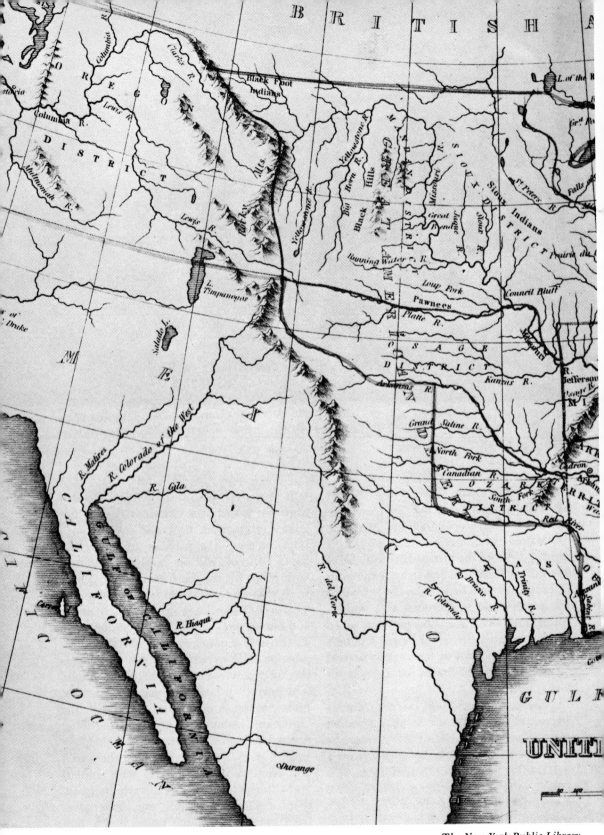

"THE GREAT AMERICAN DESERT," 1835. From Thos. G. Bradford, *Comprehensive Atlas.*

PROBLEMS OF THE PLAINS

The trappers and traders of the early far West had memorized half a continent in their ceaseless quest of game. Translated into print their knowledge would have made an encyclopedia of the wilderness. But generally speaking, Americans knew very little of the area between the Missouri and the Rockies until passing emigrants started to eye it with a view to settling there. Even then, and for some years after, it commonly appeared on accredited maps as "The Great American Desert," a dry and treeless immensity edged by formidable mountains—fit for nomads but not for settlers.

In 1819 Secretary of War John Calhoun dispatched Major Stephen H. Long to clarify geographical matters along the western limits of the Louisiana Purchase and to awe the savages en route. Long toured the Platte, the foothills of the Rockies, and the Arkansas River and returned to St. Louis to report: "In regard to this extensive section of country, I do not hesitate in giving the opinion, that it is almost wholly unfit for cultivation, and of course uninhabitable by a people depending on agriculture for their subsistence." He referred to a territory that today includes parts of Kansas, Colorado, New Mexico, Oklahoma, and Texas. That area would best serve, according to a contemporary of Long's, as an everlasting barrier to the further emigration of restless Americans.

By the middle of the nineteenth century all eyes were set on distant horizons beyond the hostile Indians and the "desert"—Santa Fe, Oregon, California. American pioneers were coming out of the woods into the open for the first time. They faced a land that, like the sea, held no shelter. New techniques of travel and transport must be evolved to conquer the almost illimitable space between the forest's edge and dream's end.

By the time the great migration was well started letters from early travelers, published guides, and the yarns of seasoned plainsmen had outlined the problems of the trail. Every manner of locomotion had been tried, but the prairie schooner—the covered wagon—soon became the standard vehicle of empire.

AN EARLY VIEW OF THE ROCKY MOUNTAINS. Engraving after a drawing by S. Seymour. Illustration from *Account of an Expedition from Pittsburgh to the Rocky Mountains ... 1819 and '20 ... under the Command of Major Stephen H. Long*, 1822–23.

The Library of Congress

CARAVAN EN ROUTE. Painting by Alfred J. Miller. The American Fur Company's outfit heading west in 1837, a small contingent compared with the emigrant trains about twenty years later, but one of the most faithful and dramatic pictures of such a scene that has survived. "For miles, to the extent of our vision," wrote one traveler in 1849 when great crowds were crossing the Plains, "an animated mass of beings broke

upon our view. Long trains of wagons with white covers were moving slowly along, a multitude of horsemen were prancing on the road, companies of men were traveling on foot, and although the scene was not a gorgeous one, yet the display of banners from many wagons, and the multitude of armed men, looked as if a mighty army were on its march."

SCENE ON THE EMIGRANT TRAIL, 1849. Drawing by Joseph Goldsborough Bruff.

In all the great, early migrations to the far West the problems of the Plains were much the same. Guides to the trail, published in growing abundance during the 1840's, were of small help in the face of sudden, often incalculable emergencies. Almost every slender diary that has survived describes some peril met on the way that seemed far different as an immediate, raw actuality than as a printed caution in a guidebook. "We cannot rely upon the truth of anything we hear of having transpired 5 miles ahead . . ." complained one bewildered traveler. "We hear all kinds of bug-bear stories about Indian depredations but when we come a little closer to the scene of action we can hear nothing of it." On the other hand, the truth of the matter was often silently recorded by rude graves that lined the long road, graves anxiously and curiously scanned by those that followed along the trail.

In a crisis beasts came first, for the lives of humans depended on those of their animals. Many pioneers walked most of the way across the country, in fair weather and foul, to spare the animals. Even so the route was often nauseous with the stench of decaying beasts, victims of overdriving, poisonous water, or poorly selected forage. The rotting carcasses of 4000 cattle lined one forty-mile stretch of the route to the West in 1850. In the course of one day a traveler in 1849 counted the wrecks of seventeen wagons along twenty-four miles of trail.

Every detail of the overland journey required careful planning. To carry too much equipment meant putting a hazardous burden on the animals when delay in crossing the barren stretches was perilous; to carry too little meant hastening that leg of the journey to a pace that might exhaust the beasts before good forage could be reached. Oxen had great endurance but traveled slowly; mules were fast but intractable. To start too soon in the season meant that enough grass might not yet have grown on the plains to feed the animals whatever they were; to start too late meant that those moving on ahead might have exhausted the forage. "How narrow must appear to any the chance of hitting the precise point of time," wrote one emigrant, "when the grass is barely sufficient and before the masses shall begin to crowd in." Smaller groups, naturally, could find more ample stock feed than larger outfits; but the fewer the company, the greater the menace of Indian attacks.

The duty of the camp, like that of a ship at sea, called for a night watch. Francis Parkman adventuring out of Boston took his turn standing guard on the Oregon Trail, wrapped to his nose in a blanket against the icy dew of the prairie night and awed by the majesty of the wilderness. It was an inescapable tour taken in rotation by each able man, the common law of the Plains. This was, after all, invasion of a country that only a

few years before had been earnestly pledged by the United States Government to the Indians as their inviolable preserve. It may have been Manifest Destiny but it was also larceny on a grand scale duly resented and sometimes punished by the Indians. Isaac Jones Wistar reported an incident on his overland trip in '49: "At daylight, though there had been no special alarm during the night, and the mules were all right, H. of the night guard was found dead and cold with several arrows sticking in him. He had evidently been still-hunted, his gun being undischarged, and as his body was otherwise undisturbed, the marauders were plainly reserving that pleasure till we should roll on and leave the coast clear. To frustrate such

THE NIGHT WATCH, 1849. Lithograph by C. Gildemeister after a drawing by J. W. Audubon from his *Illustrated Notes on an Expedition through Mexico and California*, 1852. The bulk of Audubon's sketches made on this expedition were shipped from the West Coast and lost at sea.

The New York Public Library

PAWNEE INDIANS WATCHING A CARAVAN, 1837. Another of Miller's early pictures of the West, a prospect that changed little during the next twenty years.

designs, the body was buried in the corral, and the mules herded over it for an hour, to destroy the traces."

Unobserved an Indian would follow a slow-moving column of wagons for miles until the number and character of armed men defending it were exactly known. Then, if the numbers or carelessness of the party warranted an attack, the savages chose a place where the ground was unfavorable for corralling the wagons, lay in wait, and at the right moment swooped down, whooping and shooting arrows into the animals to frighten them into panic. "Cool heads and steady hands are required at such moments," wrote Colonel Dodge, "and if the whites fail in these their fate is soon decided." The classic defense against attack was to drive the wagons into a circle with the heads of the beasts towards the center and the fore wheel of one wagon locked with the hind wheel of the next.

However, it was the stragglers and the

AN INDIAN ATTACK. Engraving after a painting by Seth Eastman. From Henry Schoolcraft, *History of the Indian Tribes*, 1853.

CROSSING THE QUICKSAND. Painting by John Russell Bartlett (?), 1850. The original painting for an illustration in Bartlett's *Personal Narrative*, etc., a summary of his trip with the United States and Mexican Boundary Commission, 1850–53.

herds which were the chief victims of attack. The full-dress raid on a wagon train with which the movies have made us familiar was a rare event, and Indians were less of an obstacle to a safe passage than were the rigors of travel. Disease, downright hardship, accidental shootings, and drowning took a much heavier toll of lives. Inexperienced people, heavily armed, shot themselves and one another in a constant succession of accidents. Crossing swift streams with treacherous bottoms added the risk of drowning to the major hazards of the trip.

"The river where we were to cross is pronounced over a mile wide," recounted one pioneer, "with a strong current quite red with mud. Nothing about its appearance was encouraging, and to plunge the wagons into it was a strong act of faith, as from its looks it might well be a hundred feet or any other depth. But it had to be crossed, and the mounted men scattered with a wide front to feel the way, and plunged in, the wagons in a long line following close. The bottom was sandy and shifting, making constant motion necessary to prevent settling down in it, besides incessant attention to the team leaders which alarmed by the swirling current, rushing noise, unstable footing, and deep holes, were with difficulty prevented from being swung round and forced down stream. . . . It was an exciting scene, the long train half submerged in the wide expanse of water, the splashing and the floundering of the mules, the whoops and yells of the men, and the foam and roar of the dashing waters."

FORT LARAMIE, 1837. Painting by Miller.

The series of forts that had been extended along the trail since the earlier days of the century served as rendezvous for emigrants, hunters, traders, and Indians. For thirty years Fort Laramie, in what is now Wyoming, remained a strategic point in the center of the Sioux country. It had been built about eight hundred miles west of St. Louis on the crossroads of the trail running north and south, used by the Indians time out of mind, and the main route to the South Pass through which the bulk of emigrants would pass going from east to west. The original quadrangle was built as a private fur-trading post in 1834, taken over by the American Fur Company, rebuilt in adobe, and finally invested by the army as a military post. The artist Miller described its "cannon or two sleeping in the towers over the two main entrances," ready to rake the sides of the quadrangle in case of attack. His painting, the only graphic record of the old building, clearly shows the loopholes for the artillery.

From the fort was conducted a lively trade in buffalo robes, blankets, guns, calicoes, and spirits. It was also a clearing house for news of the trail. "We went in to the Fort," wrote one traveler in his diary, "& was kindly & genteely receivd by Mister Bordeaux the maniger or master of the Fort   he invited us in to a room upstairs which look verry mutch like a bar room of an eastern hotel   it was ornamented with several drawings Portraits &c   a long desk a settee & some chairs constituted the principle furniture of the room   it wass neat & comfortable   Mr Bordeaux, answered the meney questions that was asked by us a bout the country the Natives, &c . . . some traders ware thare yesturday that said that 6 days drive ahead that the Snow was

THE INTERIOR OF FORT LARAMIE, 1837. Painting by Miller.

midled deep 10 days ago & that it would be difficult to find feed for our teams he said that thare ware buffalo 2 days drive ahead & some grisseley Bairs   that he expected some oregon emegrants soon he said that the next fort of trading post we came to was fort Bridgeer the other side of the mountains."

In 1846 Francis Parkman, pausing at the adobe successor of the earlier fort, was outraged by the prices the Company charged. Sugar sold for two dollars and a half, other commodities in proportion. But on the remote frontier a 2000 per cent markup on St. Louis prices was not unusual. Parkman was also offered the swap of an Indian girl for his horse by a visiting chief. Like a proper Bostonian he passed up the bargain.

Emigrants were expected to register at Fort Laramie. In 1850 during the rush to the gold fields, 37,570 men, 825 women, 1126 children, 9101 wagons, 31,502 oxen, 22,878 horses, 7650 mules, and 5754 cows had checked in by July 8. Several thousand persons and many hundreds of wagons were apparently missed in the registration. Later the fort was a relay point for the Pony Express and a station of the overland stage.

A day's journey out from the fort travelers found fresh evidence of what might be in store for them. The route became littered with the discarded paraphernalia of earlier emigrants, with beans by the sackful, bacon by the hundred-weight, bonnets, boxes, trunks, stoves, cooking utensils, carpenters' tools, wagons, and "almost every article of household furniture"— all abandoned for want of strength and means to carry them farther. Advice to those who followed was written on the skulls of dead oxen.

THE PLATTE RIVER FERRY. After a drawing by Charles C. Nahl. Illustration from Alonzo Delano, *Life on the Plains*, 1854. Those who by-passed the ferry to save the fare often did it at the risk of their lives.

Beyond Fort Laramie the North Platte River presented a critically dangerous crossing of the trail. Drowning was a common experience at this point. For several years the Mormons drove a thriving trade ferrying gentiles across the treacherous stream. Wrote one of the brethren: "Br Chesley who came back & met us was buiseyly engaged in ferreing 2 of the small bands of the oregon emegrants 25 waggons in all for which they

ALONG THE OREGON TRAIL. Photograph of gravestones marked 1844 and 1845.

received a bout 33 dollars in remuneration they took the loading acrost in the Leather Skift & drawed the waggons through the river by means of a rope fastend to the end of the tonge & thus drawing them through they rec in payment flour at $250 per hhd Bacon at 6 cts per lb &c." This crossing was a bottleneck of traffic and as wagons piled up on the riverbank traders did a lively business while the emigrants waited their turn.

Beyond the South Pass that led through the Rockies and past the post established just beyond by Jim Bridger, one of the most famous of mountain men and the Nestor of the wilderness, the emigrant came to Fort Hall. This was the last stop of consequence before a route to California split off from the Oregon Trail, and here the emigrant was likely to be persuaded by early California propàgandists to take the southern path. "Mr. Greenwood, an old mountaineer, well stocked with falsehoods," wrote Joel Palmer in 1845–46, "had been dispatched from California to pilot the emigrants through; and assisted by a young man by the name of

McDougal, from Indiana, so far succeeded as to induce thirty-five or thirty-six wagons to take that trail." For the most part, however, the first surge of transcontinental emigrants kept steadfastly on for Oregon.

Beyond the last range of the Rockies the Oregon settlements along the Columbia and Willamette had flourished under the good management of the Hudson's Bay Company. Only an occasional American had added to the population from Astor's day until the 1840's. But the groundwork for a great migration had been laid. Almost a thousand went to Oregon in 1843, half again as many in 1844, and a tide of over 3000 in 1845. By 1846, Captain Warre reported, the American Village was flourishing, "with two churches, and 100 houses, store houses, &c. all of which have been built within five years. . . . The Hudson's Bay Company was so completely over ruled by the number of Americans, that they were obliged . . . to submit to the laws of the very people whose settlement and oc-cupation of the land they contributed so generously and largely to effect." The Congressman who had asked "Who wants to go to Oregon?" in 1828 had his answer. The Oregon Trail had become a national highway and the American Village had become an outpost of empire.

The migration that crossed nearly two thousand miles of raw country to reach the wooded and watered lands of the west coast, in Horace Greeley's words, wore "an aspect of insanity." It was a phenomenal wandering of peoples that can all too easily be romanticized in history. Each of those miles, through the pioneer years, cost the lives of seventeen people, thirty-four thousand in all. The cost to the spirit can never be estimated. Tales of the man and wife who cut their wagon in two and divided their oxen in a stormy quarrel, or of the two men who carried their argument to mutual extermination, bear witness to the bitter strain of hardship.

THE AMERICAN VILLAGE IN OREGON IN 1846. Drawing by Warre. Another of Capt. Warre's original sketches.
The American Antiquarian Society

THE COUNCIL BLUFFS CROSSING ON THE OVERLAND TRAIL. Engraving by C. Fenn. After a painting by F. Piercy used for an illustration in James Linforth, *Route from Liverpool to the Great Salt Lake Valley*, 1855. The engraving, although slightly modified, reproduces more clearly than Piercy's original painting.

FIRST VIEW OF GREAT SALT LAKE VALLEY FROM A PASS IN THE WASATCH MOUNTAINS. Lithograph by Ackerman. From Howard Stansbury, *Exploration and Survey of the Valley of the Great Salt Lake of Utah,* 1852.

THE MORMON EXODUS

On the heels of the first rush to Oregon another swarm of pilgrims gathered to take the overland trail, this group headed for the virtually unknown land by the Great Salt Lake. Brigham Young, a man of great spiritual force, but a zealot who invited persecution, had moved his people to the Mississippi frontier. Unable to live his dream there, he gathered them near Kanesville, Iowa, later Council Bluffs, for a final move beyond reach of persecution, beyond the province of American authority altogether. In search of sanctuary he headed into uninhabited Mexican territory across the Rockies. The first body of Mormons, with Young in the lead, started west in the summer of 1847 to choose the exact site of the new state, leaving behind at Council Bluffs a forwarding station for future emigrants. About that town, as at previous points between Independence and Council Bluffs, several thousand acres were planted with wheat, corn, and vegetables to provision not only the present community but the stream of Mormons that would pass through from the East en route to a new Zion in the West.

Four years earlier Lieutenant John Charles Frémont with Kit Carson as guide had dipped down into the Great Salt Lake Valley, a land little known even to roving hunters, and had seen "the waters of the inland sea stretching in still and solitary grandeur far beyond the limits of our vision." At first sight of that same view Young recognized the Promised Land, but to some of his followers it seemed more like a desolate waste. Within a month of their arrival the well-regimented brethren had, in the words of one of them, "broke, watered, planted and sowed upwards of 100 acres with various kinds of seeds, nearly stockaded with adobes one public square (ten acres)," and

Statens Museum for Kunst, Copenhagen. Courtesy of L. Artur Svensson
THE VISIT OF A MORMON AGENT TO A DANISH CARPENTER'S HOME, 1856. Painting by Christen Dalsgaard.

built "one line of log cabins and stockades." There was discouragement and suffering, but in time the crops flourished, the people prospered, and followers swarmed after the firstcomers. Within two years travelers en route to the gold fields of California found at the Great Sale Lake a city of 8000 inhabitants, laid out on a magnificent scale, with a

THE BOWERY, MINT, AND PRESIDENT'S HOUSE IN SALT LAKE CITY, 1849. Lithograph by Ackerman. Illustration from Howard Stansbury, *Exploration and Survey of the Valley of the Great Salt Lake of Utah,* 1852.

Bowery serving as a temporary place of worship until a Great Temple ("to surpass in grandeur of design and gorgeousness of decoration all edifices the world has yet seen") could be built, and a mint stamping coins from California gold dust, needing only trees to make it a "Diamond of the Desert."

The overland trek of the Mormons differed little from other expeditions except for its more orderly regulation. Many groups that crossed the continent were organized in a semi-military manner to fight the "battle of the Plains," but few preserved the enduring, high discipline of these sectarians. When they paused for the night Young's crusading caravans had lectures on the land they were in, musical directors led entertainments to bolster spirits tried by travel, sanitary inspectors and overseers watched the health and hygiene of the travelers.

With agents, port representatives, and

emigration funds, the Mormons attracted a host of converts both at home and abroad. In less than a generation their numbers increased from 6000 to 200,000 and their wealth in proportion. Polygamy provided an ample, cheap labor supply and Young's patriarchal government was administered firmly and, with the purpose in mind, wisely.

Everything had seemed to conspire to confound the prophets and undo the best-laid plans. In 1834 Congress had forbidden any white person without a special license to set foot in Indian country beyond Missouri. "A barrier has been raised for their protection against the encroachments of our citizens," said President Andrew Jackson. Within a decade the Oregon migration was already making a dead letter of that solemn pledge. Even Brigham Young's vision to escape any government but his own—to secure a place where the Devil himself could not dig him out—could not outdistance the advance of the frontier. Before the Mormons had finished their new home the United States had taken over the entire area as part of its booty from the Mexican War.

Under Young's discipline the State of Deseret thrived as an unprecedented example of state socialism. About ten years after the picture below was drawn Mark Twain "enjoyed the pleasant strangeness of a city of fifteen thousand inhabitants with no loafers perceptible in it; and no visible drunkards or noisy people; a limpid stream rippling and dancing through every street in place of a filthy gutter; block after block of trim dwellings, built of 'frame' and sun-burned brick—a great thriving orchard and garden behind every one of them, apparently —branches from the street stream winding and sparkling among the garden beds and fruit trees—and a grand general air of neatness, repair, thrift, and comfort, around and about and over the whole. And everywhere were workshops, factories, and all manner of industries; and intent faces and busy hands were to be seen wherever one looked; and in one's ears was the ceaseless clink of the hammers, the buzz of trade and the contented hum of drums and flywheels."

SALT LAKE CITY, LOOKING SOUTH, 1853. Wash drawing. The central building in the group of three buildings to the right of the large house with pediment at extreme left is Governor Brigham Young's "White House." The large building at the extreme right is the first Mormon Tabernacle, built in 1851.

The New York Public Library, Stokes Collection

Santa Manuela Rancho, California, 1851. Drawing by William Rich Hutton.

CALIFORNIA GOLD RUSH

On the other side of the Rocky Mountains, south of Oregon, lay a Zion ready-made, according to most reports. California, wrote an early French trapper, was "a perfect paradise, a perpetual spring," a land where a man with chills was such a curiosity that people traveled eighteen miles to watch him shake. It was a land, according to the candid description of one returned Kentuckian who published his memoirs in 1831, where the ardor of the señoritas would quicken the blood of any trail-worn emigrant.

Fired with one incentive or another Americans in growing numbers were, by the early 1840's, filtering into California through the mountain passes or coming by sea, some to settle, some to return home with tales of a fertile land, a land of genial climate, of picturesquely decaying missions, and of tranquil ranches. The people were so pleasantly unacquisitive as to torture a Yankee conscience. California hides were shipped off to Lynn, converted into shoes, and sold back to Californians at a fancy profit. Even lumber was imported rather than exert the effort

necessary to cut it from the abundant growth of California soil. "In the hands of an enterprising people," wrote Richard Henry Dana, Jr., in 1834, "what a country this might be."

At Fort Hall and elsewhere along the transcontinental routes California-boosters were already deflecting a flow of emigrants away from Oregon. "These emigrants," wrote the Reverend Walter Colton, U.S.N., in the fall of 1846, "will change the face of California. We shall soon have not only the fruits of nature, but of human industry. We shall soon be able to get a ball of butter without churning it on the back of a wild colt; and a potatoe without weighing it as if it were a doubloon. Were it possible for a man to live without the trouble of drawing his breath, I should look for this pleasing phenomenon in Califorina." The "enterprising" people Dana had wished for were arriving in earnest.

The most active focus of American interest was the semi-feudal fort that John Augustus Sutter had completed directly in the

San Luis Obispo Mission, California, 1848. Drawing by Hutton.

line of overland travel from the States, near the present site of Sacramento. When California "revolted" against Mexico General Vallejo and his brother were imprisoned in Sutter's Fort and in July, 1846, the American flag was raised over it.

Near Sutter's mill on Monday, January 24, 1848, according to a contemporary record, "some kind of mettle was found in the tail race that looks like goald. First discovered by James Martial, the Boss of the Mill." Marshall's findings in the millrace were, of course, an early trickle of the torrent of gold that all but swamped men's imagination the world over during the years that followed. Gold had been found in traces almost everywhere in California, but this was the first advertisement of a bonanza.

When Dana visited Yerba Buena, the future San Francisco, the peninsula site had nothing to show but a few adobe huts besides its presidio and Mission Dolores. An English sailor who had quit his ship in 1822 lived in the *casa grande,* next door to a native Ohioan who ran a village store. But, like others before him, Dana foresaw the ultimate importance of that site with its magnificent harbor and impressive hills.

Sutter's Fort, 1847. Lithograph published by Snyder and Black, 1850–54.

By the winter of 1847–48 the little settlement had grown into a modest trading community with about eight hundred people, two small hotels, a few shops, and a fair sprinkling of private dwellings. That placid development was completely disrupted by the news from Sutter's Mill. By May, 1848, the *California Star* reported, it had become "a town topsy turvy in a twinkling . . . now completely quiet." The newspaper explained: "A terrible visitant we have had of late—a FEVER which has well nigh depopulated the town . . . and but for a few gracious interpositions of the elements, perhaps, not a goose would have been spared to furnish a quill to pen the remainder. It has preyed upon defenceless old age, subdued the elasticity of careless youth, and attacked indiscriminately sex and class, from Town Councilmen to tow-frocked cartmen, from Tailors to tipplers. . . . And this is the GOLD FEVER. . . . The insatiate maw of the monster, not appeased by the easy conquest of the rough-fisted yeomanry of the north must needs ravage a healthy, prosperous place beyond his domaine. . . ."

Eastern newspapers did not carry the news of Marshall's discovery of gold until the late summer of 1848. According to the *California Almanac* of 1849 Colonel Mason, Governor of California, excused himself from delaying his report to the War Department for six months because he could not countenance the wild claims of wealth being made until he had personally visited the mines. The stories were all but incredible. "You are now all incredulous," wrote one Californian to a friend in the East in September, "you regard our statements as the dreams of an excited imagination; but what seems to you mere fiction, is stern reality. It is not gold in the clouds, or in the sea, or in the centre of a rock-ribbed mountain, but in the soil of California—sparkling in the sun, and glittering in its streams. It lies on the open plain, in the shadows of the deep ravine, and glows on the summits of the mountains, which have lifted for ages their golden coronets to heaven." Such gilt-edge reports seemed to secure the truth. In his message to Congress in December President Polk solemnly acknowledged that a real and important strike had been made, one that would make Cortez seem like a small-time operator.

SAN FRANCISCO, 1847. Drawing by Hutton. One of the very few views of the city during its pre-boom period.
The Huntington Library

Collection of Ward Melville

NEWS FROM THE GOLD DIGGINGS, 1850. Painting by William Sidney Mount.

The timing of the revelation was perfect to precipitate a mad rush to the diggings. The East lay covered with mortgages, westward migration was in the air, and the national pulse had not yet quieted down from the Mexican War excitement.

As the news spread other cities throughout the world suffered the same excitement San Francisco had known. In January, 1849,

Philip Hone, the New York diarist, reported: "Gold! Gold! The California fever is increasing in violence; thousands are going, among whom are many young men of our best families; the papers are filled with advertisements for vessels for Chagres and San Francisco. Tailors, hatters, grocers, provision merchants, hardware men . . . are employed night and day in fitting out the ad-

"The California Company Going from the Town of York (Pennsylvania) in 1849." Sketch by Lewis Miller.

venturers. John Bull, too, is getting crazy as Brother Jonathan on this exciting subject."

How Everyman was to get there, poor as he often was, said one of the first guides to the gold mines, lay "in a single word—a word of vast and untold power, destined in the

A French Commentary on the Gold Fever by One of France's Great Artists. Lithograph after Honoré Daumier from *Le Charivari*.

bright hereafter to revolutionize and glorify man, and his dwelling place the earth—Association. Let fifty poor families, or a hundred young men, associate themselves together lending all their united thoughts and energies, and combining all their resources, to the one absorbing purpose of going to california—what should prevent them?... Companies are forming in all directions, under the leadership of shrewd and energetic men; and, as private speculators, deserve to be encouraged by all young men who have nerve and heart enough to break from the enfeebling conventionalities of a corrupt and corrupting civilization, and carve out for themselves a name and a fortune."

At least one hundred and twenty-four such companies left from Massachusetts alone in 1849 and others joined from every state in the Union. California companies sprang up the world over—in France, Germany, Japan, China, Australia. Methodists and Cherokees each sent a company to join large contingents of Peruvians, Chileans, Mexicans, and deserters from the American Army, Navy, and merchant marine, who were early on the spot. The phrase "qu'est-ce qu'il dit?" was heard so often about the mines that the large number of Frenchmen were generally dubbed "Keskydees."

A Section of a Map Showing the Routes to the Gold Regions. Published by J. H. Colton, New York, 1849.
The full map shows the all-sea route around Cape Horn and the routes by way of Nicaragua and the Isthmus
of Panama as well as the northern and southern overland routes. Both the Oregon and Santa Fe trails are
also indicated.

THE STEAMER *Hartford*, CAPTAIN LE FEVRE, BOUND FOR CALIFORNIA OUT OF NEW YORK, FEBRUARY, 1849. Painting by Joseph B. Smith. The *Hartford*, encountering difficulties, took nearly a year to get to California. Photograph courtesy of the Frick Art Reference Library.

The gold rush had something of the fervor of a crusade. Men from every walk of life—farmers, clerks, mechanics, doctors, lawyers, and ministers—left their callings. Men of leisure joined with those who quit hard labor to search for gold and ease. Companies went to church to receive blessings and advice before setting out. Sometimes the preacher left his pulpit to join them. One group marched off in uniform with attendants and musicians. Men of high moral character were urgently recruited. Many who had never before dreamed of leaving home found themselves swept into one of the great pioneering adventures of the age — or of any other age, for that matter.

John Woodhouse Audubon, son of the famous naturalist, left by ship from New York in February, 1849. "The last words of ministers," he wrote, "as they gave their parting advice and blessing, were drowned by the bell of the steamer. Its tolling went to my heart like a funeral bell. I was much too excited to answer the hurrahs of the hundreds who came down to see us off; and in silence I waved my cap . . . for the red eyes of fathers, wives, brothers, and even timid sweethearts, had, added to my grief, killed the boisterous man within me, and mentally I prayed God for courage and ability to perform my engagements faithfully."

No route to the West, by sea, by land, or by both, promised anything but adventure for which many left home blithely unprepared. Even those who chose the quiet inland waters as shortcuts to their jumping-off places to the golden West met perils that sometimes quickened, often tempered, and occasionally ended forever their spirit of adventure. Isaac Jones Wistar wrote of a race between two rival steamers, each crowded with California emigrants, down the Ohio River between Cincinnati and St. Louis, where every frequent threat of collision brought forth a flourish of rifles and pistols from the well-armed passengers. On the Missouri River the shipful of dirty, impatient adventurers broke out with cholera and the noisiest braggarts suddenly turned deathly still with apprehension. "Some eighteen or twenty poor fellows died," wrote Wistar, "and were laid out on deck till enough corpses accumulated, when they were buried, wrapped only in their blankets, in shallow holes hastily dug by the deck-hands on river islands, the boat barely stopping long enough for the purpose."

The route by way of the Panama Isthmus promised the quickest arrival and was the most traveled. Any hulk that could float was pressed into service from Eastern ports, and from Europe, to Chagres. Crossing the few miles of tropics in face of the difficulties of climate and terrain and unhurriable natives was high adventure for some, despair and death for others. "Trees were rolled upon trees," wrote a *Tribune* correspondent, "woven into a sheet by parasitic vines, that leaped into the air like spray, from the top-most boughs. The path ... became finally a narrow gully, filled with mud nearly to the horses' bellies. The only sounds in that leafy wilderness were the chattering of monkeys as they cracked the palm-nuts, and the scream of parrots, flying from tree to tree. In the deepest ravines spent mules frequently lay dead, and high above them, on the large boughs, the bald vultures waited silently for us to pass. ... Scrambling up ravines of slippery clay, we went through swamps and thickets, urging forward our jaded beasts by shouting and beating. Going down a precipitous bank, washed soft by the rains, my horse slipped and made a descent of ten feet, landing on one bank and I on another. He rose quietly, disengaged his head from the mud and stood, flank-deep waiting till I stepped across his back and went forward, my legs lifted to his neck."

The all-sea trip around Cape Horn was hazardous enough in its different way, and expensive. But it appealed to people with a sea-going tradition even though it took a half-year on an average, and time was a big factor in the mad race for wealth. Getting men and merchandise to the gold coast was a gamble with high stakes. Every hour wasted on the way might be a fortune lost.

CROSSING THE ISTHMUS. After a drawing by Marryat. Illustration from Frank Marryat, *Mountains and Molehills,* 1855. Drawn from the recollections of an English traveler who made the crossing.

The New-York Historical Society

The Best Chance Yet, for

CALIFORNIA!

A Meeting will be held in COHASSET, at the Office of

H. J. TURNER,

On SATURDAY, January 27th, at 11 O'Clock, for the purpose of forming a Company, to be called the " South Shore and California Joint Stock Company;" to be composed of 30 Members, and each Member paying $300.

COHASSET, JANUARY 24, 1849.

The Bostonian Society

SHIP CARD, 1849

When the clipper ship *Sea Witch* made San Francisco in ninety-seven days from New York man seemed to have captured the speed of the winds at long last. In 1851 the *Flying Cloud* sailed through the Golden Gate just eighty-nine days out of New York, sustaining a pace that today's cup racers would like to match. Travel and cargo space on the swiftest ships afloat in their race around the Horn sold at a high premium. Nothing and nobody could wait for anything slower.

The overland route was the cheapest and most popular, if not the quickest, way to the mines. The promise of gold attracted the largest and most motley group that had yet attempted to cross the Plains. As in the Oregon and Utah treks, some went in wagons, some trundled carts or wheelbarrows, and others simply hiked the several thousand miles to the rainbow's end. As the Fort Laramie registrations indicate, the forty-niners were preponderantly male. The trip made demands on the traveler's vitality that even some of the stoutest could not meet, yet

The Huntington Library

COOKING ON THE PLAINS WITH BUFFALO-CHIP FUEL, 1849. Drawing by Bruff.

many women, including one ninety-year-old grandmother, successfully made it.

The German artist Kurz watched the passing parade at St. Joseph which, with tents pitched all about to house the migrant hordes, he likened to a city besieged by an army. As thousands of adventurers, "all in a heat from gold fever," waited impatiently for the prairie grass to grow, prices skyrocketed. The poorer emigrants went broke just waiting, and had to defer their hopes. Others put on a merry spectacle trying to master the stubborn mules and wilful oxen which would take them overland when forage was high enough.

The least traveled route, but in many ways the most picturesque, was by way of northern Mexico, along the padre's trail through Sonora, over Guadalupe Pass to the Gila River and the Colorado, and thus up through southern California. The way led past living fragments of old civilizations, through passive white villages of humble huts and splendid churches, into regions terrorized by Apaches and Comanches, and by the ruins of ancient Aztec monuments overgrown with poppies and lilies. It was a land of quaint pueblos and drowsy haciendas built of sun-dried brick, a land of *monte* and cock fights, where ladies smoked and Americans were already at work trading and mining for precious metals.

"THE EXTRAORDINARY LITTLE TOWN OF JESUS MARIA." Lithograph by C. Gildemeister. A Mexican mining village on the Southern Route to California, 1849. After a sketch by John Woodhouse Audubon, son of the naturalist. Audubon, whose touching account of his departure we have read, took the southern route. "Passing through one of the wildest and most picturesque gorges I have ever seen," he wrote, "we came to the extraordinary little town of Jesus Maria, situated at the junction of two little torrents of clear, beautiful water, tumbling in noisy, joyous splashing from rock to basin, and carrying away the rubbish from this half-civilized settlement of mines as it passes through town."

The New York Public Library

SAN FRANCISCO IN 1849. Painting by Henry Firks. The original of a better-known lithograph.

After a brief abandonment San Francisco came to life again as the main trading post of the gold country. With months' old newspapers selling at a dollar apiece, eggs, laid on the other side of Cape Horn, at ten dollars a dozen, flour at fifty dollars a barrel, and almost every commodity from old shoes to tacks priced in proportion, the profits of the supply trade were enormous. One mercantile house was said to have paid fifty thousand dollars for a single-story building of twenty feet front.

In September, 1849, Bayard Taylor reported: "A gentleman who arrived in April told me he then found but thirty or forty houses; the population was then so scant that not more than twenty-five persons would be seen in the streets at any one time. Now, there were probably five hundred houses, tents, and sheds, with a population, fixed and floating, of six thousand. People who had been absent six weeks came back and could scarcely recognize the place."

Houses were going up at the rate of fifteen to thirty a day. Some were imported from Canton to be put up by Chinese carpenters, others were ordered prefabricated from the East and from London. The booming town continually outgrew its civic "improvements." At the corner of Clay and Kearney Streets a sign was posted:

> *This street impassable,*
> *Not even Jackassable!*

Sacramento City was first laid out in the spring of 1849 about a mile and a half from Sutter's Fort and was a humming community before the end of the year. "Stages run regularly to the mines," wrote one visitor that year, "steamboats run on the river; a theatre, church and several large handsome hotels with billiards saloons and bowling alleys and all the fixings, have been put up. Even a couple of girls are around with a hand organ and tambourine. Civilization is making rapid strides. . . ."

The New-York Historical Society

THE WINTER OF 1849. After a drawing by Marryat. From Frank Marryat, *Mountains and Molehills*, 1855. During the fall and winter of 1849–50, wrote Samuel C. Upham, the streets of San Francisco "ran rivers of mud—swallowed up every living thing that attempted to cross them. It was no uncommon occurence to see at the same time a mule stalled in the middle of the street with only his head above the mud, and an unfortunate pedestrian, who had slipped off the plank sidewalk, being fished out by a companion."

SACRAMENTO CITY IN 1849. Lithograph by Wm. Endicott after a sketch by G. V. Cooper.

The New York Public Library, Stokes Collection

San Francisco Harbor, Winter of 1852-53. Part of a panorama taken by William Shew when the harbor was filled with rotting sailing vessels whose crews had deserted to go to the gold fields.

In 1849 the steamship *Senator,* shown in the foreground of the illustration on the previous page, made the first "through by daylight" trip from San Francisco to Sacramento. To be able to breakfast at the Bay and sup in Sacramento was a welcome convenience for the weary miner whose overland trip often took ten days. A year or two later J. D. Borthwick, a British traveler, classed high among the wonders of California "the number of these magnificent river steamboats which, even at that early period of its history, had steamed around Cape Horn from New York, and now, gliding along California rivers at a rate of up to twenty-two miles an hour,* afforded the same rapid and

*The paddlewheeler *Chryssie,* in 1861, on a trip from Sacramento to San Francisco, averaged 22.7 miles per hour. Her record for the trip—5 hours, 19 minutes—still stands.

comfortable means of travelling . . . as when they plied between New York and Albany."

The ships of all nations used the superb harbor at San Francisco for their anchorage, many of them old and unseaworthy vessels that had been hurriedly pressed into service to handle the vast number of emigrants to the gold coast. Once arrived, many were not worth the expense of manning to sail away and they were left to rot. During 1849, reported several early annalists of the city, nearly 40,000 hopefuls had landed at the port. "Beside that great number," they added, "some three or four thousand seamen deserted from the many hundred ships lying in the bay. . . . At the time of which we write there were between three and four hundred large square-rigged vessels [in port], unable to leave on account of want of hands. Many

of these vessels never got away, but in a few years afterwards, rotted and tumbled to pieces where they were moored. As stores and dwelling-places were much needed, a considerable number of the deserted ships were drawn high on the beach, and fast imbedded in deep mud, where they were converted into warehouses and lodgings for the wants of the crowded population. When subsequently the town was extended over the mud flat of the bay, these ships were forever closed in by numberless streets and regularly built houses both of brick and frame. When by and by the runaway seamen returned from the mines, crews could be more easily had, though still at a great increase in wages, and gradually the detained vessels were enabled to leave port, to make room for new fleets."

During those frantic years San Francisco Bay rarely held less than four or five hundred ships. In July, 1850, there were 526, not counting the hundred or more anchored off Benecia, Sacramento, and Stockton. In the fall of the same year "the following accurate list" of anchored vessels was recorded:

	Ships	Barques	Brigs	Schooners	Ocean Steamers
American	42	64	67	50	9
British	5	23	5	3	
French	9	1	1	(2 others)	
Chilean	1	2		1	
Bremen	1	4	4	1	
Austria	1				

not to mention several Swedish and Italian brigs, a few German and Dutch barques, and about 150 storeships of various nations. The grand total was something over 450 at that moment.

Before roads were built, carrying supplies to the mines by mule train was a profitable, though often perilous, business. On August 23, 1850 the *Marysville Herald* reported: "One hundred mules, in one train, well packed at one store, passed our office last evening, bound to the mines. Four or five trains, of from ten to thirty, went up in the morning. The mules speak for Marysville and Marysville speaks for herself." In 1853 over four thousand mules used for packing to the mines were owned in Marysville alone.

Few of those who flocked to California were experienced miners, nor did they feel they had to be. "Any reports that may reach you of the vast quantities of gold in California can scarcely be exaggerated for belief," advised one authoritative witness. Some early comers averaged $300 to $500 a day for weeks on end. A few of the luckiest made as much as $5000 in a single day. Sailors who skipped ship, soldiers on leave from the army, hopefuls from every walk of life might expect to hit it rich by the most ama-

The Newberry Library, E. E. Ayer Collection
PACKING IN THE MOUNTAINS. From Alonzo Delano, *Pen-Knife Sketches*, 1853. The illustrator, Charles Nahl, has been called the "California Cruikshank" for his aptitude in humorously delineating the mining scenes that Delano wrote about.

teurish methods. In the general haste to pick up wealth as cheaply as possible scientific mining techniques that would have saved years of time and labor, and countless lives, were ignored. Even so, during the first six

Collection of Mrs. Angus Gordon Boggs
BOB REAM PACK TRAIN, 1853. Bob Pitt, a well-known character in the mining districts, is shown riding the lead animal ahead of his squaw (afoot) and pack train. The lead animal of the train was belled and ridden by one of the men, the loaded animals following in single file with one man at the end of the procession.

PLACER MINING, 1854. Painting by Chadwick.

years of mining in California, gold production in the United States increased seventy-three times. By 1855 this country was producing almost half the gold mined in the world, virtually all of it in California.

The Argonauts mined the river valleys by washing deposits of sand and gravel, called placers. "We tell when it will pay by trying the dirt with a pan," wrote one forty-niner. "This is called prospecting here. If it will pay from six to 12½ pr pan full, then we go to work. Some wash with cradles some with what is called a tom & various other fixings. But I like the tom best of any thing that I have seen. It is a box or trough about 8 or 9 feet long, some 18 in. wide & from 5 to 6 in. high, with an iron seive in one end punched with ½ in. holes. Underneath this is placed a ripple or box with two ripples across it.

The tom is then placed in an oblique position, the water is brought on by means of a hose. The dirt, stone, clay & all is then thrown in & stirred with a shovel until the water runs clear, the gold & finer gravel goes through the seive & falls in the under box & lodges above the ripples. Three men can wash all day without taking this out as the water washes the loose gravel over and all the gold settles to the bottom. One man will wash as fast as two can pick and shovel it in, or as fast as three rockers or cradles."

Many prospectors, however, found that digging and washing out gold was just about the hardest way to get it. Mining, as it was done in California, took brawn and endurance—and luck. "Those who, retaining their health, return home disappointed," wrote an eastern newspaper correspondent, "say that

251

The New-York Historical Society

THE PAY-OFF. Lithograph by Augusto Ferran. One of a series of unusual lithographs, entitled "Tipos Californianos," by a Havanese artist.

they have been humbugged about the gold, when in fact, they have humbugged themselves about the *work*.... Of all classes of men, those who pave streets and quarry limestone are best adapted for gold digging." After the first eager horde of prospectors had swept up the easy findings it became increasingly difficult to make a living, let alone a fortune, sifting and digging for pay dirt in the withering sunshine and the bitter chill of the California hills.

On week ends the miner descended upon the nearest town to convert his dust and nuggets into coin and his coin into gambler's luck, whisky, and, if all went well, supplies for the week to come. Villages that were heavily populated on Saturdays and Sundays and all but empty by Monday morning sprang up with all the speed necessary to catch the trade. More than one merchant found *his* gold mine in a jerry-built store so small that half his stock hung from sticks projecting outside. Miners customarily

The New-York Historical Society

A FAIR EXCHANGE AT THE DIGGINGS. Lithograph published by Robert H. Elton.

MERCHANDISING AT THE McIVOR DIGGINGS, JULY 26, 1853. Lithograph by Julius Hamel.

bought their necessities at auction. In the hands of the right auctioneer anything from sad and weary horses to rancid butter could be disposed of at a profit. After luring a crowd of curious and interested samplers with such luxuries as dried apples or a keg of butter, Frank Marryat explained, "Joe Bellows [the auctioneer] takes his stand on a cask in the midst of his samples, and startles you suddenly with: 'And I'm only bid one dollar for a dozen of mixed pickles; one dollar, one dollar, one doll —— try them, gentlemen.' In the meantime Joe nods to an imaginary bidder in the distance, and rattles on, 'One and a half, one and a half, one and a h——' 'Doo,' says a Dutchman, with his mouth full of pickled gherkins. 'Two dollars I'm offered for a dozen of mixed pickles.' 'Dos y medio,' says a Spaniard, under the influence of the green bean. 'Ah! Senor Don Pacheco,' says Joe, 'son los escabéches d'Inghelterra, muy buenos, muy finos!'

'Have I any advance on two dollars and a half?' 'Trois piastres,' says a French restaurateur. 'Three dollars I am bid for a dozen of pickles that cost five dollars in the States, Tenez! Monsieur Leon voici des cornichons comme il faut. Three dollars, three doll's, three doll's——' 'Dree-and-a-half,' says the Dutchman, to whom they are finally knocked down, just as an old miner observes that 'darn him if his knife aint turned blue with the darned vitriol juice.' "

Sunday was also the day the miners stitched and washed their clothes, wrote home, read any old papers they could get hold of, and celebrated the week's toil. For all of them California was a long way from home and for most of them a strange land they never planned to stay in. Strangers from all parts of the earth—from the East, Europe, Latin America, and Asia—were thrown together in a hodge-podge of humanity with only one common interest, to make a fortune as quickly as possible and to return home with it. Normal values and normal restraints

253

SUNDAY MORNING IN THE MINES. Painting by Nahl.

THE FANDANGO. Painting by Nahl.

were fondly remembered—but readily forgotten. "There is a good deal of sin and wickedness going on here," one of them, a New Englander, wrote to his family. "Stealing, lying, swearing, drinking, gambling and murdering."

The census of 1850 recorded that more than nine-tenths of the population of California was male. Nine years later the proportion of men to women was estimated as still more than six to one; and of the few women, according to one well-informed witness, most were "neither maids, wives, nor widows." Those who could be classified in the latter groups were celebrated creatures.

The easy gaiety of the native Californians, leading their own normal life, was an exotic and appealing spectacle. Letters home told of Spanish fandangos with fiddles and guitars making "pretty good music," the men dressed in sky blue velvet pants, white drawers, and red sashes, and the women with silk stockings and white muslin dresses "starched

so stiffly that you could not get very near." The señoritas, wrote one wistful Yankee miner, "looked very pretty." Virtually no women, as we have seen, had come west.

"The miner, notwithstanding his toil," wrote Delano on that subject, "has his fun and frolic as well as *white men*." Early one Sunday morning, "our mess was awakened by the discharge of a musket at our heads. Jumping up we exclaimed:

" 'What's the matter, what has happened?'

" 'What's the matter!' shouted the stentorian voice of one of our neighbors, 'turn out, turn out; new diggins, by Heaven! a live woman came in last night. . . .'

"We knew that delays were dangerous, so shouldering our picks and shovels, pistols and rifles, and taking a bottle or two of *aguardiente,* we marched to the new tent . . . and gave three cheers and a discharge of firearms. The alarmed occupants rushed to the door to see what was up. Our captain mounted a rock, and addressed the amazed

256

husband in something like this strain.

" 'Stranger—We have understood that our mothers were women, but it is so long ago since we have seen them, that we have forgotten how a woman looks, and being told that you have caught one, we are prospecting to get a glimpse.'

"The man, a sensible fellow, by the way, entering into the humor of the joke, produced the *animal.* . . ."

At dances held only for long-bearded men in flannel shirts and heavy boots the absence of ladies was easily overcome. Every miner with a patch "on a certain part of his inexpressibles" was, for the occasion, considered to be on the distaff side. His brightly colored canvas replacements made him quite as conspicuous as if he had been swathed in lace and muslin.

San Francisco, the principal focus of western life, attracted a congregation of all nations, creeds, and colors, dressed in every

The Newberry Library, E. E. Ayer Collection
A LIVE WOMAN IN THE MINES. After a drawing by Nahl. Another illustration from a book by Delano. His better-known pen name, "Old Block," was a household word in the diggings. At different times a packer, merchant, miner, land speculator and town promoter, and author, Delano played a prominent part in early California life. Samples of his good humored, on the spot reporting are given in these pages. When he died the flags in Grass Valley were half-masted and business stopped.

The New York Public Library
"LADY'S CHAIN" OR THE "MINER'S DANCE." After a drawing by J. D. Borthwick. From *Harper's Weekly,* 1857.

THE BAR OF A GAMBLING SALOON IN SAN FRANCISCO. After a drawing by Marryat. From Frank Marryat, *Mountains and Molehills*, 1855. Note the minstrel show in the rear.

"CALIFORNIA COMFORT." Lithographed by Ferran.

variety of costume, and babbling a medley of tongues—"Yankees of every possible variety, native Californians in *sarapes* and sombreros, Chilians, Sonorians, Kanakas from Hawaii, Chinese with long tails, Malays armed with their everlasting creeses, and others in whose embrowned and bearded visages it was impossible to recognize any special nationality." Most who came to the city in the early days arrived with the intention of staying only long enough to make a fortune. Many of them were men of culture and education but the idea of impermanence subverted normal standards.

The almost barbaric splendor of the city's numberless saloons, with their plate-glass mirrors, gaudy pictures, crystal chandeliers, and mahogany woodwork, was a measure of the uninhibited vitality that flowed through early San Francisco life. "At the corner of Montgomery, and Leidesdorff, and Sansome streets," wrote Alonzo Delano, "are musical gambling hells where your loose

THE SAN FRANCISCO POST OFFICE DURING THE GOLD RUSH. Lithograph by Wm. Endicott & Co. after a drawing by H. F. Cox.

change can be fiddled away ... and where your losses can be drowned, for an addlepate, in the flowing bowl."

Like an army in the field, Californians cherished every word from the world they had left behind in their rush for fortune. When the express arrived in the mining camps every pick and shovel was dropped, every rocker laid aside with its half-washed dirt, every living individual crowded around the distribution center with the eager cry: "Have you got a letter for me?" Next to the trader who sustained life with his provisions, the expressman was the most important man in the fields. Bayard Taylor recalled that one day in San Francisco "the *Panama's* mail-bags reached the Office about nine o'clock. The doors were instantly closed, the windows darkened, and every preparation made for a long siege. The attack from without commenced about the same time. There were knocks on the doors, taps on the windows, beseeching calls at all corners of the house

... with the first streak of daylight the attack commenced again. ... When finally, the windows were opened, the scenes around the office were still more remarkable. In order to prevent a general riot among the applicants, they were recommended to form in ranks. ... The lines extended in front all the way down the hill to Portsmouth Square, and on the south side across Sacramento Street to the tents among the chapparel, while that from the small newspaper window in the rear stretched for some distance up the hill. The man at the tail of the longest line might count on spending six hours in it before he reached the window."

By 1860 the flow of gold from California mines had started to dwindle. Once-roaring camps all but vanished. Countless adventurers returned home to pick up life where they had left off upon their attack of "fever." Others moved restlessly along looking for new strikes. But many stayed on, men of all races, putting roots into the rich soil.

259

SEVEN VIEWS OF DENVER, 1859. After a drawing by A. C. Warren. From Albert D. Richardson, *Beyond the Mississippi*, 1867.

NEW ELDORADOS

Abating interest and hope in the California gold fields let loose a floating population of prospectors eternally searching for another rich strike somewhere in the western mountains. At the close of 1858 reports of a new Eldorado broke through from the land at the foot of the Rockies, some ninety miles from Pike's Peak. That area, between the Oregon and Santa Fe trails, was known almost only from Pike's explorations early in the century. A new list of guidebooks rolled off the presses to give the fifty-niners "a realistic description of the country, climate, streams, scenery, etc; different routes from the Mississippi River to the mines, the best camping places on each route, and a reliable map of the same, etc." About twenty-five thousand people left Fort Leavenworth for the new diggings before any of the reports were authenticated. "Besides the large emigrant trains, hundreds of single wagons with 'Pike's Peak or bust,' or some similar legend displayed on the covers, line pretty much the

entire 600 miles of road," wrote Isaac Jones Wistar, who had taken the trail himself. Like many others he misjudged the prospects, sold out, and returned home. The first strike had been overadvertised and the road back East was soon crowded with disgruntled prospectors. One hopeful group still pressing on reported having passed fifteen hundred wagons west of Fort Kearney returning empty-handed and disillusioned in May, 1859.

Out of the excitement Denver took shape as the budding capital of a large territory. In 1859 approximately 1000 people had

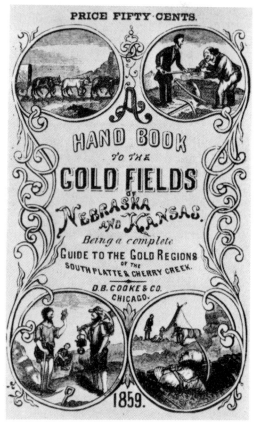

GUIDE TO THE NEW GOLD FIELDS. Cover from Byers and Kellom, *Hand Book*, etc., 1859.

The Yale University Library, Coe Collection

THE END OF THE TRAIL. After a sketch by J. C. Beard. From Richardson, *Beyond the Mississippi.*

The New-York Historical Society

BLACKHAWK POINT, COLORADO, 1862. Looking up Gregory and Chase's Gulches. Lithograph by Charles Shober after a drawing by J. E. Dillingham.

swarmed to that spot and formed a typical frontier community. About 300 buildings, most of them of hewn logs and many of them left unfinished, had been thrown up. A sprinkling of Indian lodges housed the native population.

In May a more promising strike was made in a gulch forty miles northwest of Denver. Within a month, when Horace Greeley visited the diggings, five thousand people were already there and hundreds more were arriving daily. Little towns shot up amid the mountains. "The whole string of four *cities*," wrote Bayard Taylor of the towns in Gregory Gulch, "has a curious, rickety, temporary air, with their buildings standing as if on one leg, with their big signs and little accomodations, the irregular, wandering, uneven streets, and their bald, scarred and pitted mountains on either side." The amenities of life struggled through the frontier chaos. At Blackhawk Point, 8000 feet above

sea level, a group of miners organized a singing school that shook the tin dishes off the shelves. In one mining gulch Albert D. Richardson, the Hartford journalist, met an old Boston merchant successfully running a quartz mill, and an ex-banker, a Presbyterian deacon from Kansas, selling pies and retailing whisky on Sunday. At Blackhawk, Taylor, a confirmed traveler, met one Herr Bergen, a Norwegian merchant he had last seen in the arctic wastes of Lapland. In Colorado as in California, and earlier in the forests of trans-Appalachia, the dream of freedom and plenty made a cosmopolis of the frontier, drawing hopefuls from all quarters of the globe. Here, too, the scarred and mutilated countryside gave evidence that their dreams of avarice were being realized at the expense of the land itself.

Unlike the gradual, continuous advance of the agricultural frontier east of the Mississippi, the early rush to the farther West was explosive and erratic. In the California and Colorado back country the wandering prospector replaced the frontiersman and the farmer as the first tester of the unsettled land. Roaring camps on the pattern of Blackhawk sprang up wherever gold and silver were traced—Tarryall, Fairplay, Buckskin Joe, and, in later years, Leadville and Cripple Creek of fabulous history. But here, again as in California, ranching and farming quickly gave a stability to both the economic and social life of the area.

Like so many western communities Denver, "Queen City of the Plains," was born with a rugged vitality. Once swept away by an inundation of Cherry Creek, several times burned almost to the ground, cut off from the East by Indian outbreaks, deprived of much of its expected trade in its early years by the Civil War, and made to pay a heavy premium for all its necessary supplies because of transportation difficulties—still, within a few years of its founding, the community not only endured but blossomed into a flourishing city, capital of a huge region.

Within two years, in February 1861, the Territory of Colorado, cut away from Kansas, Nebraska, Utah, and New Mexico, was formed. As a central station and supply depot for the mines, Denver gave the "desert" its first concentrated attack of civilization. Richardson returned there in 1865. "With fresh memories of the log-cabins, plank tables, tin cups and plates, and fatal whisky of 1859," he wrote, "I did not readily recover from my surprise on seeing libraries and pictures, rich carpets and pianos, silver and wine—on meeting families with the habits, dress and surroundings of the older States. Keenly we enjoyed the pleasant hospitalities of society among the quickened intelligences and warmed hearts of the frontier. Western emigration makes man larger and riper, more liberal and more fraternal. . . . Now Denver boasted a population of five thousand, and many imposing buildings. The hotel bills-of-fare did not differ materially from those in New York or Chicago."

F Street, Denver. After a drawing by A. E. Mathews. From A. E. Mathews, *Pencil Sketches of Colorado*, 1866. The elegant carriage threading its way through the ox-trains that supplied the outlying frontier suggests the rapid social evolution and remarkable contrasts that characterized community development in the early West. Guns, coffee pots, stills, and sundries, as the shop signs indicate, were staples in the trade with the mining camps for which Denver was the main base of supplies.

The Huntington Library

In California vastly improved mining techniques had developed since 1849. "Hydraulicking" was but one of the organized and expensive methods that were getting metal out of rocks and hills that would have utterly defeated the amateur miner of earlier days. When the greatest bonanza of all was uncovered at the Comstock Lode, in what is now Nevada, in 1859, Californians were the first to rush back across the mountains, bringing capital and experience to exploit the new find in proper fashion. "The wondrous city of Virginia" perched halfway up the Nevada mountains, leaped into the international spotlight and stayed there for twenty years while the mines yielded over $300,000,000 worth of gold and silver. Again a metropolis blossomed in the desert almost overnight. "Here has sprung up like Jonah's gourd a city upon a hill, which cannot be hid," reported Richardson; "a city of costly churches, tasteful school-houses, and imposing hotels; many telegraph wires, many daily coaches, two theaters, three daily newspapers —one nearly as large as the eight-page journals of New York!" It seemed that a man could take his hat and wheelbarrow and in half an hour gather enough pelf to last a lifetime.

One "Sandy" Bowers, a teamster who struck it rich, built a fabulous house and before it was finished left the West to spend more money abroad. As Bowers said: "I've had powerful good luck in this country, an' now I've got money to throw at the birds. Ther arn't no chance for a gentleman to spend his coin in this country, an' so me an' Mrs. Bowers is goin' ter Yoorup...."

HYDRAULIC MINING; PIPING THE BANK IN NEVADA COUNTY, CALIFORNIA. From *California Scenery* by Lawrence and Southworth, 1866 (3d edition).

The Library of Congress

SANDY BOWERS' MANSION, VIRGINIA CITY.

SIX-MILE CANON FROM C STREET, VIRGINIA CITY. From *California Scenery* by Lawrence and Southworth, 1866 (3d edition). "A city of costly churches, tasteful school-houses, and imposing hotels...."

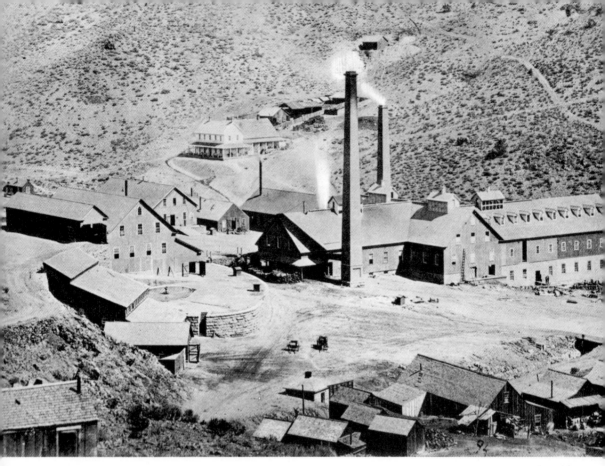

THE GOULD AND CURRY MILL, 1867–8. Photograph by T. H. O'Sullivan.

WORKING THE GOULD AND CURRY MINE, 1867–8. Photograph by O'Sullivan. One of the earliest known photographs taken by magnesium light.

The individual panning and placer mining of the earlier diggings could not get silver out of the quartz veins of the Comstock. Here mining became big business incorporating expensive machinery, engineering skill, and large organization. As a proverb ran, it required a gold mine to work a silver mine and often another to find one. Outside capital poured into the Nevada fields to extract the wealth that was there. By 1865 the Gould and Curry Mine had invested almost a million dollars in its stamp mill alone. It was a new era when the American frontier came under the control of outside interests. It was a new era in the diggings, certainly, when in 1863 a labor union was established on the Comstock Lode to protect the interests of the wage-paid miner. The carnival of individual exploitation had given way to organized industry and the coupon-clipping of an international body of bond holders.

Experts came from many countries of Europe to examine the engineering achievements on the Comstock. The great width and varying intensity of the vein made cave-ins an awful menace, until a German miner from San Francisco devised a system of mortised and tenoned "square sets," like the cells made by a honeybee, to replace the ore as it was removed. The Sutro Tunnel that cut three miles into the heart of a mountain was rightfully considered one of the engineering marvels of the age.

For some time to come the whole mountain area of the West was kept in a ferment as new strikes were made in Nevada, Colorado, Idaho, Montana, and Utah. Bull whackers, grizzled miners, footpackers,

The New-York Historical Society
BATTERY ROOM, GOULD AND CURRY MINING COMPANY, VIRGINIA, NEVADA TERRITORY. Lithograph by Britton & Co. From a company brochure. The equipment for the Gould and Curry quartz mill cost almost two-thirds of a million dollars and included eighty stamps that reduced one hundred tons of ore daily. Mining on such a scale was beyond the means of any individual.

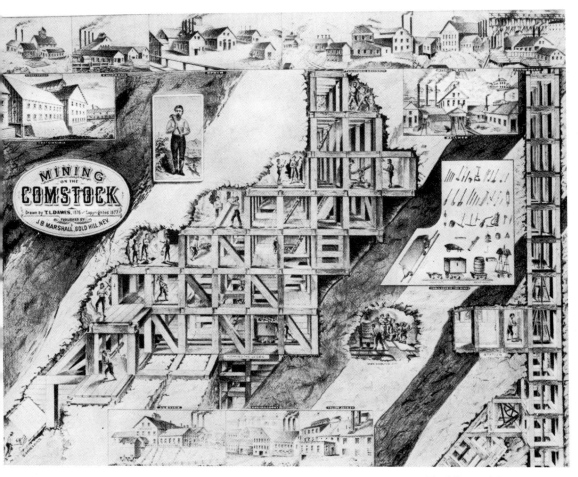

The Library of Congress
MINING ON THE COMSTOCK, 1876. Lithograph by Le Count Brothers after a drawing by T. L. Dawes.

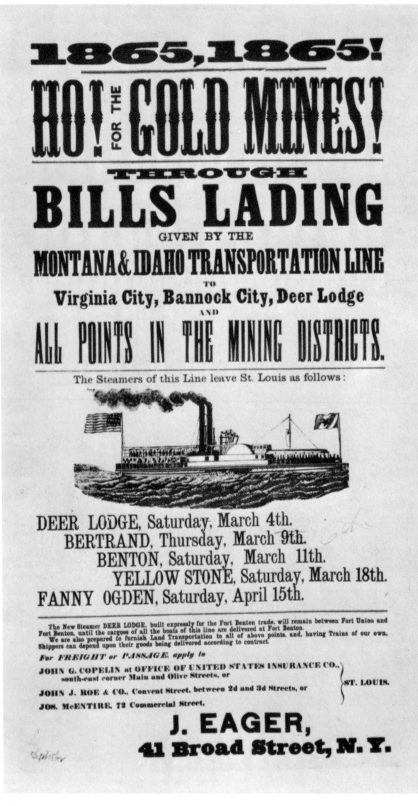

greenhorns, Jezebels, Indians, and Chinese hit the trail to each new find, some on foot, some on horseback, some in wagons. Mules and oxen dragged wagons to the mining centers with supplies of every description—"mill machinery, whiskey, provisions, whiskey, mule feed, and whiskey again," one correspondent wrote.

Where steamboats could go they carried brimming shiploads of pilgrims headed for some mining Mecca. When gold was discovered in Montana in the 1860's the upper Missouri River bore a parade of light-draft steamers, each weighted to the limit with cargo and passengers destined for the gold camps. Navigating the Missouri at low water, wrote one traveler, was like putting a steamer upon dry land and sending a boy ahead with a sprinkling pot. At best the river was "a little too thick to swim in but not quite thick enough to walk on . . . a stream of liquid brick dust." Only the decision of a jury and the state of a woman's mind were more uncertain than the condition of the Missouri, according to one editor. Against the certainty that they would strike innumerable and incalculable obstacles on each journey the hulls of ships were made to give five or six inches before cracking with the strain. Yet, in 1869, forty-two steamboats, each a floating, cosmopolitan world in itself, unloaded at Fort Benton, the extreme head of navigation, thirty to seventy days upstream from St. Louis.

The Geological Survey, Department of the Interior

THE INTERIOR OF SAWTELL'S RANCH IN IDAHO, 1874. Photograph by William H. Jackson. The noted photographer Jackson and his companions are being entertained by Sawtell and his partner, Wurtz, in their "very comfortable quarters." The two men had developed a profitable business hauling fish from Henry's Lake in the northern bulge of Idaho to Virginia City, Montana, fifty miles away.

HELENA, MONTANA, 1872. Photograph by Jackson.

Some of the richest placer-mining regions of all were discovered in Montana. Here as everywhere else the gulches were quickly worked for their readiest yield and as quickly deserted for new finds, leaving a dreary succession of abandoned huts, well-worn gallows, and the complete vacuum of an intensely busy place suddenly gone dead and quiet. Virginia City, Montana, had sprung up within a hundred yards of a profitable diggings. "In flush times," Richardson reported, "streets were thronged; stores choked with a stream of commerce; sidewalks monopolized by auctioneers hoarsely crying horses, oxen, mules, wagons and household goods. Drinking saloons, whose name was legion, were densely crowded. Theaters, which always spring up in mining regions, were closely packed. At hotels, beds were hardly obtainable for love or money. Gaming-tables were musical with clinking coin and shining with yellow gold. Hurdy-gurdy houses, where whisky sold at fifty cents a drink and champagne at twelve dollars per bottle, were filled with visitors, ranging from judges to blacklegs, in every costume, from broadcloth to buckskin. And all this, in a town less than one year old, in the heart of the Rocky Mountains, a thousand miles from everywhere!" Little boys who swept out the stores made five dollars a day in gold dust among their sweepings.

Some towns shot up out of nothing and grew with time into enduring, thriving communities, as Last Chance Gulf matured into Helena, Montana. In some, life flickered on and off with the passage of years and the shifting of circumstance; fading into oblivion as hope diminished; reviving into fitful activity as new hunches were played, new prospects discovered, or new values placed on precious metals; and waning again as times changed. Others died into ghost towns without having lived a human generation. In the West people got used to communities that boomed and boomed again, changing their populations within a lifetime, and others that boomed and busted, leaving the shells of old hopes as picturesque landmarks for the touring motorist.

The East has its dead cities too, historic sites where community life has languished or has even disappeared utterly from the face of the land. From Roanoke Island, Virginia, to Rough and Ready, California, and from Pithole Creek where oil once gushed to the last deserted settlement where government contracts briefly flourished during World Wars I and II—from one end of the country to the other patriotic and local historical societies have been obliged to raise markers identifying obscure spots abandoned by populations in quest of more promising futures. To Europeans the capricious destiny of American communities remains one of the curiosities of our history. To Americans it repeated the prevailing faith that progress was normal, that the future—most likely in some other location—always promised more than the present had yet realized.

EUREKA, COLORADO, GHOST GOLD-MINING TOWN, 1940. Photograph by Russell Lee for the Farm Security Administration.

The Library of Congress

THE LAST WEST

Miners rebounding eastward from the Pacific Coast and emigrant farmers advancing westward from the Mississippi valley caught the Plains Indians, 25,000 roving buffalo hunters, in a rapidly contracting clamp. For a score or more years after 1861, as the implacable squeeze on their homes and hunting grounds tightened, the redskins burst out periodically in wars of desperation.

The free and wild life of the open plains had to them meant security. Their liberty to lead the only kind of life they understood or wanted, their very life indeed, was threatened anew by every advance of civilization into the once boundless territory they had roamed and fought over among themselves. In 1862 six hundred and forty-four whites were massacred in Minnesota and South Dakota alone. In 1864 lines of communication between East and West were cut at every point—the overland stage and freight lines were attacked, telegraph wires torn down, trains stopped and captured, and people caught and killed.

American border troops had the triple duty of protecting white settlers from the Indians, protecting the Indians from the white settlers, and enforcing a completely anomalous international policy. Under some circumstances the frontier soldier associated with the savages, used them as scouts and allies, and even intermarried with them. But between 1865 and 1875, during the Indian Wars, hundreds of pitched battles were fought between the Army and the redmen. In 1866 near Fort Kearney a memorable massacre took place. The army had been commissioned to cut a new trail from Fort Laramie to the mines of western Montana, through the heart of the Sioux buffalo coun-

ATTACK ON AN EMIGRANT TRAIN, 1856. Painting by Wimar. Another of Wimar's reconstructions painted in Düsseldorf, this one after a description of a French chronicler of the Gold Rush.
The University of Michigan, Museum of Art

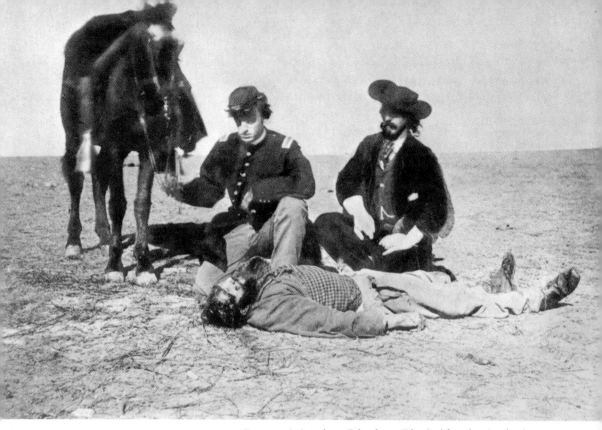

A SCALPED HUNTER (RALPH MORRISON) SLAIN BY INDIANS NEAR FORT DODGE, KANSAS, 1868. Photograph by William Stinson Soulé. Lieut. Reade, 3d Infantry, and John O. Austin, "a noted frontiersman," are the witnesses. Soulé, the photographer, was a wounded Civil War veteran of Antietam serving as a clerk at Fort Dodge. His photograph is a grim classic of the post Civil War Indian troubles.

try. Just before Christmas the wood-cutting detail of Colonel Carrington's command signaled that it was completely cut off by hostile Indians. A relief detail under Colonel Fetterman dashed out of Fort Kearney to the rescue. A few days later another relief group set out to find Fetterman, and did. "Clustered on a space less than forty feet square were the bodies of Captain Brown, Colonel Fetterman, and sixty-five of the men. . . . They were stripped naked, scalped, and so terribly gashed and mangled as to be almost unrecognizable. Years afterwards the Sioux showed a rough, knotty war-club of burr-oak, driven full of nails and spikes, which had been used to beat their brains out."

Such tales made lurid reading for Easterners. The Plains Indian was every inch a barbarian, a barbarian goaded to frenzy by the remorseless onward push of the whites. If he was in a good humor and unhurried he was the master of exquisite tortures. The goriest literature of the nineteenth century came from the pens of plainsmen and Indian campaigners who had seen white men roasted by bits, delicately skinned alive, and in other more ingenious ways brought to lingering, excruciating deaths.

Between 1784, when Congress first negotiated with the Indians at Fort Stanwix, and 1871, three hundred and seventy other treaties had been signed in a hopeless effort to ensure the white man's getting what he wanted without retribution from the red. But the Indians had no comprehension of the full meaning of a treaty and no social institution by which to enforce one—nor did the whites have any adequate laws to make the negotiated agreements effective. Any alleged breach of contract or petty misdemeanor of the Indians was punishable by

273

American troops who revenged any and all alike with a heavy hand. In 1868, two years after the Fetterman massacre, Major General George A. Custer, heading a punitive expedition against Black Kettle, whose record was as black as his name but who claimed to want peace, wiped out the Indians' village and killed without discrimination braves, women, and children—thousands all told.

It was grim poetic justice that General Custer was the tragic hero of the most dramatic Indian conflict of all. An army expedition under his command, sent to investigate conditions on the Sioux reservation in the Black Hills during the summer of 1874, had helped to advertise a fresh gold strike in that area of Dakota. Following a familiar pattern, prospectors converged from all points of the compass to try their luck. Neither the fact that the land was reserved by solemn treaty for the Indians, nor the fact that United States troops were sent to halt their inroads, could hold back the flood of eager fortune hunters.

Before this fresh encroachment into lands they were to have and to hold "as long as water runs and grass grows," the legal title

The National Archives
GENERAL GEORGE A. CUSTER. Photograph by Mathew Brady. Whether Custer disobeyed orders at the Battle of the Little Big Horn, whether he made a desperate attempt to regain prestige, or whether he was simply the tragic victim of unforeseen circumstances, will probably always be lovingly and heatedly debated by every student of the West.

THE BLACK HILLS EXPEDITION UNDER GENERAL CUSTER ON THE PLAINS, 1876. Photograph by W. H. Illingsworth.
The National Archives

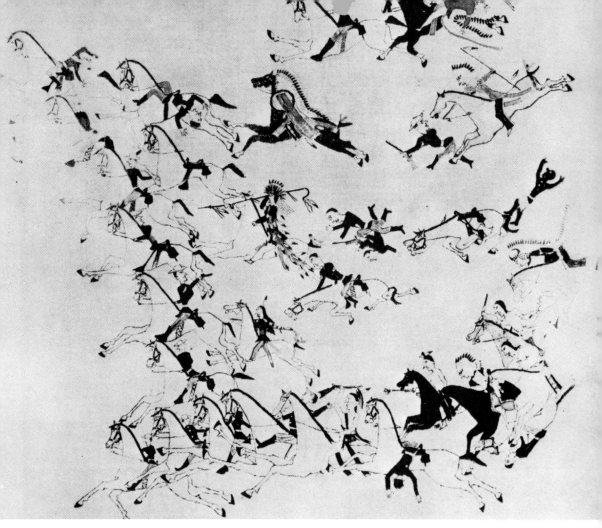

AN INDIAN VERSION OF RENO'S RETREAT. Pictograph by White Bird, painted about 1894–95.

holders scattered in hostile bands and far overran their treaty lands. The army was dispatched to bring them back to their designated reservations. On May 17, 1876, Custer went back into the hills in command of one claw of a pincer movement against the Sioux. With the regimental band playing "The Girl I Left Behind Me" and "Garry Owen" a two-mile column of cavalry, infantry, scouts, and artillery left Fort Abraham Lincoln.

Custer had distinguished himself in the Civil War, as well as on the Plains. Although not entirely trustworthy when operating independently, he had a reputation for victory that recommended him for the job.

Awaiting him in ambush were more In-dians than probably had ever been brought together for a single battle, Indians sore to the point of fury at being pushed around by the faithless opportunism of white policy. Custer and his troops were last seen alive by Major Reno's flanking command as they passed over a bluff towards the historic bat-tlefield.

Two weeks later the *Daily Press and Da-kotaian* reported the bloody Battle of the Little Big Horn, one of the few battles in American history in which an American force was completely annihilated. Major Reno later testified that in his area "the very earth seemed to grow Indians, and they were running towards me in swarms, and from all directions." There were too many of

TELEGRAPHIC.
4 O'clock, a. m.

DEATH.

Custer and His Entire Command Swept Out of Existence.

By the Wards of the Nation and the Special Pets of Eastern Orators.

A List of the Officers Killed in the Fight.

The Seventh Cavalry Completely Surrounded and Litterly Annihilated.

Reno Cuts His Way Out With a Loss of 100 Men.

CONFIRMATION.

CHICAGO, July 6—News confirmatory of Custer's fight with the Indians on the Little Horn has been received at General Sheridan's headquarters.

THE FEELING AT WASHINGTON.

WASHINGTON, July 6—The news of the death of General Custer and the terrible disaster reported from the west creates a profound senation here, particularly in army circles. Up to noon there has been no official advices received at the war department. Secretary Cameron and General Sherman and Lieutenant General Sheridan are now in Philadelphia. A number of persons anxious as to the fate of friends in the Indian country have visited the war department to day.

AT CUSTER'S HOME.

TOLEDO, July 6—A special to the Blade from Monroe, Michigan. the home of Gen. Custer, says the startling news of the massacre of General Custer and his family by Indians has created the most intense feeling of sorrow among all classes. Gener-

Yankton Carnegie Library

REPORT IN THE *Daily Press and Dakotaian*, July 7, 1876.

them, certainly, to enable him to look for Custer, and Custer was beyond help at that point anyway.

General George Crook who commanded another force in the over-all strategy had already suffered the only major defeat of his long military career at the Battle of the Rosebud a few days earlier. The whole wide area was alive with Indians that harassed white troops to a point where effective liaison between the separate army commands was impossible. Savages, armed with modern repeating rifles, outnumbered the army troops at least three to one.

Immediately after Custer's death Crook set off in pursuit of the recalcitrant Indians.

His command started with a minimum of clothing and supplies, intent on a rapid march. The redmen seemed always just beyond the next horizon and the futile chase continued day after unexpected day. Buffalo Bill Cody, guide for the march, had to leave his assignment and rush east to fill theatrical engagements. Finally Crook himself had to turn about and start a desperate march back to his base of supplies. Half his beasts died of exhaustion, others were killed to feed starving soldiers. The ragged troops barely managed to cross the gumbo of the Bad Lands during a ten-day rain. That "Starvation March" was one of the grimmest forced marches in Army history.

276

LOADING A PACK MULE WITH FLOUR ON GENERAL CROOK'S EXPEDITION TO THE BLACK HILLS, THE "STARVATION MARCH" OF 1876. Photograph by S. J. Morrow.

A SOLDIER SHOOTING AN ABANDONED HORSE FOR FOOD DURING THE RETURN OF GENERAL CROOK'S EXPEDITION, 1876. Photograph by S. J. Morrow.

The Library of Congress
MARTHA JANE CANARY BURKE, BETTER KNOWN AS
"CALAMITY JANE." This represents one of the three
women whose photos have been labeled Calamity
Jane, probably Mrs. Burke herself.

For another ten or fifteen years the Indians continued a sporadic resistance to white intrusions. But, as was earlier pointed out, the natives were being despoiled of their ancestral lands by irresistible forces; there was no country on earth to which they could migrate; they had no recognized claims upon the government; and they were compelled to steal or to starve until they were subdued.

The Custer massacre and the subsequent army campaigns had attracted increased attention to the undeveloped lands of the West. Miners poured into the Black Hills region in the long-familiar, intemperate scramble for wealth. The road from Cheyenne on the Union Pacific to Deadwood, Dakota Territory, became in short order one of the most celebrated routes in our highway history, as fortune seekers and colorful characters, good and bad, flocked to the mines. Wild Bill Hickock, Calamity Jane, and Buffalo Bill were only a few of the passengers, famous and infamous, who rode the Deadwood stage.

Continuing to police both the reds and the whites the United States Army stayed

THE UNITED STATES PAYMASTER AND GUARDS ON THE DEADWOOD ROAD TO FORT MEADE, 1888. Photograph by J. C. H. Grabill. Other photographs of the early West by Grabill are reproduced in a subsequent chapter.
The Library of Congress

The Library of Congress

"GENERAL MILES AND STAFF VIEWING THE LARGEST HOSTILE INDIAN CAMP IN THE UNITED STATES, NEAR PINE RIDGE, S. DAK., JAN. 16, 1891." Photograph by Grabill. The Wounded Knee Trouble had been settled the month before.

in the field until ordinary civilian agencies were adequately established. But the Indian wars were about over. One of the last unhappy incidents in the long struggle took place at Wounded Knee Creek, in December, 1890. Excited by the anticipated coming of a red Messiah the Sioux Indians frightened the frontier into calling for additional troops. An overwhelming force under General Nelson A. Miles settled the issue by virtually slaughtering the natives in a brief, pitiless, and probably unnecessary struggle. The survivors were rounded up in the Pine Ridge Agency and the Wild West, tamed at home, went on tour. When Colonel William F. Cody took his celebrated Wild West show to England it was the Prince of Wales's special pleasure to ride around the arena sitting on the box of the Deadwood Coach.

Chief Joseph of the Nez Percés summarized the tragedy of his race when he said: "I am tired of fighting. Our chiefs are killed. Looking-Glass is dead. Too-hut-hut-sote is dead. The old men are all dead. It is the young men now who say 'yes' or 'no.' He who led the young men is dead. It is cold and we have no blankets. The little children are freezing to death. My people, some of them, have run away to the hills and have no blankets, no food. No one knows where they are, perhaps freezing to death. I want to have time to look for my children and see how many of them I can find. Maybe I can find them among the dead. Hear me, my chiefs. My heart is sick and sad. I am tired."

The Library of Congress

EPILOGUE OF THE WILD WEST, 1899. Courier Litho. Co.

Long before the anticlimax at Wounded Knee Creek the Indian's future had been settled by the virtual extermination of the buffalo. Lacking buffalo, the Plains Indian was without the means of his traditional life—without food, fuel, shelter, clothing, and a dozen other essentials. He could settle down to farming on the fixed acreage prescribed by the Dawes Act of 1887. He could learn the white man's ways and become a fellow citizen, or go on a dole. But his life as a roving hunter was over. The free, nomadic Indian bowed off the scene with the buffalo.

When he was surveying the North Carolina–Virginia boundary in 1729 the urbane squire of Westover, Colonel William Byrd, had run across buffalo in the eastern piedmont. They were but a trifling overflow from the stupendous herds that crowded the western plains, single herds that may once have run as high as twelve million animals. The world probably never knew a quadruped that bred in such astronomical numbers. When the first white men ventured out into the sunny grasslands of the West they sometimes saw buffalo packed solidly as far as the eye could reach, mile after mile to the distant horizon. Killing them off became a major international sport, widely advertised. European royalty came to the West to shoot shoulder to shoulder with grizzled

The New-York Historical Society, Bella C. Landauer Collection

HELD UP BY BUFFALO. Painting by Newbold Hough Trotter.

frontiersmen and common emigrants. Buffalo Bill helped to arrange a great buffalo chase to amuse the Grand Duke Alexis when he traveled across the Plains with his entourage in 1871–72. To kill 120 in forty minutes or 6000 in sixty days was a record the buffalo hunter could celebrate. Between 1871 and 1874 almost four million buffalo were slain. There never was such wholesale slaughter. By 1876 not many of the early herds were left for targets.

For a time, and while the supply lasted, buffalo robes were the rage in the East. No fashionable cutter or carriage was without one. The hides, it was also discovered, made excellent machinery belts. But the waste in providing them for the market, particularly the waste of meat, was prodigal. The prairies were left littered with skinned and rotting carcasses. "Where there were myriads of buffalo the year before," reported one observer, "there were now myriads of carcasses. The air was foul with sickening stench, and the vast plain, which only a short twelvemonth before teemed with animal life, is a dead, solitary, putrid desert." At Dodge City, Kansas, a large industry grew up in the bone trade as a by-product of the slaughter. Hundreds of tons of bones lay piled in great, white stacks beside the railroad tracks. There were not enough freight cars to carry them away to market. The buffalo was following the beaver toward virtual annihilation.

The New York Public Library
CURING BUFFALO HIDES AND COLLECTING BONES. After a drawing by Frenzeny and Tavernier. Possibly at Dodge City, Kansas, 1873. From *Harper's Weekly.*

281

The Wyoming Stock Growers Association Archives

GENERAL SPRING ROUND-UP, HORSE CREEK, WYOMING, 1885. Photograph by Kirkland (?).

CONSTRUCTION CAMP OF THE CENTRAL PACIFIC RAILROAD IN UTAH, APRIL, 1869. Photograph courtesy of the Association of American Railroads.

The Southern Pacific Company

The Library of Congress
A CATTLE SHOOT ON THE KANSAS-PACIFIC RAILWAY AT ABILENE, KANSAS, 1871. From *Leslie's Weekly*.

No land that had comfortably supported millions of herbiverous bison could remain on the maps of the country as the Great American Desert. Before the slaughter of either those animals or the Indians was finished, the area that Major Long had broadly described as a wasteland was threaded with long trails of Texas cattle grazing their way towards eastern markets. In 1871 more than 600,000 cattle crossed the Red River headed north. Within a decade after the Civil War herds numbering in the millions were filling in the gaps left by the vanishing buffalo, spreading out over almost one quarter of the total area of the United States.

The objectives of the early cattle drives were the spearheads which the railroads were pushing across the country in the late 1860's. The primary aim of the transcontinental railroad had been to unite West and East by a secure and rapid means of communication across the intervening wasteland. Jefferson Davis looked upon such a project as "a herculean undertaking. I believe," he added, "that that country between the Mississippi and the Pacific, which has been well denominated the desert, is to remain so." It *was* a herculean undertaking, an epic achievement that the mythical giants of antiquity might well have envied. But for the rest Davis was a bad prophet. As the tracks leaped ahead in the late 1860's and in 1870, as fast as two, three, and more miles a day, thousands of well-fed longhorns gathered from the desert and from the northern grasslands to await transportation. At every shipping point — at Abilene, Dodge City, Newton, and elsewhere along the stretching rails—shanty towns sprang up to handle a business that grew to enormous proportions. And at every "cow-town" the shaggy, trailweary cowboy found wide-open house.

The Association of American Railroads

A PHOTOGRAPH OF UNDETERMINED ORIGIN. Probably dating from the 1870's.

THE CHEESE CREEK RANCH, 1864. Photograph by S. D. Butcher (?). A road ranch on the Oregon Trail.

The Nebraska State Historical Society

Across the open range the flow of emigrants from the East never slackened. It had continued unabated during the Civil War when at least 300,000 persons crossed the Plains. Below Council Bluffs, wrote Jonathan Blanchard in 1864, "long wings of white canvas stretch away on either side. . . . Myriads of horses and mules drag on the moving mass of humanity toward the setting sun." At Omaha, the year before, a train of 900 wagons was spotted and one traveler on the Kansas route counted over 8000 in a little more than a week.

The character of the long wagon trains was changing. Horses and mules were more often in the traces than oxen. It was less necessary to transport large stores of supplies. Provisioning posts of a sort were increasingly frequent along the trail. These road ranches did a thriving business supplying westbound travelers with food, shelter, and occasional entertainment. On his return trip across the Plains in 1859 Richardson awakened one ranch owner from his sleep between two whisky barrels to learn that he had for sale, beside whisky and tobacco, only pickled oysters and sardines. At the next road ranch, however, the traveler dined admirably upon a snowy tablecloth.

Some of the emigrant horde were headed for gold and silver mines in the farther mountains, others for the distant coast. Still others, in growing numbers, were reaching for the free lands made available by the Homestead Act of 1862, gradually pushing a solid frontier of civilization into the Prairie Plains and tentatively cutting their plowshares into the very heart of the Great Desert. In 1872, within a single year, one pioneer Nebraska settler saw the naked prairie near his homestead transformed into farmlands stippled with houses. With every onward thrust the dogged, pedestrian "nestor" was closing in on the open range of the hard-riding cowboy, forcing the old, familiar issue between the desert and the sown to its inevitable conclusion and putting the American frontier forever behind fences.

EMIGRANTS MOVING INTO LOUP VALLEY, NEBRASKA, 1886. Photograph by Butcher.
The Nebraska State Historical Society

The Baker Library, Harvard University
A LAND AD' OF THE UNION PACIFIC, 1867.

The farming West found its most importunate promoter in the railroad companies. To speed work on the first transcontinental line Congress had lent huge sums of money and granted enormous areas of land to the Union and Central Pacific Companies. A mad rush by other groups for similar favors followed. Spasms of "railmania" gripped the country, lacing it with railroads it wasn't ready for as well as those it sorely needed. The public was burdened with speculative organizations that sank or swam in their own watered stock, according to their luck. By 1871 an area three times as large as New England had been given to railroads by government grant, well over one and a half hundred million acres, far more than would ever be needed for rights of way.

With such huge tracts to dispose of, and with the prospect of further profits from hauling farm products back to the East, the western roads advertised their holdings on an international scale. In New York, Liverpool, and Berdiansk, in Canada, Germany, and Iceland, the old story of the fabulous West—"a fruitful champayne country of pleasant meadows," as the earlier Jesuits had described it—was told in up-to-date fashion. The way to rich lands with easy payments, to opportunity and freedom, was paved with steel rails. Everything from free lunches to free transportation was at one time or another offered as an inducement to entrain for the land of plenty. In the American railroad companies the British colonial trading companies had their nineteenth-century counterparts as great colonizing agents of the New World.

In Europe railroad agents built expectations higher than William Penn had ever done, and they tapped a wider audience with their propaganda. Western stations became meeting places and points of parting for an unheard of variety of peoples—emigrants from Europe, Orientals, wandering Easterners, redmen, hunters from the vanishing frontier, and settlers from everywhere. For that very reason, according to Lord Bryce and others, the West was the most American part of America—the part where the newcomer, whatever his origin, was most quickly swept into the common whirlpool of expectant, hurried activity. The sight of such congregations about the Omaha station in 1868 moved one progressive Kansan to propose the immediate removal of the national capital to that city. It was not only close to the geographical center of the United States but it looked like the crossroads of the wide world in motion. The prairie schooner lingered on, but to the aspiring emigrants peering out the windows of "the modern ship of the plains," hurtling along at twenty miles or more an hour over the smooth rails, it might have been, and sometimes was, mistaken for a traveling circus.

A SCENE AT OMAHA, 1868. From *Leslie's Weekly*.

THE MODERN SHIP OF THE PLAINS, 1886. After a drawing by R. T. Zogbaum. From *Harper's Weekly*.

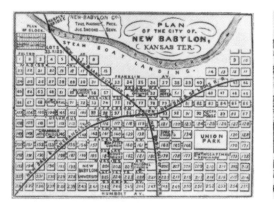 

THE CITY OF NEW BABYLON ON PAPER AND IN FACT. After drawings by A. C. Warren. From Alfred D. Richardson, *Beyond the Mississippi*, 1867.

A long line of celebrated boosters and speculators had "sold" America to the world over a course of three centuries. Richard Hakluyt, John Smith, William Penn, Benjamin Franklin, and George Washington were only a few of the leading spirits of each generation who, from the first days of colonization, advertised their faith in the western country. Just where faith gave way to speculation, and public policy to private interest, would be hard to say. American history could be told in terms of a gigantic, continuous real-estate boom in which the successful operators were often men high in the councils of the nation, men whose expansionist fervor closely paralleled their expectations of personal profit.

In any case the optimism and overstatement needed to attract settlers to an unknown wilderness in the seventeenth century had, by the nineteenth, become a fixed habit with Americans. Every new settlement in the West was located squarely in the center of "God's Country," or would be when and if it was built. "On paper," said Richardson, "*all* these towns are magnificent. Their superbly lithographed maps adorned the walls of every place of resort. The stranger studying one of these fancied the New Babylon surpassed only by its namesake of old. Its great parks, opera houses, churches, universities, railway depots and steamboat landings

made New York and St. Louis insignificant in comparison. . . . It was not a swindle, but a mania. The speculators were quite as insane as the rest." The whole country seemed constantly to be trading in futures. When one bubble burst someone blew another and crowds chased it.

Not every bubble burst by any means. Towns sprang up like magic, fattening on the produce of the surrounding prairies. The farmlands were almost as rich as the tallest tale had suggested. In western Missouri, it was said, cornstalks were used as telegraph poles, or power-sawed into cordwood lengths for winter firewood. When Nebraska pumpkins were bruised by the speed with which the growing vines pulled them over the ground, they were eased along on little wheeled trucks. Probably no one has yet measured the tallest tale told about the size of the potatoes grown in Idaho, let alone taken the dimensions of the larger examples. This whole inland empire, as one Irish immigrant very solemnly put it, had been "scooped out by the Omnipotence with wonderful adaptation to the wants of man."

The prairie farmer, often born in a static European hamlet, became a titanic figure in the world at large, replacing the hunter, the miner, and the pioneer in the rôle of the hero of the West. Within fifteen years of the Custer massacre enormous trains of agricultural machinery were clanking over the Dakota prairies, reaping a harvest that seriously modified the economy not only of America, but of a large part of Europe. With meat from the cattle range and cereal from the tilled lands, America had become by far the world's greatest single source of cheap food.

This was no tall tale but a matter of simple, statistical truth. Between 1860 and 1900 over 400,000,000 acres were added to the farming area of America, most of it in land beyond the Mississippi. This fertile basin was, as Lincoln claimed during the Civil War, the Egypt of the West, an incalculably rich granary that had then been barely tapped. In the years that followed, the immense flow of American produce upset the habits of Europe as completely as the importation of American gold and silver had done during the days of the *conquistadores.* Nothing that happened with such explosive

The Library of Congress
THE PRAIRIE FARMER, 1869. The Chicago Lithographing Co. "Engraved especially for the Patrons of the *Prairie Farmer."*

The Library of Congress
WHEAT HARVESTING IN DAKOTA, 1887. After a drawing by R. T. Zogbaum. From *Harper's Weekly.*

289

suddenness as the filling-up of the American West could properly be called a westward *movement*. Contrasted to the pace of earlier historic migrations this rapid appropriation of a new land seemed like an instantaneous operation. The driving restlessness of people was brought to a crescendo by the railroad, the harvester, the telegraph, and other mechanical aids that killed time and space with new efficiency. But the primary human bent was to do in a brief lifetime, by any means possible, what Europeans had been content to accomplish over centuries of time. From the East it looked like a frantic disorganized flight after the Golden Opportunity. In 1889 when the government threw open to homesteaders a large, fertile area in Oklahoma, "the beautiful land" of the Indians who had sold out under pressure, the whole drama of the westward movement was summarized in a few intense hours. Land-hungry whites had been eyeing that vacant corner of the West for years. The signal to enter the promised land was to be given at high noon on the twenty-second of April. Soldiers held back the twenty thousand boomers who toed the line, a shouting, milling, fighting horde, more like a herd of penned-up beasts than humankind, until the last second of the morning had ticked off the clock. When the signal was seen—it was not heard; sight was faster than hearing and every fraction of time was an eternity—the cloud of dust that rose from the stampede across the line was like a flood pouring over a broken dam. When it settled it covered the last clear traces of the frontier. The unique American experiment of colonizing and consolidating a continental empire was all but complete. Within little more than a score of years the remaining territories were organized into states of the Union "on an equal footing with the original states, in all respects whatever."

THE RUN, CHEROKEE STRIP, APRIL 22, 1889   *The Oklahoma Historical Society*

In the summer of 1896 a roving miner found signs of rich gold deposits near Klondike Creek in Yukon, Canadian Alaska, almost within the Arctic Circle. Ten months later the S.S. *Excelsior* and the S.S. *Portland* arrived at San Francisco and Portland, respectively, with more than a half-million dollars in gold dust from those remote diggings. That news in itself, together with the best advertising efforts of railroads, steamship companies, and chambers of commerce, was enough to induce another stormy bout of gold fever in America. New strikes were made along the Yukon River and elsewhere in American territory. During the next few years several hundred thousand Argonauts set off to the new frontier of the North. Not more than a fraction of that number reached the forbidding interior.

The Chilcoot Pass was the "easier" of two alternative routes through the mountains to the Klondike and for several years gold hunters streamed through it to the mining districts. It was a precipitous, zigzag trough of glistening ice and snow ascending over 3550 feet through a jumble of ice peaks. Yet, wrote one ninety-eighter, "frequently every step would be full while crowds jostled each other at the foot of the ascent to get into single file, each man carrying from one hundred to two hundred pounds on his back. . . . I reached Dawson with nine tons of my outfit and sold my first potatoes at $36 a bushel."

The frozen wastes claimed a full share of wrecked hopes and lives as they reluctantly delivered up in the next few years $140,000,-000 worth of precious metals. Together with the wealth of gold discovered in South African fields at the same time, the Alaskan yield replenished the world's stock of gold just at the moment when that seemed vitally necessary for its financial health. The Klondike bubble burst, but "Seward's Folly," 586,400 square miles of territory, held still uncounted riches in fish, furs, timber, coal, and produce. According to the air maps of a half-century later that frontier of dog sleds and tundra had been moved to the strategic center of global travel.

The Library of Congress
WOMEN PROSPECTORS ON THE WAY TO THE KLONDIKE, OCTOBER 31, 1898.

BOUND FOR THE KLONDIKE, CHILCOOT PASS, ALASKA, JULY, 1898.

The Library of Congress

THE ROCKY MOUNTAINS. Painting by Albert Bierstadt, 1863.

The census of 1890 reported that the earlier unsettled areas of the country had been so broken into by isolated bodies of settlement that a line for the frontier could no longer be traced on the map. The line that had been drawn and redrawn so dramatically and so repeatedly across American history from Jamestown on, had finally disintegrated into a jumble of small, vanishing circles.

Yet, from census to census during the decades that followed, America's center of population continued to move westward. The West remained the stage for ancient dreams, a land of wonders that were magnified and multiplied when seen through the windows of sedate eastern parlors.

"Every sunset which I witness," wrote Thoreau in the name of a multitude of wondering Easterners, "inspires me with the desire to go to a West as distant and as fair as that into which the sun goes down. He appears to migrate westward daily, and tempt us to follow him. He is the Great Western Pioneer whom the nations follow. We dream all night of those mountain-ridges in the horizon, though they may be of vapor only, which were last gilded by his rays. The island of Atlantis, and the islands and gardens of the Hesperides, a sort of terrestrial paradise, appear to have been the Great West of the ancients, enveloped in mystery and poetry. Who has not seen in imagination, when looking into the sunset sky, the gardens of the Hesperides, and the foundation of all those fables?"

GIANT REDWOOD TREES OF CALIFORNIA. Painting by Bierstadt.

III
SQUARE RIGGER
EMPIRE

SQUARE RIGGER EMPIRE

INTRODUCTION

AMERICA was born of the sea and spent a great part of its youthful energies on deep water. In a day of tiny vessels even villages far upstream, farming communities, had access to the ocean. They had to have. The few roads that cut through the wilderness were never better than adequate, usually far worse. Even after turnpikes and railroads were easing overland travel and transportation, fresh eggs were for a time still delivered to the Providence market by a sailing sloop. The old and agreeable habit of using water routes for trade and travel died hard. But in the beginning, communities that had been conceived as plantations turned to seafaring out of stark necessity. Like fish, the early colonists would have died if removed from the water. Ocean lanes were life lines and every beginning settlement clung to the water's edge with grim purpose.

Between going to sea in order to live and living in order to go to sea was a short step quickly taken. Wealth and adventure, as well as salvation, could be found offshore—and a welcome freedom from landsmen's conventions, which was salvation in itself for some. "The inclination the youth have . . . to the sea," observed Governor Cranston of Rhode Island in 1700, "[leads] the greater part to betake themselves to that imployment." So long as almost every village was

a seaport few lads could escape the thought of a sailor's life. They acquired a taste for salt water with their mother's milk. Before the Pilgrim Century was out America's course as a maritime nation was set. For New Englanders, at least, the land became "only a shelter from the storm, a perch on which they build their eyrie and hide their young, while they skim the surface and hunt the deep."

By the time the colonies struck for independence American sails and American seamen were freighting miscellaneous cargoes all about the Atlantic and Mediterranean world. The country had become a great nursery of seamen and the interminable forests provided ships to carry them all and more beside. By 1776 not only was three-quarters of the country's commerce carried in colonial bottoms, but a good third of the British merchant marine was colonial built. "The northern colonies have nearly beaten us out of the Newfoundland fisheries," complained one English author just before the Revolution, ". . . the share of New England alone exceeds that of Britain . . . the trading part of the colonies robs this nation [England] of the invaluable treasure of 30,000 seamen, and all the profits of their employment; or in other words, the northern colonies, who contribute nothing either to our riches or our power, deprive us of more than twice the amount of all the navigation we enjoy in consequence of the sugar islands, the southern, continental, and tobacco settlements!"

War put a stop to that. Most of the American fleet was beached or captured during the Revolution. But with peace and the lifting of the British blockade the new nation returned to the sea by a strong reflex action. During the next twenty years the growth of American shipping in all its forms was extraordinary. This people who were, as Edmund Burke described them to Parliament, "still . . . but in the gristle and not yet hardened into the bone of manhood," performed prodigies everywhere the sea would carry their little craft. "Whilst we follow them among the tumbling mountains of ice," said Burke, "and behold them penetrating into the deepest frozen recesses of Hudson's Bay, and Davis Strait, whilst we look for them beneath the Arctic circle we hear that they have pierced into the opposite region of polar colds, that they are at the Antipodes, and engaging under the frozen serpents of the South. . . . Nor is the equinoctial heat more discouraging to them than the accumulated winter of both the poles. . . . No sea but what is vexed by their fisheries. No climate that is not witness to their toils. Neither the perseverance of Holland nor the dexterous and firm sagacity of English enterprise, ever carried this most perilous mode of hardy industry to the extent to which it has been pursued by these recent people."

Burke was referring specifically to the whalemen, most of them at the time from that "mere hillock," that little "elbow of sand" in the Atlantic, as Melville called Nantucket. But without tempering his words he might have gone on to describe the myriad trading ships that were swarming out of every American seaport to markets around the globe in search of economic independence, and fortune beyond that. In 1791 more than seventy ships sailed from Boston alone in one day. They were not all bound for foreign markets by any means, but there were few ports on earth, from then until the Civil War, where the Yankee seatrader was

not a familiar figure. In those years, before the West put in its counterappeal, the sea attracted the pick of American manhood. Cosmopolitan they were, these seafarers, in the richest sense of the term—equally at home fighting a howling gale off Cape Horn, coping with barbarians in any uncharted wilderness that promised likely cargoes, or exchanging elaborate civilities with the ranking mandarins of ancient Canton. Not all who went to sea were so resourceful and accomplished, but among them were the merchant princes of the rising generation.

Cotton Mather had once remarked that the youth of New England were "verie Sharp and early Ripe in their Capacities." He could have wanted no better witness than the teen-age skippers and crews who followed the sea to find and better their fortunes—boys like the three Silsbee brothers of Massachusetts, each of whom commanded vessels and the consignment of their freight before they were twenty. At any age those early shipmasters drove an extraordinary trade peddling codfish and rum, it might be, for elephants' teeth and chintz, shifting their course and their cargo at their own discretion with every fresh trading possibility, pyramiding the profits of a single, meandering voyage by constant swapping, selling their very ships from under them if the bargain was right, sometimes losing everything at a single turn of fortune, and withal, living a latter-day Odyssey of fabulous variety.

"Lord" Timothy Dexter of Newburyport —he who according to his legends successfully sold warming pans in Bermuda, coal in Newcastle, and cats in Malta, was the archetype of the ingenious and intrepid Yankee trader. But the simple record outdoes any fable. Sleighing across the winter snows of Russia to tap the inland markets (ninety American vessels arrived at St. Petersburg in 1803), gathering sandalwood—incense for "heathen idols"—in the South Seas, or trading beads and bells for sleek pelts with barbarians along the northwest coast of our own continent was all part of an endlessly varied saga of real accomplishment. Thoreau enjoyed rich reflections on the theme as he watched Irish laborers near his hut at Walden cutting ice that would be peddled all around the earth, from New Orleans to Calcutta, wherever shrewd merchandising could create a market for such unheard-of hot-weather luxuries. Thus, he wrote, "the pure Walden water is mingled with the sacred waters of the Ganges. With favoring winds it is wafted past the site of the fabulous islands of Atlantis and the Hesperides, makes the periplus of Hanno, and, floating by Ternate and Tidore and the mouth of the Persian Gulf, melts in the tropic gales of the Indian seas, and is landed in ports of which Alexander only heard the names."

To such epic seafaring the War of 1812 called a temporary halt. Once again a British blockade beached the American merchant marine. But with the peace, American ships thronged back onto the seven seas in greater numbers than ever. Better ships, too. The packet lines took over the cream of the Atlantic trade from all comers by the regular, repeated, and unrivaled superiority of their performances. Fair weather or foul, wind high, wind low, these full-bodied vessels, relentlessly driven by hand-picked masters, challenged every menace and uncertainty of the Atlantic passage to keep on schedule—or do better. Every record was hailed as a national triumph. In 1824 Captain Fox kept the lee rail of the *Emerald* buried for seventeen consecutive days to make a record westward passage from Liverpool to Boston.

Ralph Waldo Emerson crossed in the *Emerald* in 1833. "The sea to us is but a lasting storm," he complained in his Journal. "My sides are sore with rolling in my berth. . . . We have torn a sail and lost a hencoop and its inmates, but the bulwarks are firm. Captain Fox, who went in 14 days from Liverpool to Boston, slept in the cable tier to keep the mate from taking in sail." In repetition, the story of the *Emerald's* earlier fast crossing had dropped three days, but such yarns fed the excitement.

With the evolution of the incredibly fleet clipper ships in mid-century, America climaxed its glory on the seas. In the China tea trade and the California gold rush the stakes were huge, the race was to the swift, and the clippers took over. Nothing had ever sailed so fast before—nor has it since. The log of the *Flying Cloud* off Valparaiso on its maiden voyage in 1851 laconically reports on July 31: "Latter part high sea running ship very wet, fore and aft. Distance run this day by observation 374 miles, an average of 15 7/12 knots . . . during the squalls 18 knots of line was not sufficient to measure her . . . speed!" Faster runs were as casually recorded.

With its "bows turned inside out," its mainmast reaching as high as 200 feet above the water line, its slender, graceful hull, and its enormous capacity for speed, the clipper won an enduring hold on American imagination. Unfortunately romance and royalties did not mix. While they were still creating legends the clippers were losing money. In the tremendous enthusiasm they excited more were built than the trade could support. Steam-powered iron hulls were stolidly and ploddingly taking over the old dominion of wooden ships. Pardonable but stubborn pride in its superb "canvas-backs" left America blind to new opportunities and necessities and, from 1860 on, the nation relinquished its prestige on the high seas.

Over the years the sea had lost much of its whilom enchantment for American youth. Man and boy, the early seamen had been drawn from the most enterprising, the most capable, and the most adventurous part of the country's population. They were men of discernment and reflection as well as men of action. From the corners of the earth they brought back, along with freight and the "curiosities" with which they embellished their homes and local museums, intellectual cargoes and a vision of the world that shaped the thought and tradition of their country in no small way. With time the lure of the West outgrew the lure of the waves, and the lure of the city outgrew both. As its magnificent fleets faded from the seas, America turned in upon itself for generations to come.

SHIPBUILDING, LATE 18TH—EARLY 19TH CENTURY. Transfer-printed design from an English (Liverpool) pottery bowl.

RETURN TO THE SEA

American shipping all but disappeared from the seas during the Revolutionary War. For a time during the conflict the country's maritime resources were largely diverted to privateering, with some spectacular consequences. During the years Washington was having such serious trouble defending the homeland, "rebel" ships, the London *Spectator* bitterly complained, were brazenly cruising along the English coasts, even in sight of the island's garrisons, picking off choice prizes "to the great terror of our merchants and shipowners." There were few more heroic actions in the war than the exploits of Captain Jonathan Haraden in his letter-of-marque ship *General Pickering* out of Salem. On his way to Bilbao, heavily laden with a cargo of sugar, he first beat off a British privateer of twenty guns; next— by sheer bluff—captured another one, also larger than his own ship; and then put to rout still another enemy craft three times larger and more heavily armed than the *General Pickering*. Later, in the same vessel, he captured three armed British merchantmen in one action by the simple expedient of "going alongside of each of them, one after the other."

However, when the full force of the British fleet was brought to bear, privateering rapidly lost its profits, and America most of its ships that were not sealed in port. For a nation that had been a breeding ground for seamen, whose forests had subsidized a booming shipbuilding industry, and whose most vital commerce had been over the ocean lanes, the last cruel blow came in 1783 with the English Orders in Council, designed specifically to stifle the American merchant marine.

But the sea ways still offered the main road to recovery from the war and towards economic independence. Timber was everywhere and skilled shipbuilders to work it shipshape. New fleets could be built and, with once familiar ports closed, new avenues of trade must be found.

On Washington's Birthday, 1784, barely

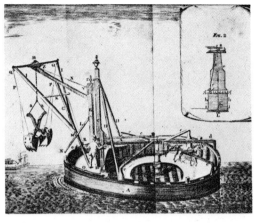

The Metropolitan Museum of Art

"A New Invented Machine for Deepening and Cleansing Docks." Engraving from the *American Magazine*, January, 1788. The gradual increase in the size of vessels made deeper anchorages, safer harbors, and larger docks a matter of vital concern to port authorities and merchants wherever the bigger ships concentrated.

The New York Public Library

The Philadelphia Waterfront in 1799. Engraving by William Birch & Son. The Arch Street Ferry is shown in the foreground.

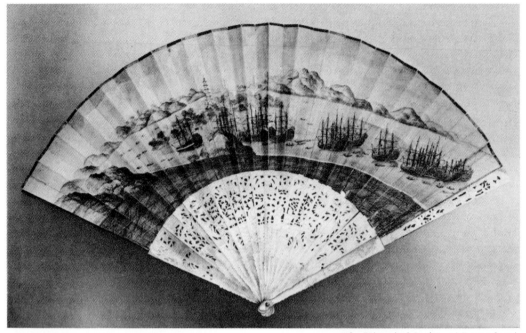

The Historical Society of Pennsylvania

THE *Empress of China* AT THE WHAMPOA ANCHORAGE IN CHINA, 1784. Painting on a Chinese fan. The only known picture of this famous pioneer ship. The fan was presented to Captain Green by the officials of Canton.

three months after New York had been evacuated by the British, a former privateer of Revolutionary days, the *Empress of China,* set sail from that port for Canton. Robert Morris, the chief financier of the Revolution, helped to back the venture and Samuel Shaw, a brilliant army veteran, sailed as supercargo. The ship was loaded principally with ginseng, a root worth its weight in gold in the Orient where it was considered the "dose of immortality."

America's first direct bid for a share in the profits out of the Far East, a field the British and Dutch East India Companies had fairly monopolized up to that time, was a bold stroke, but only the first. Almost in the wake of the *Empress of China* the tiny sloop *Enterprise*, 84 tons, sped off to the Orient and returned a year later with handsome profits.

At the start of the China trade America had little enough to offer the Orient in return for the teas, silks, nankeens, porcelains, and other products the home market demanded. In 1790, three years and 41,899

miles out of Boston, the ship *Columbia,* Captain Robert Gray, returned there, the first American vessel to circle the globe. En route to China Gray had visited the northwest Pacific coast and had found its sea-otter furs the prime commodity America needed to trade profitably at Canton. In trade, wrote Gray's clerk, the Indians "do not seem to covet usefull things but anything that looks pleasing to the eye, or what they call riches." It was not always easy trading, as George Davidson's sketch on the opposite page indicates. But with a weather eye wide open for trouble, and with good luck, exchanging notions for pelts could be a rewarding business.

The way to fortune out of China was cleared and it soon became a broad, heavily traveled thoroughfare. Few American ships had such fateful voyages as the *Columbia.* Two years after its return with the key to Eastern wealth the same vessel discovered the Columbia River and gave this country its first valid claim to empire in the Northwest.

"CAPT. GRAY, COMMANDER OF THE SHIP *Columbia*, FACING HIS SHIP WHILE DISCUSSING WITH A FRIEND UPON THE DISCOVERY OF OREGON." So reads an old legend written on the back of the drawing's frame. The view has also been said to represent "Capt. Gray ashore at Whampoa," which might account for the lady with the parasol but not for the Northwest Indian-type dugouts. George Davidson, an artist aboard the *Columbia*, signed both of these eye-witness sketches.

"CAPT. GRAY OBLIGED TO FIRE UPON THE NATIVES WHO DISREGARD HIS ORDERS TO 'KEEP OFF.'" The attack took place in Juan de Fuca Strait, between the present state of Washington and Vancouver Island.

HOUQUA, THE SENIOR HONG MERCHANT IN CANTON. Painting after George Chinnery, about 1825.

By 1789 fifteen American vessels were trading at Canton. A year later that thriving trade accounted for about one seventh of all this country's imports. Contrasting with the lumbering, kettle-bottomed British East Indiamen of fifteen hundred tons, few of the American vessels were as large as two hundred. Some were as small as thirty-five or fifty tons—so small, indeed, as to be mistaken at times for the tenders of larger ships. But it was the daring seamanship, fast sailing, and shrewd dealing of the American China traders that ultimately exposed the slow inefficiency of the British East India Company's monopoly.

The foreign trade of China was officially restricted to a section of the Canton waterfront where, in factories or "Hongs" leased by European nations and America, merchandise was bought and sold. Dealings with foreigners were monopolized by a small, powerful group of Chinese merchants, imperial appointees, who were held responsible for the credit and deportment of their clients. Among those Hong merchants none was more respected by American traders than Houqua. He was, wrote Thomas W. Ward of Salem in 1809, "very rich, sends good cargoes & [is] just in all his dealings, in short is a man of honour and veracity—has more business than any other man in the Hong and secures twelve or fourteen American ships this year.... Houqua is rather dear, loves flattery, and can be coaxed."

A number of American men formed lasting friendships with the powerful Hong merchants who dealt personally with the foreign traders and were privileged to glimpse behind the commercial front. Bryant Tilden of Salem, a youthful supercargo on the *Canton* in 1815, paid a memorable visit to the home of Paunkeiqua, one of the richest of the Chinese dignitaries who alternated with Houqua as head of the Hong. After viewing the famous gardens and being viewed by the shy, curious children and the unseen females of the house, Tilden entered a room with "a curious invaluable collection of *ancient copper and bronze articles,* principally vases, urns, house and field utensils,

THE GARDENS OF HOUQUA. Painting by a Chinese artist, early 19th century.

The Nantucket Atheneum

and pottery, old china ware, some of which bear marks of being very aged . . . were I an antiquary, as well as a supercargo," he wrote home, "valuable discoveries might here be made. Paunkeiqua tells me that many of these now out of date objects were dug up at very remote periods or found in different parts of China and Tartary." In 1819 Paunkeiqua, a mandarin of high rank and an Oriental millionaire, was made a member of the Massachusetts Agricultural Society.

Until the *Empress of China* entered the Canton River probably not a dozen Americans had ever seen a Chinese. The Orient was still a fairyland peopled by whimsical folk whose eyes were askew and whose thirst for tea out of fragile cups was quenchless. The first Americans to witness the actual scene saw sights their countrymen could hardly have dreamed of. "In coming up the river," wrote one American trader, "a stranger is completely absorbed in contemplating a scene, without parallel in any country." Craft of every description—myriad boats moored in regular streets—fleets of canal boats, revenue cutters painted the brightest colors and with a red sash tied about the muzzle of their guns and vermilion-figured white flags floating from their sterns, ferry boats carrying coolies or elegant beaux luxuriating on clean mats, junks gaudily painted with dragons, gold leaf, and huge eyes for the vessels to "see with," all moving in every direction—the din of business by day and of a thousand gongs and the discordant music of the flower boats by evening—at night the glare of flaming papers set on fire in the boats and thrown blazing into the stream. . . . It was something to witness and to recount in the trim coastal villages of New England. During the heyday of the China Trade thirty or forty American

THE FOREIGN FACTORIES AT CANTON. Painting by an unknown artist, early 19th century.

The Peabody Museum of Salem

Collection of Mrs. James B. Drinker

CAPTAIN GEORGE HARRISON OF THE *Alliance* AND HIS FRIENDS IN CANTON. Painting on glass by a Chinese artist, late 18th century.

ships a year, operating through the American factory on the waterfront, were doing an annual trade of about ten million dollars against such a background.

Foreign women were not allowed in Canton although they occasionally tried to sneak into the city from their residential areas in Macao. Soon after George Chinnery, the English artist, arrived in China in 1825 his wife threatened to join him in Macao. He fled for safety to Canton remarking: "Now I am all right. What a kind providence is this Chinese government that it forbids the softer sex from coming and bothering us here." A few years later all trade with Americans was temporarily suspended when two adventurous ladies from Boston were discovered to have slipped into the forbidden city in disguise. One of them had her portrait painted by the misogynistic Chinnery the following year.

The men themselves were supposed to retire from Canton to the Portuguese settlement at Whampoa, about twelve miles down the river, as soon as they had transacted their immediate business. However, a few representatives of the trading companies usually remained in residence in the Canton factories. Some traders, Americans among them, ignoring another law, built up their credit by bootlegging opium past the Chinese customs.

The New York Society Library

SLAYING SEALS AT BEAUCHEENE ISLAND, SOUTH SEAS. Lithograph by Endicott and Sweett from Edmund Fanning, *Voyages around the World*, 1833.

Another source of profitable exchange for the China Trade was the fur-seal rookeries on the bleak shores of Antarctica. In and about the Falkland Islands, South Georgia, the Aucklands, and other remote southern islands seals were clubbed to death by the million, their pelts removed, and their carcasses left to rot. "The method practised to take them," wrote Amasa Delano of Duxbury, a pioneer in the trade, "was, to get between them and the water, and make a lane of men, two abreast, forming three or four couples, and then drive the seals through this lane; each man furnished with a club, between five and six feet long; and as they passed, he knocked down such of them as he chose; which are commonly the half grown, or what they call the young seals. This is easily done, as a very small blow on the nose effects it. When stunned, knives are taken to cut or rip them down on the breast, from the under jaw to the tail, giving a stab in the breast that will kill them. After this all hands go to skinning. I have seen men, one of whom would skin sixty in an hour. . . . They have been sold [in Canton] as high as three or four dollars a skin, and as low as thirty-five cents; but the most common price which they have brought has been about a dollar. Three fourths of the payment for them is generally made in tea."

"So anxious were the officers and men to make sure of filling the ship," wrote Edmund Fanning who cruised the Southern Seas from 1792 to 1832, "that even after the hold was stowed so as not to have room for any more, then the cabin, and finally the forecastle, were filled, leaving just enough space for the accommodation of the ship's company; and yet there was remaining in stacks on shore, more than four thousand skins." On his first voyage to Canton in 1798 Fanning

A SEALERS' ENCAMPMENT AT BYERS' ISLANDS, SOUTH SEAS. Lithograph by Endicott and Sweett from Edmund Fanning, *Voyages around the World*, 1833.

cleared $52,300 for the owners of his ship.

Under Fanning's command the ship *Sea Fox* stopped at Byers' Islands to pick up a cargo of seal skins. The plate illustrating the account of his voyage, wrote Fanning, "represents an encampment of sealers at these islands; in the foreground, part of the crew are engaged in preparing a supper of upland geese ... opposite to them a seaman is picking a goose, while another is dipping some loggerhead ducks in a kettle of boiling water ... others of the crew are backing skins from the landing, a short distance around the point ... on the opposite beach, in the background, is seen some small hair seal rookeries, with six or eight clapmatches (female seal) as usual huddled around each sea lion, their protectors; on the upland hillocks, the tussuc grass appears, while over the more elevated ground in the interior, the albatrosses are hovering, and directly over the back of the cook, a whale-boat is seen crossing, and coming round the point with a load of skins."

Other vessels peddled their way about the Pacific Islands picking up sandalwood, tortoise shell, sea slugs, and edible birds' nests to tickle Chinese palates, and a fantastic variety of oddments to meet the peculiar and shifting demands of the Oriental market. Some crews fell victim to cannibals; others succumbed to the amorous welcome of island natives. A century and a half later the journals of those early adventures make exciting reading. But when Delano, as rugged a shipmaster as there was, returned to Boston in 1807 after a four-year voyage to distant parts of the earth he concluded: "I should rather prefer an honourable death, than to undergo such hardships and severe trials as I experienced during this passage and had frequently before endured while at sea."

CROWNINSHIELD'S WHARF, SALEM. Painting by George Ropes, 1806.

For more than a generation after the Revolution the small town of Salem, just north of Boston, was one of the celebrated ports of the world. "The citizens of this little town," wrote one of its historians, "were despatched to every part of the world, and to every nook of barbarism which had a market and a shore." They wrote brilliant pages in America's maritime history, swapping, bargaining, buying, selling, adventuring with life and fortune about the seven seas of the earth. In some remote parts where Salem's gaily decorated little ships were everywhere to be seen it was believed that the town *was* the United States — an immensely rich and important country.

To the docks and warehouses of Salem, for distribution in a hundred different directions, was fetched exotic freight whose simple listing in the customs records carries vi-

sions of an oriental bazaar—ivory and gold dust from Guinea, gum copal from Zanzibar, coffee and palm oil from Arabia, teas, silks, and pepper from the Far East, whale oil from the Antarctic, hemp from Luzon, hides from the Rio de la Plata, iron from Gothenburg and St. Petersburg, silk slippers from somewhere east of Good Hope, and, among an interminable variety of other things, one elephant in good condition—the first seen in America.

The people of Salem, wrote Harriet Martineau, spoke of distant places of the globe as if they were close at hand. "The fruits of the Mediterranean are on every table," she said. "They have a large acquaintance at Cairo. They . . . have wild tales to tell of Mosambique and Madagascar. . . . Anybody will give you anecdotes from Canton and descriptions of the Society and Sandwich

Islands. They often slip up the western coasts of their two continents; bring furs from the back regions of their own wide land; glance up at the Andes on their return; double Cape Horn; touch at the ports of Brazil and Guiana, look about them in the West Indies, feeling there almost at home; and land, some fair morning at Salem, and walk home as if they had done nothing very remarkable."

These pages are not many enough to give an inkling of how remarkable some of those voyages were. There is an often-told tale of Captain Nathaniel Silsbee who, at the age of nineteen, took Elias Hasket Derby's ship *Benjamin* to the East in 1792. His first mate was twenty, his clerk eighteen. At the Cape of Good Hope the young captain learned that the Napoleonic War had enormously increased prices and he sold his cargo on the

spot for Spanish dollars. While he was detained in port by an embargo his Spanish dollars tripled in value and, released, off he went to the Isle of Bourbon with them to buy coffee and spices. En route home he again paused at the Cape and picked up another tip. Sending most of his cargo home by other Salem vessels then in port the youngster, before he could be stopped, raced back to the Isle of France with a fresh cargo. Selling and reloading he again gave port officials the slip and reached Salem with cotton, pepper, sugar, and indigo which netted Derby 100 per cent profit.

Silsbee's younger clerk, Richard Cleveland, made an even more remarkable Odyssey a few years later. Picking up a little cutter at Le Havre he manned it with a weird international crew and, after being beached by a gale, reached Cape Town where he sold both

CAPTAIN . . . CARNES OF SALEM. Painting by an unidentified artist, about 1790.

cargo and vessel. With the proceeds he shipped to Canton and bought another small craft and manned it with an even more motley group of characters. On a round trip from China to the northwest coast of America and return young Cleveland was obliged to put down a mutiny among his renegade crew and to beat off attacks by savage Indians. In Calcutta, a bit later, he bought a twenty-five-ton pilot boat and by way of Mauritius and Copenhagen reached Hamburg where he again sold out and bought still another vessel. With it he sailed for the western coast of the Americas whence, with contraband furs, he returned to Canton. And so home at the age of thirty with a fortune in his pockets after more than seven years of trading and adventure which had led him twice around the globe.

For Yankee lads the sea was a playground and a training field. The dream of adventure on salt water and in exotic surroundings lured generation after generation of New England youths from the farm to the forecastle. But they rarely stayed there. Those who quickly rose to master a ship of their own, which many an ambitious boy did while still in his teens or early twenties, gained prestige and, frequently, fortune while life was still young. From shipmaster to shipowner, to eminence and greater wealth, was but another step often taken. Those whom the sea did not favor with promotion and those who did not favor the sea after a trial of life on deep water left their place before the mast for new adventures. Except on the fishing fleets the "old salt" of European tradition was not a usual type on American ships. The land, as well as the sea, had too much to offer.

Chestnut Street, Salem.

The Essex Institute

Fishing was a specialized and altogether different salt-water business, and just about the most vital business of New England. Even before the Pilgrims left Leyden Captain John Smith had witnessed and pointed out the possibilities of "mining" the coastal waters of the northeastern Atlantic. "Let not the meanness of the word fish distaste you," he had advised prospective emigrants, "for it will afford as good gold as the mines of Guiana and Potassie." During the next several centuries those fishing waters did in fact prove to be "gold mines." From kid apprentices on their families' vessels—fishing was often a family venture—to long-weathered oldsters, Yankee fishermen swarmed over every likely ground, hand-lining for the sacred cod, "jigging" for mackerel, harpooning for whales, and with their catches of every nature pumping life's blood into New England's economy, feeding the local populations up and down the American coast, shipping vast quantities of dried fish to France, Spain, Portugal, and the West Indies, and providing abundant currency for the general trade of the northern colonies.

During the negotiations of the alliance with France the French Minister wondered if the rebellious colonies could subsist deprived of their fisheries. They could and did, of course, but the end of hostilities found the once-thriving industry prostrate and England loath to have it revive. But New England clung stubbornly and desperately to its rights to fish where it must and by the early years of the nineteenth century the British colonists once again complained that the Yankees, by their numbers and their enterprise, were ruining them.

The Napoleonic Wars helped revive not only the American fishing industry but deepsea enterprise in general.

In 1793 with most of Europe at war America remained the only important trading neutral in the world. England, however, refused to view any trade with France or her colonies as neutral. France, in her turn, considered any trade with England subject to seizure. For a while American shipping was in a serious situation and American ships

THE SHIP *America* "HAND-LINING" ON THE GRAND BANK. Water color by Michele Felice Corné, 1789.
The Peabody Museum of Salem

suffered all manner of indignities on the high seas and in foreign ports. Differences with England were patched up after a fashion. Differences with France developed into an unofficial war which did not, however, keep American ships from trying their fortune through the gauntlet of hostile sails that lined the trade routes.

Captain Elias Hasket Derby, Jr., of Salem, reported his brush with a French fleet of sixty vessels in the Mediterranean: "Off Algeria Point we were seriously attacked by a large latineer who had on board more than one hundred men. He came so near our broadside as to allow our six-pound grape to do execution handsomely. We then bore away and gave him our stern guns in a cool and deliberate manner, doing apparently great execution . . . he was thrown into confusion, struck both his ensign and his pennant. . . . It was . . . a satisfaction to flog the rascal in full view of the English fleet." Not all shipmasters were so successful but, in general, the undeclared war remained popular in Massachusetts seaports.

Naval Records and Library
UNIFORM OF AN AMERICAN SAILOR OF A CARGO CREW AT THE END OF THE EIGHTEENTH CENTURY.

THE LETTER-OF-MARQUE SHIP *Mount Vernon* OF SALEM, CAPTAIN ELIAS HASKET DERBY, JR., ESCAPING FROM A FRENCH FLEET OFF NAPLES. Painting by Corné, 1799.

The Peabody Museum of Salem

PREPARATION FOR WAR TO DEFEND COMMERCE, BUILDING THE FRIGATE *Philadelphia*. Engraving by William Birch & Son, 1800.

The imminent threat of a declared war resulting from the repeated insults and depredations of the French united the country in a patriotic fervor it had not known since the Battle of Lexington. The merchants of eastern seaports combined to subscribe money for building vessels of war to lend the government; to provide "millions for defense but not one cent for tribute."

"All true lovers of liberty of your Country!" called out one appeal, "Step forth and give your assistance in building the frigate to oppose French insolence and piracy. Let every man in posession of a white oak tree be ambitious to be found foremost in hurrying down the timber to Salem where the noble structure is to be fabricated to maintain your

rights upon the seas and make the name of America respected among the nations of the world. Your largest and longest trees are wanted, and the arms of them for knees and rising timber. Four trees are wanted for the keel which altogether will measure 146 feet in length, and hew sixteen inches square."

Newburyport promised a twenty-gun craft in ninety days. Boston speedily laid the keels of two frigates and subscribed one hundred and twenty-five thousand dollars for the projects in a few weeks time. New Yorkers pledged thirty thousand dollars in one hour. From Portland to Charleston in the shipyards of the young nation war vessels took rapid shape on the stocks. More money was raised to throw up harbor defenses all along the Atlantic coast, from Maine to Carolina.

In the Harvard Chapel, June 22, 1798, the students sang out their defiance of France in an ode whose chorus ran:

Yankee Doodle (mind the tune)
Yankee Doodle dandy,
If Frenchmen come***
We'll spank 'em hard and handy.

When Stephen Decatur in the sloop-of-war *Delaware* chased down and brought back to port a French privateer that had just robbed an American trading ship and, the next year, when Commodore Truxton in the Frigate *Constellation* defeated the renowned French frigate *L'Insurgente,* pride in the new navy knew no bounds. The American frigates were, in truth, superior to any other frigates of their day.

The *Mount Vernon* returned from its adventurous eleven months' journey showing a profit of about two hundred and fifty per cent. New ships to carry such wartime harvests were in constant demand, whether the frigates saw service or not. Launching the *Fame* was just one of a succession of gala launchings at Salem.

"April 14, 1801. This day a vessel was launched at Becket's yard, and a fortnight ago one at Brigg's. Another is up at Becket's and another at Brigg's." The report of launchings runs as a constant theme through the diary of William Bentley of Salem.

For the launching of the *Essex* in 1799, wrote the diarist, "everything was in full preparation. The morning gun was fired and nothing remained to be done but to prepare the tallow, drive the wedges, remove the blocks and let her go. Seats were prepared and given to such as paid their quarter of a dollar, on the western side of the ship and near the water. Within were seats for the Committee, in Banks, so as to accommodate many Spectators. Above 12,000 persons passed the Causeway and entered upon Winter Island, crowds were on Naugus' head on the opposite side, numbers in boats, and the whole adjacent shore was covered. She moved easily and the Launch was happy. No accident interrupted the joy of the day."

LAUNCHING THE SHIP *Fame* AT SALEM. Painting by George Ropes, 1802.

The Peabody Museum of Salem

"NON INTERCOURSE OR DIGNIFIED RETIREMENT," A SATIRICAL COMMENT ON JEFFERSON'S POLICY. Engraving by "Peter Pencil," 1809.

In spite of his aversion to war it was during Jefferson's administration that the American Navy was despatched to put an end to the depredations of the Barbary corsairs against American commerce in the Mediterranean. Bainbridge, Decatur, Preble, and others in 1804 all but ended that infamous hold-up, and in a few years Decatur finished it once and for all. But "civilized warfare" with European nations still threatened and Jefferson dreaded it.

His futile embargo of 1807-1809, intended to avoid conflict, caused real privation in the maritime states. England could hardly complain when American ships, the rivals of her commercial supremacy, were held in port. But New England could. The profits of trade had risen with the risks and the one was easily worth the other. An act of the United States Government, that section complained, did more harm to its commerce in one year than all the seizures of European governments had done in ten. New England moved towards secession. "I did not expect a crop of so sudden and rank growth of fraud and open opposition by force could have grown up in the United States," remarked Jefferson. Three days before his retirement he bitterly signed the repeal of his hopeful experiment.

Free of the Embargo, pent-up ships winged out of American harbors for world ports. Even with Napoleon grabbing every American ship he could take, merchant marine tonnage rose to a higher level than ever. New

The Harry Shaw Newman Gallery

THE BOMBARDMENT OF TRIPOLI UNDER COMMODORE PREBLE, 3 AUGUST 1804. Painting by Corné.

THE SHIP *Hercules* OF SALEM, CAPT. EDWARD WEST, PASSING THE MOLE HEAD OF NAPLES, COMING TO ANCHOR, 1809. Painting by an unidentified artist.

The Peabody Museum of Salem

THE IMPRESSMENT OF AN

American Sailor Boy,

SUNG ON BOARD THE BRITISH PRISON SHIP CROWN PRINCE, THE FOURTH OF JULY, 1814
BY A NUMBER OF THE AMERICAN PRISONERS.

THE youthful sailor mounts the bark,
    And bids each weeping friend adieu :
Fair blows the gale, the canvass swells :
    Slow sinks the uplands from his view.

Three mornings, from his ocean bed,
    Resplendent beams the God of day :
The fourth, high looming in the mist,
    A war-ship's floating banners play.

Her yawl is launch'd ; light o'er the deep,
    Too kind, she wafts a ruffian band :
Her blue track lengthens to the bark,
    And soon on deck the miscreants stand.

Around they throw the baleful glance :
    Suspense holds mute the anxious crew—
Who is their prey ? poor sailor boy !
    The baleful glance is fix'd on you.

Nay, why that useless scrip unfold ?
    They damn'd the " lying yankee scrawl,"
Torn from thine hand, it strews the wave—
    They force thee trembling to the yawl.

Sick was thine heart as from the deck,
    The hand of friendship wav'd farewell ;
Mad was thy brain, as far behind,
    In the grey mist thy vessel fell.

One hope, yet fondly bosom clung,
    The captain mercy might impart ;

Vain was that hope, which bade thee look,
    For mercy in a Pirate's heart.

What woes can man on man inflict,
    When malice joins with uncheck'd power ;
Such woes, unpitied and unknown,
    For many a month the sailor bore !

Oft gem'd his eye the bursting tear,
    As mem'ry linger'd on past joy ;
As oft they flung the cruel jeer,
    And damn'd the " chicken liver'd boy."

When sick at heart, with " hope deferr'd,"
    Kind sleep his wasting form embrac'd,
Some ready minion ply'd the lash,
    And the lov'd dream of freedom chas'd.

Fast to an end his miseries drew :
    The deadly hectic flush'd his cheek ;
On his pale brow the cold dew hung,
    He sigh'd, and sunk upon the deck !

The sailor's woes drew forth no sigh ;
    No hand would close the sailor's eye :
Remorseless, his pale corse they gave,
    Unshrouded to the friendly wave.

And as he sunk beneath the tide,
    A hellish shout arose ;
Exultingly the demons cried,
    " So fare all Albion's Rebel Foes ! "

fortunes were to be made everywhere ships could ply. When war with England was finally declared in 1812 it was no paradox that New England again objected. Confiscation and impressment were objectionable and costly. But profits were to be made over and above such nuisances and in any case Napoleon seemed a greater ogre than John Bull. The West with its concern over British rivalry along the frontier had a bigger stake in the war than the coastal states, however much was said of impressment and sailors' rights. The "War Hawks" of the West would end the menace to their well-being by driving the British out of Canada, putting an end to Indian troubles with the same move. "Is it nothing," Henry Clay demanded of the Senate, "to acquire the entire fur trade connected with that country, and to destroy the temptation and the opportunity of violating your revenue and other laws?"

At the start of the War of 1812 the United States Navy consisted of sixteen sea-going ships carrying from twelve to forty-four guns and ranging from one hundred and fifty to fifteen hundred tons. Only five were ready for sea when war was declared. A good part of the naval warfare, particularly in the earlier stages, was commissioned to privateers. Not intended for fighting regular naval battles these privately operated marauders were built for speed, maneuverability, and all-weather sailing qualities. They could not be built too big. Ports were so quickly stripped of enthusiastic privateersmen that large crews could hardly be found at any one time.

With lightning speed, and for a while with notable results, American privateers

A CARTOON OF 1812.

Collection of Titus C. Geesey

THE PRIVATEER HERMAPHRODITE BRIG *Rambler* OF MEDFORD. Painting by an unidentified artist, 1812.

THE PRIVATEER SCHOONER *Surprise* OF BALTIMORE CAPTURING THE BRITISH MERCHANT SHIP *Star*, 1815. Painting by an unidentified artist.

THE *United States* AND THE *Macedonian*, 1812. Water color by Thomas Birch.

THE *Constitution* AND THE *Guerrière*, 1812. Painting by Corne.

The Maryland Historical Society

ADMIRAL COCKBURN BURNING AND PLUNDERING HAVRE DE GRACE ON THE 1ST OF JUNE, 1813. From a sketch made at the time.

Yale University Art Gallery, Mabel Brady Garvan Collection

"THE *Shannon* VS. THE *Chesapeake*," 1813. A BRITISH CARICATURE. Aquatint by George Cruikshank.

carried on a form of private warfare with the enemy. More than five hundred of them captured some thirteen hundred prizes costing England about forty million dollars. The unpopularity of "Mr. Madison's War" in the northeastern states, however, was shown by the fact that, for once, New England ports were overshadowed by others in maritime enterprise. Baltimore was building the most and the swiftest privateers.

The early successes of the small American navy, as well as the actions of the privateers, stunned England. After the *United States* brought the *Macedonian* into New London and the *Constitution* knocked out the *Guerrière* and then the *Java*, all in 1812, a London journal reported: "Lloyd's list shows five hundred British merchantmen taken by the Americans in seven months. Five hundred merchantmen and three frigates! Can this be true? . . . Any man who foretold such disasters this day last year would have been treated as a madman or a traitor. . . . Yet not one of the American frigates has struck. They leave their ports when they choose and return when it suits their convenience. They cross the Atlantic, they visit the West Indies,

they come to the chops of the Channel, they parade along the coast of South America. Nothing chases them; nothing intercepts them. . . ."One impudent seacaptain, Thomas Boyle in the little *Chasseur* of Baltimore, sent ashore a proclamation to be posted in Lloyd's Coffee House announcing that the United Kingdom of Great Britain and Ireland was blockaded.

Despite its early great successes the United States Navy was, in the long run, no match for England's huge fleet on the high seas. The war proved little or nothing else. After the *Chesapeake* surrendered to the *Shannon* in 1813, against the dying command of Captain Lawrence—"Don't give up the ship"— most of the American men-of-war were blockaded in port for the rest of the war.

But the experience gained by American designers in planning faster and larger ships, vessels built to carry heavy burdens with a minimum sacrifice of speed, was an inestimable boon to merchant shipping in years to come. Without those wartime lessons the packet ships and clippers that were to win peacetime glory would not have been possible.

The New-York Historical Society
THE CAPITOL AFTER THE BRITISH ASSAULT ON WASHINGTON. Water color by George Heriot, 1815.

BLACK BALL LINER, *New York I*, BUILT IN 1822. Painting by Robert W. Salmon (?).

PACKETS

An announcement in the fall of 1817 that a small fleet of packet boats, operated out of New York by what was to become the Black Ball Line, would cross the Atlantic on a "frequent and regular" schedule opened a new era in maritime history. The pioneer, square-rigged ships that were built for the job were bigger, swifter and safer than most other vessels afloat at the time and were captained by men who mercilessly used every ounce of their crews' endurance to keep to schedule. At the start the Black Ball "Liners" sailed on the first of every month averaging twenty-three days from Sandy Hook to Liverpool and forty days for the trip back against the head winds. Occasional trips were much faster in both directions. But in all cases they sailed in foul season or fair, "full or not full."

This unmatched punctuality and efficiency in spanning the western ocean during the most savage winter storms or the summer's mildest winds was a portentous development and it immediately inspired competition by other American lines. The successful operators, it was soon pointed out, were "with their packet ships, scarcely less of public benefactors than Fulton and Whitney were with their steamboats and cotton gins." Within a few years American packets were taking over most of the passenger and freight trade of the Atlantic. For a generation they knew no rivals except among themselves. Their numbers were relatively few—there were never more than fifty afloat—but they reduced the shuttle service across the Atlantic to what looked in the port entries deceptively like an ordinary routine.

Within a decade after the War of 1812 New York became the nation's chief seaport. Geographically its advantages were great. The Erie Canal gave it easy access to the interior of the country, made it a close neighbor of the West. Its merchants were alert. Its steamboats paddled incessantly about adjacent waters. England had chosen it as the American dumping ground for manufactures after the war. Its early packet service helped to concentrate transatlantic trade in its direction. New Yorkers, wrote J. Fenimore Cooper in 1824, were daily constructing great ranges of wooden piers "in order to meet the increasing demands of their trade, while the whole of the seven miles of water which fronts the city, is lined with similar constructions," excepting the Battery.

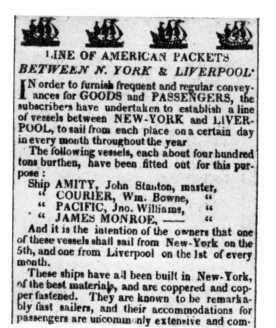

LINE OF AMERICAN PACKETS BETWEEN N. YORK & LIVERPOOL.

IN order to furnish frequent and regular conveyances for GOODS and PASSENGERS, the subscribers have undertaken to establish a line of vessels between NEW-YORK and LIVERPOOL, to sail from each place on a certain day in every month throughout the year.

The following vessels, each about four hundred tons burthen, have been fitted out for this purpose:

Ship AMITY, John Stanton, master,
" COURIER, Wm. Bowne, "
" PACIFIC, Jno. Williams, "
" JAMES MONROE, ——— "

And it is the intention of the owners that one of these vessels shall sail from New-York on the 5th, and one from Liverpool on the 1st of every month.

These ships have all been built in New-York, of the best materials, and are coppered and copper fastened. They are known to be remarkably fast sailers, and their accommodations for passengers are uncommonly extensive and com-

The New-York Historical Society
NEWSPAPER ADVERTISEMENT, 1817.

"PACKET ROW," SOUTH ST., NEW YORK, FROM MAIDEN LANE, 1828. Aquatint by William J. Bennett after his own painting. The Swallowtail packet *Leeds*, in the left foreground, was wrecked shortly after this view was made.

The New York Public Library, Stokes Collection

NEW YORK HARBOR FROM THE BATTERY, A BLACK BALL LINER INCOMING. Lithograph by Thomas Thompson, about 1828.

The New York waterfront, Battery included, was lined with dreaming landsmen as well, wrote Herman Melville, "posted like silent sentinels all around the town . . . thousands upon thousands of mortal men fixed in ocean reveries. Some leaning against the spiles; some seated upon the pier-heads; some looking over the bulwarks of ships from China; some high aloft in the rigging, as if striving to get a still better seaward peep. But all these landsmen, of week days pent up in lath and plaster—tied to counters, nailed to benches, clinched to desks. . . . Strange! Nothing will content them but the extremest limit of the land. . . . They must get just as nigh the water as they possibly can without falling in. And there they stand—miles of them—leagues. Inlanders all, they come from lanes and alleys, streets and avenues—north, east, south, and west. Yet here they all unite."

In the years following Melville's observation it became possible to live in New York unaware of the incessant and increasing activity of the port; to partake of the metropolitan activity with only a rare view of the ocean traffic restlessly swarming on every tide. But when Melville wrote, New York was a city of ships, hemmed by masts and ever conscious of the salty lick of the sea at the end of every short crosstown street.

The sight of its ample bay teeming with craft of every description and from every port of the world was enough to tempt a landsman's eye. To Manhattan came earliest and quickest the main flow of news from abroad. Thanks to the prevailing westerly winds of the North Atlantic, reports from Europe were never less than a month or two old when they reached America, but they were none the less vital for the delay. America was still more curious about and dependent upon overseas conditions than Europe was about the state of affairs in the New World. Men and women waiting impatiently to hear the latest gossip and to read of or see the most recent fashions; merchants nervously expecting information that might improve or reduce their fortunes; newsmen determined to get the most vital intelligence into print before their rivals—all these joined the curious along the water's edge anxious to end their suspense. Some sped out to sea to gather the news from a ship halted by calm or fog and put their advance knowledge to good use in the market or on their presses.

The packets reduced the average time for the westward crossing from more than seven weeks to barely over five. Two Black-Ballers made the trip in sixteen days as a result of a freakish reversal of the winds.

"THE COOK ENRAG'D AT THE STEERAGE PASSENGERS BEING LATE WITH THEIR BREAKFAST," ABOARD THE BLACK CROSS PACKET *Acasta*, 1824. Painting by J. Gear.

Packets attracted the cream of transatlantic passenger travel. Cabin passage was expensive; the cabin appointments were luxurious and the food and service celebrated. At the start steerage passengers were few and their accommodations bad. "The passengers turned out on deck like bees in the Spring," recalled one of them. "Some stand about the stove, cooking, or waiting their turn at the fire. Others take a walk round the jolly-boat, which I may call the ship's farmyard, and talk to the cow, or sheep, or pigs, or poultry in their several tongues; or, they sit upon the water-barrels amusing themselves with a book, or, by the aid of tobacco fumes, wonder what sort of a world it is they are bound for, and build castles in the air." "It will be better for Jack and the girls when they come out," another steerage passenger wrote home, "to make some arrangement with the cook . . . as in rough weather it is impossible to cook at the passengers' fire. If possible bring out some good apples and some preserved fruit to make puddings and tarts of, as you can often eat something of that kind when you have no relish for meat. . . . Seidlitz powders are very good things to bring."

As time passed packets took over an ever-larger share of the immigrant trade and that trade grew to an enormous size. The potato famine in Ireland brought 163,000 Irishmen to the port of New York alone in 1851. "Every corner, tree, and pump and public place in the city of Dublin," it was said, "and for forty or fifty miles in the surrounding country" were placarded in a systematized effort to persuade Irishmen to leave home for the world of opportunity and equality—at about twenty dollars a head steerage passage. It was a booming business for the shrewd men who organized the traffic in human freight.

"Outward Bound." Lithograph by T. H. Maguire after a drawing by J. Nichol, 1854.

The Metropolitan Museum of Art
STEERAGE PASSENGERS BELOW. Engraving after a drawing by A. Boyd Houghton from *The London Graphic,* 1870.

Following the War of 1812 the improvement of chronometers and compasses, the better charting and marking of dangerous shores, and the disappearance of warring privateers, all added certainty and swiftness to ocean travel. But a mass migration of humans across the Atlantic became economically possible only as Europe's demand for American products kept a large and steady stream of vessels busy on the eastward passage. As that demand developed the immigrant became the ever-ready "back freight" for the return trip. He became, in fact, a leading article of commerce, a highly durable cargo much sought after by rival shippers anxious to carry a full load on the westbound voyage. The largest flow of human freight was directed towards New York, arrivals at that port increasing from 3000 in 1820 to 327,000 in 1854.

However you travel, advised one of the most popular guidebooks to emigration of the 1820's and '30's, "let the ship be American; remember he is going home, and the captain will never pull off his clothes to go to bed during the whole voyage." Those who could not find passage on an American ship or afford the rates on a packet took what they got, egged on to the adventure by persuasive and sometimes unscrupulous agents of transportation companies.

That every bit of 'tween-decks space might be put to profitable use the shippers often built rough pine bunks close enough together to compress humanity and luggage into an almost impassable, tight jumble. Ventilation and light were neglected or totally ignored. Privacy was next to impossible. In some ships—too many—officers and crews treated steerage passengers with brutal contempt. Not all emigrant ships were pestholes by any means, but a fetid squalor was common enough to keep the death rate from disease pathetically high.

Those who could afford the rates, "thirty guineas, wines included," took to the best ships—the American packets whose comforts, sumptuous fare, and swift crossings attracted such noted travelers as Lafayette, Joseph Bonaparte, Charles Dickens, S. F. B. Morse, Longfellow, and a host of other celebrities.

The New-York Historical Society
TO AMERICA IN STYLE ON BOARD THE *Peruvian*. From a sketch book by H. S., about 1831.

New York was becoming America's great entrepôt not only for immigrants but also for merchandise gathered from within the country and from foreign lands. Even the other large coastal cities used New York as a port of distribution for the goods their own fleets had imported from markets throughout the world. In the 1830's brigs and schooners out of Gotham, for example, were carrying to Caribbean markets for resale large quantities of inexpensive cottons, originally imported from Calcutta to Boston.

New York firms had a good share of that thriving commerce with Latin America. From the East River docks were shipped Windsor chairs, Duncan Phyfe furniture, carriages, machinery, livestock, flour, European re-exports, textiles, and a bewildering variety of goods in vessels which often resembled "country stores on a mammoth scale." Back came sugar, coffee, hides, "segars," molasses, and sundries. It was during this period that America developed its great taste for coffee—coffee from Rio, Haiti, Venezuela, Jamaica, and other parts of the Latin South.

For fifteen or more years following the War of 1812 most vessels went into the Caribbean armed against trouble. The succession of revolutions by which the Spanish-American colonies gained their independence kept that whole southern area in an unsettled state.

Vessels of war and privateers from the various warring countries (sometimes built in American shipyards and manned by American crews) preyed on shipping of any nationality regardless of their mission, guided usually by the size of the "take" that might be expected. It was just a cut above piracy and often not even that. In 1829, a year after the Secretary of the Navy reported that West Indian piracy had been crushed for good, a New York-bound brig was boarded six hours out of Cuba and its captain and all but one of its crew "one by one . . . butchered in detail." More than one of those latter-day pirates was hanged in New York before enthusiastic audiences.

The New York Public Library

INCIDENTS ON A TRADING VOYAGE TO THE WEST INDIES, 1838–9. *a*) Taking an observation of the sun; *b*) Mending a pair of breeks "which had gone adrift"; *c*) dining in the cabin. Water colors from a manuscript journal by William H. Meyers. Meyers, a Philadelphian, commanded the brig *Lucy* on the trip illustrated in part by the above drawings. In 1841 he was recommended by Master Thomas Harry, U.S.N., for naval service as a "good seaman, a good navigator and of moral worth." For the next eight years he served with the U.S. Navy (see pages 337, 338, 343). The gay illuminations of his journals constitute a lively graphic record of life on the high seas a century ago.

BOSTON HARBOR, ABOUT 1826. Lithograph by Deroy after a painting by J. Milbert.

FAR WESTERN WATERS

Boston may not have been the "hub of the solar system" but it became the hub of New England's foreign commerce. Its numerous docks and its gathering and distributing system of turnpikes, railroads, and coastal fleets were the envy of rival seaports north of New York. Salem's day at sea was not yet over but it was waning. At mid-century in the Salem Custom House Nathaniel Hawthorne, son of a Salem skipper, had time enough to dream without being distracted by the great activity that a generation earlier had been staged at Crowninshield's and Derby's wharves. Most of the other small New England seaports whose ships had once traded in the earth's distant markets turned over their carrying to the "hub," feeding its growing commerce with the products of their more localized efforts.

Until the 1840's Boston still owned more ships than even New York, ships that gathered cargoes in every harbor of the world and carried them where they were wanted: ice from Saugus to the West Indies; shirtings from the Lowell Mills to Montevideo; sugar from Cuba to Sweden and Russia; Peruvian bark via Boston to Tunis; goat skins and ostrich feathers from South Africa to America; sandalwood from Hawaii to China and, as exchange, palm-leaf hats to Hawaii! and hides from California to Lynn.

Boston's trade with Spanish America, like New York's, was so lively that practically every ship that could keep out water was pressed into service, even vessels that were best sold for firewood when their cargoes were delivered. Rounding the Horn to get to the western coast in such "whistle divers" was no uncommon experience, and rounding the Horn could test the stoutest ship.

334

The diary of James A. Rogers, boatsteerer on the *Mentor,* a whaler out of New London, laconically recites one episode of a more or less typical journey. It happened on Friday the thirteenth of August, 1839.

"Begins with fresh N. E. trades and squally, steering S. About quarter before 7 A.M. the fore topgallant mast broke off to the cap, carrying away the main royal mast with it. The man at the mast-head forward was sitting on the royal yard at the time. He was thrown off and caught the end of the fore topsail yard, and from there down between the rail and swing-boom, where he caught by the studding-sail outhall and hung on 'till he was bent on and hauled in-board and carried aft. The captain bled him and took him down in the cabin. He was hurt very little, for the distance he fell was about 120 feet. The man at the mast-head aft was thrown from the yard, but he caught hold of one of the stays. Turned to and cleared away the remains of the wreckage and got up another gear in its place. Thus ends these twenty-four hours."

The Metropolitan Museum of Art

SAILORS ALOFT. Engraving from a bank note. The marine news of contemporary papers was studded with accounts of seamen who fell to their deaths while coping with sails one hundred or more feet above a ship's deck.

THE SHIP *Ringleader,* BUILT AT MEDFORD IN 1868, ROUNDING THE HORN. Painting by A. V. Gregory, 1889.

The Peabody Museum of Salem

MAKING TALLOW, MONTEREY, CALIFORNIA.

CURING HIDES, MONTEREY. CALIFORNIA. Both sketches by William Rich Hutton, 1847.

THE AMERICAN SLOOP-OF-WAR *Dale* AND OTHER VESSELS OF THE PACIFIC SQUADRON LYING AT LA PAZ, LOWER CALIFORNIA, IN 1847. Another water color from a journal by Meyers (see next page).

Sending fleets of small, copper-bottomed (by Paul Revere's process), heavily armed (against Indian attacks) brigs and ships through the enormous seas and destructive winds around Cape Horn (by the grace of God and resourceful seamanship) to the northwest coast of America, Boston merchants had practically monopolized the lucrative fur trade of that section. As that traffic declined Boston ships slipped down the coast to California collecting tallow and hides ("California bank notes") for New England shoe shops in exchange for shoes made of California hides at Lynn, notions, and "everything that can be imagined from Chinese fireworks to English cart-wheels." Emerson's pupil Richard Dana gave the picture its full color in *Two Years before the Mast:* stout New England ships standing off from a surf that roared and rolled in upon the beach; white missions and dark towns; stark mountains; a land where mañana was,

for the natives, ever the day of action; tales of soaking, curing, hauling, and lading the hides—of lazy sunshine, squalid Indians, and gracious Latins—of the journey home down through "thrilling regions of thick-ribbed ice and freezing, tempestuous gales and, finally, the sight of the State House dome atop Beacon Hill fading in the western sky and the unexpected anticlimax of homecoming" after long months of nostalgia.

To the Kanakas who manned many of the foreign ships doing business in California the United States was nothing more—nor less—than Boston. Nearly two thirds of all the articles carried around the Horn were imported by the single Boston house of Bryant, Sturgis, & Co., the firm that owned Dana's ship. At Monterey and Santa Barbara Dana discovered that most of the chief alcaldes were Yankees by birth, men who had "left their consciences at Cape Horn" and renounced their Protestantism to enjoy politi-

Adios Senorita

Teatro Aleigra

SCENES IN A SAILOR'S LIFE, 1845. Wash drawings from a manuscript journal of a cruise on the U.S. Ship *Cyane* by William H. Meyers. These and the preceding sketch were made while the artist was serving with the U.S. Navy in Pacific waters. "Gunner" Meyers served on the sloop-of-war *Cyane* for almost three years. (Herman Melville, returning from various adventures in Honolulu and other Pacific areas, served on the frigate *United States* in the same squadron.) Later Meyers served as gunner on the *Dale* during the Mexican War.

cal liberty and trading opportunities in the land of sun-soaked, decaying Catholic missions. What a land it *could* be, mused Dana, if it were governed and worked by people with Yankee enterprise.

California hung like a ripe plum at the tip of Spanish empire, tempting the imperialists of more aggressive nations. For a dozen years before the Mexican War American squadrons eager to improve their country's opportunities up and down the length of Spanish America, kept watch on the war vessels habitually maintained in the eastern Pacific by Russia, France, and England.

Merchants had been there long since. From an early date there were American commission houses, often preceding diplomatic representatives, at Valparaiso, Lima, Guayaquil, and other western cities. Sealers, whalemen, China traders, and Northwest men had also for years past put in at west-coast ports to provision, swap, and smuggle. At mid-century came fleets of northern ships, many of them from Baltimore, to collect guano on the Chinchas Islands off Peru's coast. Guano —the collected droppings of seabirds—was valued as a natural fertilizer.

North Americans had played their parts in the liberation of the South American republics. Yankee-built ships had sailed as privateers and blockade runners in the cause of liberty in the Southern Hemisphere; Yankees had served in the armies and navies of the infant republics, and a few had founded distinguished South American families.

In 1818 the American warship *Ontario* was detailed to protect American shipping along South America's west coast and in later decades a succession of others followed in its wake. Yankee sailors along with the merchant mariners were getting a fair chance to know their neighbors to the south and, by the record, were improving their opportunities. At the bullfights and the theater, at carnivals and picnics, in society and out of it, American navy men were interested onlookers and participants.

One prim chaplain found South American conduct to be "at war with our sentiments of propriety," although he conceded that out of many a peasant cabin stepped "beauty . . . in a combination of charms that might stir the chisel of a Praxiteles." "I know not how or why," more appreciatively recorded another, less inhibited representative of the Pacific Squadron in 1849, "but there certainly is an irresistible charm, that floats like a mist around Spanish creoles . . . they have soft, languishing eyes, rich, dark hair, and pliant graceful forms, combined with the greatest possible charm in woman, earnest, unaffected, and amiable dispositions."

THE NITRATE FLEET AT THE CHINCHAS ISLANDS. Painting by an unknown artist.

The Peabody Museum of Salem

A Whaling Scene. Painting by an unidentified artist.

WHALING

An occasional whale may still be seen sporting in the waters about New York. But long ago, it was said, all the wiser ones had learned to avoid New Bedford and Nantucket by a much wider margin. Before the end of the eighteenth century whalemen from those towns had chased their game around Cape Horn into what Melville called "the remotest secret drawers and lockers of the world." By the beginning of the next century American whalers had practically staked out the broad Pacific as their own green pasture.

With its combination of sordid horror and wild adventure whaling was for years one of the leading industries of Massachusetts. For-

The New York Society Library
"Cutting in and Trying Out" the Blubber. From J. Ross Browne, *Etchings of a Whaling Cruise*, 1846. Lithograph by J. Halpin after a drawing by A. A. Von Schmidt.

tunes literally poured into the towns that sent out successful fleets, until the advent of cheap kerosene made the whale-oil lamp and the spermaceti candle obsolescent. Between 1804 and 1876 the value of the whaling industry amounted to a third of one billion dollars. The whole wide world was witness to this herculean labor, from one frozen pole to the other, from Africa to Brazil, from Chile to Japan.

It is easy to forget the stench and the cruelty in the game and to think, rather, of young Herman Melville, in pursuit of symbols high in the crow's-nest of the *Acushnet,* fancying himself striding across the Pacific on giant stilts. But the routine of whaling— cutting the blubber from the whale in strips, mincing it into thin slices, boiling it, cooling the oil, and straining it into casks—was an infernal and stinking business, a small-scale hell for whalemen.

"Their tawny features, now all begrimed with smoke and sweat," wrote Melville, "their matted beards, and the contrasting barbaric brilliancy of their teeth . . . their unholy adventures, their tales of terror told in words of mirth; as their uncivilized laughter forked upwards out of them, like the flames from the furnaces; as to and fro the harpooners wildly gesticulated with their huge pronged

forks and dippers; as the wind howled on, and the sea leaped, and the ship groaned and dived, and yet steadfastly shot her red hell further and further into the blackness of the sea and the night, and scornfully champed the white bone in her mouth, and viciously spat round her on all sides; then the rushing *Pequod,* freighted with savages, and laden with fire, and burning a corpse, and plunging into that blackness of darkness, seemed the material counterpart of her monomaniac commander's soul."

The ordinary whaleman, concluded one author who had served on a whaler, belonged to "the most oppressed class of men in existence." For months on end he was subject to severe labor, he fed on the poorest and meanest fare, he toiled in constant peril, and for the slavery to which he was bound while at sea he received but a pittance. Hardly a whaler returned to port, it was said, without bringing a tale of mutiny. Yet, with every returning season crews were found to man the growing fleets.

SOUTH SEA WHALE FISHING. Painting by Robert W. Salmon, 1835.

NEW BEDFORD IN 1807. Painting by William Allen Wall, 1857. Photograph courtesy of the Frick Art Reference Library.

A WHALE OIL LAMP. Engraving by John W. Barber, about 1840.

While the larger ports of Boston, New York, Philadelphia, and Baltimore gradually tightened their hold on the ocean trade routes hardly a town on the coasts of New England and Long Island—even Poughkeepsie, Hudson, and others far up the rivers—but had its whaling fleet. In 1787 Burke, in his memorable speech, traced the endless exploration for blubber to places which seemed "too remote and romantic an object for the grasp of national ambition." But, he added, that was only "a stage and a resting place in the progress of their victorious industry." New Bedford became the whaling metropolis of the world, outdistancing Nantucket, New London, Edgartown, Mystic, and the others until, in 1857, its three hundred and thirty vessels were more than all their fleets combined. At New Bedford, wrote Emerson, "they hug an oil-cask like a brother." The opulent houses of the town, said Melville, were "one and all . . . harpooned and dragged up hither from the bottom of the sea."

With the China traders whalemen made

Hawaii practically a suburb of Boston and almost a facsimile of it in some spots, according to one visiting mariner. For years the most conspicuous building in Honolulu—a landmark for seamen—was the large Stone Church built of coral blocks by American missionaries in the image of a New England clapboard meeting-house.

The New-York Historical Society
THE STONE CHURCH AT HONOLULU. Illustration from Rufus Anderson, *The Hawaiian Islands*, 1867.

Whalers and other seamen long and far removed from home town conventions added to the problems of missionaries in the tropical islands of the Pacific. More than a few jack-tars foundered on the temptations of a carefree life in the South Seas. Looking back on the inhuman shipboard conditions during his whaling voyage to Polynesia, and farther back to the unhappy drudgery of his workaday life in America, Herman Melville earnestly thought for a while that his countrymen had much to learn from the pagan cannibals, the Typees, among whom he had found refuge. "In this secluded abode of happiness," he wrote, "there were no cross old women, no cruel step-dames, no withered spinsters, no lovesick maidens, no sour bachelors, no inattentive husbands, no melancholy young men, no blubbering youngsters, and no squalling brats. All was mirth, fun, and high good humour. Blue devils, hypochondria, and doleful dumps went and hid themselves among the nooks and crannies of the rocks."

Collection of Kenneth K. Bechtel
MORE SCENES IN A SAILOR'S LIFE, 1845. Another water color from Meyers' manuscript journal.

HARPOONING A WHALE. Lithograph by Martens after a painting by Ambroise Louis Garneray.

INCIDENTS IN WHALE FISHING. Lithograph by Martens after a painting by Garneray.

Whatever the reasons men chose to go to sea in a whaler they found one in the chase. Here was a transporting excitement that made exultant adventurers out of the slaves of the forecastle and the quarterdeck. Melville, as always, best described the agonizing thrill of the experience.

"It was a sight full of quick wonder and awe!" he wrote. "The vast swells of the omnipotent sea; the singing, hollow roar they made, as they rolled along the eight gunwales, like gigantic bowls in a boundless bowling green; the brief suspended agony of the boat, as it would tip for an instant on the knifelike edge of the sharper waves that almost seemed threatening to cut it in two; the sudden profound dip into the watery glens and hollows; the keen spurrings and goadings to gain the top of the opposite hill; the headlong, sledlike slide down its other side—all these, with the cries of the headsmen and harpooners, and the shuddering gasps of the oarsmen, with the wondrous sight of the ivory *Pequod* bearing down upon her boats with outstretched sails, like a wild hen after her screaming brood; all this was thrilling. Not the raw recruit, marching from the bosom of his wife into the fever heat of his first battle; not the dead man's ghost encountering the first unknown phantom in the other world—neither of these can feel stranger and stronger emotions than that man does, who for the first time finds himself putting into the charmed, churned circle of the hunted sperm whale. . . . A short rushing sound leaped out of the boat; it was the darted iron of Queequeg. Then all in one welded commotion came an invisible push from astern, while forward the boat seemed striking on a ledge; the sail collapsed and exploded; a gush of scalding vapor shot up near by; something rolled and tumbled like an earthquake beneath us. The whole crew were half suffocated as they were tossed helter-skelter into the white curdling cream of the squall. Squall, whale, and harpoon had all blended together . . ."

Not many men chose to repeat a whaling cruise. "There is a murderous appearance

LIFE IN THE FORECASTLE. From Browne, *Etchings*, etc., 1846.

about the blood-stained decks, and the huge masses of flesh and blubber lying here and there . . ." reported J. Ross Browne of his own experiences. "The forecastle was black and slimy with filth; very small, and as hot as an oven. It was filled with a compound of foul air, smoke, sea-chests, soap-kegs, greasy pans, tainted meat, Portuguese ruffians, and sea-sick Americans. . . . From the time he leaves port [the whaler] is beyond the sphere of human rights, he is a slave until he returns. All this time he is subject to . . . such treatment as an ignorant and tyrannical master . . . chooses to inflict upon him."

"A PICTURE FOR THE PHILANTHROPISTS." From Browne, *Etchings*, etc.

CLIPPERS

New York City was growing into such a huge, swarming pile that the metropolis tended to overshadow the seaport. Yet during the mid-years of the last century more shipping activity concentrated along its East River than anywhere else in the country. At New York in 1845 Smith and Dimon launched the *Rainbow*, 750 tons, the first extreme clipper ship. American ship designers always have been noted for the speed of their vessels and in this revolutionary new type the fast-sailing cargo ship reached its ultimate development. Along certain world trade routes, notably on the China run, speed, even at the sacrifice of carrying capacity, was of first importance. Clippers supplied that in quantities mariners had only dreamed of. The *Sea Witch* launched at the same yard in 1846 made the voyage from Canton around the Horn to New York in seventy-four days. The next year she sailed around the world in 194 days.

With the discovery of gold in California new clippers for the Cape Horn route were in enormous demand. Eagerness of traders to capitalize on the boom market in San Francisco where fabulous prices were paid in gold dust for ordinary merchandise, eagerness of adventurers to get to the mines before any more treasure hunters reached there, gave fast-sailing ships inordinate importance. Clippers were on the ways everywhere. Ordinary shipping around the Horn to California took from 150 to 200 days even as much as eight full months on one occasion. On her maiden voyage in the summer of 1851 the clipper *Flying Cloud* dropped anchor in San Francisco Harbor just eighty-nine days out of New York.

With the repeal of the British Navigation Acts in 1849 the carrying trade between China and London at last was opened to American vessels. British firms in Hong

THE SMITH AND DIMON SHIPYARD, NEW YORK, 1833. Painting by James Pringle.

The New York State Historical Association

Kong paid almost triple freight rates to get their tea aboard the swift American clippers. British East Indiamen waited for cargoes day on day while Yankee ships, one after another, sped off for the London market with a full hold, often earning a considerable part of their cost in a single voyage. Driven by masters of consummate skill and daring, these clippers became prodigies of swiftness. Carrying towering clouds of sail over an immaculately finished, pencil-slim hull they seemed to some like maritime cathedrals, a glorious tribute to the human spirit that conceived them.

The logs of the clippers tell their own story: "Passed a ship under double reefs, we with our royals and studdingsails set. . . . Passed a ship laying-to under a close-reefed maintopsail. . . . Split all three topsails and had to heave to. . . . Seven vessels in sight and we outsail all of them. . . . Under double-reefed topsails passed several vessels hove-to." So reads the log of the *Great Britain* in 1849. Driven without caution through the heaviest weather until their top masts "bent like

The New-York Historical Society
SHIPCARD, about 1851.

whips" and sails shredded before the gale, they performed incredible feats. The *Red Jacket* logged a day's run of 413 nautical miles. The *Sovereign of the Seas* logged 424 in twenty-four hours, 3562 miles in eleven days. Before a strong gale, with her lee rail under water, the *Lightning* ran 436 nautical miles in twenty-four hours—an average of 18.2 knots. Racers for *America's* cup, with no cargo, do not often average more than half that speed over a thirty-mile course.

CLIPPER SHIP *Red Jacket*, IN THE ICE OFF CAPE HORN ON HER PASSAGE FROM AUSTRALIA TO LIVERPOOL, 1854. Lithograph by N. Currier after a drawing by J. B. Smith & Son.

The Harry Shaw Newman Gallery

The American Clipper Bark *Zephyr* in Messina Harbor, Sicily. Painting by William Bygrave.

THE SAILOR'S WEDDING, 1852. Painting by Richard Caton Woodville.

By the clipper ship period—by the middle of the last century—the working crews of American ships were no longer the eager native youths who had manned the earlier merchant marine. In his heyday the American seaman had been well paid and enterprising; and with his colorful, distinctive outfit—from shiny hat to bell-bottomed dungarees—he was "the best dressed of mankind," according to Emerson. The tender hearts that followed every American ship out of port had expectations they could reasonably hope to capitalize on. "Jack" was a freeman with decent wages and with a career before him.

By 1850 he had just about passed into history. The forecastles of packets and clippers, at least, housed a mixed breed who worked as cheap labor, often involuntarily shanghaied into service because no self-respecting youth would stand the gaff of brutal mates and masters, low pay, and the relentless demands of a hard, routine performance. Not when the workshops of New England, the prairies of the Midwest, and the mines of the distant coast offered brighter chances. Shipowners could not, or would not, compete with those better opportunities ashore and a peculiar type of sailor vanished from the seas. More men were needed than ever before and they were recruited by fair means or foul, and kept at their dangerous tasks, if need be, by the threat of a belaying pin or heaver in the hands of a tough "bucko mate." Frequent juries of landsmen were called to decide whether mutiny or abuse of authority had caused a fracas at sea. When a ship was manned by a dissolute, fractious crew and ruled by demanding, despotic officers, it was usually impossible to fix blame.

A NEW ERA

For a generation after the sailing of the first Black Ball liner the square-rigged American packet ships ruled the Atlantic shuttle. By 1845 there were on an average three regular transatlantic sailings a week out of New York alone, and other ports had their own packet services. Stoutly constructed by skilled builders out of apparently inexhaustible supplies of fine timber, officered by the best of seamen, and astutely managed, these fleets had become the main link between Europe and America. Speedy and remarkably dependable for all the caprices of wind and weather, they held dominion of the Atlantic as the early clippers did of other waters a very few years later. As their trade grew the sailing packets increased in size, reaching a climax in the 1771-ton, 215-feet-long *Amazon* built at New York in 1854. To the major ports where the finest and biggest packets and clippers were built, came an endless parade of ships carrying live oak from Georgia and Florida swamps, red cedar and locust wood from Chesapeake Bay, light pitch pine from the Carolinas and Georgia, and white pine spars from Maine—the best woods that could be procured for their various purposes in building the world's stoutest and most perfect sailing vessels. No other single country could command within its own borders such a supply of superb wood. And in the early 1850's no other country was launching such a succession of matchless wooden ships. It seemed, and not only to local pride, that American "Canvas-back" wooden ships might inherit all the seas.

SHIP *Bavaria*, UNION LINE OF HAVRE PACKETS, BUILT 1846. Painting by an unidentified artist.

Kennedy & Co.

THE ARRIVAL OF THE *Great Western* AT NEW YORK, APRIL 23, 1838. Painting by Joseph Walter.

Even while the trustworthy sailing packets were growing in size, numbers, and speed, they were obsolescent. At the very time when they were demonstrating their finest qualities, steam and iron were taking over the important traffic on the Atlantic. To one learned observer in 1835 the project of crossing the ocean solely by steam power had seemed as chimerical as flying to the moon. Three years later the S. S. *Sirius* arrived at New York in nineteen days from Cork, the first ship to make the ocean crossing to the United States wholly by steam power.

"The news of the arrival of the *Sirius* spread like wild fire through the city," reported the New York press, "and the river became literally dotted over with boats conveying the curious to and from the stranger. There seemed to be an universal voice of congratulation, and every visage was illuminated with delight. . . .

"Whilst all this was going on, suddenly there was seen over Governor's Island, a dense black cloud of smoke, spreading itself

upwards, and betokening another arrival. On it came with great rapidity, and about 3 o'clock its cause was made fully manifest to the multitudes. It was the steamship *Great Western*.... This immense moving mass was propelled at a rapid rate through the waters of the Bay; she passed swiftly and gracefully around the *Sirius,* exchanging salutes with her, and then proceeded to her destined anchorage in the East River. If the public mind was stimulated by the arrival of the *Sirius,* it became intoxicated with delight upon view of the superb *Great Western.*"

New York has rarely known such a day of thrills. Twice within a few hours the harbor had welcomed an innovation in ocean travel that in the years soon to come would drive America's best sailing ships into discard. Within the next ten years England's Cunard Line was operating a fleet of steam vessels between Liverpool and Boston, then also to New York, that first skimmed the cream of transatlantic trade and then threatened to take over the whole substance.

The New-York Historical Society

THE NOVELTY IRON WORKS, NEW YORK. Lithograph by Endicott. The boilers and engines for New York's first ocean steamship were built here; also the engines for several of the Collins liners.

Determined to regain American supremacy and to "drive the Cunarders off the ocean," the Collins Line, subsidized by the United States Government, launched the *Atlantic,* the first of four super-steamships for the transatlantic run, in 1850. The three others, the *Pacific, Arctic,* and *Baltic,* followed later in the same year. They were all almost one thousand tons larger than the Cunarders then operating and their straight-stern design was a novelty that was soon generally accepted as standard.

To beat the Cunarders was a mania of the moment. Costs were not reckoned and in a frenzy of general excitement records for the Atlantic voyage tumbled one after another. Two Collins liners made the run in 9 days 18 hours—even the hours were counted now. Cunarders could not match such speed, nor could they vie with the comfort and cuisine the Collins Line provided.

Captain McKinnon of the Royal Navy made a round trip between Liverpool and New York, one way on a Cunarder and re-

turn on a Collins ship, and in July, 1853, published a piece in *Harper's New Monthly Magazine* about his adventures. After long centuries during which the passage either way across the North Atlantic had threatened a trying ordeal, he concluded, the voyage had been reduced finally to "a mere pleasure trip" by the magnificent new steam liners. He took the Collins liner *Baltic* from New York and arrived at Liverpool ten and a half days later. The Collins ships, he wrote, were "beyond any competition, the finest, the fastest, and the best sea boats in the world . . . they are as well officered and manned as any ships afloat; they treat their passengers with as much, or more civility and attention than any other line; and, finally, their food and wine, and all arrangements of the table . . . are as good as any person can require, even if spoilt by Sybaritic luxuries of the great Metropolitan cities of the world."

Swarms of well-to-do Americans bought passage to Europe on the new steamships, parading their bad manners along with their opulence on their tours abroad, it seemed to Walt Whitman and other critics. There were other lines than the Collins, of course, but the latter provided America's most conspicuous experiment, and failure, in this new competition on the high seas. They burnt up all hopes of profit along with a wealth of coal in their furious race against time. In the flush of victory that hardly mattered, even with the hardheaded businessmen who kept the ledgers. In 1852 Congress more than doubled the line's subsidy. But in 1854, while hurrying on to New York, the *Arctic* of the Collins fleet crashed another ship and sank with a loss of 318 persons, including Collins's wife, son, and daughter. Two years later the *Pacific*, another ship of the same line, utterly disappeared at sea. Congress lost interest in mail subsidies which had given the line its working margin and the Collins ships ended operations. Gradually the ocean steamship business passed to foreign companies and remained there.

America's heavy iron industry, needed to build large fleets of ocean steamships, was in its infancy at the time of the Collins-Cunard competition. With its endless forests

The Maryland Historical Society
SCENE ON BOARD THE S.S. *Arago*, June 7, 1857. Painting by John Hazlehurst Boneval Latrobe. The artist was the son of Benjamin Henry Latrobe whose distinguished work as an architect and artist is illustrated in various other chapters. The son was a lawyer, inventor, architect, and author, as well as an artist.

A COLLINS LINE STEAMSHIP. Lithograph by C. Parsons after a painting by S. Walters, about 1851.
The Harry Shaw Newman Gallery

CROWELL'S WHARF, SAN FRANCISCO, 1868. In the foreground, the *Valparaiso* loading for New York; in the background, the *Midnight* just in from China; other ships, the *Summer, Sacramento, Lookout, Dashing Wave*, and *Gold Hunter.*

of fine timber to draw upon, this country was slow to recognize the industrial revolution that was replacing wood by iron and steel for so many different purposes. On America's myriad inland protected waterways wooden-hulled steamboats, boats that could be fueled at almost any point along their routes from the forests that still lined the riverbanks, adequately carried their share of the nation's enormous and increasing domestic trade. But ocean traffic was passing to bigger, iron-hulled vessels and when the challenge was first posed America's production of iron was Lilliputian beside England's.

When, during the Civil War and the years immediately following, America's iron and steel factories made their first giant strides,

the nation's vision had been distracted from the sea. There was now no urgent need, as there was in some other lands, to live by the sea, to live by the sea or perish. But from the great continent behind the coastal range, unfolding its latent resources at a bewildering rate, there came insistent calls for the tools of progress—for railroads to span the land and knit it together, for mining machinery to gather the incredible riches of the Comstock and other lodes, for agricultural machinery to harvest the wealth of the immense prairies.

No nation on earth had such a huge and varied domestic market to claim its own manufactures. And in the zeal to satisfy the landsman's need, industry gave relatively little heed to the requirements of a new, up-to-date merchant marine of iron ships.

356

Steam and iron relegated the sailing packets to humble work. New York's Chamber of Commerce addressed Congress in 1860 stating that its members had "lived to see the noble vessels, which once stood so high in the estimation of the traveller, and which bore to our shores the most costly merchandise, degraded to the service of the emigrant, to the carrying of coal, crockery and iron and the bulky products of our own soil." So with the clippers. Like the Collins liners their day of glory was brilliant but brief. Their spectacular bursts of speed no longer counted against the regularity of steamship schedules. They left the country a golden maritime legend. But within a few years after their peak activity they were reduced to carrying guano, coolies, lumber, and flour at modest rates—searching unfamiliar seas for the limited cargoes they could pick up and carry in their slim, graceful, and uncapacious hulls.

Some of the once majestic square-riggers knocked about from port to port as tramps for years to come. Some were wrecked on distant coasts, winning but a scant obituary in the shipping records. Others lay deserted and rotting on the Pacific coast, or were hauled ashore to serve as rooming quarters. One, the Medford-built clipper *Phantom,* was plundered by Chinese pirates during America's Civil War. Still others utterly vanished during some ignominious voyage.

For years following the Civil War the sailing ships of Maine carried on the old tradition with even increased spirit and profit. Such ports as Portland, Rockland, and Bangor were white as ever with sails that moved lumber, ice, lime, and transshipped goods to widespread markets. Then here, too, slowly but inevitably the drama ended.

SOUTH STREET FROM COENTIES SLIP, NEW YORK. Photograph by Alfred Stieglitz, about 1898.

Estate of Alfred Stieglitz

IV

AGRICULTURE

AGRICULTURE

INTRODUCTION

$\mathbf{A}$T THE CLOSE of the Revolutionary War farming was, as Benjamin Franklin remarked, "the great business of the country." So it had been throughout the colonial period and so it continued to be for many years to come. Practically everyone lived on a farm. What was more significant in the world of that day, almost every farmer owned and, to a large extent, lived off the land he worked. It was a nation without peasantry, a nation of small-scale, freeholding farmers. "No wonder," wrote Crèvecoeur, about the time of the Revolution, "that so many Europeans who have never been able to say that such a portion of land was theirs, cross the Atlantic to realize that happiness."

The relation between man and land in America was unlike anything that had obtained in Europe for long centuries past. Here, for the first time in remembered history, man was confronted with far more free and desirable land than he could cultivate in a month of lifetimes. In other parts of the world people were hungry and clamoring for food. As Thomas Paine remarked at the time, it seemed as though so long as eating was a custom of Europe the American farmer could always find a ready market for his produce.

Commercial farming on a large scale was an early development in the South. The concentration on a few important staples, tobacco, rice, sugar, and cotton—largely for export —fixed the plantation system on a large region with a fateful certainty. The demand from abroad for those exotic cash crops was undeniable, the land was for a time rich and plentiful, and, by the approval of an old tradition, the cheapest human labor could fill the crying need for man-power. For the two generations before 1860 the production of cotton alone dominated almost every aspect of southern life. It became far and away the South's largest crop and the nation's most important export. The plantation was accepted by the world as a social and economic unit representative of half of America. Actually, even in the tobacco and cotton kingdoms, small, owner-operated farms greatly outnumbered large, slave-worked holdings. And the outlook of that sizeable yeomanry was little different from that of its northern counterpart.

North of the Mason-Dixon Line the rural scene was, for the most part, unrelieved by the spectacle of great plantations. The self-sufficing farmer was not only the typical, but almost the only, representative of rural life. Pennsylvania, and later the Genesee Valley of New York, offered exceptions to that general pattern. From an early date these regions, with areas of Maryland and Virginia, were the leading wheat-producing districts of the country and for years supported commercial agriculture on a considerable scale for the time. But generally, and especially in New England, subsistence farming was long a way of life for a substantial part of the population. The lot of a typical New England farmer, reported the *American Museum* in 1787, consisted of ". . . One miserable team, a paltry plough, and everything in proportion; three acres of Indian corn,— as many acres of half-starved English grain from a half-cultivated soil, with a spot of potatoes, and a small yard of turneps, complete the round of his tillage, and the whole is conducted, perhaps, by a man and a boy. ·.. All the rest of the farm is allotted for feeding a small stock. . . . Pastures are never manured and mowing lands seldom."

Mean as that picture was, it characterized the slovenly attitude toward the soil that featured almost all farming in early America, north or south. The colonial farmers and those who came later faced problems, many of them unprecedented in Europe, which unfolded in fresh variety as the country moved westward—the dense woods, the prairie, the different soils and climates, but, most of all, the land in itself. In relation to the "two billion acre farm" that lay before them, theirs practically for the taking, the farmers have ever been few in number. Their problem was not how much could be raised on an acre, but how much by one hand or man, "the land being nothing in comparison with labor."

Everywhere the haste to reap a quick harvest, regardless of consequences to the soil, encouraged a steady movement toward new lands to the west. "Scarcely has a family fixed itself," wrote one witness in 1826, "and enclosed a plantation with the universal fence—split rails laid in the worm trail, or what is known in the north by the name of Virginia fence—reared a suitable number of log buildings, in short, achieved the first rough improvements that apertain to the most absolute necessity, than the assembled family about the winter fire begin to talk about the prevailing theme—some country that has become the rage as a point of immigration. They offer their farm for sale and move away." Few farmers stayed long enough on one spot to learn by careful experiment the best use of their land.

Lands suitable for growing cotton ran out in Texas (although the land-hungry looked to Cuba, Mexico, and Central America beyond that) but fresh lands fit for northern produce seemed almost limitless. With the rise of industrial cities clamoring to be fed, those fresh lands were called upon for all the corn and wheat they could so easily grow. Northeastern farmers were driven by such competition to concentrate on perishable items they could more quickly get to near-by markets, and to more progressive methods of production.

Surveying the West of his day Jefferson saw there "room enough for our descendants to the hundredth and thousandth generation." Hardly two generations after his death the good lands seemed to be almost all taken up. Even parts of the "Great American Desert" were yielding crops to the charging advance of the farmer. In that brief interim the traditional pattern of agricultural life changed beyond recognition. Within a generation America adopted, invented, and improved enough agricultural machinery to bring about a complete revolution in farming. Land was still worked with realistic fervor. Mounted on a machine, the farmer could spread over a lot more acreage, far more rapidly and with much less human labor. And the new western lands offered ideal ground in limitless quantity in the race for plenty. The most fertile soils of all were being tapped by increasingly efficient mechanisms. America seemed ready to feed the world, as Anthony Trollope observed, for generations to come.

Production reached unheard of heights, accumulating vast surpluses for marketing. The farmer acquired a large stake in world trade and a new, complicated relation to the rest of the industrialized, urbanized world.

"The old rule that a farmer should produce all that he required, and that the surplus represented his gains, is part of the past," reported the *Prairie Farmer* in 1868. As in all other businesses, such periodicals argued, the object of farming was no longer primarily to grow a living, but to make money. The time had come "when the farmer must be a business man as well as an agriculturist."

By then the relative number of farmers necessary to feed the non-farming population was dwindling fast. In 1870 each farm worker was supporting about five and a half persons, the actual number of farmers in America was already a minority of the population, and there was a growing surplus of food for export. By 1945 each farm worker was supporting more than fourteen persons, barely one fifth of the gainfully employed population was engaged in agriculture, and the largest crops on record were being grown.

Long before that the habits and attitudes bred of a close association with the soil had become fixed. "The philosopher's stone of an American farmer," Crèvecoeur explained, "is to do everything within his own family; to trouble his neighbors by borrowing as little as possible; and to abstain from buying European commodities. He that follows that golden rule and has a good wife is almost sure of succeeding." And for all that has happened in the meantime we continue to recognize in that homespun vision of independent and versatile resourcefulness a vital part of the national character. The figure of Uncle Sam still resembles his prototype, Brother Jonathan, a country fellow with a good deal of horse sense and a cracker-barrel philosophy. Recent efforts to urbanize him by shaving off the rustic beard were quietly ignored.

The situation has almost exactly reversed since Crèvecoeur's day. Specialization and interdependence have replaced self-sufficiency on the farm. Most farmers subsist to a considerable degree on the factory-packaged produce of other specialized farms. With reports of miraculous, machine-contrived production—and of overproduction—are mingled warnings that the land itself is complaining. Large areas lie exhausted by extravagant misuse in the past.

During the depression of the 1930's that long neglect belatedly captured the public attention. By then it was an old story, told in its beginnings in colonial days and remarked constantly ever since. A century ago one observer wrote that even the relatively new lands of the West, in Mississippi, that had first been scratched by a plowshare only thirty years before, already resembled Europe after the Thirty Years' War, with "deserted homesteads and fields of broomsedge. lone groves of peach and China trees by the roadside, amid a growth of forest trees" to recall the passage of the plundering farmer. The total area of American soil reported perhaps with some exaggeration as "destroyed" by the first Soil Conservation Service surveys of the early 1930's amounted to eighty thousand square miles, an area equal to that of Scotland and England combined.

Since then the nation has learned better how to rebuild productive soil. Since then, too, the machine has increasingly taken over the problem of labor, or, more accurately. has shifted it elsewhere. Where once crops went unharvested, even with women and children in the fields, because hands were too few, now men stand idle while machines do the harvesting. Of the one in four families who now live on farms only a minority own the land they operate. And in the majority of the actual farmers, the tenants, migrants, and share croppers could be forming a new peasantry, American style.

THE OLD SOUTH

In the years immediately following the Revolution, as in colonial days, the pattern of life in a large section of the South was determined by tobacco culture. Despite periodic efforts at crop curtailment and price fixing by the Colonial and British governments to reduce the disadvantages of overproduction, the volume of tobacco exports had almost quadrupled in the century before the Revolution and increased by a third more before the close of the century. In 1790 more than $4,000,000 worth of tobacco was shipped from America, a value exceeding that of any other commodity shipped from the new Republic. The "evil weed" was grown everywhere in the East, from Que-

bec to Carolina, but the most concentrated planting was in the upper South. During the 1790's more than half the population of Virginia, Maryland, and North Carolina was engaged in or dependent on its production.

For a while yet lowland Virginia and adjacent lands retained strong traces of their colonial grandeur. It was here, wrote one late eighteenth-century traveler, that "numbers of English gentlemen, who migrated when Virginia was a young colony, fixed their residence; and several of the houses which they built, exactly similar to the old manor houses of England, are still remaining.... Some of these, like the houses in Maryland, are quite in ruins; others are kept

A VIRGINIA PLANTER'S FAMILY, 1845. Drawing by August Köllner.

MOUNT AIRY, RICHMOND COUNTY, VA., BEFORE THE FIRE OF 1844. Lithograph by Pendleton. Perhaps the finest colonial mansion still standing in America.

in good repair by the present occupiers, who live in a style which approaches nearer to that of English country gentlemen than what is to be met with anywhere else on the continent, some other parts of Virginia alone excepted."

With the close of the eighteenth century the Tidewater's Golden Age was fading. Even before the Revolution a careful reporter noticed that "plantations are every day left by tobacco planters, who quit and sell them at low prices in order to retire backwards for fresh lands." The wealthy could amass huge holdings in various sections and move their slaves onto fresh, fertile soil when worked fields refused to yield. The poorer moved on to new homes, first "backwards" to Piedmont, then up and over the mountains to still more distant virgin land.

By the early 1840's more tobacco was raised west than east of the Alleghenies. Virginia planters ruefully saw the tobacco inspections at New Orleans double the Virginia figure.

HOUSES ON A TOBACCO PLANTATION. Water color by George Harvey, about 1840.

ROLLING A HOGSHEAD OF TOBACCO EQUIPPED WITH WOODEN HOOPS. From William Tatham, *An Historical and Practical Essay on the Culture and Commerce of Tobacco*, London, 1800.

TRANSPORTING TOBACCO BY AN UPLAND BOAT. From Tatham.

TOBACCO WAGON. From Benjamin Lossing, *Field Book of the American Revolution*.

RICHMOND, ABOUT 1822. Thomas Jefferson's famous capitol building, the world's first "modern" public structure in the style of a classical temple, shows prominently in the upper left. Water color by an unidentified artist. In the foreground a market wagon and a rolling hogshead.

Richmond was the heart of the eastern tobacco region and the Mecca of the planter aristocracy which for a few years yet led a charmed and charming life on tobacco profits. When the Assembly met in the early days of the capital city it seemed to one visitor like an Arabian village, with its congregation of carefully bred, pedigreed horses that converged from the countryside around and about—fine horses that "must be mounted, if only to fetch a prise of snuff from across the way," bearing "Generals, Colonels, Captains, Senators, Assembly-men, Judges, Doctors, Clerks, and crowds of Gentlemen, of every weight and caliber and hue of dress."

Every early plantation "had a river at its door" and the prized tobacco, cured on the spot, was often simply rolled from the growing field down the slope to the near-by wharf. As the quest for unspoiled land led planters farther back into the Piedmont, getting the leaf to deep water without consuming all expected profits became a vital phase of plantation routine. Especially constructed hogsheads, "closer in their joints than other hogsheads" and raised on wooden tires for additional protection, were drawn like so many giant rolling-pins over the roads hacked through the thick forests for the purpose.

Heavy market wagons, drawn by mules, frequently six or eight in a team, with a shouting Negro driver astride the wheel mule, filled the few passable roads with picturesque tobacco-laden caravans during the summer marketing season. But the roads were often deep in mud, adhesive as tar, and at best rolling or wagonage was expensive and difficult.

Where possible the roads were used simply as feeders to the inland waterways. Until canals were constructed to ease the flow of traffic from the hinterland, shallow-draft, lightly constructed *bateaux* made good use of the Piedmont rivers, picking up hogsheads at likely points along the shore and hurtling downstream with them to their destination. The risks of transport, however, together with the dubious reputation of the professional boatmen made the freight costly if rapid.

All in all, concluded Thomas Jefferson, tobacco growing was "a culture productive of infinite wretchedness. Those employed in it are in a constant state of exertion beyond the power of nature to support. Little food is raised by them; so that the men and animals on these farms are illy fed, and the earth is rapidly impoverished." One planter complained that he had to sell a few slaves each year to buy food for the others. "Thus," he expressively observed, "they eat each other up."

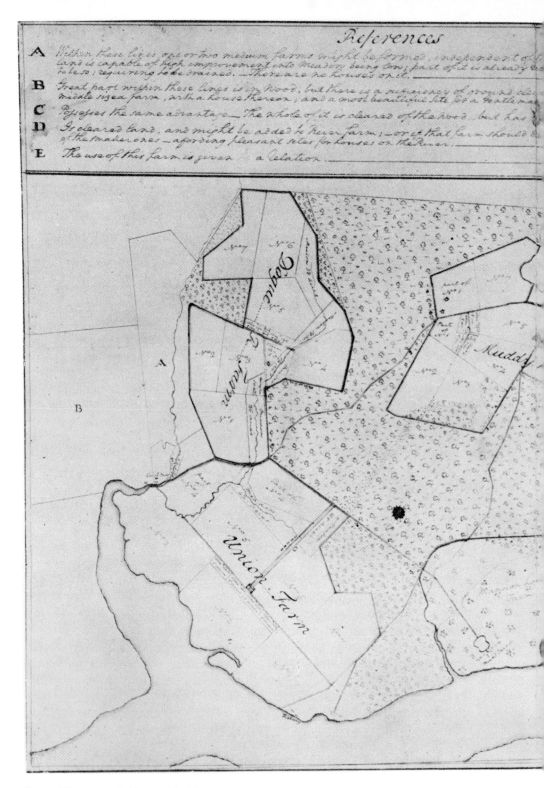

GEORGE WASHINGTON'S MAP OF MT. VERNON, 1793. It was drawn by the President, then in residence at Philadelphia, to a scale of 1 inch to 100 rods (16½ ft.). Washington referred to the map as "a rude sketch of the farms," but it is the best map of an American farm remaining from the 18th century.

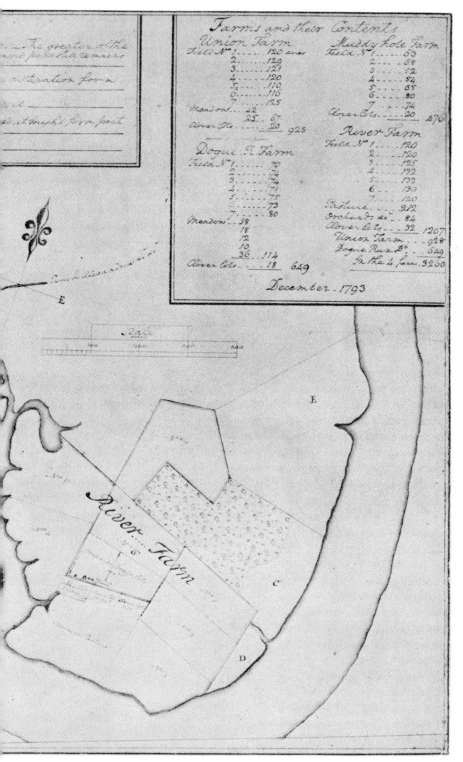

Farms and their Contents

Union Farm

Field N° 1	120 acres
2	120
3	121
4	120
5	110
6	116
7	125
Meadow	42
	25 67
Clover No.	20 928

Dogue R. Farm

Field N° 1	70
2	71
3	74
4	71
5	75
6	73
7	80
Meadow	38
	18
	12
	10
	36 114
Clover Lots	18 629

Muddy Hole Farm

Field N° 1	63
2	58
3	52
4	54
5	65
6	80
7	74
Clover Lots	30 476

River Farm

Field N° 1	120
2	120
3	125
4	132
5	132
6	130
7	120
Pasture	212
Orchards &c	84
Clover Lots	32 1207
Union Farm	928
Dogue Run Do.	629
In the 4 farms	3260

December — 1793

Scale

E

River Farm

E

C

D

The Mount Vernon Ladies' Association
MOUNT VERNON.

Like other Virginia plantation owners George Washington found the growing population of his slaves an embarrassment, an annoyance, and an expense. "Were it not that I am principled against selling negroes as you would cattle in the market," he wrote in 1794, "I would not in twelve months be possessed of a single one as a slave. I shall be happily mistaken if they are not found to be very troublesome species of property ere many years have passed over our heads." In his will Washington provided for the manumission of his human chattels.

While he lived Washington's estate grew to include more than 8077 acres. It was divided into five farms, each independently managed by an overseer (at one time a slave adequately managed one of the units) and each with its separate equipment, stock, and buildings. Distracted as he was by his career as a warrior and a public servant and by his duties as an indefatigable host to curious visitors, Washington was nevertheless one of the most progressive farmers of his day. His fields were constantly open to experimentation with new seeds, new fertilizers, and new methods of cultivation; he was in frequent correspondence with the leading agriculturists of America and England; he imported asses from Spain and France to breed mules in this country; and, when in residence, he was tirelessly in the saddle watching over the husbandry of his beloved plantation.

Through war, peace, politics, and a plague of visitors (he once referred to Mount Vernon as "a well resorted tavern") Washington's devotion to his estate—to its architecture, its furnishings, its gardens, and its husbandry—remained deep and constant. "No estate in United America," he wrote, "is more pleasantly situated than this. It lyes in a high, dry and healthy Country 300 miles by water from the Sea . . . on one of the finest Rivers in the world. . . . It is situated in a latitude between the extremes of heat and cold, and is the same distance by land and water, with good roads and the best navigation [to and] from the Federal City, Alexandria and George town; distant from the first twelve, from the second nine, and from the last sixteen miles."

Without his indomitable resolution to improve the land Washington's plantation would have soon resembled the worn-out, deserted farmlands that were everywhere to be seen in Tidewater Virginia in his day. As it was, The Father of His Country almost made his plantation pay, although it was too large for his convenience and he tried unsuccessfully to rent four of the farms.

Like Jefferson, Madison, and other for-

The Library of Congress
STACKING WHEAT, CULPEPPER COUNTY, VIRGINIA, 1863.
Drawing by Edwin Forbes.

ward-looking southern planters of the day, Washington turned from the continual tobacco cultivation that impoverished the soil to a conservative plan of rotated crops. A slave, it was estimated, could cultivate ten times more acreage of wheat than of tobacco. Wheat had always been an additional staple in Virginia, Maryland, and North Carolina. During the first half of the nineteenth century it often rivaled tobacco as the primary cash crop of that region. In the ante bellum period grain milling, indeed, became one of the "tobacco kingdom's" most important manufacturing enterprises.

About the middle of the century, however, the development of tobacco manufacturing in Virginia helped to stabilize and revive the languishing cultivation of that crop. By the time the Civil War broke out Virginia tobacco factories were employing more hands than any other industry in the state. Richmond became probably the most important tobacco-manufacturing center in the world.

In 1858 the Richmond Tobacco Exchange was formally opened. Here buyers and commission merchants met for the sale of the leaf by samples. Earlier warehouses had been in the nature of public utilities to encourage and protect the planter. The formal printed receipts of good-quality tobacco, issued first by the colonial government and later by the state legislature, were used as currency throughout a wide area, quite replacing paper money as such. As state inspection grew lax buying agents came in person to observe the official sampling for quality and first-hand sales took place on the spot. The warehouse once reserved for official inspections became an auction room, and a system of warehouse auctioning had evolved that differed only slightly from today's practice.

TOBACCO AUCTION IN A DANVILLE, VIRGINIA, WAREHOUSE, 1940. Photograph by Marion Post Wolcott for the Farm Security Administration.

The Library of Congress

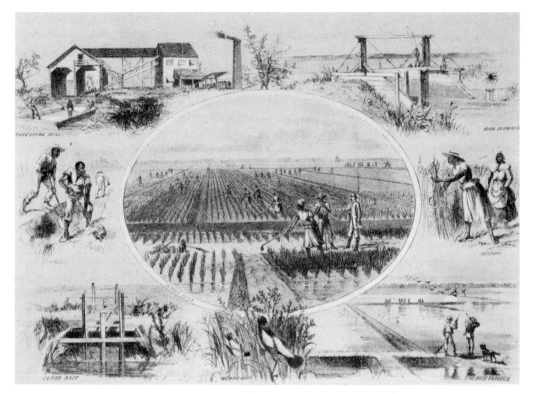

RICE CULTURE IN GEORGIA. From *Harper's Weekly*, 1867.

RICE HOPE, THE SEAT OF DR. WILLIAM READ ON THE COOPER RIVER, ABOUT 1803. Water color by Charles Fraser.

With its extensive and expensive operations rice culture in the Carolina lowlands flourished on a larger scale than tobacco did farther north, wealth became more highly concentrated, slavery more deeply entrenched. Negro slave labor was necessary to perform the ditching, the successive hoeings, the harvest, and miscellaneous tasks in the malarial fields—labor which white workmen could hardly have survived in any case. "Rice can only be cultivated by negroes," wrote one observer, "... Slavery, therefore, confirms the planter in his prejudice for rice; and the cultivation of rice, on the other hand, attaches him to slavery." Out of 1600 heads of family in the rural part of the Charleston district in 1790, 1300 held 43,000 slaves. Even Negroes in Charleston owned Negro slaves.

Ultimately the alluvial soil of the lower Mississippi Delta proved better suited to rice growing than the Carolina and Georgia coasts. But until the Civil War the river bottoms of the Ashley, Cooper, Santee, and Edisto supported plantations of great pretension, scattered as the swamps permitted. The more wealthy planters occupied several different residences according to the season, retiring in June or July "for four months into the town, for fear of the pestiferous effluvia" of the swamps.

The town was Charleston and on their city homes the rice aristocracy lavished wealth from their swamps. In urban retreat they lived out the summer season, giving themselves "every pleasure and convenience to which their warmer climate and better circumstances invite them." The city itself seemed unpleasantly exotic to some visitors. Picturesque houses built to suit the climate and the polyglot background of the people broke too many rules of proportion and academic form. "In Charleston persons vie with one another, not who shall have the finest, but who the coolest house," wrote La Rochefoucauld-Liancourt. The aristocratic nature of the city's social life was maintained long after wealth had shifted to new sections, and in a region of few cities its pre-eminence was indisputable.

CHARLESTON, SOUTH CAROLINA, 1831. Painting by S. Barnard.
The Yale University Art Gallery, Mabel Brady Garvan Collection

AN AMERICAN SLAVE MARKET, 1852. Painting by Taylor.

The colorful affluence of early Charleston, as of some of the tobacco plantations farther north, was an apex of an economic system built on slave labor. With the invention of Whitney's cotton gin, the development of the cotton industry, and the rapid, vast expansion of cotton growing in America, slaves took on an economic importance of new and tremendous magnitude. Cotton production doubled by the decade, jumping from 73,222 bales in 1800 to over four and a half million in 1859. It fed the mills of England and New England alike with an ever-growing quantity of a staple whose culture was admirably suited to unskilled, gang labor of the slave system. Breeding chattels for the increasing market became a big business in itself. The auction hammer rose and fell in a tattoo wherever "black gold" could be peddled and the sales held a morbid attraction for every visitor to the South. The cost of a "prime field hand," at about $1500 just before the Civil War, was probably greater than the relative cost of a tractor in the 1940's.

The growing textile industry of Europe and America was geared to the production of southern American soil and a vast human machinery slaved to meet the increasing demands. The fields of cotton in the United States and the manner of working them were a phenomenon that focused world-wide attention on the southern plantation system. "The whole plantation," wrote Frederick Law Olmsted of one he visited, "including the swamp land around it, and owned with it, covered several square miles.

It was four miles from the settlement to the nearest neighbor's house. There were between thirteen and fourteen hundred acres under cultivation with cotton, corn and other hoed crops, and two hundred hogs running at large in the swamp. It was the intention that corn and pork enough should be raised to keep the slaves and cattle. This year, however, it has been found necessary to purchase largely, and such was probably usually the case, though the overseer intimated the owner had been displeased, and he 'did not mean to be caught so bad again.'

"There were 135 slaves, big and little, of which 67 went to field regularly—equal, the overseer thought, to 60 able-bodied hands. Beside the field-hands, there were 3 mechanics (blacksmith, carpenter and wheelwright), 2 seamstresses, 1 cook, 1 stable servant, 1 cattle-tender, 1 hog-tender, 1 teamster, 1 house servant (overseer's cook), and one midwife and nurse. These were all first-class hands; most of them would be worth more, if they were for sale, the overseer said, than the best field-hands. There was also a driver of the hoe gang who did not labor personally and a foreman of the plowgang. These two acted as petty officers in the field, and ultimately in the quarters.

"There was a nursery for sucklings at the quarters, and twenty women at this time who left their work four times each day, for half an hour, to nurse their young ones, and whom the overseer counted as half-hands—that is, expected to do half an ordinary day's work. . . . We found, in the field thirty plows, moving together, turning the earth from the cotton plants, and from thirty to forty hoers, the latter mainly women, with a black driver . . ."

As long as new lands, cheap and plentiful, beckoned from the West, quick fortunes were wasting in any efforts to conserve the eastern fields by long-sighted, careful tillage. As early as 1820 the old lands presented a sad picture of wasteful erosion. Scrubby growths moved in to replace once fertile fields. Nothing that wiser southern leaders could plan stayed the inevitable shift of the cotton belt towards the Piedmont and then beyond it to the rich soils of the Alabama-Mississippi black belt.

A COTTON PLANTATION. Painting by S. Giroux.

The Museum of Fine Arts, Boston, M. and M. Karolik Collection

A HOME ON THE MISSISSIPPI, ABOUT 1850. Painting by an unidentified artist. The original of a well-known Currier and Ives print.

A FARM IN MONTGOMERY COUNTY, TEXAS, ABOUT 1850. Pencil drawing by William Bollaert. "1. Dwelling house; 2. Well; 3. Negro houses; 4. Smoke house; 5. Out house; 6. Crib for corn for horses; 7. Water trough; 8. Honey stand; 9. Filler for ashes for soap making; 10. Stumps of pine trees; 11. Gin house; 12. Cotton screw or press."

Cotton plantations varied widely in size and character throughout the South. In 1828 Mrs. Basil Hall stopped at one where the bed rooms had "their snow-white quilts and draperies, delightful arm chair and sofa, nicely set out toilet tables, and, in short, everything that is luxurious. . . . The house is small but very comfortable," she wrote. "On the first floor is a small drawing room and dining room opening upon a deep piazza, as they call them here. From this piazza a few steps lead down to a delightful garden filled with all sorts of flowers in full bloom, and close to the piazza is an orange tree covered with the flower and fruit in all stages."

In Texas, on the other hand, Olmsted stopped overnight at a plantation house which was but "a small square log cabin, with a broad open shed or piazza in front, and a chimney, made of sticks and mud, leaning against one end. A smaller detached cabin, twenty feet in the rear, was used for a kitchen. A cistern under a roof, and collecting from three roofs, stood between. . . . Three hundred yards from the house was a gin-house and a stable, and in the interval between were two rows of comfortable negro cabins. . . . The [plantation] house had but one door and no window, nor was there a pane of glass on the plantation." But the soil would yield. In 1853 a Texas newspaper noted that the cotton crop had been "doubling itself for the last twelve or fourteen years," and wondered where the ox teams could be mustered to cart the enormous crops promised for the future.

Here in Texas was the fateful boundary of the Cotton Kingdom. Cotton, it was firmly held, could not move on to the ultimate West as wheat marched into the distant valleys of California and Washington, its limits being set by soil and climate. But in the 1850's "Cotton was King"—or seemed to be. It comprised more than half the value of all American exports and three quarters of the slaves of the soil were engaged in its production. "In the three million bags of cotton the slave-labor annually throws on the world for the poor and the naked," reported *De Bow's Review* in 1853, "we are doing more to advance civilization . . . than all the canting philanthropists of New and Old England will do in centuries."

Three quarters of the total world's supply

The Newberry Library, Edward E. Ayer Collection

THE LEVEE AT NEW ORLEANS. Drawing by T. K. Wharton.

of cotton, it was plausibly estimated, was furnished by the Gulf States. Most of it was shipped from New Orleans, the old capital of France's Louisiana Colony.

"The most animated and bustling part of all the city is the Levée, or raised bank running along immediately in front of the river, and extending beyond the houses and streets, from 100 to 150 yards, for a length of at least three miles, from one end of the city to the other," wrote the English lecturer J. S. Buckingham in the 1840's. ". . . It may be doubted whether any river in the world can exhibit so magnificent a spectacle as the Mississippi in this respect . . . even New York, splendid as is the array of ships presented by her wharfs, is not so striking as New Orleans, where a greater number of large, handsome, and fine vessels seemed to me to line the magnificent curve of the Mississippi, than I had ever before seen in any one port. . . .

"The Levée itself, on the edge of which all these ships and vessels are anchored, is covered with bales of cotton and other merchandize; and in the busy season, such as that in which we were in New Orleans, in March and April, it is filled with buyers and sellers, from every part of the Union, and spectators from all parts of the world. There are no less than 1,500 drays for the conveyances of the merchandize, licensed by the city; and they seem to be all in motion, flying to and fro on a brisk trot, whether laden or empty— the horses never walking, and the drivers never sitting, either on the shafts, or in the drays, as in Europe. The bales of cotton, on their arrival in the rafts or steamboats, from the upper country, are carried off to the numerous establishments of steam presses, where they are compressed into about half their original bulk, and repacked in this reduced shape for shipment to foreign ports. All this, with the arrival and departure every day of many hundreds of passengers up and down the river, from Cincinnati, Louisville, St. Louis and Pittsburgh, to the Havannah, to New York, and to Texas. . . . Such incessant bustle, that every body and every thing seems to be in perpetual motion."

More than cotton passed through the colorful Crescent City en route to distant markets—lead from Illinois; tobacco from Kentucky; furs from the far-reaching tributaries of the parent river; ham, bacon, pork, lard, and flaxseed from various farming areas of the hinterland; specie from the silver mines of Mexico; and, among other things, sugar from near-by regions.

Sugar had been successfully cultivated in Louisiana under French rule in the eighteenth century. Behind a high protective tariff, production expanded rapidly—more than thirteenfold during the last four decades before the Civil War. The cane fields of over fifteen hundred sugar plantations spread back in a solid expanse from the banks of the Mississippi and its bayous. The highly mechanized character of the various refining operations of the plantation encouraged big production units, large-scale cultivation, and many slaves to work the fields. "A plantation well-stocked with hands," wrote "A Yankee" in 1835, "is the *ne plus ultra* of every man's ambition who resides in the south . . . not till Mississippi becomes one vast cotton field, will this mania, which has entered into the very marrow, bone and sinew of a Mississippian's system, pass away. And not then, till the lands become exhausted and wholly unfit for farther cultivation."

New Orleans became the world's leading market for slaves, many of them shipped there from eastern regions, sometimes in trainload lots, to be sold at the best advantage. Not all who took part in America's great westward migration were gloriously free and independent pioneers!

Sugar Mill on Bayou Teche, Olivier Plantation, 1861. Water color by Adrien Persac.
The Louisiana State Museum

The Bland Gallery, Inc.

COTTON PICKER'S HOME, 1883. Painting by W. A. Walker.

NEGRO QUARTERS, DRAYTON'S HOUSE, HILTON HEAD, SOUTH CAROLINA, 1862. Photograph probably by Henry P. Moore.

The New-York Historical Society

Two different accounts of slave conditions rarely agreed. Conditions differed widely and witnesses often came to see what they were prone to believe. "The negro cabins were small, dilapidated, and dingy," wrote Olmsted, "the walls were not chinked, and there were no windows — which indeed, would have been a superfluous luxury, for there were spaces of several inches between the logs, through which there was unobstructed vision." Fredrika Bremer, on the other hand, saw slave villages of "small, whitewashed, wooden houses, for the most part built in two rows, forming a street, each house standing detached in its little yard or garden, and generally with two or three trees around it. The houses are neat and clean, and such a village, with its peach trees in blossom, presents an agreeable appearance."

In *Uncle Tom's Cabin* Harriet Beecher Stowe spotlighted the seamy side of slavery in a sentimental manner that reached the heart of an international audience. Her tale easily became the best seller of its day and was published in several dozen different languages. In Europe it was reviewed by Heine, Macaulay, and George Sand; Tolstoy compared it with the work of Dostoevsky and Victor Hugo. In America it was read by millions, freemen and slaves. It was dramatized and remained on the boards somewhere in this country for at least sixty-seven years running.

More than a dozen pro-slavery novels were published in the three years following Mrs. Stowe's great tract. None of them enjoyed anything like the widespread popularity of *Uncle Tom* but something was achieved by a few impartial witnesses who supported the Southerners' contention that the slave was, all in all, well off.

The New-York Historical Society

ELIZA CROSSING THE ICE. Lithograph by Bour (Paris) after a drawing by Bayot, about 1852.

A Kitchen Ball at White Sulphur Springs, Virginia, 1838. Painting by Christian Mayr.

An inordinate curiosity about southern slavery seized the world. The prospect of a considerable area of the earth's surface, situated in a nation ostensibly dedicated to freedom and equality, farmed on an unprecedented scale, and profiting mightily by the exploitation of a peculiar institution which had been discarded almost everywhere else as barbaric, was enough to excite the world's wonder. On every score—political, economic, moral, ethical, and religious — the subject inevitably aroused passionate interest. The South, it would seem, was constantly thronged by sight-seers, many more curious than earnest, few capable of grasping the scene in its entirety, but all eager to make a personal investigation and report.

Out of the conflict of testimony it seems likely that the slave frequently suffered no more from the system than anyone else and that the average slave owner treated his chattels with care and consideration, often with fondness and respect. A "Massa sleeping in de cold, cold ground" set many a darky "a-weeping" tears of real and deep sorrow.

The Negro's capacity for gaiety, even on the auction block or slaving in the fields, confused or charmed many visitors to the South. "To everyone, whether in Old or New England," wrote Fredrika Bremer, "who is troubled by spleen or dyspepsia, or overexcitement of brain or nerves, I would recommend as a radical cure, a journey to the South . . . to see the negroes and hear their songs. They are the life and good humor of the South. The more I see of this people, their manners, their dispositions, way of talking, of acting, of moving, the more I am convinced that they are a distinct stock in the great human family, and are intended to present a distinct physiognomy, a distinct form of the old type man, and this physiognomy is the result of temperament. . . ."

There were tales of the lash, of chains, and of branding. But Southerners might point to the white "slaveys" of the North, captured in the toils of mechanized industry that was growing even more rapidly, and inexorably, than the Cotton Kingdom. There was no community responsibility to assure employment, shelter, food, and clothing for the industrial worker of the North or of England as there was for the Negro on the average decently managed plantation.

Many Southerners like Robert E. Lee, and like George Washington and Thomas Jefferson before him, deplored slavery. But the problem had grown to a desperate complexity. "I surely will not blame them," said Lincoln in 1854, referring to southern slaveholders, "for not doing what I should not know how to do myself. If all earthly power were given me, I should not know what to do as to the existing situation." The pressure on the South was relentless. The cotton crop leaped from two and one half to almost five million bales in the last decade before the Civil War, but with all the slaves in the country at work, the mills of New England and Europe were still not satisfied.

The American Antiquarian Society

NEW ENGLAND MILL SCENE, 1867. Lithograph advertisement of E. C. Cleaveland & Co., Worcester, Mass.

PENNINGTON MILLS, BALTIMORE, 1804. Painting by Francis Guy. Photograph courtesy of Walters Art Gallery.

NORTH OF THE POTOMAC

North of the Mason and Dixon Line methods of agriculture in the post-Revolutionary period were, on the whole, little better than they were in the South. Conservative habits and traditional equipment handicapped the farmer from getting anything like the best yield from his fields. Hauling produce to deep water here, too, remained a prime factor in the development of new lands. For, until the urban population of America grew to a relatively larger size, the main impetus to large-scale farming lay in exporting crops to European markets. In 1790 more than nine tenths of the American people who were gainfully employed were engaged in agriculture and, being self-sufficient, pro-

vided little market for their fellow farmers.

Northern farmers were generally small-scale husbandmen, like most of those in the South. But the North had its cash crops, too, especially the rich back country of Pennsylvania, the adjoining areas of Maryland, and, later, the Genesee Valley of New York. In the first two years of the nineteenth century alone almost a third of a million quarters of wheat were exported to England, much of it from Pennsylvania and Maryland. The Napoleonic struggles in Europe created an insistent demand on American agriculture and gave the American farmer a vital stake in world affairs. While Europe warred he was no isolationist.

BALTIMORE, 1802. Aquatint by T. Cartwright, London, after a drawing by G. Beck.

"The prosperity of the town of Balti-more," wrote one observer in 1799, "has been greater than that of any *seaport* town of the United States, judging by its exports." Mary-land's wheat was as highly thought of as its tobacco and, in the early days of the Repub-lic, Maryland flour was considered by many as the best produced in America. Ample wa-ter power and a proximity to the wheat fields of upland Maryland and to those west of the Susquehanna River in Pennsylvania, gave Baltimore its start as a city. Its flour mills helped give it the reputation of "the most flourishing commercial town on the conti-nent" during the late eighteenth and early nineteenth centuries. The revolutionist Mo-reau de Saint-Méry, who fled to America until the Terror subsided in France, esti-mated the city's exports in 1794 at almost five and a third million dollars. That growth of trade, explained apologists for Pennsyl-vania, was direct proof of the prosperity of that neighboring state, since many of Penn-sylvania's richest and most productive coun-ties lay nearer to Baltimore than to Phila-delphia.

Unlike most commercial farmers of the time, the Germans of Pennsylvania often settled at a distance from navigable streams. But, as one traveler noted, "hauling is done to better advantage in Pennsylvania than in most of the other provinces." To get the produce of the rich fields to market, wheel-wrights and wainwrights of what is now Lan-caster County, near the Conestoga River, developed the famous Conestoga wagon. "In this waggon, drawn by four or five large horses of a peculiar breed, they convey to market over the roughest roads, between 2 or 3 thousand pounds weight of the produce of their farms. In the months of September and October, it is no uncommon thing, on the Lancaster and Reading roads, to meet in one day from fifty to one hundred of these waggons . . . most of which belong to German farmers."

Whether the easier road to market led to Baltimore or Philadelphia, the typical Pennsylvania German farmer settled on land to remain there. Even first settlers built barns "as large as pallaces, while the owners live in log hutts, a sign of thriving farmers," wrote Lewis Evans in the middle of the eighteenth century. A generation later Benjamin Rush pointed out that the German farm could be distinguished from the farms of other citizens of the state, "by the superior size of their barns, the plain but compact form of their houses, the height of their enclosures, the extent of their orchards, the fertility of their fields, the luxuriance of their meadows, and a general appearance of plenty and neatness in everything that belonged to them."

Another writer of about the same period remarked on the "immense quantities" of wheat which the German farmer harvested from his fields. The habit of thrifty husbandry and unstinted labor, deeply impressed upon him in the fatherland, led the immigrant settler from Germany to utilize every inch of the rich soil he acquired in the New World. Those bountiful yields of his farm were the result of the freshness of the soil and the tireless labor with which it was worked rather than of any especially skilled husbandry. Like his ancestors and his new compatriots, the Pennsylvania farmer prepared the ground, grew his crops, and gathered his harvest in a tedious manner and with archaic equipment. The need of greater conservation of manpower in a country where men were so few, where desirable land was everywhere to be had, and which gave increasing promise of becoming the granary of Europe, was clear to every thinking farmer.

John Beale Bordley of Maryland, an earnest advocate of better agriculture and a founder of the Philadelphia Society for Promoting Agriculture, drew the accompanying sketch to suggest one way human labor might better keep up with the potential yield of the soil—a pre-machinery effort to allevi-

A PENNSYLVANIA BARN.

THE RESIDENCE OF DAVID TWINING, PENNSYLVANIA, 1787. Painting by Edward Hicks.

ate the shortage of manpower and to make what there was more efficient.

"The Drawing is intended to represent part of a Wheatfield," he explained, "and the Manner in which S. C. conducted his Harvesting in the Summer, 1787; whereby a smaller Portion than usual of Straw was gathered, the Labour of reaping lightened, the Grain more safely secured, and the Business of getting it out greatly expedited." A—P are the reapers cutting wheat, filling, emptying, and tying their bags. Q—T are lads or girls stationed in furrows holding larger bags to receive wheat from the reapers. V—W carry the bags to a cart. X loads the cart and Y is the driver. For the edification of his fellow Americans Judge Bordley's sketch was engraved and published in the *Columbian Magazine* the following year.

The Philadelphia Society for Promoting Agriculture
HARVESTING WHEAT, 1787. Drawing by Judge John Beale Bordley.

Collection of the late Harry T. Peters

A COUNTRY FAIR IN PENNSYLVANIA, 1824. Painting by John A. Woodside.

THE PROCESSION OF VICTUALLERS OF PHILADELPHIA, 1821. Aquatint by J. Yeager after a drawing by J. L. Krimmell.

The Historical Society of Pennsylvania

The Philadelphia society was only one of a large group of agricultural organizations which sprang up in America following the Revolution in imitation of those in Europe. By 1800 such societies were active in six states. Their purpose was to spread scientific information; to encourage experimentation with new methods and new implements; to breed fleecy sheep, sleek cattle, and strong horses; to promote modern equipment of every sort; and to encourage tidy, efficient farms with well-tended fences and large, airy, clean barns—an ideal glorified in the painting illustrated opposite.

Notable leaders lent their names and influence to the cause of better farming—Washington, Jefferson, Madison, among numerous others. But in America the little farmer was independent of pressure from above. He was rarely a tenant and could move about with more freedom than his European cousin. Customarily, as was often pointed out, he scratched over a great deal of ground but cultivated none, then moved west to repeat the performance in fresh fields, leaving conservation to the occasional landed gentry whose stake in stability was big.

The efforts of progressive farmers, notably about Philadelphia, were not altogether wasted. "The occasion that gave rise to this SPLENDID PROCESSION," reads the caption to the lower illustration on the opposite page, "was conveying the meat of the stock of exhibition Cattle to Market, which for number, quality, beauty and variety, has never been slaughtered at any one time in this, or probably in any other country, 100 carts were required to convey them to market, and the whole was sold within twenty four hours," etc.

Penn's city, grown large, was in an even better position than Baltimore to tap the rich farming hinterland; it became not only an important center of the grain trade, exporting 420,000 barrels of flour as early as 1792, but a marketing point for produce of every kind. The market itself, according to another observer, was "the great boast of the Philadelphians. . . . It is well supplied; and its regularity and cleanliness indicate good living and wholesome regulation. No article can be offered for sale here without first being submitted to the inspection of one of the clerks of the market, who seizes unwholesome articles, and a fine is inflicted upon the owner."

THE HIGH STREET MARKET, PHILADELPHIA, 1800. Engraving by William Birch.

The New York Public Library

NEW ENGLAND

Rural New England, as ever, had its own distinctive pattern which changed only gradually during the half-century following the Revolution. In spots, indeed, it seemed unchanged almost until the present day. However, the character of the earlier agricultural village, so typical of colonial New England, with its surrounding cultivated lands to which the yeoman made his daily journey, had already altered by 1776. The framework of the old village remained—still does here and there about the New England countryside—with the meetinghouse facing the common ground, the school near by, and the trees and old houses set in pleasant patterns along the adjoining roads. But as the population of such villages increased, the daily stint of traveling to ever more distant plots of ground became burdensome, then impossible. The new owner built his homestead, not in the central village, but on the land he farmed by day.

With time those farms became so widely separated from any center of population that the farmer could make only the necessary trips to meeting and to the miller, blacksmith, doctor, and other individuals who provided the more specialized services offered by a community. That transition from agricultural village to farm marked a profound change in New England rural life. As farms multiplied, their isolation increased and the farmer's family, thrown largely upon its own resources, became virtually a self-sufficient economic microcosm.

The household had, according to the author of *American Husbandry*, writing in 1775, "the necessaries of life and nothing more.... Their farms yield food—much of cloathing—most of the articles of building—with a surplus sufficient to buy such foreign luxuries as are necessary to make life pass comfortably: there is very little elegance among them." Separated even from neighboring farmers by long stretches of very bad roads and a continuous series of demanding chores, the Yankee farmer inevitably was "individualism incarnate." Independent and self-reliant, he constituted the backbone of Jefferson's ideal republic. His soil may

A CONNECTICUT FARM, 1789. From the *Columbian Magazine*

The New-York Historical Society

The Springfield Museum of Fine Arts

SMITHTOWN, LONG ISLAND, ABOUT 1860. Water color by A. Milne.

have been so rocky and sterile that even a single grasshopper could not find a square meal on it, the noses of his sheep sharpened so that they could nibble between the rocks, his pigs so thin it took two of them to cast a shadow, as local humor sometimes boasted. But with what little he may have had the Yankee farmer shaped a way of life, tightly centering around his family and his home, that later generations have given a hallowed place in the American tradition.

Nothing more clearly distinguished the rural life of New England from that of the South than those tidy villages to which the Yankee farmer looked for his "foreign luxuries"—for his salt, sugar, tea, and tobacco—and for much of his limited social activity. They were not planned primarily to be attractive, as were so many garden cities of later date. But, shaped by the vital community interests they served, villages and houses recalled the complete and intelligent partnership between earth and man that once

existed in old New England communities. And they reached, as Lewis Mumford has written, "a pretty fair pitch of worldly perfection" which the passage of time has in many instances not yet obscured.

That perfection was apparent to much earlier witnesses, both native and foreign. "New-England may justly glory in its villages," wrote James Fenimore Cooper. "... In space, freshness, an air of neatness and of comfort, they far exceed any thing I have ever seen, even in the mother country.... I have passed, in one day, six or seven of these beautiful, tranquil and enviable looking hamlets, for not one of which have I been able to recollect an equal in the course of all my European travelling."

As New Englanders emigrated, their typical villages appeared in other sections of the country—in Long Island, New Jersey, Ohio, and occasionally farther west, clustered about the village green or strung along the main road.

391

The New York Public Library

RURAL LIFE IN THE FIRST HALF OF THE 19TH CENTURY. 1. plowing; 2. sowing seed; 3. harrowing; 4. harvesting with a cradle; 5. and with a sickle; 6. threshing wheat; 7. a mill; 8. making butter; 9. breaking flax; 10. country store; 11. sewing bee. Woodcuts by Alexander Anderson.

The stern virtues that marked the character of the early Yankee farmer were hard-earned. In the techniques of husbandry he was no more progressive than his southern counterparts. Sowing his seed by hand in a manner unchanged since the time of Jacob, plowing and harrowing with cumbersome devices hardly better than those used in Caesar's day, reaping his harvest with the sickle and scythe of ancient tradition (only slowly accepting the cradle), and threshing his grain with a flail, or treading it out with horses and cattle, his routine was primitive and relentless. Under such circumstances men's and women's work alike was never done. "So sudden is the succession of labors," wrote Jeremy Belknap, "that upon any irregularity in the weather they run into one another; and if help be scarce, one cannot be completed before the other suffers from the want of being done. . . . It is partly for this cause . . . and partly from a want of education, that no spirit of improvement is seen . . . but everyone pursues the business

of sowing, planting, mowing and raising cattle with unremitting and undeviating uniformity."

Inland, at least, there were few markets to encourage the growing of surplus crops. The farm family lived unto itself, supplying its own needs and finding its recreation in close association with its work—in "bees" and other productive social gatherings. The mill and the country store provided the main specialized services necessary to an otherwise self-sufficing pattern of life.

The best and boldest of the New England farmer's sons and daughters moved on to more fertile fields as the West opened up, or quit the soil altogether for the more varied and promising opportunities offered by the city. "Every farmer's son and daughter," complained the *New England Farmer* in 1840, "are in pursuit of some genteel mode of living." A steady flow of Yankee youths streamed from the quiet village streets, the lonely farms, and the hillside cabins of rural New England, leaving the "honorable pro-

A NEW ENGLAND FARM SCENE, ABOUT 1860. Painting by George H. Durrie. A number of Durrie's oils were reproduced as popular lithographs by Currier and Ives.

"OCTOBER," 1867. Painting by John W. Ehninger.

fession of their fathers" for broader adventures in the rapidly changing world outside.

The small-scale farmer, laboriously working just as much of his holdings as unaided family enterprise could accomplish, enough to supply most of the family wants and little more, was the typical figure of early American society. The complete economic independence which he sweated to attain through seedtime and harvest became a symbol of the good life in America that persisted long after changing conditions had reduced what had once been a reality to a daydream. A century and a half after Jefferson's pronouncement, the self-sufficient family farmer was quite likely an illiterate and ill-nourished member of society, as the Okies and hillbillies of the country made sadly evident. But the antique ideal persists and from it many legends of the traditional American character have grown.

Thus Charles Miner Thompson has recently summed up the Vermonter—typical American for so many of us—in these words: "What manner of men are . . . the people whose turbulent history I have tried to tell? . . . Their experience had made them strong,

and the ceaseless training of a lovely but exacting land was enough to keep them so. A mountainous country that, although it had . . . rich stretches of fertile soil and abundant rain, also had long, rigorous winters and a short growing season; it exacted hard and resolute labor to make it yield its none too lavish rewards."

Hard as it was, rural life was never unmitigated toil. But recreation was usually made a part or by-product of work that had to be done. "Poor as we are," wrote the American Farmer Crèvecoeur to a friend, "if we have not the gorgeous balls, the harmonious concerts, the shrill horn of Europe, yet we dilate our hearts as well with the simple negro fiddle, and with our rum and water, as you do with your delicious wines. In the summer it often happens that either through sickness or accident some families are not able to do all they must do. Are we afraid, for instance, that we shall not be able to break up our summer fallow? In due time we invite a dozen neighbors, who will come with their teams and finish it all in one day. At dinner we give them the best victuals our farm affords; these are feasts the goodness of

CIDER MAKING. Painting by W. M. Davis.

The New York State Historical Association

A MAPLE SUGAR CAMPFIRE, FRYEBURG, MAINE. Painting by Eastman Johnson.

which depends on the knowledge and ability of our wives. Pies, puddings, fowls, roasted and boiled,—nothing is spared that can evince our gratitude. In the evening the same care is repeated, after which young girls and lads generally come from all parts to unite themselves to the assembly. As they have done no work, they generally come after supper and partake of the general dance. I have never been so happy in my life as when I have assisted at these simple merriments, and indeed they are the only ones I know. Each returns home happy and is satisfied, and our work is done."

Crèvecoeur's idyllic picture of solid rural happiness was redrawn over and over again in the century following. Audubon delightedly wrote of the "bursts of laughter, shouts, and songs," the general merrymaking, that greeted his approach to a maple sugar campfire where harvesters had gathered to make the most of the short season when the sap flowed.

"The husking of Indian Corne whereunto all the neighboring Swains are invited" was only one other of the customs that made light of work and that lingered on until the old-fashioned farm completely lost its place in the nation's changing economy. "Both sexes join in the pleasant labor," wrote Thomas L. Nichols, "with songs, stories, chaffing, and the understanding that the fellow who husks a red ear has the privilege of kissing the girl next to him. The corn baskets are filled, the pile diminishes, the stalks and husks are cleared away. Then comes a profuse supper of pork and beans, pumpkin-pie, doughnuts, apples and cider, if these have been produced, or other stronger beverages. Then, if the Puritanism is not too strong, a fiddle and a dance; if it is, games of romps and forfeits, certainly quite as objectionable, and a walk home by moonlight." The pleasant habit of making social entertainment of the necessary work of harvesting, when things had to be done on a large scale and quickly, developed into a memorable tradition in American rural life.

The Museum of Fine Arts, Boston, M. and M. Karolik Collection

RUSTIC DANCE, 1830. Painting by William Sidney Mount.

CORN HUSKING AT NANTUCKET. Painting by Eastman Johnson.

The Metropolitan Museum of Art

An Agricultural Fair at Auburn, N. Y., 1846. Lithograph by G. & W. Endicott after a drawing by Sanford. From the *Monthly Journal of Agriculture*.

The rocky and hilly New England countryside offered little incentive to experiment with the agricultural machinery and the new implements that were being developed for the rural market. The ordinary dirt farmer was, as well, conservative by nature and suspicious of anything that smacked of book farming. "I used to farm some," said one still unregenerate old-timer years later (President Harrison's Secretary of Agriculture!), "and made money at it; now I'm engaged in the pursuit of agriculture and can't make ends meet." But there were Yankees and Yorkers, as well as Pennsylvanians and Southerners, who were interested in something better than the traditional scratch-soil methods and who could prove the advantages of newer techniques.

Earlier agricultural societies were sponsored principally by the American equivalents of what Disraeli called those "squires of high degree" in England. In 1807, to demonstrate the value of improved stock to his neighbors, Elkanah Watson publicly showed his two imported merino sheep on the Pittsfield green. By popular demand he organized the Berkshire Agricultural Society

to perpetuate such a neighborhood cattle show on a broader basis and, in 1811, the first important American county fair blossomed out of those earlier exhibitions.

Unlike the buying and selling fairs of colonial times and those of European precedent this new American type developed into a social institution meant for education and recreation. The announcement of the first Berkshire fair read: "We take the liberty to recommend to farmers to select and prepare prime animals for exhibition, also for manufacturers to exhibit their best cloth, etc., for inspection and sale ... innocent recreation will be permitted, but everything tending to immorality will be discountenanced."

In time the fair associations and agricultural societies lost their early aristocratic flavor and more and more attracted the interest of the dirt farmer. In time, too, a wide variety of recreational features tended to overshadow the customary exhibits of livestock, fruit, vegetables, preserves, and fancywork at the fair. "There was two yoke ov oxens on the ground," said Josh Billings, "beside several yokes ov sheep and a pile ov carrots, and some worsted work, but they didn't seem to attrakt enny simpathy. The people hanker fur pure agrikultural hoss-trots." Horse racing in various forms became a standard feature and a great drawing card on the usual program. There were those who "would bar the gate forever to gamblers, jockeys, whiskey vendors, and oleomargarine frauds, and leave reptilian monsters, with acrobats, pigmies and fat women to the showman, Barnum. . . ." But, for all that, the fair did provide a discussion ground for common problems, for the formulation of policies, and for the fixing of agricultural and social standards.

Under the aegis of manufacturers, as well as of the societies, contests were held to prove that such modern contrivances as plows with cast iron shares would not poison the soil and would function better than traditional equipment. By the 1830's the value of better tools had been clearly demonstrated and old-fashioned resistance to progress was generally broken down.

The county fairs, contests, and other such periodic get-togethers, apart from satisfying the farmer's deep-lying need for social contacts, helped him to meet an increasing demand for his produce. The total population of southern New England more than doubled between 1810 and 1860. The non-farming population, often in the small factory towns that were scattering over the countryside, increased with much greater rapidity in the same period. Here, for the first time, the inland New England farmer found a handy market for surplus foods and raw materials. Under that stimulus the difficult change from farming for a living to farming for profit gradually got under way. "The Yankee," wrote the French traveler Michel Chevalier in 1839, "is the laborious ant; he is industrious and sober, frugal, and, on the sterile soil of New England, niggardly." Transplanted into the rich frontier lands, the Frenchman continued, the Yankee "passed miracles." "Fatigue has no hold on him. . . . He grapples with nature in close fight, and more unyielding than she, subdues her at last, obliging her to yield whatever he wills, and to take the shape he chooses."

The Essex Institute, Salem, Mass.

A PLOWING MATCH AT WORCESTER, MASS., 1841. Advertisement of the Boston Cultivator.

399

A NEW ROAD TO THE WEST; THE JUNCTION OF THE ERIE AND NORTHERN CANALS, ABOUT 1835. Aquatint by J. Hill.

The Collection of Regional Art, Cornell University
THE WEST DRAWS NEARER, 1857.

The productiveness of the West was prodigious. "Indeed," wrote one pioneer Westerner, "the two greatest objections to the West, in my judgment, are that the land is too cheap and too productive." During the first decades of the nineteenth century transporting crops to eastern markets by itself cost far more than growing the food in the East. However, when an easy passage through the Erie Canal cut those costs to a fraction of earlier rates, wool, wheat, pork and other commodities poured eastward at prices which the New England farmer on his older, hard-worked soil seldom hoped to match.

The rapid extension of railroad service throughout the country hastened changes already started. The canal and the railroad gave the West the outlet that it so badly needed. By 1860, Minnesota, Iowa, Nebraska, Kansas, and other western states were sending huge food surpluses to the East.

But by the same token, New England farmers found it easier to transport their produce to the cities. "Probably, in our state," wrote one Yankee in 1850, "there are now few farms not within ten or twelve miles of a railroad. They are thus enabled to send many articles to market, for which before they had none; while the transit of what they sell and what they consume is wonderfully cheapened."

Showing the genius for adaptation with which she shifted from commerce to industry in these same years, New England also changed her farming habits, concentrating on "the production of livestock—cattle, hogs, sheep, and to some extent horses."

The greater variety of ready-made goods on the shelves of the country store was a measure of the decline of the old economy of self-sufficiency. His new relation to a commercial market supplied the farmer with a cash income with which to buy factory-made clothes, tools, furniture and other useful equipment in place of that he had once made for himself. Home industries gradually declined towards a vanishing point and rural life underwent a fundamental transformation. "This transition from mother and daughter power to water and steam-power is a great one," wrote Horace Bushnell, "greater by far than many have as yet begun to conceive—one that is to carry with it a complete revolution of domestic life and social manners.... If our sons and daughters should assemble, a hundred years hence ... they will scarcely be able to imagine the Arcadian picture now so fresh in the memory of many of us.... Everything that was most distinctive of the old homespun mode of life will then have passed away. The spinning-wheels of wool and flax ... will be no more forever; seen no more, in fact, save in the halls of the Antiquarian Societies, where the delicate daughters will be asking, what these strange machines are, and how they were made to go?"

NEW ENGLAND COUNTRY STORE, 1873. Painting by Thomas W. Wood.

Anonymous Owner

AN AMERICAN FARM SCENE, 1853. Lithograph by N. Currier after a painting by F. F. Palmer.

PREPARING FOR MARKET, 1856. Lithograph by N. Currier after a drawing by L. Maurer.

A DESERTED FARM HOUSE IN THE SAVOY MOUNTAINS, MASSACHUSETTS, 1941. Photograph by John Collier for the Farm Security Administration.

Throughout the northeastern states farmers had to adapt themselves to the needs of near-by, growing cities, which were their best markets. Perishables could not yet be transported from the West and concentration on dairying and market gardening as we have seen, offered one solution to the East's problem. By 1860 New England and the Middle Atlantic states supplied seventy per cent of the country's cheese and almost half its butter. New York became for a while the leading dairy state in the nation.

Through the efforts of horticultural societies improved varieties of apples were grown. In Crèvecoeur's day a good share of the apple crop went to the hogs or to the press for as little as a half-dollar a barrel. "Situated as we are," he wrote, "it would not quit cost to transport it twenty miles." By 1870, Oneida County, New York, shipped nearly 18,000 barrels of apples to the city by canal or railroad.

To meet the new competition the Yankee farmer, like his counterpart in the Middle Atlantic states, overcame his indifference to new tools and techniques. The wooden plow was replaced by better-designed models of iron and steel; the sickle gave way to the grain cradle; the cultivator superseded the hand hoe; some lands were reclaimed and soil was restored by planting clover and using gypsum; more labor was hired and good farm land increased in value.

On the darker side of the picture many farms had been neglected or improvidently "skinned" to worthlessness. New England was spotted by abandoned farmhouses, once-cultivated clearings that had reverted to brush, and forgotten orchards. In years to come new pioneers would move in to recover the wilderness the original lords of the soil had left behind; Frenchmen, Portuguese, Finns, Swedes, Greeks, Syrians, and Jews, all ready to work with the same grim purpose that had once inspired the Puritan inhabitants.

FARMER GOES WEST

The farmer who moved westward during the generation following the Revolution repeated the experiences of the first American colonists. First, and quickly, he had to make a clearing in the interminable woods to let the sun in, then plant a crop for immediate needs around and about the remaining tree stumps. In 1803 Washington Irving reported the dreary fields of western New York where the occasional pioneer farmer had built a rude cabin amid the charred stumps of yesterday's forests.

To Irving that seemed a desolate, lonely prospect. Yet such solitude was a condition of life along the early frontier. The first settler was as dependent upon the stream and forests for fish and game as on the slim yield of his crudely fenced-in clearing, and to the hunter a neighbor was a competitor. The sight of another chimney's smoke was a signal to move on to an undisturbed wilderness.

In a second or third generation American that restless, primitive activity was an acquired characteristic. To the immigrant such a way of life was all but impossible. No system of agriculture with which he was familiar succeeded in the virgin West. In America, warned one disgusted student of agriculture, the European farmer would have to learn a new trade: "He will have to chop up trees, and cultivate the land by the

The New York Public Library

PLAN OF AN AMERICAN NEW CLEARED FARM, 1793. Engraving by McIntyre from Patrick Campbell, *Travels in the Interior Parts of North America.*

The New-York Historical Society

FLOUR MILLS ON THE UPPER FALLS OF THE GENESEE RIVER AT ROCHESTER, N. Y., 1835. Lithograph by J. H. Bufford after a drawing by J. Young.

hoe and the pick-axe, instead of the plough and harrow." Plowing a new-cleared wilderness farm was indeed at first practically impossible. An early settler in the Genesee Valley recalled that "he merely struck his axe into the ground and in each cleft planted a grain of Indian corn." Yet he expected to reap from fifty or sixty bushels per acre. Optimism was the prevailing spirit of the frontier.

That particular pioneer was not only an optimist but a prophet. In the decades to follow the Genesee Valley became one of the principal wheat fields of the country and Rochester the foremost flour-milling center. In 1852 *Gleason's Pictorial*, with typical American brag, boasted: "What Sicily was to Europe, and Egypt to the States of the Mediterranean—store-houses and granaries—

the Valley of the Genesee is to the world. The starving millions of Europe wait upon the action of its mills. . . . The flour mills of Rochester are among the most stupendous works of modern art, being built of granite, and of such size and strength as to be analogous only to the massive workmanship of ancient Egypt. These mills are so constructed that the grain can be delivered from the boat into the hoppers of the mills, and the returning boat receives, from another side of the building, the same grain converted into the most beautiful flour ever manufactured."

Much of that rapid progress had followed the opening of the Erie Canal. By the 1850's the canal was already carrying even heavier produce from the newer West—from Ohio, Michigan, Illinois, Indiana, and Wisconsin.

The great migrations of earlier history

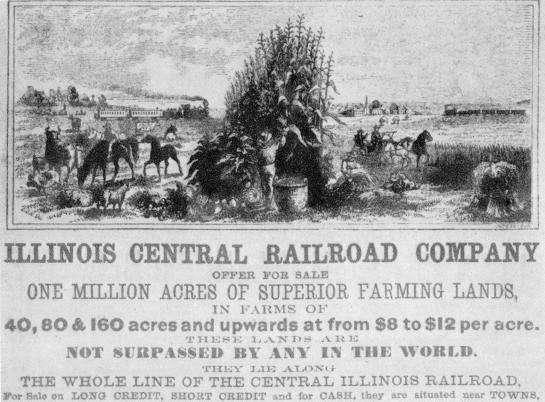

ILLINOIS CENTRAL RAILROAD COMPANY

OFFER FOR SALE

ONE MILLION ACRES OF SUPERIOR FARMING LANDS,

IN FARMS OF

40, 80 & 160 acres and upwards at from $8 to $12 per acre.

THESE LANDS ARE

NOT SURPASSED BY ANY IN THE WORLD.

THEY LIE ALONG

THE WHOLE LINE OF THE CENTRAL ILLINOIS RAILROAD,

For Sale on LONG CREDIT, SHORT CREDIT and for CASH, they are situated near TOWNS, VILLAGES, SCHOOLS and CHURCHES.

The Illinois Central Railroad Company

ADVERTISEMENT OFFERING LAND ALONG THE RAILROAD.

were like thin, erratic streams compared with the current that surged into western America following the War of 1812. When the study of our present civilization becomes the sport of archaeologists, that epic migration may be seen in its true perspective and its sweeping outlines. Neither the tall tales nor the statistics of today begin to suggest the real proportions of the story.

To witnesses in the East the older parts of the country seemed to be pouring out their people onto the new lands beyond the mountains. For vast numbers of migrants the Genesee Valley, the nearer West in general, was only a stopping place on the way to more distant goals. By 1830 the states beyond the mountains held more than a quarter of the population of the nation. Ohio had more inhabitants than Massachusetts and Connecti-

cut together. In 1818 Illinois entered the Union with a population of slightly over 40,000—less than was legally required for statehood. A generation later the number of people in the state had multiplied more than twenty times. A whole new world of political, economic, and social importance had suddenly appeared.

When the canal, and the railroad, brought it closer to eastern markets the great basin of the Mississippi seemed brighter than ever. The East, and Europe as well, was bombarded with rhapsodic claims of this land foaming with creamy milk and of hollow trees trickling with honey. It was a poor man's Paradise, more than anything else reminiscent of the Heaven on Earth of medieval legend.

Ohio and Illinois comprised "the finest

region in the world." The Wisconsin Territory was "the finest product of North America." The Mississippi Valley above Cairo embraced "the greatest tract of fertile land on the surface of the globe"—"the most magnificent dwelling-place prepared by God for man's abode." Iowa, too, was "as fine a region as ever the sun cherished by its beams."

Optimism could hardly go further. Railroads with millions of acres of lands to sell cheap, speculators with a stake in the new country, and boosters of a typical native strain, all appealed to eastern farmers, who, under any circumstances, were usually all too ready to move West.

Despite the influx of fresh hordes of European immigrants who settled in the cities of the seaboard the drain of people from the East was serious. Long before Dickens described the bitter disillusionment of Martin Chuzzlewit, the extravagant advertising of the West was lampooned by Eastern counter-propagandists. In 1839 "Major Wilkey," a New England prototype of Chuzzlewit,

pointed out that in Illinois innumerable droves of accommodating, well-fatted wild hogs, ripe for slaughter, did *not* amble up to the barnyards each week to be butchered, nor did extensive wheat fields sow themselves with grain. There was no special tonic in the air, water, or climate. Wilkey returned to his beloved New England from a year's residence in Illinois with "a broken down wagon!—a broken winded horse!—a broken hearted wife!—a broken legged dog! —and, what is still more to be lamented, the irreparable broken constitutions of my three Fever and Ague sons, Jonathan, Jerry and Joe!"—all as illustrated below.

But the "Major" preached a lost cause. In 1841 a "New England Farmer" bemoaned an undiminished emigration. "A great portion of our young men, on arriving at the age of manhood," he wrote, "push their fortunes in the West ... leaving the agricultural portions of New England, with help scarcely sufficient to cultivate their lands in the ordinary way."

The Library of Congress

A Satire on Western Emigration, 1839. "Major Walter Wilkey's unhappy return to New England from a twelve months' miserable half-starved residence" in Edensburgh, Illinois.

The Göteborgs Konstmuseum, courtesy of S. Artur Svensson
"Per Svensson's Farmstead in America: How He Dreamed It To Be and How It Really Was." From the weekly *Förr och nu*, Sweden, 1870.

Europeans also disbelieved or ridiculed the booming stories from the American West. To distinguish the "whopper" from the simple truth was indeed no easy matter at a distance of thousands of miles. Potato hills that might be confused with Indian mounds, beets so large that they looked like tree stumps, cucumber seeds that sprouted so fast the growing vines all but strangled the farmer as he briefly napped after sowing them—that sort of gravely told jest was not much more incredible than sober tales of a land where a man could easily earn a farm of his own and be free of burdensome tithes and taxes, want, and social oppression.

"If you wish to see our whole family living in . . . a country where freedom of speech obtains," a German farmer in Missouri wrote home to his relatives in 1834, "where no spies are eavesdropping, where no simpletons criticize your every word and seek to detect therein a venom that might endanger the life of the state, the church and the home, in short if you wish to be really happy and independent, then come here." To people accustomed to periodic famine and depressions, to people dissatisfied with religious and political controls, to people with frustrated hopes and ambitions, that sort of prospect must have seemed almost as chimerical as the wildest promises of the agents for railroad and steamship companies. In some European communities coded letters and secretly devised seals were adopted by correspondents to make sure that the truth and not censored propaganda came through from emigrant friends.

Occasional disillusioned visitors returned from America to spread true stories of their own unhappy adventures in novels and tracts. Dickens' classic caricature of the bitter aspects of emigration was varied by dozens of lesser-known writers according to their personal experiences. "In part," concluded one German author thoroughly disenchanted by the theme of emigration to America, "one deceives oneself, in part one is deceived; the result, total ruin."

Intermittently the darker reports from America diverted the main current of emigration to more promising countries—to Russia, Brazil, Canada, or Australia. At other times the call of the West was countered by official propaganda that vividly pictured the enormous gap between the restless peasant's poetic hopes and the grim reality that awaited him in the New World.

Between the accounts of Cooper, Chateaubriand, Byron, and other romancers of the early American West, and the reality of frontier life the gap was indeed wide. But the land, once cleared, was in truth almost incredibly rich. There was no fooling those who had tasted its fruits, and Europe was deluged with their simple letters home. Enough wheat was left ungleaned in the average farmer's fields, it was reported, "to keep a whole parish" in England; the peaches and apples left to rot in Ohio orchards were more than enough to sink the British fleet. The typical nineteenth-century emigrant was a son of the soil and such stories were enough to head him to the nearest port of embarkation. "Day after day it goes on so," read a descriptive German novel of the period; "band after band come down over the mountain with bag and baggage, with wife and child—all are emigrating, all are emigrating."

As earlier noted, the European immigrant was rarely a full-fledged pioneer. But when the native American pathfinder had cleared the land and pushed west it was often the newly arrived foreigner who took over. "My Yankee neighbor wants to move," wrote one newcomer to a friend abroad; "he is asking ten dollars an acre for his farm, but it will spare you the trouble of starting in the woods. The bank will lend the money, and I will go security for the note." By the numbers and speed with which they answered such calls, filling in behind the restless natives, the "ragged regiments of Europe" gave American expansion much of its epic, and much of its disorganized and reckless, character.

AN EMIGRATING PEASANT FAMILY ON ITS WAY TO GOTHENBURG TO EMBARK FOR AMERICA. Painting by Geskel Saloman, 1872.

The Göteborgs Konstmuseum, courtesy of S. Artur Svensson

THE OHIO CHILLED-STEEL PLOW.

Beyond the eastern forests lay the immense, treeless and trackless prairies of Middle America. A steady note of enchantment sounds through the descriptions by the first French explorers of these "vast meadows." This, La Salle had written, "was the best land in the world." Louis Joliet, companion of Marquette on his great adventure to the Mississippi, had reported that "a settler would not there spend ten years cutting down and burning the trees; on the very day of his arrival, he could put his plough into the ground."

However, after hacking his way through a thousand miles of gloomy forest the pioneer American farmer viewed that treeless expanse with a suspicious eye. It was beautiful enough—"a garden of delight in a dreary wilderness," wrote one immigrant English farmer. True, too, the land needed no girdling nor grubbing. "Why, thar aren't no stumps to plow around," was a typical farmer's reaction. But a land that grew no trees might not support farm crops. There was a lack of good water and little timber for fuel and for building. There were no nuts for the hogs. The thick and tough prairie soil

BREAKING SOIL ON A KANSAS PRAIRIE. Engraving after a sketch by Theodore R. Davis. From *Harper's Weekly*, 1868.

"Hazen Grove Farm, Fulton County, Illinois, Owned, Settled, and Improved from Wild Prairie, September 1842." Illustration from a county atlas.

was in itself a formidable challenge for the first plows to try it. Three to seven yoke of oxen were required to break new fields. Even the iron shares of improved plows could not scour or clean in the sticky, heavily root-matted earth.

In some ways trying to improve the "wild prairies" was a more heroic adventure than trekking across those inexpressibly lonely wastes to the tamer, more friendly wooded lands of Oregon or California. But when the tough sod was mastered the farmer unearthed all the riches La Salle had foreseen.

The first necessary step in that mastery came in the 1830's with the development of steel plows that would cut and turn the sod and scour cleanly. Other steps came in quick succession in the decades that followed. By the end of the 1830's the prairie farmer was already a towering figure. In 1839, one farmer in South Michigan wrote: "You can be-

hold the vast plain of twelve thousand acres, all waving in golden color, ripe for the cradle. . . . At this moment every man and boy, and even women are actively engaged in cradling, raking, binding and shocking the golden harvest. . . . But, after all, a large portion will be left out, and be destroyed. There is not *help* enough in the country to secure the crop."

Manpower enough to tap the unfathomable resources of the country never had been found in America. In every field mechanical aids to offset the lack of labor were a crying need. The American Philosophical Society was told in 1789 that "agriculture has the first claims to the exertions of mechanical genius." Fifty years later in the immensely fertile West those claims were pressed with undeniable insistence. Half a continent would waste its plenty until the solution was found.

411

The McCormick Agricultural Library

THE McCORMICK REAPER, 1851, "numbered and marked with paint, showing the connection of the parts one with another that they can readily be put together by the farmer." From a company advertisement.

Solutions were offered in a frenzied competition of manufacturers of agricultural machinery during the middle years of the nineteenth century. The mechanical reaper was probably the most significant single invention. For years Europeans and Americans had struggled to meet the need at that crucial point of the harvest when the work must be done quickly to save the crop. With the perfection of the reaper that problem was solved. Geared to the wheels of the device, a reciprocating knife cut the standing grain and dropped it on a platform for the worker to gather and toss aside.

At the Crystal Palace Exposition in London where it was displayed in 1851, Cyrus McCormick's Virginia Reaper was at first described as "a cross between a flying machine, a wheelbarrow and an Astley chariot." ... "An extravagant Yankee contrivance." ... "huge, unwieldy, unsightly and incomprehensible." But, when the field trials proved it would cut the cost and labor of harvesting by a third, the London *Times* conceded that the reaper alone was worth

more to England than the cost of the entire exhibition, it conferred "so great a benefit upon the Old World."

Nowhere in the world at that time was there a market for such agricultural mechanisms to compare with the American prairies. "He who has not seen corn on the ground in Illinois or Minnesota," wrote Anthony Trollope, "does not know to what extent the fertility of land may go, or how great may be the weight of cereal crops. ... This country is larger than England, Ireland, Scotland, Holland, Belgium, France, Germany and Spain together, and is undoubtedly composed of much more fertile land. ... The land bursts with its own produce, and the plenty is such that it creates wasteful carelessness in the gathering of the crop. It is not worth a man's while to handle less than a large quantity." McCormick had the foresight to move his manufactory in 1847 to Chicago, the heart of the midwest farming area, and by 1851 was turning out a thousand reapers a year. With the Civil War the reaper came into its own, enormously benefiting the Union cause by its work in western fields. It was a curious chance that it should have been the invention of a Virginian while the cotton gin that so thoroughly committed the South to cotton growing and the slave system should have been invented by a Connecticut Yankee.

In 1854 Chicago claimed to be the greatest primary grain market in the world. By 1860 there was hardly any doubt of it. During the 1860's more than eight million acres of new land was brought under cultivation in Illinois alone. The fertility of the cheap land and the increasing use of agricultural machinery soon reduced the cost of growing and reaping crops to a small percentage of the cost of handling the harvest and transporting it to distant markets. To cope with so much gathered grain and to offset the perennial scarcity of labor mechanical handling and storage was necessary.

The grain-elevator system, first used in Buffalo in 1842, not only solved that problem but in the half-century to come was a key factor in revolutionizing the grain trade of the world. Visiting the elevators at Chicago during the Civil War, Anthony Trollope wrote of "corn measured by the forty bushel measure with as much ease as we measure an ounce of cheese, and with greater rapidity . . . the work went on, week day and Sunday, day and night incessantly; rivers of wheat and rivers of maize ever running. I saw men bathed in corn as they distributed it in its flow. I saw bins by the score laden with wheat, in each of which bins there was space for a comfortable residence. I breathed the flour, and drunk the flour, and felt myself to be enveloped in a world of breadstuff. And then I believed, understood and brought it home to myself as a fact, that here in the corn lands of Michigan, and amidst the bluffs of Wisconsin, and on the high table plains of Minnesota, and the prairies of Illinois, had God prepared the food for the increasing millions of the Eastern world, as also for the coming millions of the Western."

GRAIN ELEVATORS AT THE GRAND CENTRAL DEPOT GROUNDS, 1866. From *Chicago Illustrated,* published by Jevne and Almini.

The Library of Congress

Step by step, and at a rapid pace, the manual labor of farming was being eliminated by horse-powered mechanical contrivances. With the Marsh harvester, patented in 1858, the grain was raised by a continuous canvas apron to a table where two men could bind it and toss the bundles aside as rapidly as it was brought to them, without the need of stepping or stooping in the process. It halved the time of the binding operation. With the automatic binder even that human operation was eliminated by a machine that seized the bundles, bound them, cut them loose, and laid them aside, all with power supplied by horses. The speed of harvesting was enormously stepped up, horses were increasingly in demand, and men were freed for other work in other fields. "The saucy machine has driven the scythe from the field," reported one exuberant Philadelphia editor, "almost tempting old Time to choose a new weapon ... and the principal work of harvest, now, is to drive the horse about the field a few times and lo!, the harvest is gathered."

No one who had sweated through a prairie harvest would have recognized that pretty picture. The time needed for preparing the soil and reaping the harvest had, indeed, been phenomenally reduced. The brute labor of many operations had been transferred from the farmer to his horses, oxen, and mules. The farmer was in a better position to secure his crop regardless of weather and scarcity of man-power. But it is doubtful that the labor-saving machines shortened the working day of many farmers, as the advertisements suggested.

America was still being farmed exploitively rather than intensively and conservatively. Yield per acre was less important than quantity produced by one worker. The European farmer gleaned more per unit of land than his American cousin. But the latter, astride his "saucy machine," produced more in a

THE MARSH HARVESTER. From an advertisement.

The McCormick Agricultural Library

414

THE AUTOMATIC TWINE BINDER. From an advertisement.

day from much larger fields to which he added year by year. William H. Seward once asserted that the reaper had pushed the farming frontier forward at the rate of thirty miles each year. Not many were yet worrying about what happened to the land itself in that surging progress. In 1860 more than a billion acres still remained in the public domain, and results of rapid expansion were spectacular.

Even during the Civil War, under the burden of feeding the Northern army as well as the civilians, western production was so high that 138 million bushels of wheat could still be exported. The spectacle of a nation fighting a great war with large numbers of its young farmers in service, and producing a surplus of foodstuffs at the same time contradicted all logic.

After the war, despite a large increase in domestic consumption, grain exports continued to rise. But the growing concentration of people in the cities of the world provided a ready market for the bounty of a land blessed with every resource.

THE ADVANTAGES OF MECHANIZED FARMING. "Owning a McCormick twine binder he has time to spare." From a company advertisement.

415

HARVEST TIME, A HORSE-POWERED THRESHER IN ACTION. Engraving after a drawing by W. M. Cary from *Harper's Weekly.*

The solution of one farm problem usually throws a searching light on some other need at a different point in crop production. After the introduction of the mechanical reaper, turning the soil took a disproportionate amount of time and labor. The invention of the modern plow, quickening and easing that step, shifted the peak load of farm labor to threshing.

For long centuries the farmer had threshed his grain with hickory flails or by his horses' hoofs. One way or the other it was one of the slowest and most laborious, expensive, and wasteful operations on the farm. Even before better plows, reapers, and cultivators had stepped up other phases of farm activity the traditional methods of threshing constituted a wearisome delay. By the 1830's the need for some machine to break through that bottleneck was so urgently felt that more than seven hundred different small inexpensive models were being advertised.

In the next decade the Pitts thresher, operated by a horse-powered treadmill, which cleaned and separated the grain as well as threshed it, was operating in the leading wheat fields of the West. But horse-driven threshing was still inadequate to keep pace with the improving harvester and binder. The produce of the prairies was developing into a golden torrent. The wheat harvest of 1840 amounted to 85,000,000 bushels; in 1860 it was more than twice that; by 1890 it was more than five times the 1840 figure— one sixth the total crop of the world.

The development of a steam-powered thresher that would not only separate the grain from the chaff but would move the apparatus itself from point to point, released both human crews and animal teams for other waiting chores. It was not an immedi-

ately popular innovation—to many farmers
the machine seemed dangerous—but it pointed to the day when much of the traditional,
often ugly drudgery of farm life would be
taken over by self-powered machines.

"Threshing by steam is a comparatively
new feature in agricultural industry," wrote
a reporter for *Frank Leslie's Magazine* in
November, 1860, "new even in the West,
where almost everything is as yet new. . . .
There are now . . . within a range of ten
miles from [here], twelve of these steam
threshers running steadily during the threshing season, which generally lasts from July
to February, and all are doing a good business. . . . Grain threshing in the West is not
generally done by each farmer doing his
own work, but is done by men who purchase
a threshing machine and go from farm to
farm threshing each man's crop for so much
per bushel." The newly applied machines,
he added, were capable of processing a thou-

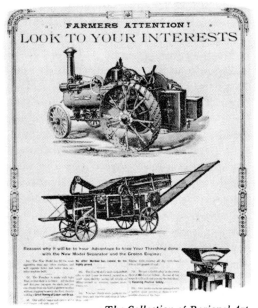

*The Collection of Regional Art,
Cornell University*
STEAM-POWERED THRESHER WITH PORTABLE ENGINE.
Advertisement.

The Library of Congress
STEAM-POWERED THRESHING IN DAKOTA, 1879. Engraving from *La Ilustracion Española y Americana.*

sand bushels of good wheat in ten hours and sometimes were worked at that rate for days at a time.

Machine farming as it developed in the last quarter of the nineteenth century found its perfect proving ground in the American West. The enormous sweep of tillable land, together with the demands for food from a rapidly increasing non-farming population in Europe as well as America, encouraged always quicker and simpler means of working the soil. Every advance in mechanization suggested larger farming units for economical and profitable production. In turn, as farming areas increased, more and speedier mechanized appliances were wanted to work them. There would never in the wide world be men enough to do the job manually.

In the bonanza farms of the Northwest and California that spiral of agricultural development reached a grand climax. The Dalrymple farm in Dakota consisted of over one hundred and fifteen square miles of land bought up from the vast Northern Pacific Railroad holdings that Jay Cook's failure in 1873 had dumped on the market. Six hundred men worked on the harvest; one hundred and fifteen self-binding reapers cut through the wheat in a seemingly endless file, cutting a swathe one fifth of a mile wide; seventy-one steam threshers passed the load on to waiting trains.

In California by the 1880's, giant combines that reaped, threshed, cleaned, and bagged wheat in a single operation were moving over other vast fields, working as many as forty-five acres a day. (Less than two generations earlier it had taken the single farmer more than two working days to harvest one acre.) Even before that California had become the second wheat-producing state of the Union—and, soon after, steam-driven combines were pouring out twelve bushels of grain a minute. Here were gold diggings, indeed!

The bonanza farms lasted only briefly;

HARVESTING ON A BONANZA FARM. Engraving after a drawing by W. A. Rogers, from *Harper's Weekly*, 1891.
The Library of Congress

they were mostly broken up in profitable sales by the 1890's. But while they lasted their huge, cheaply acquired, productive lands, worked by highly organized, mechanically efficient methods, yielded handsome profits. The nation was eager to boast of that sort of large-scale accomplishment. But the nation was also conditioned to the ideal of the free and independent farmer and where was he here? This was Big Business and the independent farmer was often either an absentee owner or a company. "In no case," remarked one traveler in the Red River wheat country in 1880, "was the permanent residence of a family to be found upon them, nor anything that could be called a home. In fact the idea of a home does not pertain to them; they are simply business ventures."

On the larger farms the man in the field was more like a cog in an industrial system than like Crèvecoeur's happy freeholder. Huge harvests, machinery notwithstanding, needed many extra hands temporarily at the peak of the load. Migratory laborers worked their way northward from Kansas to Canada following the season. The old, informal relationship of farmer and hired hand was giving way on the great wheat farms to a business agreement between proprietor and laborer. As free and cheap lands disappeared, and as farming became increasingly capitalized, the traditional progress of the hired hand to a farm of his own was blocked. It projected the alarming possibility of a disinherited rural caste in parts of the country.

At that rate Jefferson's dream of an expanding agrarian democracy could turn into a national nightmare. Even worse, at the rate the soil was, in many places, being skinned by careless farming — hurriedly, recklessly, prodigally—large areas of the bountiful continent could be turned into a wasteland long before Jefferson's "hundredth and thousandth generation" of Americans had tried their crops.

MIGRANT HARVEST HANDS ON THEIR WAY TO THE WHEAT FIELDS OF THE NORTHWEST. Engraving after a drawing by W. A. Rogers, from *Harper's Weekly*, 1890.

The Library of Congress

From the first days of the Republic the land laws of America have been designed to establish, maintain, or recover the freehold family farm as an essential working unit of our society. The Ordinance of 1785 which at the beginning shaped the course of our public land policy (see Chapter II), and the Pre-emption Law of 1841 which legalized squatting on the unsurveyed public domain were both directed toward that same end. Lincoln, who was "in favor of settling the wild lands into small parcels so that every poor man may have a home," readily signed the Homestead Act of 1862 which assured that virtually any mature American, actually or potentially a citizen, could acquire 160 acres of free land after proving five years' residence on or cultivation of the site for which he had filed a claim.

In theory the Homestead Act was a democratic formula for distributing and populating the remaining public domain. But in practice there arose many complications to the full achievement of its purpose. For one thing, both the federal and state governments as well as the railroads were, at the same time, offering for sale other huge, usually more desirable tracts of unoccupied land. Although a larger area was patented under the terms of the act than the combined area of Great Britain and France, even more land was sold than homesteaded. In either case the speculator or the monopolist often profited at the expense of the individual settler—and the proportion of tenant to free farms continued to increase.

Much of the land opened by the Homestead Act was west of the 100th meridian, a sub-humid, treeless region. Little in their experience could have prepared the settlers for their new life. Nature was violent. Floods, droughts, and hot winds; hordes of earth-blackening grasshoppers that by sheer weight broke the limbs of trees they could find to settle on, that thunderously fed on everything in sight; prairie fires that leaped sizeable rivers; blizzards that mocked description; and, worse, the anguishing, mind- and heart-breaking loneliness of an isolated prairie home that resulted in "alarming

EMIGRANTS MOVING INTO CUSTER COUNTY, NEBRASKA, 1886. Photograph by S. D. Butcher.

The Nebraska State Historical Society

A Sod Dugout in Nebraska, 1892. Photograph by Butcher.

amounts of insanity" according to the *Atlantic Monthly* in 1893. The bad with the good was on a magnificent scale.

Whatever the conditions in unoccupied lands America knew the greatest land boom of all in the 1870's and '80's. Urged on by their inherent mobility, by reports of wondrously black soil, by government and railroad persuasion, migrant hordes swept in a gigantic wave over the lands west of the Missouri. Restless veterans of the Union Army, Confederate soldiers fed up with carpet-bag rule in the South, emigrants from Europe, people of every variety joined the stampede. A large portion was merely moving on from recently settled lands just to the east of the "boom belt."

Whole colonies of Germans, Russians, English, French, Swiss, Belgians, Canadians, Scandinavians, Icelanders (one third of Denmark's Icelandic subjects crossed the ocean to find their fortune), and colored people from the South, not to mention a variety of religious and utopian groups, came credulously to lands advertised without restraint by agents of territories and railroads. Everett Dick in *The Sod-House Frontier* quotes a revealing report home from Nebraska's salesman in Scandinavia in 1871: "Dear Sir: Victory! The battle is won for our state, but it was a hard fought battle; a great deal harder than I imagined. The fall emigration to Nebraska of people with sufficient capital to commence work on our prairies will be very large. On Monday I go to Sweden and Norway, and will have easy work there. I shall try my best to beat the agent for Minnesota, Col. Mathison, formerly secretary of state. but now in Sweden. The truth must and shall be known all over the country.

"All the papers here will now come out in favor of our state; but I had to face them by threatening to lecture publicly about Nebraska—a step now unnecessary."

The farmer's contribution to America's unique success story was beyond calculation. He fed the hungry swarms that crowded into cities; he provided the huge freights that kept the railroads at their gigantic task of knitting the continent together; he supplied the ships of the sea with return cargoes—in exchange for their incoming human shipments; by the bulk and value of his produce, he profoundly changed America's position in world affairs and moved his country towards economic independence. Yet, with the 1860's, the tiller of the soil, "oldest of nobles," was threatened by vassalage to the barons of industrial power. To grow and market his crops he must cope with the corporate interests of finance, manufacture, and railroads—interests that often seemed diametrically opposed to his own. For the first time in American history agricultural production, for all its impressive statistics, was overshadowed economically by the output of factories and shops, and the organizations that controlled it. What at first seemed quite as serious, the farmer's social status was being undermined by city attitudes. "Rube" and "hayseed" were creeping into the vernacular.

To consolidate and improve the farmer's position, to justify farming as a good and dignified way of life, an astonishing rural organization—The Patrons of Husbandry, or Grange—was founded in 1867. Within six years a million and a half farmers had joined fifteen thousand local granges "to develop a better and higher manhood and womanhood among" rural folk, to enhance the comforts and attractions of their homes, and to reaffirm their faith in farming as a direct path in the pursuit of happiness—as one Grange convention announced. "We propose," another convention proclaimed, "meeting together, talking together, working together, buying together, and in general acting together for our mutual protection and advancement as occasion may require."

All those resolves and purposes were hardly realized, but they were a token of a new and lasting rural self-consciousness. The social program of picnics, meetings, and get-togethers, all of which specifically included women, at least promised some escape from the monotonous toil of farm life.

The revolt went much farther than mere social endeavor, vital as that was. It was in part directed against those who carried and handled the farmer's produce and those "middlemen" who raised the price of foodstuffs many times en route from farm to consumer. By their complaints against the arbitrary and excessive charges imposed by grain warehouses and railroads, the crusading farmers opened a whole new era in the relations of government and industry. In the "Granger" cases decided by the Supreme Court in 1877, state laws controlling railroad and warehouse charges were upheld and the fundamental principle that government could control privately owned business of a public character, in the interest of the general welfare, was clearly and permanently established. Although in 1886 a state's power was limited to control of strictly intra-state business, yet government "meddling" was officially approved in spite of private enterprise's cry against "communism."

In many places where local granges were established some sort of co-operative buying and selling was attempted. By direct dealings between producer and consumer the farmer hoped to eliminate the oppressive charges of the middleman and force local merchants to keep their prices fairly in line. In spite of occasional spectacular successes most of these early enterprises failed. However, the idea never died and those first efforts at co-operation not only saved the farmer considerable sums of money but also threw a lasting scare into the manufacturers and merchants who hoped to sell to him. Speaking of the early Grange, John D. Hicks has said, "Many of these ventures were unsuccessful . . . but the farmers who had participated in the movement did not soon forget the fright they had given the politicians by their independence, the victory they had won over the railroads, and the good times they had had at lodge meetings and picnics."

THE PURPOSES OF THE GRANGE, 1873. Lithograph by Strobridge & Co.

The Library of Congress

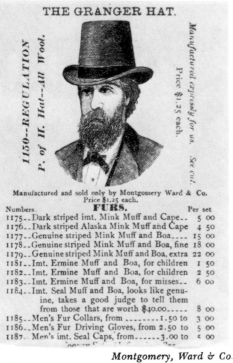

THE GRANGER HAT.

1150—REGULATION
P. of H. Hat—All Wool.

Manufactured expressly for us. See cut.

Price $1.25 each.

Manufactured and sold only by Montgomery Ward & Co.
Price $1.25 each.

Numbers.	FURS.	Per set
1175..Dark striped imt. Mink Muff and Cape..		5 00
1176..Dark striped Alaska Mink Muff and Cape		4 50
1177..Genuine striped Mink Muff and Boa....		15 00
1178..Genuine striped Mink Muff and Boa, fine		18 00
1179..Genuine striped Mink Muff and Boa, extra		22 00
1181..Imt. Ermine Muff and Boa, for children		1 50
1182..Imt. Ermine Muff and Boa, for children		2 50
1183..Imt. Ermine Muff and Boa, for misses..		6 00
1184..Imt. Seal Muff and Boa, looks like genuine, takes a good judge to tell them from those that are worth $40.00.....		8 00
1185..Men's Fur Collars, from ....1.50 to		3 00
1186..Men's Fur Driving Gloves, from 2.50 to		5 00
1187..Men's imt. Seal Caps, from......3.00 to		5 00

Montgomery, Ward & Co.
AN ADVERTISEMENT FROM A CATALOGUE OF MONTGOMERY, WARD & CO., 1875.

Another answer to the farmer's protests came with the beginning of mail order merchandising. Montgomery, Ward and Co., established in 1872 specifically "to meet the wants of the Patrons of Husbandry," won quick and widespread rural support by its program of direct cash sales. In the "wishing books," as their illustrated catalogues were called, the farmer's family could review not only the necessary equipment for the farm but also the less essential accessories of life made popular by city fashions—all priced to attract the rural market.

The first and most lasting benefit of Grange activity was in breaking down the intolerable isolation and monotony of rural life. In *A Son of the Middle Border* Hamlin Garland recalled that the periodic Grange meetings were dates of very great importance in the Garland calendar.

"We all looked forward to it for weeks and every young man who owned a top-buggy got it out and washed and polished it for the use of his best girl, and those who

Montgomery, Ward & Co.
THE BEGINNINGS OF THE MAIL-ORDER BUSINESS. From the Montgomery, Ward & Co. catalogue, 1878.

THE IOWA AGRICULTURAL FAIR, 1884.

were not so fortunate as to own a 'rig' paid high tribute to the livery stable of the nearest town. Others, less able or less extravagant, doubled teams with a comrade and built a 'bowery wagon' out of a wagon-box, and with hampers heaped with food rode away in state, drawn by a four or six-horse team. It seemed a splendid and daring thing to do, and some day I hoped to drive a six-horse bowery wagon myself.

"The central place of meeting was usually in some grove along the Big Cedar to the west and south of us, and early on the appointed day the various lodges of our region came together one by one at convenient places, each one moving in procession and led by great banners on which the women had blazoned the motto of their home lodge. Some of the columns had bands and came preceded by far faint strains of music, with marshals in red sashes galloping to and fro in fine assumption of military command.

"It was grand, it was inspiring—to us, to see those long lines of carriages winding down the lanes, joining one to another at the cross roads till at last all the granges from the northern end of the county were united in one mighty column advancing on the picnic ground, where orators awaited our approach with calm dignity and high resolve. Nothing more picturesque, more delightful, more helpful has ever risen out of American rural life. Each of these assemblies was a most grateful relief from the sordid loneliness of the farm. . . .

"The County Fair on the contrary was becoming each year more important as farming diversified. It was even more glorious than the Grange Picnic, was indeed second only to the Fourth of July, and we looked forward to it all through the autumn.

"It came late in September and always lasted three days. We all went on the second day (which was considered the best day), and mother, by cooking all the afternoon before our outing, provided us a dinner of cold chicken and cake and pie which we ate while sitting on the grass beside our wagon just off the race-track while the horses munched hay and oats from the box. All around us other families were grouped, picnicking in the same fashion, and a cordial interchange of jellies and pies made the meal a delightful function. However, we boys never lingered over it,—we were afraid of missing something of the program."

The Library of Congress

The County Fair, Princeton, Illinois, 1909.

No other writer knew so well the bad with the good of life along the Middle Border as Garland. Together with the youthful adventures of picnics and fairs he remembered, as vividly, the poignant sight of his own family and neighbors breaking under the savage toil of early midwestern farm life. Garland himself retreated to the city, to Boston, to find the perspective for his grim classics of the prairies.

The National Archives

Time out of mind the farmer had looked on the city and its works with distrust and resentment. Even the tiny urban communities of colonial days had been occasionally castigated by rural opinion as parasites on the body politic and social. Jefferson's denunciation of "the mobs of great cities" was a classic variation on a traditional theme. Yet, decade by decade since his pronouncement, the proportion of people living in cities has increased. And as urban centers grew and multiplied the contrast between city life and country life seemed to become constantly sharper.

The relative advantages of the city never appeared so great as during the days of agrarian revolt that Garland described. Neither Grange meetings nor county fairs with their "female equestrianism," balloon ascensions, and divers other excitements could slow the constant, heavy drift of people from farm to village, from village to town, and from town to city.

Even those who by choice or necessity remained on the farm were being linked to the city in ways that were reshaping the immemorial pattern of rural life. The progressive husbandman of this latter day was becoming a commercial operator whose work in the fields was increasingly geared to the demands of distant city markets; whose own table often served the produce of other com-

The County Fair, Princeton, Illinois, 1909.

mercial farms, delivered through the trading channels of cities; and whose idea of the good life stemmed less from the agrarian philosophy of Crèvecoeur and Jefferson than from the most recent notices from the metropolis.

For almost a hundred years the urbanization of the countryside has proceeded at an accelerating rate. Each improvement in transportation and communication not only turned more farm youths to the city but, for better or worse, returned city standards of culture to the farm. As long ago as 1885 the farmer was warned by one rural observer that he must make a wide distinction between "true refinement" and the false glitter of city manners. "We do not believe you will find any better manners in the city than in the country," wrote the author, "though you may find more awkwardness and restraint in society, simply the result of isolation or lack of society."

As isolation and lack of society diminished so did the distinction between true refinement and city manners. With the coming of the automobile and better roads the farmer's mobility was vastly increased and the range of his contacts broadened. The gas buggies took the country to the city and the city to the country on rubber tires. The telephone brought rural neighbors within the range of immediate conversation—frequently all on the same line at the same time—and gave the farmer a quick way of talking back to the city. Rural mail delivery brought daily news of the world beyond the farming belt. The radio, in time, brought news of the whole wide globe to the farmer's fireside, news which well might tell the fate of his crops. As Garland wrote in later years it all seemed far away from his days on the Middle Border.

427

THE WESTERN RANGE

To turn back in time, the farming frontier had paused at the edge of the Great Plains, a land of forbidding novelty to the traditional farmer. "This strip of country," wrote one observer in 1866, "which extends from the provinces of Mexico to Lake Winnipeg on the North, is almost one entire plain of grass, which is, and ever must be useless to cultivating man." A few years earlier a writer in the *Atlantic Monthly* had pointed out that that "strip of country," comprising at least one quarter of all the United States, was "inevitably set apart for the one sole business of cattle-raising." While the farmer-settler briefly halted his westward march to ponder the problems that stretched before him, that huge territory did indeed become the kingdom of the cowman and the theater for one of the most colorful phases of American history. People around the world know the cowboy's story in one form or another. Even deprived of its Hollywood and pulp magazine trimmings it remains America's most distinctive legend. Yet it was a very brief pastoral, hardly more than an interlude in the development of the West.

Long before the western cowboy staged his great drama cattle owners and drovers of the East had held their rodeos, or roundups, had corraled their beasts — gathered them into cowpens, that is — branded or marked them, and herded them on long drives to distant markets. The eastern arena was relatively small and wooded contrasted with the boundless and treeless Plains; but the end efforts were the same in either case, to gather in and identify roaming, often half-wild kine and get them to the most

AN EARLY CATTLE DROVER. Lithograph by August Köllner, about 1845.

The Harry Shaw Newman Gallery

CALIFORNIA COWBOYS, 1839. Lithograph by L. M. Lefevre after a drawing by Captain W. Smyth. From Alexander Forbes, *History of Upper and Lower California.*

promising markets. In colonial days cattle were sometimes driven from as far south as Carolina to the splendid market in Philadelphia. Before the eighteenth century was out the youthful Davy Crockett drove a large stock of cattle 400 miles over the mountains from Tennessee to Virginia.

On the opposite coast another very different breed of cowhand also made an appearance before the end of the eighteenth century — the hard-riding California *vaquero.* The first of these true American cowboys were often trained to their work by the padres of the missions whose vast and wandering herds of cattle later provided those hides known as "California bank notes" that Yankee traders sailed so far to collect. In the farthest West succeeding generations of superb horsemen developed a pattern of dress and equipment and techniques in the saddle that were admirably suited to hard work on the cattle range.

Richard Dana thought the Californios were the world's finest riders and they seemed always on horseback. "They are put upon a horse when only four or five years old . . ." he wrote, "and may almost be said to keep on him until they have grown to him. The stirrups are covered or boxed up in front, to prevent their catching when riding through the woods; and the saddles are large and heavy, strapped very tight upon the horse, and have large pommels, or loggerheads, in front, round which the lasso is coiled when not in use. . . . Their spurs are cruel things, having four or five rowels each an inch in length, dull and rusty. . . . I have seen men come in from chasing bullocks, with their horses' hind legs and quarters covered with blood."

But it was on the Great Plains of the West that the ancient art of cattle droving reached its most picturesque climax and the cowboy his most heroic stature. Most of the tools, the techniques, the language, and the accessories of his vocation the western cowboy borrowed from the early Mexican *vaqueros.* The bulk of the cattle, too, which swarmed out of Texas after the Civil War, and with magical suddenness spread out over a great

C. F. Doan's Store. Trading Outpost for Cowboys and Indians at the Red River Crossing on the Texas Cattle Trail, built about 1879. Photograph taken about 1889.

empire of grassland, stemmed from Mexican stock—distant, wild descendants of the Andalusian cattle imported centuries before by the *conquistadores*.

The Great Plains area, with its forbidding, arid distances and its murderous, mounted savages, had discouraged the early Mexican *rancheros* from advancing their frontier beyond the southernmost tip of Texas. During the days of the Lone Star Republic the long-horned kine grew wild and multiplied enormously. From 1830 to 1860 it has been estimated that the cattle in Texas increased from 100,000 to almost 5,000,000 head. They seemed to "spring up out of the earth . . ." wrote one amazed correspondent for an Eastern magazine, "beyond being numbered, roaming, undomesticated, over a thousand plains."

These cattle-breeding grounds of Texas were a long distance from the giant markets of eastern and northern cities hungry for meat. From the 1830's to the Civil War sporadic efforts were made to drive longhorn stock to New Orleans, St. Louis, Los Angeles, Chicago, and Cincinnati—at least one herd of Texas longhorns was driven all the way to New York—but the movement was irregular and did nothing to relieve Texas from what threatened to become a plague of fast-multiplying, wild beef. Two new factors in the latter 1860's changed matters almost overnight. The Pacific railroad pierced across the Plains, ready and eager to haul eastward all the cattle that could be driven to its tracks; and it was discovered that beeves could winter and flourish on the northern plains as well as the buffalo and come out fat and sleek in the spring. With explosive suddenness the "cow country" burst out of its Texas corner and spread over an enormous domain stretching from the Rio Grande to Canada and from central Kansas to the Rocky Mountains.

The first great trail north out of Texas led to Abilene, Kansas. As the railroad advanced the main paths of the drives shifted successively westward to meet it at more convenient points. When Dodge City, Kansas, became the principal shipping point, Doan's Store, near the ford where hundreds of thousands of cattle splashed across the Red River, became a famous landmark of the main trail north.

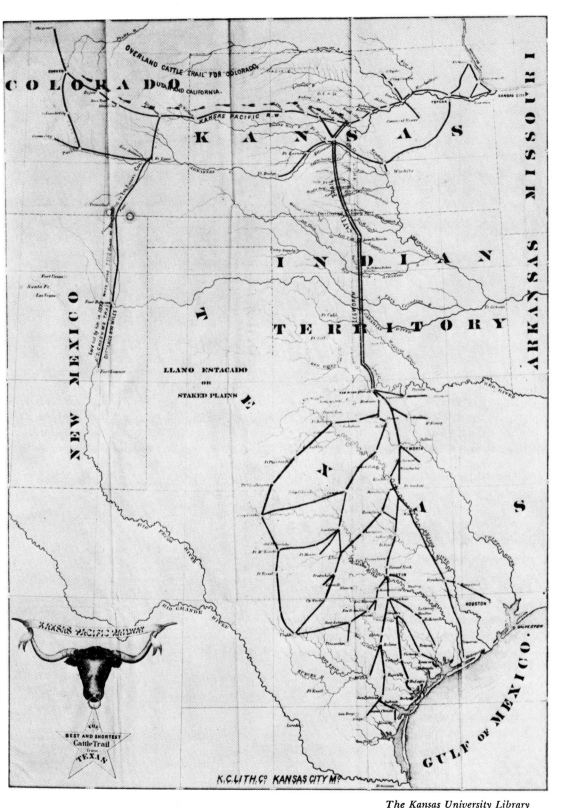

CATTLE TRAILS TO THE RAILROAD, 1875. From a *Guide Map to the Best and Shortest Cattle Trail (from Texas to the Kansas Pacific Railway)*.

431

LONGHORNS

The wild longhorns that ranged the Texas brush country were ferocious, muscular beasts, "fifty times more dangerous to foot-men than the fiercest buffalo," fleet as a horse, and as long of horn as they were short of good eating beef. Writing of his days in Texas during the 1850's Colonel Richard Dodge recounted an old story of one infuriated longhorn bull that scattered several regiments of General Taylor's army "like chaff, and finally escaped unhurt, having demoralized and put to flight an army which a few days after covered itself with glory by victoriously encountering five times its number of human enemies."

During the fifteen years following 1866, Texas cattle by the million streamed northward, some to be shipped by rail to eastern abattoirs, others fanning out to stock the great ranges to the north and west. Only tough cattle could stand the long drive over a thousand miles of open, dry country to the railroad, and then on, occasionally, for an-other thousand and more across Montana to the Canadian Pacific near Moose Jaw and Regina. And men and horses had to be quite as tough. Every rod of the way threatened the success of the drive, and, along with that, the very lives of the "cows," horses, and men on the trail—Plains Indians who had kept white men at bay for several centuries; outlaw white men in armed mobs, a worse menace than the worst Indians during the early drives; drought which blinded and maddened the beasts and drivers alike; wild animals that stalked the wilderness; choking dust and pouring rain with its floods.

Any incident of the day and night, from a casually struck match to a lightning bolt—or no apparent incident at all—might start thousands of nervous brutes on a furious stampede that could be brought under control only by men of eternal vigilance and resourcefulness. Of such perils there was no end. Andy Adams, "the cowboy's Boswell," has left a classic description of one long drive.

TRAILING TEXAS CATTLE. Engraving after a drawing by Frederic Remington. From *Collier's Magazine*, 1904.

The Metropolitan Museum of Art

"Good cloudy weather would have saved us, but in its stead was a sultry morning without a breath of air, which bespoke another day of sizzling heat. We had not been on the trail over two hours before the heat became almost unbearable to man and beast. Had it not been for the condition of the herd, all might yet have gone well; but over three days had elapsed without water for the cattle, and they became feverish and ungovernable. The lead cattle turned back several times, wandering aimlessly in any direction, and it was with considerable difficulty that the herd could be held on the trail. Our horses were fresh, however, and after about two hours' work, we once more got the herd strung out in trailing fashion; but before a mile had been covered, the leaders again turned, and the cattle congregated into a mass of unmanageable animals, milling and lowing in their fever and thirst. . . . No sooner was the milling stopped than they would surge hither and yon, sometimes half a mile, as ungovernable as the waves of an ocean. After wasting several hours in this manner, they finally turned back over the trail, and the utmost efforts of every man in the outfit failed to check them. We threw our ropes in their faces, and when this failed, we resorted to shooting; but in defiance of the fusillade and the smoke they walked sullenly through the line of horsemen across their front. Six-shooters were discharged so close to the leaders' faces as to singe their hair, yet, under a noonday sun, they disregarded this and every other device to turn them, and passed wholly out of our control. In a number of instances wild steers deliberately walked against our horses, and then for the first time a fact dawned upon us that chilled the marrow in our bones—the herd was going blind.

"The bones of men and animals that lie bleaching along the trails abundantly testify that this was not the first instance in which the plain had baffled man."

The "cow-towns" at the rail heads—Abilene, Wichita, Ellsworth, Dodge City, and others—were the primary markets of the long drive from the South. Here the cattle changed hands. Some were shipped to slaughter; others bought as food for Indians or for army posts; still others, usually in the custody of different cowboys, driven off for a few seasons of fattening before they faced the butcher's block. Abilene, the first established of those transfer points, has been likened to Appomattox as a significant crossroads in American history. Here it was, a few short years after the Cotton Kingdom had fallen, that southern men from Texas and Northerners from Lincoln's home town met together to do business and celebrate the rise of the new Cattle Kingdom.

With eastern and foreign cities increasing their cry for beef and with cattle breeding prolifically all over the free and open land, and fattening on a "sea of grass," the progress of the American range cattle industry attracted attention the world over. Even before the real tidal wave of cattle had started to roll eastward the Illinois legislature had incorporated the Union Stockyards in Chicago, set on three hundred and forty-five swampy acres, to handle the livestock already pouring through that city. In the first year of operation the stockyards received well over a third of a million cattle—not to mention almost a full million hogs. By 1884 the figures were four or five times as large. "Were the live stock upon Uncle Sam's estate ranged five abreast," remarked Andrew Carnegie "....and marched around the world, the head and tail of the procession would overlap."

TEXAS CATTLE IN A KANSAS CORN CORRAL. Engraving after a sketch by Frederic Remington. From *Harper's Weekly.*

The New York Public Library

THE UNION STOCKYARDS, CHICAGO, 1866. Lithograph by Jevne and Almini.

The development of refrigeration and of the tin-canning machine, the extension of the railroads, and the rise of astute businessmen in the packing industry, made it possible to concentrate that industry on a new and revolutionary scale. Chicago became the largest packing center of the world, equipped to handle the endless supply of beef from the range and move it on to remote markets.

Cheap American beef in every form—on the hoof, tinned, in frozen sides, and in tubs—was inundating the European market in addition to satisfying the increasing native demand. "The merry roast beef of England in old England itself," exulted the Chicago *Times* in 1880, with perhaps pardonable exaggeration, "is giving way to American beef, which is now actually ruling the roast there." Exports of meat and meat products rose from about thirty-seven million dollars in 1865 to over one hundred and sixteen million fifteen years later.

AMERICAN BEEF FOR ENGLISH MARKETS; SHIPPING CATTLE FROM NEW YORK. Engraving after a drawing by I. Pranishnikoff. From *Harper's Weekly*, 1879.

435

MAIN STREET, DODGE CITY, KANSAS, "THE COWBOY CAPITAL OF THE WORLD." Photograph taken in 1878.

A GAMBLING SCENE IN A SALOON AT PECOS, TEXAS. Photograph taken in the 1880's. The man sitting at table with white hat on is Jim Miller, subsequently lynched with three other men at Ada, Oklahoma, in 1909.

The Metropolitan Museum of Art
Row in a Cattle Town. Engraving after a drawing by Frederic Remington. From *Century Magazine*, 1888.

There were two kinds of cow towns—those that blossomed briefly at the terminal points of the railroads and at which cattle were gathered for shipment east, and those that served as distributing points to the lonely ranches of the back country.

At either kind the cowboy's day in town at the end of a long spell on the range was a rare, important, and often violent occasion. Youthful spirits pent up after months of ascetic, monotonous, and rigorous life were discharged in a riot of carefree excitement and revelry. The towns were ready and waiting with saloons, dance halls, gamblers, liquor, and girls to provide every variety of fun and vice the frontier could muster. "Shooting the works" was more than a figure of speech during those rude carnivals where most men went armed and ready to shoot in fun or earnest as the case might be. Eleven men were killed in a single night's brawl at Newton, Kansas. Twenty-five were buried in "Boot Hill," the local cemetery, during the first year of Dodge City, "the Beautiful, Bibulous Babylon of the Frontier."

> It was hot July when we got to Dodge,
> That wickedest little town;
> And we started in to have some fun
> Just as the sun went down.
> We killed a few of the worst bad men
> For the pleasure of seeing them kick;

> We rode right into a billiard hall,
> And I guess we raised Old Nick.
> The bartender left in a wonderful haste
> On that hot and sultry day;
> He never came back to get his hat
> Until we were miles away. . . .

Against such a wide-open shanty-built setting the bad man briefly played his celebrated part in the evolution of western society. Even the wildest and woolliest West could not long tolerate such irresponsible, murderous characters as Billy the Kid. "Good men," quite as fast with a gun and often bad enough themselves—near-legendary figures like Sheriff Wyatt Earp, "the greatest gun-fighting marshal that the Old West knew," and that "prince of pistoleers" Wild Bill Hickok—lined up on the side of law and order. Aided by "substantial citizens" of the cow country, with sure eye and steady hand these forces of "law" and order first put the bad actors on the defensive and then forced them off the stage entirely, or into more conventional rôles.

NOTICE!
TO THIEVES, THUGS, FAKIRS AND BUNKO-STEERERS,
Among Whom Are

J. J. HARLIN, alias "OFF WHEELER," SAW DUST CHARLIE, WM. HEDGES, BILLY THE KID, Billy Mullin, Little Jack, The Cuter, Pock-Marked Kid, and about Twenty Others:

If Found within the Limits of this City after TEN O'CLOCK P. M. this Night you will be Invited to attend a GRAND NECK-TIE PARTY.

The Expense of which will be borne by
100 Substantial Citizens.

Las Vegas, March 24th, 1882.

The N. H. Rose Collection
A Notice to Bad Men.

AN ARIZONA COWBOY.

A GROUP OF WYOMING COWBOYS. Photograph by C. D. Kirkland.

The millions of scrawny longhorns that were driven up from Texas were not many enough to take advantage of the "inexhaustible" feeding grounds of the Northwest, nor to fill the railroad cars going east. Soon descendants of the shorthorn cattle that had accompanied the Oregon pioneers across the Great American Desert were being herded back across the dusty, lava-rock reaches of eastern Oregon and Idaho to fill the comparatively lush grasslands of Wyoming, within reach of steel rails. In a human generation their members had enormously increased and they were a better strain of stock. From Oregon to Wyoming was farther than from Texas to Kansas, but great herds made the trek, policed by men who often were veterans of the Texas Trail; men who were among the finest of America's long line of frontier types.

The western cowboy might refer to himself as an "ordinary bow-legged human," but he was by every circumstance a carefully screened and highly conditioned type of man. Only a rugged man of courage, a skilled horseman, resourceful with cattle and inured to hardship, peril, loneliness, and the pitiless torments of nature, could do a cowboy's necessary work. He might be drawn out onto the range from the East, South, North, or West, from Mexico or Canada, England, Scotland, or Australia. He might be white, tawny, or, perhaps, black. But his minimum requirements were set by the nature of his job. Beyond that the conditions of his life in the unsheltered open spaces, the specialized round of his duties, the limited circle of his associations, all made him something more than "a man with guts and a horse." It made him representative of a culture that was unique in history.

"Cowboys," wrote Theodore Roosevelt, the most famous of them all, include "wild spirits of every land, yet the latter soon become indistinguishable from their American companions, for these plainsmen are far from being so heterogeneous a people as is commonly supposed. On the contrary, all have a certain curious similarity to each other; existence in the west seems to put the same stamp upon each . . . of them. Sinewy, hardy, self-reliant, their life forces them to be both daring and adventurous, and the passing over their heads of a few years leaves printed on their faces certain lines which tell of dangers quietly fronted and hardships uncomplainingly endured."

The cowboy dressed for his work in a fashion that seems intentionally picturesque only when it is not understood. The broad,

A WYOMING COWBOY.

The Wyoming State Library

THE COWBOY. After a drawing by Frederic Remington.

heavy-brimmed hat worn on the southern range served as an umbrella in the rain, a shade against the sun, a hood—when tied down about the ears—in the bitter cold, a drinking cup when shaped into a trough, and, perhaps, a pillow at night. On the northwest plains of Montana and Wyoming where winds were strong and frequent, hat brims were smaller. His kerchief provided protection for the cowboy's neck against scorching winds or, tied over his lower face, a mask against choking dust. Calfskin chaps, and the woolly ones used on the northern range, were for warmth as well as for turning aside cactus thorns, brush, and mesquite that would rip and tear ordinary clothing. High- and narrow-heeled boots did not catch in the stirrups should a horse fall, and they anchored the wearer in the corral when roping was done afoot. They were high enough and stout enough to keep out water when the wearer forded an ordinary stream. Snugly fitted trousers, tucked inside the boots, had

"straight down" pockets in front that discouraged small articles from falling out when the cowboy sat on the ground. The vest was a handy repository for tobacco, matches, tally books, and the customary impedimenta of a life in the saddle. A six-shooter hanging from a loosely sagging belt had various obvious functions. For the work he had to do, the cowboy's regalia was sensible and modest dress. Each item had an important purpose.

The cowboy's saddle was his work bench and typically his most prized possession. Stout and heavy, it half covered his mustang and could withstand terrific strains. Its high, covered metal "horn" was firmly bolted to the "tree" to serve as a snubbing post if need be. Its cantle rose high enough to prevent the rider from being pulled backward by a roped steer. Wooden stirrups, often enclosed, protected the feet in a crush of cattle or horses. Broad cinches bound saddle and horse into a single contraption.

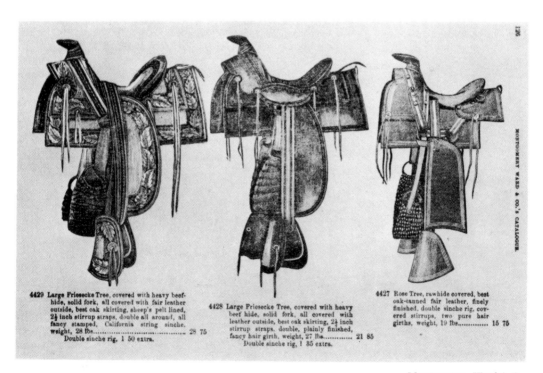

4429 Large Friesecke Tree, covered with heavy beef-hide, solid fork, all covered with fair leather outside, best oak skirting, sheep's pelt lined, 2¼ inch stirrup straps, double all around, all fancy stamped, California string sinche, weight, 28 lbs.......................... 28 75
 Double sinche rig, 1 50 extra.

4428 Large Friesecke Tree, covered with heavy beef hide, solid fork, all covered with leather outside, best oak skirting, 2¼ inch stirrup straps, double, plainly finished, fancy hair girth, weight, 27 lbs............ 21 85
 Double sinche rig, 1 35 extra.

4427 Rose Tree, rawhide covered, best oak-tanned fair leather, finely finished, double sinche rig, covered stirrups, two pure hair girths, weight, 19 lbs.............. 15 75

Montgomery, Ward & Co.

WESTERN SADDLES, 1882. From a Montgomery, Ward catalogue.

A WESTERN RANCH HOUSE, 1888. Probably in the Dakotas. Photograph by J. C. H. Grabill.

ONE OF THE BUILDINGS ON MAJOR PEASE'S RANCH ON THE YELLOWSTONE, 1872. Photograph by W. H. Jackson.

"In the northern country," wrote Theodore Roosevelt, "the ranches vary greatly in size; on some there may be but a few hundred head, on others ten times as many thousand. The land is still in great part unsurveyed, and is hardly anywhere fenced in, the cattle roaming over it at will. The small ranches are often quite close to one another, say within a couple of miles; but the home ranch of a big outfit will not have another building within ten or twenty miles of it, or, indeed, if the country is dry, not within fifty. The ranch-house may be only a mud dugout; or a 'shack' made of logs stuck upright into the ground; more often it is a fair-sized well-made building of hewn logs, divided into several rooms. Around it are grouped other buildings—log-stables, cow-sheds, and hay-ricks, an out-house in which to store things, and on large ranches another house in which the cowboys sleep. The strongly made, circular horse-corral, with a snubbing-post in the middle, stands close by; the larger cow-corral, in which the stock is branded, may be some distance off."

In that semi-arid land, control of water gave control of the grasslands for miles around. A cowman's range might cover a million acres although the owner perhaps held actual title only to his headquarters camp of one small quarter-section on a stream or near a water hole. The rest was government land—enormous, undefined areas of unfenced pasturage over which the cattle of numerous owners roamed at will.

While land was plentiful it was common courtesy not to establish a ranch too near one already in operation. Cattle could not walk more than seven miles to their watering place and back to the limit of the grazing area in a day. Fourteen miles, thus, was a comfortable distance for a neighbor. While cattle remained tough and cheap they could be left to rustle for themselves in any weather, intermingling and interbreeding with the wanderers from adjoining outfits. In later years improved and more highly valued stock demanded less casual care.

It was largely a man's world, and, for long months on end, a closed society of men who could get as weary of their isolation, as bored by empty evenings, and as irritated by the unrelieved company of their own outfit, as men anywhere else.

Cowboy Outfit of a Wyoming Ranch, about 1885.

The Wyoming State Library

The University of Wyoming, Archives of The Wyoming Stock Growers' Association
SUPPER ON THE ROUNDUP, 1885.

In the spring of the year the stockmen of a wide territory gathered with their men to comb the range for beasts that had wandered during the winter, to segregate them into separate herds, and to brand the calves of the season. The roundup often covered thousands of square miles with up to a thousand men and many times that number of horses working for weeks on end to complete their job. It was by nature a co-operative undertaking and by all odds the most spectacular phase of ranch life. It was the harvest of the open range.

The base of operations of each group was its chuck wagon. A merciless cook awakened the men before dawn with his particular "chuck call"—such as "Roll out, there, fellers, and hear the little birdies sing their praise to God"—and fed them quickly before they rode out into their district to bring in everything with hide and horn. Again at noon the riders converged upon the wagon which had moved to an appointed spot to meet the men with a mid-day meal and fresh horses for the afternoon's work. After the evening meal weary men repaired their equipment, "horsed about" the fire, and swapped tales in a language all their own.

When the entire countryside included in the roundup district had been scoured and the ranging herds were assembled, the cattle of each brand were cut out from the rest and the unmarked calves caught for branding. Roosevelt described the headlong dash of the horseman in his effort to cut out a cow marked with his brand from a herd of several hundred others, following at full speed the twistings and doublings of a refractory steer over ground where an eastern horse could barely keep its feet walking. "Cutting out cattle," he wrote, "next to managing a stampeding herd at night, is that part of the cowboy's work needing the boldest and most skilful horsemanship. A young heifer or steer is very loath to leave the herd, always tries to break back into it, can run like a deer, and can dodge like a rabbit; but a thorough cattle pony enjoys the work as much as its rider, and follows a beast like a four-footed fate through every double and turn. The ponies for the cutting-out or afternoon's work are small and quick; those used for the circle-riding in the morning have need rather to be strong and rangey."

Some calves were branded, both legitimately and illegitimately, out on the range. More generally the work was done in the rodeo corral. In the latter case the young beasts were dragged in a cloud of dust to the fire, accompanied by a bleating, bellow-

DRAGGING A CALF TO BRAND, WYOMING, 1885. Photograph probably by Kirkland.

ROPING AND CHANGING HORSES DURING A ROUNDUP ON THE CHEYENNE RIVER, 1888. Photograph by Grabill.

The N. H. Rose Collection

BRANDING CALVES ON A ROUNDUP NEAR FORT STANTON, NEW MEXICO.

The Wyoming State Library

BRANDING A CALF IN A CORRAL, ABOUT 1885.

ing, and whinnying chorus and the mingled smells of fire, burnt hide, steaming horseflesh, and human sweat.

Brand marks were the heraldic devices of the cow country, etched on rawhide and as telling to knowing eyes as the blazons of European nobility—and to the uninitiate, just as esoteric. A letter or numeral placed on its side was "lazy," a hyphen was a "bar," capital letters were "big"—thus the "4-28" or "four bar twenty-eight," "ᴸ" or "lazy m bar," "A2" or "big A two," and so on. No system was foolproof enough to eliminate

ingenious rustlers who ran or forged their brands on other men's cattle.

In time the business of cattle growing became well organized on a large scale. Eastern and foreign capital were attracted by the immense profits to be made. Huge associations of stockmen dominated the business and laid down the law, in their own mutual interests, registering the brands recognized within their territory, sending their brand inspectors as far east as Kansas City and Chicago, and, in general, functioning as *de facto* governments.

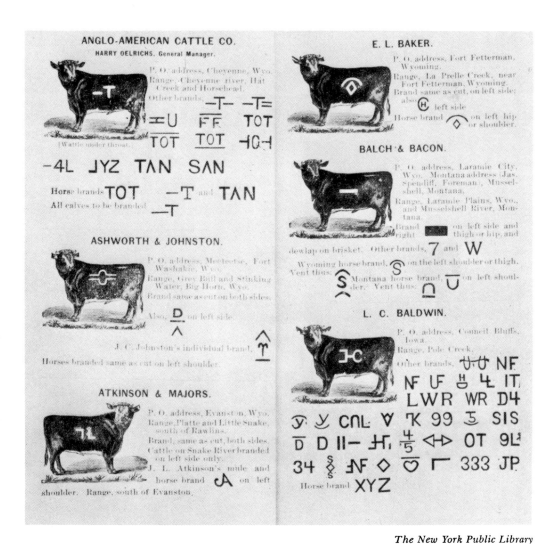

PAGE FROM A BRAND BOOK OF THE WYOMING STOCK GROWERS' ASSOCIATION.

447

Roundup Scene on the Belle Fourche, Dakota Territory, 1887. Photograph by Grabill.

The American Steel and Wire Company

POSTER ADVERTISING BARBED WIRE, ABOUT 1880.

"Much of this land," remarked one handbook for emigrants in 1845, referring to the Western Plains, "must lie unoccupied for generations for want of fencing." None of the traditional types of fences were practical in that woodless and stoneless area, and the agricultural frontier that had moved relentlessly westward from the eighteenth century on was momentarily stopped, as we have seen, at its border. In 1874 the first barbed wire was made in America and its general use in the years immediately following revolutionized life on the range. Under the protection of the cheap, new invention the farmer started moving west again. Where he encroached on the cowman's preserves there was, for a while, bitter and bloody conflict. For the nester, wire fences were a perfect defense against the cattle that crushed his crops underfoot — providing him with a chance to work his lawful homestead claim. They also made it possible for cattlemen to fence great areas of the public domain against intrusion by smaller-scale operators.

Between "fence men" and "no-fence men" it was open war. But the whole tide of history was on the side of the settler against the nomad.

"For we ourselves and the life that we lead," wrote Theodore Roosevelt in 1885 at the peak of the range industry, "will shortly pass away from the plains as completely as the red and white hunters who have vanished from before our herds. The free, open-air life of the ranchman, the pleasantest and healthiest life in America, is from its very nature ephemeral. The broad and boundless prairies have already been bounded and will soon be made narrow. It is scarcely a figure of speech to say that the tide of white settlement during the last few years has risen over the west like a flood; and the cattlemen are but the spray from the crest of the wave, thrown far in advance, but soon to be overtaken. As the settlers throng into the land and seize the good ground, especially that near the streams, the great fenceless ranches, where the cattle and their mounted herds-

FENCE-CUTTING IN NEBRASKA, 1885. "SETTLERS TAKING THE LAW INTO THEIR OWN HANDS." Photograph by Butcher.

The Nebraska State Historical Society

SETTLERS IN CUSTER COUNTY, NEBRASKA, 1886. Photograph by Butcher.

men wander unchecked over hundreds of thousands of acres, will be broken up and divided into corn land, or else into small grazing farms where a few hundred herd of stock are closely watched and taken care of." In 1885, the year Roosevelt's words were published, cattle trails virtually ceased. The next year and the one following, cruel winters almost obliterated the herds on the open range. Within a few more short years Roosevelt's prophecy was all but realized. The brief bucolic interlude in the drama of westward expansion was over. In perspective it seems incredibly brief for so complete a cycle. The Plains Indian had held the immense land as his hunting ground and he was gradually crowded into a reservation. Millions of buffalo and countless other game had fed for centuries on the luscious grasses, and in turn had fed and nurtured the Indian, and both were all but exterminated. The United States government took title to the land and the range cattlemen stocked it overabundantly with grazing beef, using it as "free air," little concerned with titles or homestead claims.

Within little more than a score of years the range cattle industry spread from a small corner of Texas to cover over a million square miles of land. It developed from a relatively informal, subsistence activity to a highly organized and heavily capitalized staple business—"a formidable vested interest," as one historian has called it. In that time ten or eleven million cattle were herded across the scene, and a million range horses took their part. Cowboys and capital from far places were attracted to the range by the adventure and profit to be found there. A new and peculiar culture, with its own folklore and balladry, evolved and in its way matured. In typical native fashion Pecos Bill, a rip-roaring Texas cowboy, picked up the tall tale where Davy Crockett

TURNING OVER THE FIRST SOD ON A HOMESTEAD IN MONTANA, 1908.

and Mike Fink had left it—west of the Mississippi. And within less than a generation the curtain dropped on that last American frontier with its fabulous heroes.

The railroad reached across the land to give the cattleman a way to market. And it also brought the landseekers who forced the cattlemen from the range into ranches. First timidly, then boldly, later rashly plowing into the heart of the Plains, the farming frontier moved forward again. Granger and nester took title under their homestead claims and advanced behind a barricade of barbed wire. The cattleman of the open range became the stockman of his own pastures, large they might be, but fenced in. The half-wild kine that had been driven a thousand miles and more to market were replaced by more carefully bred cattle that never could have survived such punishing experience. The cowboy changed from a picturesque nomad to a hired hand.

POWER PLOWING THE PRAIRIE IN 1939 IN CASCADE COUNTY, WYOMING. Photograph by Arthur Rothstein for the Farm Security Administration.

CHAFF FROM A THRESHER, WELD COUNTY, COLORADO, 1939. Photograph by Arthur Rothstein for the Farm Security Administration.

PLOW COVERED BY SAND, CIMARRON COUNTY, OKLAHOMA, 1936. Photograph by Arthur Rothstein for the Farm Security Administration.

HOW FARES THE LAND?

By the beginning of the present century there was no longer in America that endless vista of good, cheap, unoccupied land that had lured earlier generations always on to "somewhere else." There was still free land, but the best was already taken; it had proved its bounty; and there was some point in the farmer settling where he was, long enough to understand and care for the land that was his. Husbandry was no longer the way of life it had been from the day of Hesiod. Within hardly more than half a century farming techniques hallowed by three thousand years of usage had become obsolete. Agriculture was a business, machine-operated and specialized. And for the moment it was a stable business.

Even when farm mechanization was barely started nostalgia for the "good old days" was occasionally expressed. "Wooden harvesters do not sing harvest songs," lamented the *Prairie Farmer* in 1860, "iron mowers do not drink from cold springs, nor with Sancho Panza bless HIM who invented sleep. The poets and the prophets are a brotherhood, but the poets and the *profits* are

strangers, forever." However, neither did these wooden and iron thralls ache with fatigue and cry for rest. The typical farmer hailed his release from an ancient serfdom, made possible by the marvels of science. Easier means of communication and transportation; better facilities for education and recreation; more efficient farming techniques, all helped to fit rural life more pleasantly and effectively into the pattern of modern civilization. Huge agricultural exports provided a basis for the country's international trade. Within the nation the farmer's voice was heard and more often heeded in councils of state. Every prospect promised a new and tranquil era for rural people.

Then two things happened, war and the rapid development of power farming, and tranquillity became unrest overnight as history is reckoned. The First World War challenged the American farmer to produce at all costs and he met the test—at a considerable cost to himself over a score of years to come. He fed millions of Europeans who had quit their own farms for the battlefields, as well as his compatriots at home and abroad. His great crops were delivered where they were needed. "Food will win the war," he was told, and in the single year of 1915 he brought the nation's wheat crop up to a miraculous billion bushels.

With peace those abnormal demands shrank as fast as they had grown and the farmer was left holding the bag—the bag of surpluses he could not sell. Canada, the Argentine, and Australia were also growing enormous crops for the European market. The American farmer suddenly and seriously suffered from an unprecedented case of overproduction. Ironically production was becoming easier by the minute.

The application of the internal-combustion engine to farming released forces that threw rural America into a new agony of change. Compared to the titanic possibilities of power farming, the progress of mechaniza-

tion over the past century was insignificant and laggard. After gathering and pyramiding its forces for more than a hundred years in the cities and factories of the country the industrial revolution suddenly and inexorably moved onto the farm. By the 1920's the tractor and its growing list of accessories was firmly entrenched. It was driving the horse and the mules from the field, as the development of electric traction and the automobile had driven them from the city streets. It was releasing millions of acres once needed for fodder to the growing of human food crops. It stepped up the individual farmer's ability to produce at an accelerating rate. And, year by year, it shifted thousands of excess farmers—"elsewhere."

The farmer had known nothing but distress and uncertainty since the close of World War I while his city cousins sang of prosper-

Have you placed a Sentimental Value on your Horses out of proportion to the work they are able to perform?

BAILOR MOTOR CULTIVATORS

THE ADVENT OF POWER FARMING. From an advertisement in *The Country Gentleman*, 1920.

455

ity. With the depression of the 1930's the farmer's problem seemed a lot closer to everyone else's. The nation as a whole took stock of its rural resources more attentively than it ever had done before.

Self-powered machines penetrated more and more phases of farm production. Combines that united harvesting and threshing in one operation had moved onto the Plains from the far West where they had seen earlier service. Methods that had not changed in millennia had become hopelessly obsolete in a single lifetime. One veteran Plains farmer, as he watched his grandson cut and thresh thirty acres a day in 1929, remembered that it once had cost him three days of man-labor to reap and thresh a single acre of grain. Migrant harvest hands were in part replaced by a smaller crew, sufficiently mechanics to service the trucks that hauled threshed wheat to a place of storage in a non-stop automotive routine. The new-day farm had every appearance of a factory in the field. "We no longer raise wheat here," remarked one

Washington grower, "we manufacture it."

The development of an all-purpose tractor made possible the mechanical cultivation of row-crops and, with a wide variety of appliances that were evolving, it vastly extended the mechanical functions of the tractor. Corn harvesters, cotton pickers, asparagus cutters, walnut pickers, internal-combustion nutcrackers that explode the shells and leave the meat, and an increasing variety of other machines promised to replace human "stoop labor" where it was only recently considered irreplaceable. The progression was apparently endless—and the human displacement. Efficiency, overproduction, and unemployment marched lock step towards an uncertain destination.

To many observers it seemed that the expensive, powerful machines were giving every advantage to larger-scale farming, to the point where only capitalists or corporate groups who could invest heavily in land and mechanized equipment could compete for the market. One such corporation, in 1936,

HARROWING A FIELD WITH A DIESEL TRACTOR, NEW JERSEY, 1941. Photograph by Marion Post Wolcott for the Farm Security Administration.

The Library of Congress

TRACTOR-DRAWN COMBINE DELIVERING BULK-WHEAT TO A MOVING TRUCK, WALLA WALLA COUNTY, WASHINGTON. 1941. Photograph by Russell Lee for the Farm Security Administration.

MECHANICAL CORN-PICKER, GRUNDY COUNTY, IOWA, 1939. Photograph by Arthur Rothstein for the Farm Security Administration.

WHEAT COMBINES ON A WESTERN FIELD.

The Department of Agriculture

GREAT NORTHERN GRAIN ELEVATORS, SUPERIOR, WISCONSIN, 1941. Photograph by John Vachon for the Farm Security Administration. The largest working house grain elevator in the world when it was built. The total storage capacity is 12,000,000 bushels.

boasted of "the largest diversified farming organization in the world, owning and operating approximately 600,000 acres of land." The Homestead Act of 1862, framed to encourage the independent family-sized farm, had not anticipated such bonanza developments.

Another significant change was in the diet of the nation. Sedentary people were asking for less grain and beef, more fruits, milk, sugar, and succulent vegetables. Again there were changing fashions in clothes. The farmer, no matter what the rate of his production, could not quickly or easily adjust his crops to such shifting needs.

The rate of production was spiraling upwards. In the brief period from 1910 to 1930 alone, the output per agricultural worker increased forty-one per cent. The farming population that had been ninety per cent of all the people in 1790, and seventy-eight per cent in 1840, had dwindled to twenty-one and a half per cent by 1930; and was growing relatively smaller. Still the nation had the power to produce and facilities to store and handle more foodstuffs than would feed its one hundred and fifty million adequately. It seemed silly to say that American land produced too much food so long as one hungry citizen remained in the country, or anywhere else. Yet there were years when hungry and ill-clothed people and impoverished farmers who could not market their abundant crops lived within easy reach of one another. It was the paradox Henry George had suggested in his title, *Progress and Poverty*.

It was all the more paradoxical to an age that conceived of proper nutrition, like education, liberty, and decent housing, as among the fundamental rights of a citizen—that at long last, saw hunger as an avoidable folly, not as a natural condition of man.

WHEAT STORAGE IN THE NORTHERN PANHANDLE, TEXHOMA, OKLAHOMA, 1942. Photograph by John Vachon for the Farm Security Administration.

The Library of Congress

The Tennessee Valley Authority

A DESERTED FARM IN BLOUNT COUNTY, TENNESSEE.

There was another side to the story. Over more than a century of rapid expansion farmers had, in too many areas, swept over the land like a swarm of locusts, recklessly skinning the soil and leaving incipient deserts behind them. A tragedy of waste had been written that few until now had paused to read. "The dead land, shorn of its cover of grass and trees, was torn mercilessly by the rains," wrote David Lilienthal of one spot in the Tennessee Valley, "and the once lovely ... earth was cut into deep gullies that widened into desolate canyons twenty and more feet deep. No one can look upon this horror as it is today without a shudder."

In the West as well as in the East the early comers had unsettled the soil almost as effectively as they had settled the land.

"May 11, 1934, although it passed with little notice," writes Katherine Glover, "was almost as momentous in American history as April 6, 1917, when the United States entered the World War. On that date a great dust storm blew across the continent from the plains of the West. Gray clouds choked the air for several hundred miles, day turned into night, and street lights were lighted in many cities. Railroad schedules were interrupted; roads were blocked; homes could not shut out the shifting sand; the soiling debris piled in stores, ruining thousands of dollars' worth of merchandise. Following in the wake of the storm, 'dust pneumonia' took its toll in life."

Dust storms of the Great Plains, historically speaking, were not abnormal phenomena. Time and again in the past they had swept over large sections of the West. But the extraordinary publicity given to the "Dust Bowl" in the 1930's was a fair measure of the novel self-consciousness the nation felt in the presence of its land problems.

In many parts of the country, the abandoned farm stood as a memorial to the plundering methods of the past. As one author has written, it seemed like a reversal of history, with civilization retreating before the advancing wilderness of weeds and sand.

ABANDONED FARMSTEAD, OKLAHOMA, 1937.

DUST OVER THE TEXAS PANHANDLE, MARCH 1936. Photograph by Arthur Rothstein for the Farm Security Administration.

People were moving from ransacked soil—"elsewhere." That sort of migration had been going on for years in the shadow of many successes in other fields. But in the '30's the procession moved into the bright light. In *The Grapes of Wrath* John Steinbeck described the situation in a way that made everyone see it in dramatic detail: "The cars of the migrant people crawled out of the side roads onto the great cross-country highway, and they took the migrant way to the West. In the daylight they scuttled like bugs to the westward; and as the dark caught them, they clustered like bugs near to shelter and to water. And because they were lonely and perplexed, because they had all come from a place of sadness and worry and defeat, and because they were all going to a new mysterious place, they huddled together, they talked together; they shared their lives, their food, and the things they hoped for in the new country."

The American frontier had always been a new country that promised better things. That dream of brighter skies and greener pastures, so often realized in past generations, refused to die. But it was hard to recognize the spiritual heirs of Daniel Boone and Johnny Appleseed in the migrant hordes that took to the roads in the 1930's, or to find among them descendants of Jefferson's "chosen people." They were still made of flesh and blood and hope; but their relation to the land was different. The land they looked for was already owned by someone else. The "new mysterious place" was often only a migrant hands' place to stop at in a search for seasonal jobs, or a tenant's shack. Farming as a way of life was, in large areas, no fit subject for a Currier and Ives print.

DROUGHT REFUGEE FAMILIES STALLED ON THE HIGHWAY, NEW MEXICO, 1937. Photograph by Dorothy Lange for the Farm Security Administration.

The Library of Congress

"The agricultural ladder, on which an energetic young man might ascend from hired man to tenant to independent owner, is no longer serving its purpose...." President Roosevelt reported to Congress in 1937. "The agricultural ladder ... has become a treadmill.... When fully half the total farm population of the United States no longer can feel secure, when millions of our people have lost their roots in the soil, action to provide security is imperative, and will generally be approved."

The problem was not new. The Department of Agriculture had been progressively concerned with it for more than fifty years. But it came into sharper focus and into a closer relation with the misuse of the soil. Fifty per cent of the nation's farmers were producing ninety per cent of our agricultural products. Forty-two per cent of our farmers were tenants who had small incentive to respect and conserve the soil they worked. "What's the use?" was a stock reply of share croppers. "I don't get nothing but a living nohow."

No nation could afford such attitudes on the part of its farmers—any part of them— least of all a democracy professedly "on the march." Soil erosion was bad. Human erosion was worse. The two together were unthinkable, but there they were. The remaining productive soil still grew a surplus that could be plowed under or otherwise destroyed to save embarrassment, although it was against every normal instinct of the farmer to do so. (Even mules, long trained to walk between rows, stubbornly objected to trampling on growing cotton to satisfy the terms of the Agricultural Adjustment Act.) But human beings could not be plowed into

MIGRANT FARMERS. Photograph by Edward Ackerman.

The Department of Agriculture

Burleigh County

FARMERS - WORKERS
Mass - Meeting

CITY AUDITORIUM

Bismarck, Saturday, August 1st., 1:00 P.M.

Our economic struggle has become unbearable, due to the condition of drought. Starvation of humans as well as animals is facing us all.

Something must be done immediately to save mankind and beasts from real suffering.

This Burleigh County Mass Meeting has been called by The Burleigh County Holiday Association, supported by The American Federation of Labor, The North Dakota Labor Association, Inc., The State Unification Committee of WPA Workers, The Workers Labor Club of Bismarck.

This distress and condition for food is the people's question, and must be discussed by the people. For this purpose this mass meeting has been called. This is your meeting, you are expected to be present with all your friends and neighbors.

TOPICS TO BE DISCUSSED

1. The immediate relief of food for man and beast.

2. An American living wage scale for all workers on projects.

3. Pension for all old age people.

4. Winter consideration, such as coal, shelter, clothing, food for humans as well as animals.

5. How can such mass meetings spread into every county of this state, and into every state of this nation?

6. Unification of all Farm Organizations and Labor Organizations, upon the question of The Right to Live, food, clothing, and shelter.

7. Any other, non-political, question which concerns the farmer and the worker at this time.

Burleigh County Holiday Association, Fred Argast, President
American Federation of Labor, Adam Voight, Chairman Bismarck Central Labor Body
Burleigh County Labor Association, Frank Walker, President
Workers Labor Club of Bismarck, Gene Hunt, President

CAPITAL PUBLISHING CO., BISMARCK, N. D.

The Library of Congress

ANNOUNCEMENT, NORTH DAKOTA, 1937. Photograph by Russell Lee for the Farm Security Administration.

FARMERS' UNION MEETING, PROTESTING THE SALE OF LAND TO CORPORATION FARMS, WILLISTON, NORTH DAKOTA, 1942. Photograph by John Vachon for the Farm Security Administration.

the soil for compost like vegetables or slaughtered like baby pigs to bolster the trade value of those that were spared.

Whether the family-operated farm could compete with large-scale farming enterprise was an acute question. Mass-production methods were proficient and efficient; statistics tended to show a high, economical yield from large units, up to a point. Whether the total social effect was beneficial to the country was a different and more dubious matter. As one witness described a large-scale corporation-dominated farming community: "Nobody builds [here] for permanence. The laborers don't expect to stay here, the farmers figure on making a killing, and the merchants won't invest any money in their stores because they want to make their money and get out. That is why we don't have much of a community here." The family farmer, on the other hand, had a bigger stake in his community. He actively helped to make it and shape it into a wholesome social agency.

In the darkest days of the Depression em-battled farmers here and there tried to assert their proverbial independence in open revolt against the giant economic forces that threatened their livelihood and their property. Vigilantes broke up foreclosure sales, pickets prevented food from reaching city markets, and less violent groups met to discuss and promote their community welfare. But for all his classic virtues the family farmer was in no position to play savior to democracy. Yet it might be in the interest of democracy to save the small family farmer.

More than profits and efficiency were involved. Romance, tradition, and a great deal of political theory recognized the family farm as the "central point" in America's cultural background and "the cornerstone of our national land policy." When three and a half million rural households went on relief, public and private, those time-old shibboleths carried little conviction. For American agriculture this was, in the words of Franklin Roosevelt, "an unprecedented condition" that called for new and untried measures.

The state of rural affairs in America had been a concern of government as early as 1839 when an Agricultural Division was inaugurated in the Patent office for the purpose of gathering statistics, conducting agricultural experiments, and distributing seeds. Even so far back as 1776 government aid to agriculture was recommended to the Continental Congress. But it was with the establishment of a separate Department of Agriculture in 1862 that a national policy of aid and interest was formalized. Since then, through fact-finding and fact-dispensing, the Department has broadened its scope to meet the public need until it has become one of the largest of government agencies.

In the 1930's the public need had grown to monstrous size and complexity, involving city man and country man in the same problems. "The great towers of Manhattan and Chicago, the modern business streets of Omaha on the prairies," wrote David Lilienthal, "all rest on the same foundation as the old manor—the land, the waters, the minerals, and the forests. We are all in this together, cities and countryside."

Only a superagency of government had wide enough interests and powers to seek the allover balance of man and nature. But even the government could not master the problem alone any more than could the individual farmer. The two together might. For all the past efforts of the Department of Agriculture the rank and file of farmers only during the last generation conceded the value of scientific research to their workaday problems. In recent years the laboratory apron has been replacing the fringed deerskin of the pioneer as the symbol of progress —"a priestly vestment of authority for the farmer as for the rest of the world," as one Department member described it.

The help to and guidance of the farmer by the government expert backed by labora-

COUNTY LAND USE PLANNING COMMITTEE, MEETING IN A SCHOOL HOUSE, YANCEYVILLE, NORTH CAROLINA, 1940. Photograph by Marion Post Wolcott for the Farm Security Administration.

The Library of Congress

POTATO LABORATORY OF THE U.S. DEPARTMENT OF AGRICULTURE RESEARCH CENTER, BELTSVILLE, MARYLAND, 1935. Photograph by Carl Mydans for the Farm Security Administration.

tory authority was admittedly vital. But, quite as often, so was the education of the technician by the dirt farmer in particular needs and feelings at the grass roots. So, always, was a spirit of voluntary collaboration. Here as everywhere else, the test of democracy was to protect local initiative and individual freedom while promoting the general welfare.

It was with the avowed intention of fostering the voluntary collaboration of rural people that the New Deal approached the "unprecedented" problems of the farmer and the land he held in trust for "the rest of us." The efforts of the Farm Credit Administration, Agricultural Adjustment Act, Farmers' Home Administration, Rural Electrification Administration, and other acts and agencies marked the "new and untrod paths" that might lead, it was hoped, to the rehabilitation of rural society and the land itself, all within the framework of democratic practise.

REHABILITATION LOAN SUPERVISOR EXAMINING A FARM OF ONCE EXHAUSTED LAND, ST. CHARLES PARISH, LOUISIANA, 1936. Photograph by Carl Mydans for the Farm Security Administration.

AN AMERICAN LOG HOUSE, 1822. Water color by John Halkett. A realistic view by an Englishman showing many typical aspects of frontier life.

As Lilienthal wrote, the plight of the farmer, as of the city dweller, was inseparable from the plight of the land. And the American land, fertile for millions of years, had in too many regions been stripped and raped. "Suddenly this great body of land," wrote Russell Lord in the *Saturday Review of Literature,* "was thrown open to land-hungry men and women from Europe. We settled—or unsettled—it in no time at all. With gun and axe and plow we took possession, slashed down trees, tore topsoil open and beat upon it hungrily, pioneer wave by wave. The advent of steam power speeded up this business somewhat; but that was nothing compared to the acceleration of the earthy transformation which came with the development of the internal combustion motor plus tractors with rubber tires."

Conservation had long been the concern of landed people, anchored to their larger estates and fixed interests. When you couldn't profitably move away from it, the precious little layer of soil, the thin storage layer of vital substance inherited from untold ages of sun, rain, air, and decayed organic matter had to be cherished. Well over a century ago, Jefferson wrote from his beautiful hilltop to his friend, Charles Willson Peale: "Our country is hilly and we have been in the habit of plowing in straight rows, whether up or down hill, in oblique lines, or however they led, and our soil was all rapidly running into the rivers. We now plow horizontally following the curvature of the hills and hollows on dead level, however crooked the lines may be. Every furrow thus acts as a reservoir to receive and retain the waters, all of which go to the benefit of the growing plant instead of running off into streams. In a farm horizontally and deeply ploughed, scarcely an ounce of soil is now carried off from it. In point of beauty nothing can exceed that of the waving lines and rows winding along the face of the hills and valleys." (See pp. 472-73.) But for the better part of three centuries the conservationist in America was a prophet crying in a wilderness.

Before the end of the eighteenth century the New England coast had been so thoroughly denuded of trees that fuel and building timber had to be sought twenty or more miles distant; Boston imported some of its wood from as far away as New Hampshire. A few farsighted souls were already suggesting that public forests be established, that wood cutting be subject to regulation, that laws be passed for protection from forest fires, and that roadside forests be maintained for the beauty of the countryside.

Only in recent years has a broad halt been called to destruction and irresponsible exploitation. As in so many other ways of conservative living, America has gone to school in Europe to learn forest protection. It learned much from its distinguished nineteenth-century immigrants Carl Schurz and Bernard Ferrow. It was further prompted by the earlier President Roosevelt and Governor Pinchot among others. In 1935 Congress "recognized that the wastage of the soil and moisture resources on farm, grazing, and forest lands of the Nation, resulting from soil erosion, is a menace to the national welfare." By the Soil Conservation Act of that year it was "declared to be the policy of Congress to provide permanently for the control of soil erosion and thereby to preserve natural resources."

Against a long, dark history of prodigal waste and shortsighted exploitation appear the national forests and parks of today with their considerable stands of timber set aside "for the benefit and enjoyment of the people." The benefits and enjoyments have been many and diverse, including recreation and wild-life refuge as well as the simple preservation of the forests. The growing area of such government holdings today constitutes a major land use of the country.

SHENANDOAH NATIONAL PARK, VIRGINIA.

The Department of the Interior

STRIP AND CONTOUR FARMING IN GEORGIA. Photograph by O. S. Welch.

The Library of Congress

EXPLORING THE COLORADO RIVER, 1857–58. From Lieutenant Joseph C. Ives, *A Report upon the Colorado River of the West.*

From Lewis and Clark on, the body of American pioneers had been preceded into the little-known lands of the West by government expeditions. The men who reported those adventures were awed and enchanted by the spectacular panoramas that they were often the first white men to see. In 1857 Lieutenant J. C. Ives explored the Colorado River to ascertain its navigability. After describing the "strange sublimity" of that great gorge, "perhaps unparalleled in any part of the world," he argued that the region was, "of course, altogether valueless. It can be approached only from the south, and after entering it there is nothing to do but to leave. Ours was the first, and doubtless will be the last, party of whites to visit this profitless locality. It seems intended by Nature that the Colorado River along the greater portion of its lone and majestic way shall be forever unvisited and unmolested."

But majestic rivers cannot be isolated and forgotten in the midst of a growing civilization. Nature has no respect for state boundaries or man-made property lines. As dust storms and floods so tragically illustrated, neglect or abuse at one point—or a lack of concern for Nature's own destructive forces— could result in damage hundreds of miles away. Each spring the Colorado River ran wild and coffee-colored, ruining the land in its path. And then it ran dry and water for crops near its bed had to be conducted a hundred miles or more.

Just seventy-one years after the Ives Report a Senate Committee on Irrigation and Reclamation, weighing a vast accumulation of field data, favored the construction of a great dam at Boulder Canyon on the Colorado. In 1931 the Secretary of the Interior, as a beginning, awarded the largest labor contract ever let by the United States Government—almost fifty million dollars—for the construction of a dam that would impound a reservoir of ten and one half thousand billion gallons of water. Seven states and Mexico were included in the plan to control floods, provide water for irrigation and for domestic and industrial purposes, to improve navigation, to create a playground

474

BOULDER DAM, ON THE COLORADO RIVER, ARIZONA–NEVADA.

The Bureau of Reclamation

The Bureau of Reclamation

BOULDER DAM, LAKE MEAD, AND THE WORLD ABOUT.

SHASTA DAM, MT. SHASTA IN THE DISTANCE.

The Bureau of Reclamation

The Bureau of Reclamation

A CHART OF THE COLUMBIA BASIN PROJECT. The distance between the Grand Coulee Dam, in the foreground, and Mt. Hood, on the horizon, is some 220 miles.

area and a wild-life refuge, and to supply power. The dam itself, at 726.4 feet the highest in the world, was only one prominent item among the works established over a widespread region.

The Boulder (officially Hoover) Dam is but one of scores of federal dams that have been rising during the past generation—"small" beginnings of a systematized effort to conserve and reclaim the land in broad regional patterns. Great areas of the country are involved, areas considered by past generations as of inferior quality. The waters stored in Lake Mead behind Boulder Dam form the largest artificial lake in the world, with a shore line about 550 miles long—and with about two million acres of irrigable land within its reach. Shasta Dam at the head of the Central Valley Reclamation project in California stores water for and promises power to another two million acres. The Grand Coulee Dam, the largest structure ever built by man, is one element of a project that, in all its ramifications, will serve still another empire of land in the Columbia River Basin—again more than a million acres—with its growing population.

By these and other huge reclamation projects the American frontier had been reopened; not into an unmapped, untouched wilderness such as resisted the early pioneers, but into a world prepared for a fresh advance by new concepts. More than material accomplishment is involved. Underlying those colossal regional experiments is the deepening and broadening sense of public responsibility, the indication of moral purpose on a magnificent scale, that Walt Whit-

477

man had called for in his *Democratic Vistas.* "Not Nature alone is great in her fields of freedom and the open air, in her storms, the shows of night and day, the mountains, forests, seas—but in the artificial, the work of man too is equally great."

One of the most impressive vistas into the future of rural America has been opened by the Tennessee Valley Authority since its inception in 1933. In a gigantic laboratory was tested the timeless American thesis that the ideals of order and liberty, of a strong state and a free people, are compatible. Here, in an area largely rural and roughly equal in size to England and Scotland combined, it has been demonstrated that over-all planning for the general welfare is consistent with elementary democratic practices and that "a world of science and great machines is still a world of men."

The field chosen for the experiment was the valley of a river—although it was at points a mile wide, it was actually a tributary of a tributary of the great Mississippi—that wound wantonly for nine hundred miles through parts of seven states, affecting the lives of several million people; a river that year by year, encouraged by the negligence of man, clawed at its banks, leaving deep wounds of erosion and drawing off in daily drains and annual floods the life blood of the land. By 1933 the valley had become one of the most emaciated regions in the country, and one of the most depressed in terms of human life.

The rehabilitation of that region, physically and socially, has been one of democracy's most portentous recent demonstrations. The twenty-one dams incorporated into the TVA system, several of them among

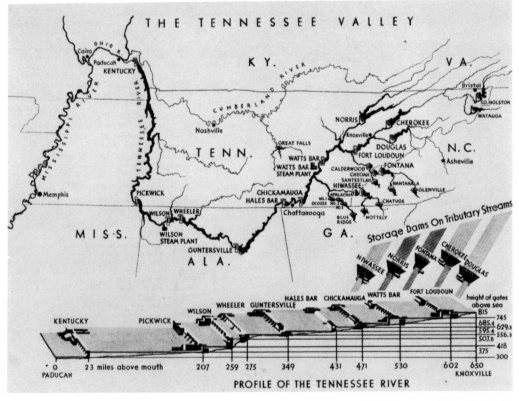

The Tennessee Valley Authority

THE TENNESSEE VALLEY AND A PLAN OF THE SYSTEM OF DAMS.

GENERATORS AT PICKWICK DAM.

the largest in America, are in a sense only markers of the total achievement. In this valley the destiny of the land, water, forests, cities, countryside, and people have been considered as a single problem, the only historic example of such a completely integrated project in regional planning. Reforestation, soil conservation, flood control, navigation, power production, civic planning, and public health, recreation, and education have been woven into a "seamless web" of common purposes.

In the fields, forests, schools, homes, and communities, in the traffic on the tamed waters, and in the huge generators that provide more than a billion kilowatt hours of electric energy a month, the success of the total venture is manifest throughout the reborn val-

ley. Yet the most significant success is in the manner that the project has been underwritten by people participating with a government agency on a level of intimacy not generally associated with large-scale planning. The plan took shape largely as an expression of individual and local public opinion. Like a chain reaction in physics, each simple element was related to others until all became part of a widespread complex.

People from the world over have come to the valley to witness the achievement; possibly to find there a model for an international agency, as Julian Huxley has suggested, that might transcend and undercut national sovereignties, as the TVA undercuts States' rights and boundaries, in behalf of the general welfare of humanity.

V

INDUSTRIAL
AMERICA

INDUSTRIAL AMERICA

INTRODUCTION

O N NEW YEAR'S DAY, 1641, John Winthrop, Jr., one of America's pioneer scientists and industrialists, resolved to give up his habit of inventing things. In that moment of reflection he doubted whether any technological improvements he could devise would ever help him, or any one else, to salvation. Winning greater control over the material surroundings of life might provide practical advantages past generations had had to do without; but the spiritual gains were dubious. A small band of people trying to convert the raw American wilderness into a New Zion needed every practical advantage it could command; but it took a painfully sharp conscience to distinguish what merely added to physical well-being from what also might contribute to the advances of God's commonwealth on earth.

Winthrop's dilemma is still with us. Rather it has returned to us. The same note of deep anxiety sounds in the reflections of today's most advanced scientists as they contemplate the ultimate value of technical progress—most obviously, of course, in the field of nuclear physics. In the meantime, nowhere on earth has human society been so profoundly modified—so richly benefited or so pitilessly tested—by the advances of technology as in America. Nowhere else have the hidden energies of nature been so assidu-

ously tapped and so widely distributed for general use. The relatively sudden emergence of a mechanized, industrial civilization in the New World is one of the most novel and significant developments of recent history. In the words of one English visitor, America had, by the 1930's, become one vast "polytechnic" with all the western world at her heels. "Technique," he wrote, "always in process of further refinement, has imposed itself on everything, invading not only the world of material objects but the world of human relations, where it has become established under the name of 'psychology.' . . . Indeed, there is little exaggeration in saying that the whole country reeks and roars with technique."

Most of the features which distinguish our machine-fed economy from the homespun system of our ancestors have developed only in the last two or three generations. At the time of Washington's inauguration the material conditions of life in America were more like those of Caesar's day than like those of the present. Except in a few respects the average citizen of the new Republic exercised no greater control over his natural surroundings than man had for ages past. Besides the muscles of his own arms and back, the horse or ox and the water wheel were virtually his only sources of prime-moving power. His tools were still hand-hewn and forged to rough measurements, made by old, familiar patterns. In few instances was even this limited equipment systematically organized in the interest of large-scale production.

The transition from that primitive technology to mass-production industry was delayed for a while by natural circumstances. In a sparsely settled land where villages were a day's journey apart and houses often out of sight of one another, where men were generally trained by experience to care for their own immediate wants, the need for more men seemed to be greater than the need for factories—men to fill the gaping distances between other men, men to clear the forest, settle the wilderness, and tame the earth. The immensity of the land, as Jefferson said, courted the industry of the husbandman. So long as there was land left to work, he argued, "let us never wish to see our citizens occupied at a work-bench, or twirling a distaff . . . for the general operations of manufacture, let our work-shops remain in Europe." With many other Americans Jefferson soberly believed that those who depended for their subsistence on the "casualties and caprice of customers," instead of their own self-sufficient efforts, were liable to corruption and subservience.

On the other hand, the shortage of manpower in a land so rich in opportunities actively encouraged labor-saving devices of every sort. As early as 1812 the Russian traveler Paul Svinin noted the short cuts Americans were finding to production. Everything in the New World, he reported to his countrymen—with some exaggeration, for he was one Russian who deeply admired American ways—seemed to be done by some special sort of machinery, even sawing rocks, cobbling shoes, making bricks, and forging nails. A quarter of a century earlier the amazing Philadelphia inventor, Oliver Evans, had already devised a mechanized flour mill where all the operations—cleaning, grinding, and bolting—were carried on without any human intervention at all. Thomas Jeffer-

son himself delighted in labor-saving gadgetry that automatically opened doors and conveyed bottles from his wine cellar in Monticello. A half-century later a group of British manufacturers reported to Parliament that "the chief part . . . of the really new inventions, that is, of new ideas altogether, in the carrying out of a certain process by new machinery, or in a new mode, have originated . . . especially in America."

The organization of such mechanical ingenuity into a large-scale system of manufacture was slow but inevitable. Docile, cheap labor to work in factories was hard to command in a country where everyone hoped soon to be his own boss, in his shop or on a farm. The potential consumers scattered so far and fast it was difficult to keep in easy contact with them until communications swiftened with the steamboat and the railroad. Modern European industry was building with coal and iron and despite America's tremendous deposits of those materials the country was so overladen with fine timber that manufacturers were slower than in other nations to switch from wood and charcoal. But once the switch was made to coal and iron, steam and steel, every circumstance favored the rapid growth of big industrial developments. While European nations searched far-off continents for new materials to feed their factories, America had more than it could quickly do to exploit the long-neglected resources of its own continental expanse. While in Europe industry became a weapon of bitter international rivalry, in America it remained for an important period principally a tool for domestic progress. Production was largely geared to the vast and rapidly growing market within the country—a democratic public that constantly expected more and better things.

To outsiders the American's faith in increased growth and endless progress appeared to keep the country in a state of constant impatience with the achievements of the present. Tocqueville asked an American sailor why his ship was built to last so

484

short a time and was told that the arts of shipbuilding and navigation were making such rapid daily progress that the finest vessel he could build would be obsolete in a few years. "In these words," wrote Tocqueville, "which fell accidentally, and on a particular subject, from an uninstructed man, I recognize the general and systematic idea upon which a great people direct all their concerns."

The lasting truth of that observation could be seen in the junkpiles of automobiles and other abandoned articles that littered the American countryside a century later. By the 1920's domestic mass production had reached such a potential that if goods were made too durable there was grave danger that replacements would not be necessary often enough to keep the assembly lines running at a paying rate. Men had applied themselves to the necessary problem of producing more so earnestly that constantly increasing production had become an end in itself. Americans, wrote one foreign visitor, had become so wrapped up in their machines that they had lost interest in anything that could not be put into mass production. Even jerry-built commodities might last too long in some cases. Not only to anticipate, but to hasten the moment of obsolescence by the invention of new fashions in things (not necessarily technical improvements), became a serious concern of modern industry and its promotion agencies.

With all its ramifications the problem of overproduction marked one of the frontiers of modern industry. Except for an occasional Winthrop it did not occur to our forebears that the advances of technics led anywhere but to salvation. It was largely assumed that with plenty made possible, at long last, the important troubles of society would automatically diminish and disappear. Democracy and technology would triumph together.

During the years of the Great Depression it became painfully clear that mass production was synonymous with neither progress nor human welfare. The machine could now deliver an abundance undreamed of in the past, but it, and those who were entrusted with its performances, had developed no equable system for distributing the plenty. People could suffer want within sight of the most efficient factory. In our mechanical civilization human beings of all sorts and ranks had become so thoroughly interdependent that unless some integrated social purpose was provided for them, all the marvelous technical instruments and processes in Christendom might lead to nothing but confusion and frustration. Unless technology were subordinated to desirable and reasonable human purposes the forces of mechanization and power might turn the American dream into a nightmare.

The conflict of that stubborn fact with the traditional American faith in free, highly competitive economic enterprise had been under way for long years before it assumed larger importance during the depression. What many people referred to as government "meddling in business" was an old story before the 1930's. "Few people notice the little vans that run about the streets collecting mail," wrote the late Carl Becker, "but they are parts of one of the largest business enterprises in the country—a business enterprise owned and operated with exceptional efficiency by the Federal Government. No one thinks that the United States Post Office is a menace to private economic enterprise; and if the government had built, owned, and operated railroads and telegraph lines from the beginning no one would now think that it was meddling in business." How much of the traditional private-enterprise system could be preserved in a society whose interrelated complexities tempted it ever farther toward socialized controls, was very far from settled when World War II ended the depression.

HOUSEHOLD INDUSTRY. Woodcut by Alexander
Anderson.

HANDICRAFT TRADITION

Thomas Jefferson's vision of a pastoral America, of a land given over to farming and a people meeting their needs by their own individual resourcefulness, almost matched the reality in the early days of the Republic. As we have seen in the last chapter, about nine of every ten families practised husbandry a century and a half ago; their freehold was their stake in life, their fields and homes were their factories. Until well into the nineteenth century visitors to this country remarked on the familiar sight of the American who, with the help of his wife and children, not only tilled his fields and subsisted largely on their produce, but who also built his own dwelling, contrived his own tools, made his own shoes, and wove the coarse stuff of his own clothing. In 1791 Alexander Hamilton said the nation was a "vast scene of household manufacturing."

That homespun economy was powered directly by human muscles, supplemented by the strength of the beasts of the field and farmyard and augmented by a few labor-saving contrivances that were usually age-old in principle and limited in performance. The only power-using plants in the nation when Washington became President were the water-driven mills, and the occasional

windmills, employed in sawing wood, grinding flour, and making such basic commodities as paper, gunpowder, and plaster. In Europe hand-sawyers had tried to delay the introduction of sawmills from the fear of losing their day's work to a machine. In America technological unemployment was undreamed of. The work that waited doing always called for more hands than could be brought to the task and every shortcut to accomplishment was welcomed.

Long before the Revolution sawmills were plentiful, converting the forests into workable timber as fast as the streams would turn the wheels. Also, according to Crèvecoeur, most people were within reach of a grist mill, which "is a very great advantage considering the prodigious quantity of flour which we . . . consume annually. . . ."

But, for the rest, production was largely geared to human endurance. Versatility was a necessary virtue and the average citizen was a jack-of-many-trades. Even the local miller was not often a highly specialized manufacturer. Seasonally his machinery might be diverted to different purposes; he inevitably remained a part-time farmer; and in disposing of his toll of the things he processed, he necessarily became a trader of sorts.

RURAL INDUSTRY; A COUNTRY CIDER MILL. Early nineteenth century. Stipple engraving by Cornelius Tiebout after J. J. Barralet.

A TIDAL MILL, ABOUT 1800. Water color attributed to Archibald Robertson.

In the growing villages and budding cities of the new Republic handicraftsmen with special training found ample patronage for their talents. Even during the colonial period every urban community had its roster of silversmiths, cabinetmakers, jewelers, coachmakers, carpenters, shoemakers, tailors, printers, and specialists in numerous other callings.

Returns for such work were relatively high in America, and the market for luxuries as well as necessities was constantly and rapidly expanding as cities grew, as trading increased, and as better highways brought city and country into a more interdependent relationship. It was an attractive field for private enterprise, as Tench Coxe pointed out in 1794 in his *View of the United States.* "A large porportion of the most successful manufacturers in the United States," he wrote, "consists of persons, who were journeymen, and in a few instances were foremen in the work-shops and manufactories of Europe; who having been skilful, sober, frugal, and having thus saved a little money, have set up for themselves with great advantage in America."

Such an enterprising and successful immigrant was the Scot, Duncan Phyfe, whose shop and warehouse in New York City are illustrated on the opposite page and whose

The New-York Historical Society
A PEWTERER'S SHOP, 1788. Painting on a silk flag carried by the Society of Pewterers of New York City in the Federal Procession celebrating the ratification of the Constitution, July 23, 1788.

superb furniture is rightly treasured by the connoisseurs and collectors of the present day. At about the time the accompanying water color was executed there were more than two dozen French cabinetmakers in New York alone, men who vied with one another, with other local craftsmen of different backgrounds, and with importers of foreign-made goods to win the patronage of an increasingly prosperous buying public.

Traditionally, shop production met demand as it arose, on an individual basis. The artisan was usually owner of his own tools and shop, or soon expected to be, and controlled the hours and conditions of his own labor. No elaborate distinctions were yet drawn between manufacturer, retailer, and middleman, although by the close of the eighteenth century all existed in their separate capacities. Craftsman and patron, producer and consumer, rubbed shoulders familiarly in the same society and all understood the amenities and necessities of life

The New-York Historical Society,
Bella C. Landauer Collection
T. S. UFFINGTON, GOLD AND SILVER BEATER, NEW YORK, 1808–09. Engraving by an unidentified artist.

from much the same viewpoint. Production was still largely aimed at essential use and the methods of production were no mystery to any reasonably enlightened consumer. When almost everyone was a fair judge of the serviceability and fitness of an object, fooling people for profit simply was not profitable. So long as production was limited to the output of unaugmented human labor there was no superabundance of manufactured goods to embarrass the manufacturer into extravagant sales techniques.

In early America the artisan, like the farmer and the miller, was rarely a specialist in any advanced degree. There was not enough demand to encourage the development of extreme virtuosity in craftsmanship such as supplied the courts and capitals of Europe with superbly wrought luxuries; and the variety of opportunity constantly tempted workmen to undertake new occupations. As a consequence, noted Tocqueville, the American was often a mediocre craftsman, not because of lack of ability but because, with such wide, inviting fields to conquer, "he would never accomplish his purpose if he chose to carry every detail to perfection." If he were less perfect in his craft, Tocqueville added—at least there was scarcely a trade with which he was unacquainted—"his capacity is more general, and the circle of his intelligence is greater."

THE FURNITURE SHOP AND WAREHOUSE OF DUNCAN PHYFE, FULTON STREET, NEW YORK. Water color by an unidentified artist, early nineteenth century.

The Metropolitan Museum of Art

In a society where no man expected to remain long in the employ of another, where every journeyman was a budding capitalist, and where, in any case, wages were relatively high, labor problems were minimal. Most early labor organizations were for benevolent purposes solely. Twenty-four such societies were incorporated in New York alone during the first decade of the nineteenth century. There were also, however, some labor societies composed of journeymen of one trade, groups usually formed for the purpose of regulating wages and working laws.

To prevent exploitation by those who hired the skill of their members, these latter organizations—incipient trade unions—early resorted to the closed shop, to collective bargaining, and to strikes, or "turnouts." The boot- and shoemakers of Philadelphia who had organized in self-protection in 1792 had by such measures considerably increased their wages by 1805 when they struck again. This time, however, the men were brought to trial and, under the common law, convicted of a "conspiracy" to raise their wages further. After their conviction the journeymen set up a warehouse of their own and appealed to the public, through the press, to save them and their families from "abject poverty." Five years later a society of New York tailors was likewise found guilty of criminal conspiracy on the same count.

Although the early courts were hostile to union demands, and an occasional strike was attended by violence, no serious unrest

The New York Public Library
CERTIFICATE OF THE NEW YORK MECHANICK SOCIETY, A BENEVOLENT SOCIETY FOR ARTISANS OF DIFFERENT TRADES, 1795.

490

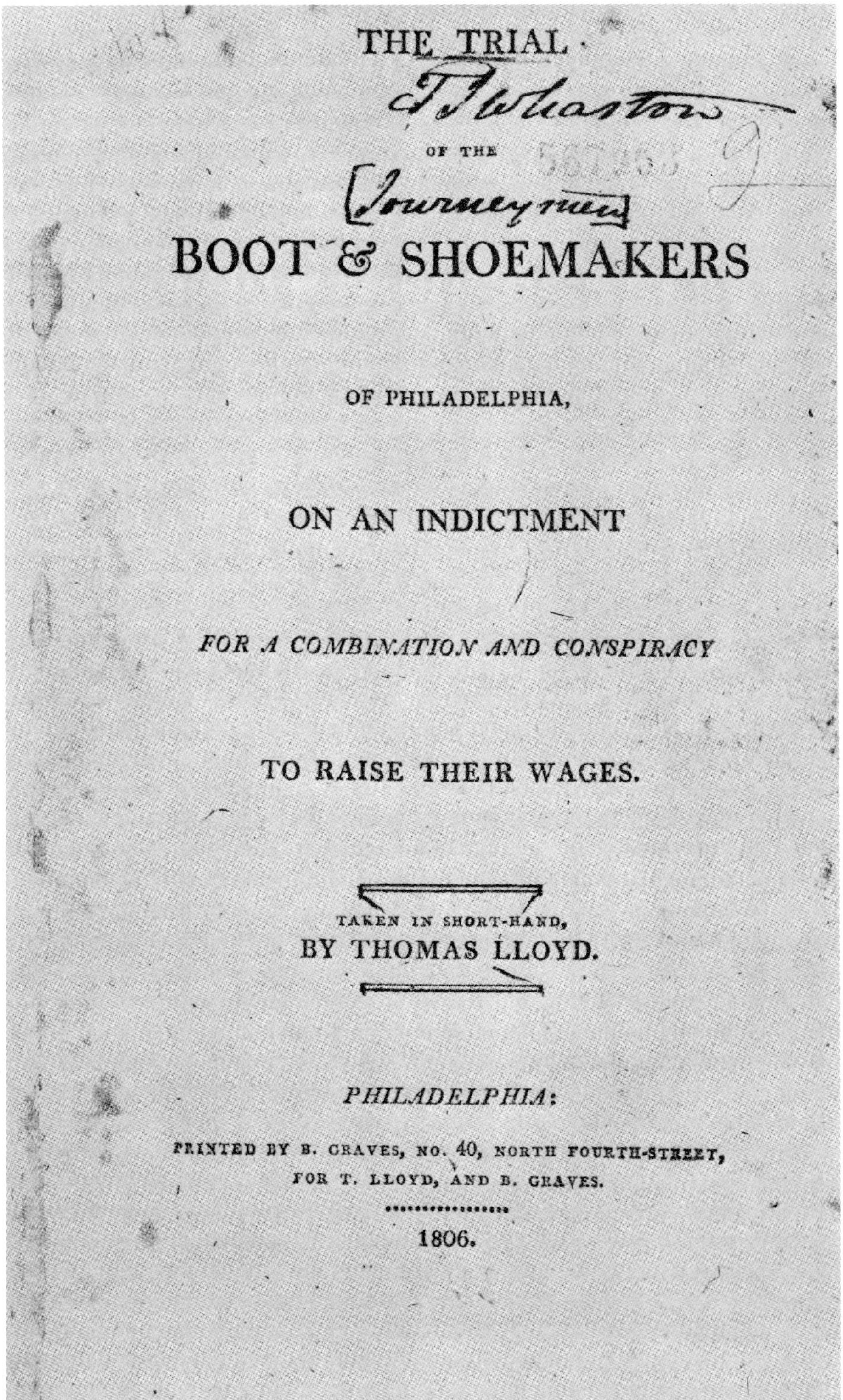

THE TRIAL

T Wharton (handwritten)

OF THE

[*Journeymen*] (handwritten)

BOOT & SHOEMAKERS

OF PHILADELPHIA,

ON AN INDICTMENT

FOR A COMBINATION AND CONSPIRACY

TO RAISE THEIR WAGES.

TAKEN IN SHORT-HAND,

BY THOMAS LLOYD.

PHILADELPHIA:

PRINTED BY B. GRAVES, NO. 40, NORTH FOURTH-STREET,

FOR T. LLOYD, AND B. GRAVES.

....

1806.

A REPORT OF AN EARLY LABOR STRIKE, 1806. Title page of a pamphlet reporting the trial of the strikers for "conspiring" to raise their wages.

developed among journeymen artisans. Everywhere and in most trades the demand for skilled labor was far greater than the supply. When New York built its third and present City Hall every known inducement was offered to attract stone cutters from other cities, even from places as distant as Charleston, South Carolina. High weekly wages were promised, work would be steady, tools would be kept in repair. Thus it also was in other trades.

Even those who by reason of their special skills found an eager and profitable welcome could not always be persuaded to stay on the job. "Scarcely a shoemaker, a joiner, or a silversmith but quits his trade as soon as he can get able to buy a little tract of land." So Governor Wentworth complained to England during the colonial period. For years to come the temptation of an independent, self-sufficient life on a freehold continued to siphon off a portion of the labor supply from the cities. The need of more workmen to man the growing industries of America remained chronic for more than a century after the Revolution.

As a consequence, any device that would save the time and cost of a day's work, or

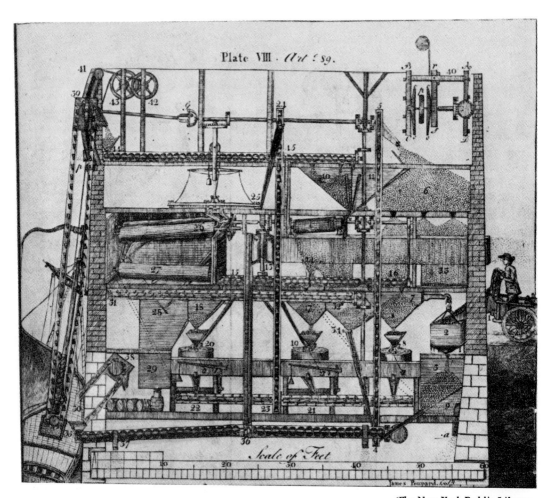

OLIVER EVANS' PLAN FOR A MECHANICAL GRIST MILL, 1783. From Evans, *The Young Mill-Wright and Miller's Guide*, Philadelphia, 1795.

that would step up the rate of an individual's production, had special value in this country. By a sort of reflex action the American developed what Michel Chevalier called "a mechanic in his soul"—an ingenuity in contriving mechanical substitutes for man-power and in finding the quickest and easiest, if often not the best, way of getting things done. That penchant for saving time became such a fixed and fundamental habit that the typical Yankee came to use the leisure he derived from a labor- or time-saving device to think up a new such device so that he would have more time to think up still other labor-saving devices in a non-stop spiral of time-consuming effort.

Probably the most spectacular early exponent of that native bent was the indefatigable Philadelphia inventor, Oliver Evans. The mechanical grist mill he invented in 1785 performed "every necessary movement of the grain and meal, from one part of the mill to another . . . through all the various operations, from the time the grain is emptied from the Wagoner's bag . . . until it is completely manufactured into flour . . . ready for packing into barrels, for sale or exportation. All of which is performed by the force of water, without the aid of manual labor, except to set the different machines in motion."

The belt conveyors, screw conveyors, and endless-chain buckets of Evans's inspired contraption, which handled three hundred bushels an hour, anticipated almost all the integrated mechanical handling devices common to modern mass production. From raw material to finished product the material was "untouched by human hands," probably "the first instance of an uninterrupted process of mechanical manufacture . . . in the history of industry."

Evans's extraordinary mill was only one contribution of his singular genius. A few years later he developed a high-pressure steam engine that was more efficient than that of James Watt, the celebrated English inventor, and shortly thereafter he drove his own amphibious steam car through the

The Library of Congress
A COTTON GIN IN OPERATION. Engraving after a drawing by William L. Sheppard. From *Harper's Weekly*, 1873.

streets of Philadelphia, much to the amazement of the citizens of that quiet city. "I have To-day seen a waggon go through our Street without Horses," wrote one of them in 1797, "—a piece of Mechanism that charms me as I look forward to having a Carriage that I can wind up and set agoing as I do my watch, without trusting my Life to the Mercy of drunken Coachmen or perhaps wild Horses."

More renowned among early American inventions was Eli Whitney's celebrated cotton gin. Several years before it was put into action, it is said, eight bales of cotton were seized at Liverpool on the ground that American soil could hardly export such a quantity at one time. By 1800 the cotton fields of the South, thanks to the impetus provided by Whitney's gin, were exporting nearly eighteen million pounds a year and by 1845 seven-eighths of the world's cotton supply

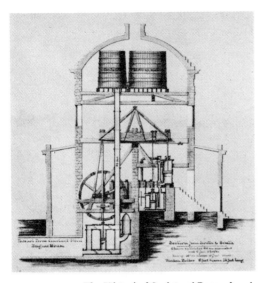

The Historical Society of Pennsylvania
THE STEAM ENGINE OF THE CENTER SQUARE WATER WORKS, IN USE FROM 1801–1815 IN PHILADELPHIA. Drawing by Frederick Graff, 1828.

came from America. Whitney, too, went on to other inventions and ingenious adaptations of equal importance in the history of industry, as we shall see. In his and Evans's achievements the whole future of the American system of mass production was foreshadowed.

During the colonial period virtually the only fuel-using plants in America were the charcoal furnaces where iron, glass, lime,

The Metropolitan Museum of Art
THE CENTER SQUARE WATER WORKS, PHILADELPHIA, 1811–13. Water color by Paul Svinin.

tar, and a few other commodities were manufactured. Occasional efforts were made, following English precedent, to convert heat into steam power. Twenty years before the Revolution a steam-powered pump was installed by English workmen at Colonel John Schuyler's copper mine in New Jersey. On the eve of the war, Christopher Colles had also set up a successful steam-pumping plant in New York; an enterprise brought to an unhappy end by the British occupation of the city. But by the end of the eighteenth century there were less than a half-dozen steam engines of any considerable power in the country.

Probably the most conspicuous early example was the pumping station of the Philadelphia waterworks, a device which gave that city the great luxury of an adequate water supply (see Chapter VII). "It is of great importance . . ." remarked a contemporary, "that [these water works] are the property of the public, and not subject to individual speculation, in consequence of which the supply is liberal, and there are fountains in every street to which the whole public have access. The water can be used for watering the streets, or extinguishing fires, as often as may be necessary; while every householder, by paying a reasonable compensation, can have a hydrant in any part of his premises that he pleases, even to the attic story."

The successful application of steam power to industry released titanic forces that completely revolutionized the relation of man to his environment. But in America the innumerable streams and rivers that coursed through the land continued to turn the wheels of industry long after the manufactories of England had been converted to steam. Not until after the Civil War did steam supplant water as this country's main source of power. *On* the waterways, however, the conversion to steam power was early and remarkable. Characteristically, America first seriously used the invention not for a stationary prime-mover, as in England, but for increased mobility. As described more fully in Chapter VIII, to America the steamboat meant unity, accomplished and sustained on a scale that would otherwise have been impossible. Although the first conquests of the new steamboats were on eastern waters, the crying need for them was on the inland rivers of the West, the great open highways of the rapidly expanding nation. "Poor John Fitch" who "reigned Lord High Admiral of the Delaware," as he exultantly described it, in the steamboat he operated on that river in the 1780's, and Robert Fulton whose later and larger success on the Hudson earned him world-wide fame, both knew that the greatest service for their craft would be on the Mississippi and its tributaries. In describing the *Clermont's* maiden voyage the *American Citizen* referred to "Mr. Fulton's Ingenious Steam Boat, invented with a view to the navigation of the Mississippi from New Orleans upwards. . . . It is said it will make a progress of two [miles per hour] against the current of the Mississippi, and if so it will certainly be a very valuable acquisition to the commerce of Western States."

Fitch was a remarkable inventor. But invention is only one link in a chain of circumstances that secures practical success. He lost his backing and died by his own hand, an embittered and frustrated genius of sorts. By Fulton's day, twenty years later, the public attitude toward such outlandish innovations had considerably matured, the need for them had grown more obvious and pressing, Fulton could control ample capital, innumerable small technological developments insured continuous production of his models, and, with the chain of circumstances complete, steamboat navigation became seemingly overnight a successful commercial enterprise. That success was America's first contribution to the technology of the Industrial Revolution.

THE WESTERN STEAMBOAT *Superior,* 1832. Lithograph after A. St. Aulaire.

Kennedy and Co.

THE SALEM IRON FACTORY, EARLY 19TH CENTURY. Reprint from a contemporary copperplate engraved by G. Graham.

THE RISE OF THE FACTORY

Tremendously important though it was, the development of steam power was only one element in a series of changes that fundamentally altered human society during the eighteenth and nineteenth centuries. Throughout the history of civilization industry had been principally in the hands of craftsmen, workmen whose individual strength, skill, and resources, largely dictated the production of goods. Now, first in England, then later in America and elsewhere, workmen in certain industries were being gathered into factories to produce larger quantities through a systematic division of their labor.

Here for the first time appeared that combination of factors that provided the foundation of modern industry—the concentration of many hands under one roof, the development of machinery and the application of mechanical power, the separation of the worker from the ownership of his tools and of the means of production, and a growing distinction between management and labor. Except in a few instances those factors had previously played no important part in the American economy. From now on they would, in combination, determine the direction and extent of the nation's industry.

The portentous change grew out of crisis. The long disturbance of foreign trade resulting from the Revolution and the Non-Intercourse and Embargo Acts practically obliged this country to supply for itself the manufactured articles which for almost two centuries had come from England and the European continent. It was during the cold war with France, in 1798, that Eli Whitney set up his factory, pictured opposite, and contracted to supply the government with ten thousand muskets which he planned to produce in such unheard-of quantity by a system of interchangeable mechanical parts —one of the earliest and the most successful application of that principle in industrial history.

During the embargoes on foreign trade that followed, Societies for the Encouragement of Domestic Manufactures were formed throughout the states. Columns of newspaper carried advertisements of American-made goods. American women were asked to put aside the gaudy trappings of imported luxuries for the plain stuff of domestic manufacture. Toast after toast was drunk to the infant Hercules of American industry which might yet strangle the serpent of European influence. Even Thomas

ELI WHITNEY'S GUN FACTORY, 1826–28. Painting by William G. Munson. In the middle distance are depicted the dwellings erected by Whitney for his employees, one of the first housing projects in the United States.

THE INTERIOR OF AN ENGLISH COTTON FACTORY, ABOUT 1825–35. Lithograph.

THE UNION MANUFACTORIES OF MARYLAND ON PATAPSCO FALLS, BALTIMORE COUNTY, ABOUT 1812. Drawing by Maximilian Godefroy. Established during the embargo, the Union Factory by 1825 employed 600 hands,

Jefferson, champion of an agrarian society, conceded that America must develop its own manufactures or America would go clad in skins.

But, as the members of the Kentucky legislature pointed out in a petition for protective measures in 1811, the strife in Europe would one day subside. "Peace will return," read this plan, "and when it does what has so long been the soul of industry will expire, and a new means will have to be sought for preserving the wealth so rapidly acquired. . . . The manufacturer in the United States contends with obstacles long since removed in England. He is poor; he has shops and factories to build; he has workmen to train, high wages to pay, and none of the bounties which enable his English rival to overcome the cost of freight, duty, and insurance, and sell goods in the markets of America as cheaply as in those of England. . . . The whole people are concerned. Should peace with England be broken, should we be forced to take up arms in defence of our honor and our rights, where would we look

for clothing and blankets for the troops and sailors, and cordage and sail-cloth for the frigates and privateers? Never shall we be truly a free people till we are independent of England commercially as we are politically."

As it turned out, hostilities with England commenced the next year, and America was soon subjected to a tight and humiliating blockade. Under the pressure of this new necessity industries sprang up with unprecedented rapidity. "Wheels roll, spindles whirl, shuttles fly," reported a Connecticut newspaper of the revitalized manufactories. Before the war was fairly started Jefferson wrote: "Of coarse and middling fabrics we never again shall import. . . . This single advancement in economy, begun by our embargo law, continued by that for nonimportation, and confirmed by the present total cessation of commercial intercourse, was worth alone all the war will cost us."

Yet, when the war ended, great fleets, carrying heavy cargoes of European goods, swarmed into American ports where there

498

who tended 80,000 spindles driven by sixteen water wheels.

were ready buyers of everything that was offered for sale. In April, May, and June of 1815 duties paid at New York's Custom House alone amounted to almost four million dollars. A few months later, twenty square-rigged ships, laden with imports from Europe, sailed up New York's bay in a single flotilla. America was becoming a dumping ground for the long pent-up manufactures of England.

Too much capital had by then been invested in American factories to abandon them, even in the face of such bitterly discouraging competition. In 1816 a protective tariff passed Congress—surety that the country was preparing for an industrial future. But the commitment was not made lightly or without opposition. Young Daniel Webster spoke for many when he told Congress he had no wish to hasten that day "when the great mass of American labor shall not find its employment in the field; when the young men of the country shall be obliged to shut their eyes upon external nature, upon the heavens and the earth, and im-

merse themselves in close and unwholesome workshops; when they shall be obliged to shut their ears to the bleating of their own flocks upon their own hills . . . that they may open them in dust and steam to the perpetual whirl of spools and spindles and the grating of rasps and saws." Furthermore, it was earnestly asked, would men who received their bread from employers instead of winning it by their own independent efforts be the faithful guardians of liberty? A decade after the conclusion of the War of 1812 America was well on its way to white adult male suffrage. Might not factory dependents and hirelings vote as they were told in the interest of their own precarious security?

Whatever the menace to democracy and despite the post-war slump in sales, American manufacturers persisted and flourished. "Factories are now multiplying," reported the *North American Review* in 1825, "built on the best instruction and with the modern improvements, and there is little reason to doubt, that the water power now unem-

LOWELL, MASSACHUSETTS, ABOUT 1833. Lithograph by Pendleton.

ployed will be converted to purposes of manufacture, chiefly of cotton."

The rise and spread of mechanized industry in America did not cause the violent upheaval that had accompanied that development in England. In the older country a widespread hand industry, carried on in the homes of the individual workers but systematically organized from above in factory fashion, was immediately and seriously threatened by the introduction of concentrated mechanical methods of production. The habits and the very livelihood of thousands of people were imperiled.

Except for a few instances, such highly organized and controlled domestic manufactures had not developed on any appreciable scale in this country. New factories merely lessened our dependence on foreign importations and offered a novel occupation to those who could be persuaded to work in them.

For, relatively scarce as labor was in America, it could not be driven into the new mill towns; it had to be tempted there by decent conditions and adequate remuneration.

Then too, because the use of coal and steam for factory power was delayed here, most of the new enterprises did not mass in existing cities but rather sought more or less isolated points along the swifter streams of the countryside where water power was plentiful. The first industrial communities that sprang up along the mill streams of New England bore small resemblance to the congested, grimy manufacturing centers of England. In Connecticut, wrote Tench Coxe, the traveler's eye was "charmed with the view of delightful villages, suddenly rising as it were by magic along the banks of some meandering rivulet, flourishing by the influence and fostered by the protecting arm of manufactures."

Of those new and tidy manufacturing settlements Lowell, Massachusetts, on the Merrimack River was a conspicuous example and for a time remained one of the show places of America. Writing of the city in 1833, eleven years after its founding, Michel Chevalier observed: ". . . it now contains 15,000 inhabitants. . . . Twelve years ago it was a barren waste. . . . At present, it is a pile of huge factories, each five, six, or seven stories high, and capped with a little white belfry. . . . By the side of these larger structures rise numerous little wooden houses, painted white, with green blinds,

MILL OPERATIVES, MID-NINETEENTH CENTURY. Engraving from a bank note.

very neat, very snug, very nicely carpeted, and with a few small trees around them, or brick houses in the English style. . . ."

Nothing impressed tourists who visited Lowell so much as that the mills were largely operated by blooming girls from near-by Yankee farms. Andrew Jackson remarked that they were "very pretty women, by the Eternal!" Davy Crockett agreed, although he remarked that the prettiest ones were kept in the forefront and the homelier ones on the outside rows. The girls were rarely forced to work there from necessity but rather looked to a brief experience in the mills as a sort of introduction to life, much as their brothers looked to a few years at sea.

For a generation or so those independent young daughters of New England farmers, comfortably housed as they were, neatly dressed, protected against every suspicion of immorality, and provided with cultural opportunities which they eagerly improved (Trollope called Lowell "a philanthropical manufacturing college") provided one of the most intriguing attractions of the New World. Chevalier compared the steeple-crowned factories at Lowell with the convents of a Spanish town, but in Lowell, he wrote, "you meet no rags nor Madonnas . . . the nuns of Lowell, instead of working *sacred hearts,* spin and weave cotton."

Quite aside from being a "commercial Utopia" the Lowell mills were revolutionary in their operations. Visitors referred to them as "a strange Yankee phenomenon . . . that took your bale of cotton in at one end and gave out yards of cloth at the other, after goodness knew what digestive process." An earlier factory of the company, started at Waltham by Francis Cabot Lowell, a Boston merchant, had incorporated the first power loom to be used in America and was one of the first in the world to combine all the operations necessary to convert raw fiber into cloth under one roof. At Lowell with its larger establishment and greater water power, according to a visiting English manufacturer, the mills produced "a greater quantity of yarn and cloth from each spindle and loom (in a given time) than was produced by any other factories, without exception in the world."

MORNING BELL AT A NEW ENGLAND FACTORY. Painting by Winslow Homer, about 1866.
Collection of Stephen C. Clark

An English lecturer who offered the Lowell operatives cut rates was promptly told that they would come at the regular prices—"on the same footing as other ladies" —or not at all. Familiar with the depressed conditions of laboring classes in Europe foreigners were not always quick to understand that labor in the New World still commanded a peculiar respect. To be sure, Lowell was not typical of industrial America nor did its model qualities long survive the importation of foreign labor. But in its earlier period it demonstrated Tocqueville's conclusion that in America every honest calling was honorable and dignified.

It was a prevailing conviction that in this country there was no such thing as a laboring class. Hirelings—in the factories, on the city streets, or on the railroad gangs—were but serving an apprenticeship to a richer life. Meanwhile, as they worked out their destiny, wages were high. "The lowest wages going in the United States for a labourer's day's work," Thomas Mooney, an Irish newcomer, advised his countrymen in 1850, "is seventy cents, or about three English shillings. . . . This would be eighteen shillings for a week; and you can obtain good board, lodging, and washing for a little less than ten British shillings, or two and a half dollars a week. So that you will be able to save seven or eight shillings a week to buy the farm, which farm you can buy for five shillings an acre. . . . Remember that, if you please, you can, as soon as you get into a regular employment, save the price of an acre and a half of the finest land in the world every week, and in less than a year you will have money enough to start for the west, and take up an eighty acre farm which will be your own forever."

With such inducement it is hardly surprising that more than two and a half million aliens poured into America between 1850 and 1860. By the latter date they were replacing the country lasses in the Lowell mills at a rapid rate.

The Museum of the City of New York

THE LURE OF AMERICAN WAGES, ABOUT 1855. Woodcut by an unidentified artist.

PAT LYON, BLACKSMITH. Painting by John Neagle, 1826–27. As compensation for false accusation and imprisonment, Pat Lyon was awarded a "handsome sum of money," with part of which he commissioned this portrait of himself showing in the background the Walnut Street prison where he had been confined.

THE AMERICAN SYSTEM
OF MANUFACTURE

By 1840 industrialism had sunk firm roots in American soil. The production of textiles, in which the new growth was most conspicuous, had become an important factor in the nation's economy. More than twelve hundred cotton spinning and weaving establishments alone employed well over seventy thousand workers and processed one and a quarter million pounds of fiber annually. Although visitors still noted the abiding prejudice of many Americans against factory work, the modern factory system had become the common frame of life for a majority of the inhabitants of Waltham, Lowell, Holyoke, and other flourishing northeastern towns.

Impressive as the rapid growth of those humming mills was, developments in some of the smaller workshops of New England promised even more remarkable changes in long established ways of working and living. Eli Whitney's effort to simplify the elementary operations of manufacture by the use of standardized interchangeable mechanisms was neither the first nor the only one in that direction. However, when that principle was combined with the use of automatic machinery, as it early was in Whitneyville, a new manufacturing technique evolved that radically changed the ratio of a workman's time and labor to the quantity of work he was capable of producing. From those pioneering efforts sprang the American system of mass production upon which our whole social structure has come to depend.

Whitney's system was early applied to the manufacture of clocks with such startling success that within a few years inexpensive American timepieces were flooding markets around the world. The first consignment of such mass-produced brass clocks sent to England were bought by the customs authorities there at the registered cost of $1.50 on the ground that they must be undervalued. Since the manufacturer lost no money on the deal other shipments followed until the truth was accepted. Before 1843 a single American firm had sold more than forty thousand clocks abroad.

The successful application of automatic mechanisms to metal manufacturing ultimately depended on the tools that made the

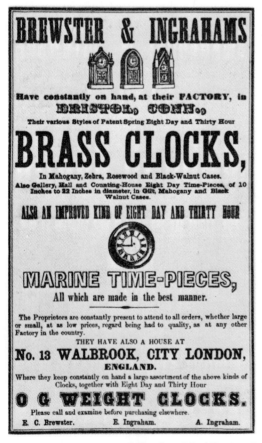

Collection of Carl Drepperd
ADVERTISEMENT OF MASS-PRODUCED CLOCKS, 1845–50.

MACHINE TOOLS: AN IRON PLANER (above) AND A PILLAR DRILL. Engraving by J. W. Orr.

tools that shaped the final product, on the machine tools—lathes, planers, millers, gear cutters, punch presses, and other basic tools— that have aptly been named the "master tools of industry." Without them sustained quantity production was impossible. The lack of machines to turn and bore and plane metal surfaces to a tolerable mechanical fit had wrecked the dreams of many aspiring mechanics and inventors, "Poor John" Fitch of steamboat hopes among them. When machine tools made possible the standardization of all machine parts to accurate measurement a technical revolution was inevitable—sewing machines, typewriters, automobiles, electric generators, linotype machines, and a thousand other props to modern civilization became mechanically feasible.

Whitney probably invented the first suc-

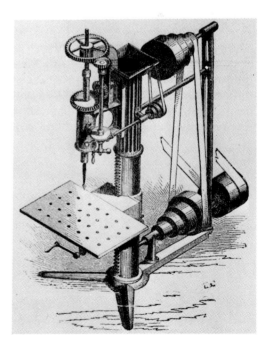

THE MACHINE SHOPS OF THE CHISEL AND STEEL SQUARE WORKS, SHAFTSBURY, VERMONT, ABOUT 1857. Lithographed by Endicott and Co. after Charles Parsons.

cessful milling machine; the turret lathe, the fully automatic lathe, and several other machine tools have been claimed as the original inventions of various other Connecticut Yankees. But it is more significant that American mechanics in general adapted the new manufacturing procedures based on their operations with uninhibited zest, boldly improvising new adaptations whenever the standard practice seemed too rigid or too cumbersome for a particular job. In 1840 British mechanics who considered emigrating to the New World were advised by one returned Englishman, who had worked for four years in America and traveled through much of the country, that they must be prepared to meet with "new and peculiar, if not improved modes and ideas," and make up their minds to accept those circumstances immediately. Fourteen years later a committee of British manufacturers told Parliament that "the contriving and making of machinery has become so common in [America], and so many heads and hands are at work with extraordinary energy; that unless the example is followed at home, notwithstanding the difference in wages, it is to be feared that American manufacturers will before long become exporters not only to foreign countries, but even to England. . . ."

In broad outline the engineering equipment of machine shops had already assumed the functions which it performs today. In latter years, to be sure, operations were on a larger scale and carried out with great refinement. But in its basic form the technol-

DIS-ASSEMBLY LINE IN A SLAUGHTERHOUSE, 1872. After a charcoal sketch by Forney.

The New-York Historical Society, Bella C. Landauer Collection

ogy of mass production was widely understood and applied in America more than a hundred years ago. Henry Ford ultimately combined Evans's system of mechanical conveyors and Whitney's system of automatically produced interchangeable parts into a modern system of manufacture; but the individual techniques were a century old when he did it.

Several recent writers have pointed out that the moving assembly line that mechanically carries a job past workmen, each of whom performs a separate operation — a technique inseparably associated with Fordism, was also a long-tried practice in America when Ford adopted it. In *Made in America* John Kouwenhoven remarks that as early as 1835 Harriet Martineau witnessed such an assembly line in a slaughterhouse in Cincinnati. "One man," reported Miss Martineau, "drives into one pen or chamber the reluctant hogs, to be knocked on the head by another whose mallet is for ever going. A third sticks the throats, after which they are conveyed by some clever device to the cutting-up room, and thence to the pickling, and thence to the packing and branding." While Miss Martineau's queasy stomach could not support a more detailed account of what went on, her description is clear enough evidence that this phase of American manufacturing technique had very early origins—and provides another effective reminder, as Mr. Kouwenhoven writes, that the technology of mass production is "as indigenous to the United States as the husking bee."

The Library of Congress

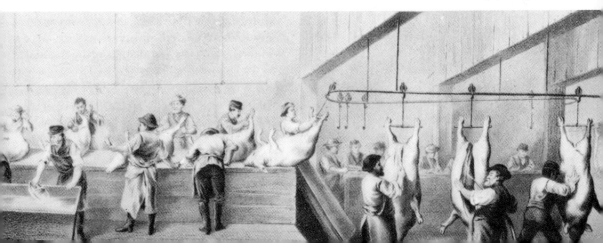

The Metropolitan Museum of Art

COLT'S REVOLVER IN ACTION. Engraving from the drum of a Colt presentation revolver.

One of the most remarkable early demonstrations of the American system of manufacture was provided by Samuel Colt at his world-famous factory in Hartford. Colt had whittled out the basic form of his revolver years before but his early production efforts at Paterson, New Jersey, had failed from his inability to find a market for his invention. As told in Chapter II, when the struggle of the Texas Republic in the 1840's focused national attention on the open warfare of

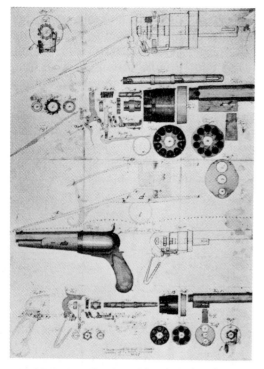

Colt's Patent Fire Arms Manufacturing Company
SAMUEL COLT'S FIRST PATENT, 1835.

the western borderlands, the search for an effective weapon against the rapid arrow fire of the Indians blazed a path from that remote market to Colt's front door and made him a captain of industry almost overnight. Equipped with his revolver, Colt was told, the Texas Rangers were willing to engage four times their number in any engagement. One group of sixteen men with revolvers had all but slaughtered a war party of about eighty Comanche Indians. "Several other Skirmishes have been equally satisfactory," Captain Samuel H. Walker wrote Colt in 1846. ". . . Without your Pistols we would not have had the confidence to have undertaken such daring adventures. . . . The people throughout Texas are anxious to procure your pistols & I doubt not you would find sale for a large number at this time."

Colt produced his first large orders at Whitney's plant, using machinery and equipment that later became his own. His subsequent operations centered in the Hartford factory where, from the start, the most advanced principles of interchangeable manfacture were incorporated in a large-scale, integrated enterprise that used about four hundred different machines performing more than that number of separate operations. In the 1850's the factory was producing almost 25,000 revolvers a year. It was soon the greatest arms factory in the world.

The famous English engineer, James Nasmyth, reported that his visit to Colt's factory affected him in a way he would never forget. "The first impression was to humble me very considerably," he wrote. ". . . I was in a manner introduced to such a skilful extension of what I knew to be correct principles, but extended in so masterly and wholesome a manner, as made one feel that we were very far behind in carrying out what we knew to be good principles. What struck me at Colonel Colt's was, that the acquaintance with correct principles had been carried out in a bold, ingenious way, and they had been pushed to their full extent; and the result was the attainment of perfection and economy, such as I had never met with before."

There is little doubt that by the middle of the last century America was making greater mechanical progress in some directions than Europe. At the Crystal Palace Exhibition in London, 1851—the first modern world's fair —this country had little more than Hiram Powers's "Greek Slave," a somewhat notorious sculpture of the period, to present beside the lavish display of art from European nations. But with its practical accomplishments America proudly won its first international distinctions. Colt's revolver, Day and Newell's locks, Charles Goodyear's India-rubber products, Bigelow's carpet power looms, and certain other industrial exhibits from America had no equal at the fair. Cyrus McCormick had sent a magnificent mechanical reaper, built of highly varnished ash, with bronzed woodwork and a canvas screen brightly decorated with an American eagle, all manned by "a brown, rough homespun Yankee." After first greeting that particular exhibit with amused skepticism the London *Times* finally conceded that it was "the most valuable contribution from abroad to the stock of our previous knowledge, that we have yet discovered" (see Chapter IV).

The yacht *America* had just beaten its English rivals in the international regatta of that same year. Steamers of the Collins Line were, for a brief few years, showing their sterns to the English Cunarders. Yankee clippers were leaving all other sailing ships in their wakes on every sea. The traditional Yankee brag could not be restrained (see pages 510-11).

THE COLT FACTORY, HARTFORD, CONNECTICUT, ABOUT 1855. Lithograph.

The Library of Congress

*Mister Bull you can now se...
of the exhibition 'to more advan...
your 'Crystal Palace' if your old...
across the pond, and you will se...
to the Pacific & China -and show...
longer, we will show you great...*

*Yankee Doodle had a craft, a rather tidy clipper,
And he challenged, while they laughed, the Britishers to whip her,
Their whole yacht-squadron she outsped, and that on their own water,
Of all the lot she went a-head, and they came nowhere arter.*

THE GREAT EX

AMERICAN

*By Yankee Doodle, too, voi...
With his machine for reaping...*

YANKEE BRAG AFTER THE CRYSTAL PALACE EXHIBITION AT LONDON, 1851. Lithograph by N. Currier.

THE SINGER SEWING MACHINE FACTORY, 1853. Woodcut.

Collection of Carl Drepperd

"The expenditure of months or years of labour upon a single article . . . solely to augment its cost or its estimation as an object of *virtù*, is not common in the United States. On the contrary, both manual and mechanical labour are applied with direct reference to increasing the number or the quantity of articles suited to the wants of a whole people, and adapted to promote the enjoyment

The American Antiquarian Society
DOMESTIC FELICITY WITH A SEWING MACHINE. Lithograph by Ehrgott, Forbriger, and Co.

of that moderate competency which prevails among them."

In that rather apologetic comment on novel American displays at the Crystal Palace, the official catalogue of the exhibition rationalized the whole development of mass production methods. To marry democracy to the machine, to provide the greatest number of people with the greatest number of the good things of life, was not only an ideal to celebrate but, once a flow of articles had been established, a practical necessity for a system based on continuous, automatic production. Once started the new industrialism developed its own independent momentum. But America was a large, prospering, and expanding country in which virtually every citizen had the confident hope of soon bettering his material position. The domestic market alone, in 1851, promised an apparently inexhaustible demand for machine-made goods of every variety.

The several exhibits of American sewing machines at the Crystal Palace excited only a mild curiosity. The first practical models had been manufactured but the year before and the mechanism was still in a primitive stage. Within a decade, however, more than one hundred thousand were being produced annually in this country. One of the most ancient forms of human art and drudgery was meeting machine competition.

The family "Singer" was a tireless seamstress, reported the *American Agriculturist*, that was "always at home when you want work done, never troubled with beaux, nor with aching shoulders, nor with mumps, nor mopes." With it available, the magazine added, mother could whip together a couple of shirts for tomorrow's trip merely by sending Johnny to the village store for the requisite muslin and buttons. Furthermore, "the little ones need no longer be turned over to the tender mercies of Bridget in the kitchen, while mother works all day to bring up the back sewing. She can spend the day in amusing them and instructing them. . . ." As a contemporary song put it:

*When woman toiled for daily bread from
    early morn till eve,
How many eyes were dimmed with tears,*

*How many hearts did grieve;
But now she has her "household pet"
    and one to which she'll cling.
For labor is a pleasure now, and she
    can toil and sing—
It works alike for rich and poor, the
    humble and the proud.*

During the decade before the introduction of the sewing machine, textile machinery showed remarkable improvement. Perhaps the most notable American contribution was the power loom patented by William Crompton for weaving fancy cotton fabrics, a loom he soon adapted to the manufacture of equally fancy figured cassimeres. The latter machine all but revolutionized the woolen industry. Products from Crompton's looms at Lowell, Massachusetts, were, it was said, indistinguishable from the best hand-loom products of the Old World and cost as little as plain goods. Production was so cheapened that a fashion for worsteds and fancy cassimeres was created that spread around the world.

The American Antiquarian Society

CROMPTON'S LOOM FOR THE MANUFACTURE OF FANCY WOOLENS, 1867. Lithograph by J. H. Bufford.

STRIVE TO EXCEL.

The Library of Congress

THOMSON'S SKIRT MANUFACTORY, NEW YORK, 1859. Engraving from *Harper's Weekly.*

The effect of the sewing machine and the new textile machinery on the clothing industry, reported *Harper's Weekly* in 1859, was "almost magical." At Thomson's Skirt Manufactory in New York a thousand girls were employed and five hundred labor-saving machines were in constant use; furnishing "an indispensable article of dress" for three or four thousand ladies daily. Elsewhere in the country, shops as large and as well-equipped were also turning out ready-mades, "from the rough garments of the boatman and the ditch digger to the elegant and costly apparel of the nabob and dandy," in a flow that kept the American public uniformly well dressed. Visitors from abroad complained that it was difficult, if not impossible, to distinguish between a clerk's wife and a banker's daughter on the score of their dress.

Ready-made clothing had preceded the sewing machine in America by at least a generation. (Some ready-made clothing, indeed, was sold in the colonies as early as 1714.) At first the trade was largely confined to furnishing sailors' outfits, or "slops." Soon, however, it was learned that transients passing through such cities as New York would willingly buy their clothes ready-made to save the time and inconvenience of bothering with a tailor, and by 1850 more than four thousand shops were in the business. With the sewing machine, however, the industry became enormously more productive. A gentleman's shirt which took thirteen and a half hours to complete by hand took barely an hour on the machine; the time for making a frock coat was reduced from almost seventeen hours to something less than three, for making a pair of "summer pants" from three hours to half an hour; and so on, according to one estimate.

In housebuilding, as in clothesmaking, a new, a quicker, and simpler method of getting the job done was evolved in America during the middle decades of the last century. For hundreds of years men had framed their wooden dwellings and other buildings of heavy timbers, often more than a foot square, that were mortised, tenoned, and pegged together and then raised into position by group labor. As a traveler pointed out, sometimes, on the prairies, where heavy timber, labor, and carpentering skill were unavailable, homebuilders were obliged "to do with make-shifts, to get a home at all."

514

AN ADVERTISEMENT FOR READY-MADE CLOTHES (AMONG OTHER THINGS), MILLEDGEVILLE, ILLINOIS, 1855. The fancy cassimeres mentioned on the previous page are much in evidence.

CONSTRUCTING A BALLOON FRAME HOUSE. Engraving by W. W. Wilson. From Edward Shaw, *The Modern Architect*, 1855.

It was such a condition, he added, "that led the well-disposed pioneer of the West to adopt the method called 'Balloon framing,' which in reality was no framing at all. . . ."

However well disposed he was, the western pioneer could not adopt the new method until cheap, machine-made nails were available in quantity, which they generally were by the 1830's. The balloon frame was a construction of light two-by-four studs nailed, rather than joined, in a close, basket-like manner, the studs rising continuously from foundation to rafters. Uninjured by mortise or tenon, with every strain coming in the direction of the fiber of some portion of the wood, the numerous, light sticks of the structure formed a fragile-looking skeleton that was actually exceptionally strong. What was more important, as one architect later pointed out, "Unlike the early dwellings of wood erected in the East, no expert carpenter was needed—no mortise nor tenon nor other mysteries of carpentry interfered with the swiftness of its growth. A keg of nails, some two by four inch studs, a few cedar posts for foundations and a lot of clapboards, with two strong arms to wield the hammer and saw—these only were needed and these were always to be had."

The balloon-frame house was far more than a "make shift"; it has been generally used throughout the country ever since it was first conceived. Without its time- and labor-saving advantages Chicago and other mushroom cities of the West could never have risen as fast as they did.

Even earlier attempts had been made to solve the housing problem by prefabricating the elements of a structure at a point where labor, materials, and manufacturing facilities were plentiful and shipping them for assembly to areas of greater need. The idea was neither new nor limited to America when it was applied to mass-production methods in this country. But America provided its most extensive proving ground. During the days of the Gold Rush all the world seemed to be manufacturing houses to be assembled in California. Twenty years later it was said that the western prairies

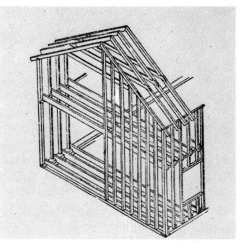

The New York Public Library
CONSTRUCTION DETAILS OF THE BALLOON FRAME, AN ISOMETRICAL PERSPECTIVE VIEW. From George E. Woodward, *Woodward's Country Homes*, 1865.

were dotted with portable buildings that had been shipped from the East, prefabricated on the principle of interchangeable parts. Such structures—schools, barns, railroad stations, barracks, and hospitals, as well as dwellings—probably enjoyed a greater popularity during the 1860's, '70's, and '80's than they ever have since.

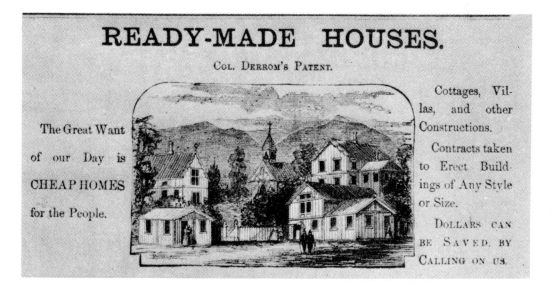

READY-MADE HOUSES.

COL. DERROM'S PATENT.

The Great Want of our Day is CHEAP HOMES for the People.

Cottages, Villas, and other Constructions.

Contracts taken to Erect Buildings of Any Style or Size.

DOLLARS CAN BE SAVED BY CALLING ON US.

The Metropolitan Museum of Art
PREFABRICATED BUILDINGS. Advertisement from the *Manufacturer and Builder*, 1871.

THE WAY TO MARKET

By 1850 man's effort to amplify, control, and vary his environment had already been freed, and with sudden swiftness, from the limitations of human energy. After millennia of struggle the conquest of want seemed near at hand. With the proper machines and a little ingenuity any necessary commodity could be produced in ample quantity.

The new machinery and methods of production were even capable of creating an embarrassment of goods unless a ready way of marketing them could be found. Until the railroads threaded the countryside the American market was largely scattered beyond easy access. To reach the extensive hinterland, self-sufficient by necessity and habit, with products it was able and willing to buy, was a test of Yankee ingenuity. If production were to be set at high levels consumers had to be "manufactured" as quickly as the commodities themselves, and brought within reach of the manufacturer.

The first and most picturesque answer to that challenge was the Yankee pedlar, that unique distributing agency, who could outwit sales resistance as cunningly as his Puritan forebears had sensed and outwitted the Old Boy himself. Even when windows and doors were closed and locked against his magic, the blandishments of his pack, as it unrolled to disclose glittering scissors and knives, gay cottons, and Connecticut clocks —notions of endless variety, including a possible wooden nutmeg, created an irresistible appeal. At every remote stop on his journey he instituted a brief bazaar. He peddled his wit with his wares in a fertile mixture of business and pleasure. Yankee notions were, indeed, a manner of thinking as well as the products of a shop. And they were distributed everywhere. "Sam Slick" put no limit to the range of his wanderings. He peddled, tricked, and swapped his way to every corner of the country—on into the shadow of the Andes—beyond all geographic bounds into the realm of myth.

A YANKEE PEDLAR AT WORK. Painting by Asher Durand.

AN AD' FOR YANKEE NOTIONS, ABOUT 1860.

The Harry Shaw Newman Gallery
A VILLAGE STORE, ABOUT 1840. Lithograph by August
Köllner.

As late as the middle of the last century, swapping remained a vital trading technique in wide areas of the country, not only of the ubiquitous Yankee pedlar and his customers, but at the stores of sizable communities. Following the War of 1812 the factories at Waltham and Lowell were among the first to pay their employees with cash. Others paid the help in mill orders. The manufacturers themselves often exchanged the products of their mills for raw materials and other necessary supplies.

Writing of his experiences early in the nineteenth century, Thomas Ashe reported that the "entire business" of the western riverways was conducted without the use of money. Storekeepers in the larger towns, he wrote, bartered manufactured goods for "flour, corn, salt, cyder, apples, live hogs, bacon, glass, earthenware, etc. . . . The storekeepers make two annual collections of these commodities; send them down the river to New Orleans; and there receive an immediate profit in Spanish dollars, or bills on Philadelphia at a short date." They then shipped to Philadelphia or Baltimore, Ashe explained, where they purchased "British and West India goods of all kinds; send them by waggons over the mountains to their stores in the western country, where they always keep clerks; and again make the distributions and collections, descend the waters, and return by the same circuitous route, of at least 5650 miles."

For many years country stores throughout the nation carried on a large part of their business by exchanging "store goods" for local produce. In the larger cities, of course,

A FREIGHT WAGON, BOUND FOR THE WEST, PASSING THE EAGLE INN, SEVENTEEN MILES FROM PHILADELPHIA ON THE LANCASTER PIKE, ABOUT 1852. From a sketch in The National Museum. *The Public Roads Administration*

merchandising on a cash basis had been common practice since early colonial days. But as industry retired first from the home and then from the immediate neighborhood to more or less remote factories, as the variety of quantity-produced articles on store shelves became yearly more impressive, the storekeeper had more serious work cut out for him. He had to familiarize the public with his changing stock-in-trade and cultivate the consumer's urge to buy.

The public, on the other hand, no longer familiar with the process of manufacture, or with the manufacturer himself, as had been generally true in the handicraft era, became more and more dependent upon what it was told about the commodities offered for sale in retail shops. On both scores advertising and salesmanship took on new importance. The more progressive merchants were increasing their store fronts and window space and giving earnest thought to the display of their wares. As told elsewhere in these pages, Captain Marryat in the 1830's found the shops of some new western towns quite as attractive and well-stocked as those of the larger English cities.

The Museum of the City of New York
An Advertisement, 1840. Lithograph by Alfred E. Baker. The copy on the elegant model's bag reads: "I'll Purchase at Bogert & Mecamly's, No. 86 9th Avenue [the store shown in the background]. Their Goods are Beautiful & Astonishingly Cheap."

The Piano, Music, and Military Goods Store of Nathaniel Phillips in St. Louis, 1842. Lithograph after F. Lemasson.

The Missouri Historical Society

A FAIR OF THE AMERICAN INSTITUTE OF NEW YORK, HELD AT NIBLO'S GARDEN, ABOUT 1845. Water color by B. J. Harrison. Photograph courtesy of the Museum of the City of New York.

With the dual purpose of spurring industry to greater performances through premiums and liberal awards, and of whetting the public's appetite for new products, the American Institute in 1828 inaugurated a series of annual fairs in New York City. Morse's magnetic telegraph, McCormick's reaper, Singer's sewing machine, and later, Bell's telephone and the Remington typewriter, all aroused wide interest through

their displays at the Institute fairs. Prominent men in every walk of life lent active support to these annual displays. Among the first honorary members of the Institute was Henry Clay. In acknowledging his election to membership Clay wrote that the association of his name with "an Institute having in view an object so patriotic as that of the American System" was to him "inexpressibly gratifying."

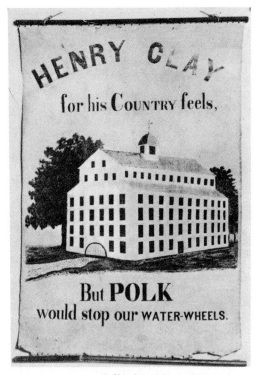

A CAMPAIGN POSTER SUPPORTING CLAY AND THE AMERICAN SYSTEM, 1844.

Clay had coined the expression "American System" some years earlier as a label for the national policy he sponsored, encouraging eastern manufacturers by a protective tariff and, with the revenue from the tariff, promoting internal improvements. Neither point won undivided support and, although a protective tariff of some sort or another has always been levied on manufactured imports, it is difficult to judge what benefits accrued to American industry from it during Clay's lifetime. The manufacturers' lobby was not strong enough, in any case, to elect Clay to the Presidency in 1844 although it pressed for higher tariffs. Nor, of course, did the water wheels stop, as the accompanying campaign poster suggests they might, with Polk's election.

Every year, indeed, the wheels turned faster; and every year a larger proportion of Americans became preoccupied with the concerns of business—with tending the complicated operations of the new industrial economy. Organizations of businessmen had been formed even during the colonial period for the purpose of exchanging the results of their experiences, of improving methods, and of stimulating trade and manufacture; groups which customarily met in the taverns and coffee houses of the larger cities.

The imposing new buildings, such as the Merchants' Exchange in New York and the one in Philadelphia (see p. 144, Vol. II), which were erected to house the activity of those organizations in the early decades of the nineteenth century, gave fair evidence of the growing importance and influence of their activities. New York's Merchant Exchange Company was incorporated in 1823 with a capital of one million dollars. Its marble "palace," built on Wall Street a few years later, was one of the city's most elaborate structures, although it was replaced by an even more costly building within fifteen years.

The "typical American business man" was already attracting the curiosity of European visitors. He was a man of extraordinary vitality who lived his business from morning to night, who was quick to speculate on greater prosperity "just around the corner," who eagerly faced the pitiless test of unrestricted competition, and for whom, some claimed, the acquisition of wealth was a form of religious exercise.

The New-York Historical Society
THE MERCHANTS' EXCHANGE ON WALL STREET, NEW YORK, 1830. Sepia drawing by C. Burton.

BUSINESS MEN AND OTHERS BEFORE THE CUSTOM HOUSE, AS SEEN FROM WALL STREET, NEW YORK, 1845. Lithograph by Robert Kerr.

In a limited sense that last characterization was true. The roots of American enterprise lay deep in the history of the country; the Puritan gospel of work by which it could be argued that man climbed to a state of grace up the ladder of success, lingered in the national psychology. Nowhere else in history, in any case, was the obligation to succeed, to better the material achievements of one's parents and to improve the prospects of one's children, so stern a duty as in this new industrial democracy.

Nowhere else, it is also true, had the individual ever had so free a field to operate in or one so generously endowed with natural resources. Neither Europe nor Asia has known the spaciousness of opportunity that opened to Americans in the nineteenth century. The invitation to explore and to exploit a land so big and so rich developed the force of compulsion. One not only *had* to

succeed, one stood an excellent chance of doing it. To conquer a continent and to hew a civilization out of the wilderness took energy, courage, and faith; but it promised immeasurable rewards to the victors in a free-for-all struggle.

In being near to the expanding western market and familiar with its peculiar demands American producers enjoyed an immense advantage over European competitors. Without hindrance from tariff walls or ocean barriers, domestic manufacturers had easy access to the most rapidly growing consuming area in the world. Their heavy sheetings, shirtings, and jeans, their charcoal-iron and bog-ore castings, their wagons and implements, while often less fine in quality than imported articles, were peculiarly suited to frontier requirements and enjoyed favor among those who were advancing across the continent.

The Chicago Historical Society

A Display of Wagons from the Peter Schuttler Factory in Chicago. Lithograph. The advertisement represents an imaginary scene at Ute Pass, Colorado.

In pursuit of his nomadic market the manufacturer developed nomadic habits of his own, moving westward with the general flow of the population. As an example, the Peter Schuttler wagon factory was established at Chicago in 1843 during the early days of the overland trail and its justly famed products were soon a familar sight from Texas to Oregon. Nine years later the Studebaker company, also manufacturers of wagons for the great migration across the Plains, was established at South Bend, Indiana, with a starting capital of sixty-eight dollars and a plant equipment consisting of two forges. In 1870 the company opened a branch farther west in St. Joseph, Missouri.

". . . here is a field for you to operate in," one Chicago magazine called to American manufacturers in 1842; "anything that you wish to have introduced into extensive use,

which you know to be really valuable, you can bring here with a good prospect of success. Bring along your machines, and also give us a chance to advertise them." Chicago was still only an infant community—in 1840 the population was less than five thousand—but Cyrus McCormick heeded the call and in 1847 left Virginia to re-establish his reaper factory in the little prairie city. His factory rose by a dreary swamp on the edge of Lake Michigan, but for McCormick that spot became the exact center of a world of promise.

Three years later a Chicago newspaper reporter ecstatically described the incessant, automatic operations of the factory where "rude pieces of wood without form or comeliness are hourly approaching [little wheels of steel] upon little railways, as if drawn thither by some mysterious attraction. They touch them and *presto*, grooved, scalloped, rounded, on they go, with a little help from an attendant, who seems to have an easy time of it, and transferred to another railway, when down comes a guillotine-like contrivance,—they are mortised, bored, and whirled away, where the tireless planes without hands, like a boatswain, whistle the rough plank into polish, and it is turned out smoothed, shaped, and fitted for its place in the Reaper or the Harvester. The saw and the cylinder are the genii of the establishment. They work its wonders, and accomplish its drudgery."

Mass production on the prairies was just in time to reap golden harvests without precedent. In the decade of 1850–60 American wheat production increased by seventy-five per cent. Single counties in Illinois produced more than a million bushels in a season.

During that decade, too, the first railroads entered Chicago from the East. The larger story of the railroads is told elsewhere. It is enough to remark here that with the spread of iron rails throughout large areas of the country, America's future as a rapidly advancing industrial state was clearly set. The railroads not only tapped the western markets, they created new markets where there had hitherto been none. They helped to people the country at a prodigious rate. They accelerated the growth of cities and furthered the concentration of industrial effort. Wherever they reached they revolutionized and systematized trade routes. By overcoming the obstacles of weather and topography they made industries continuous that had been seasonal. With the railroad the distribution of goods changed from a speculation by the manufacturer to a dependable, specialized business in itself. The way to market became a highly organized, open, and heavily traveled route.

THE LATHE AND PRESS ROOM OF THE McCORMICK REAPER WORKS IN CHICAGO. Woodcut from a company pamphlet.

The McCormick Historical Library

INTERIOR OF THE CRYSTAL PALACE, 1853. Lithograph by Endicott and Co. after C. Parsons.

In 1853 America, to take stock of its progress in comparison with the achievements of Europe, staged its own world's fair at New York's Crystal Palace. In the central court of the palace, under "the largest dome in the Western World," stood a heroic equestrian statue of George Washington modeled by the Anglo-Italian sculptor Marochetti. Had Washington, himself, visited the fair he would not have recognized the nation he had fathered hardly two generations earlier. A nation schooled in homespun frugality and asceticism was being re-educated to machine-fed prodigality and hedonism. Clothes, furnishings, and the other accessories of life that had once embodied the slowly evolving taste of an age now reflected the passing fashion of a season—the "period style" became the current year's mass-produced novelty. The craftsman had lost his place in the economic world to the skilled mechanic. The independent artificer became the wage earner. The manufacturer joined the merchant among the princes of industrial society.

The common man was becoming something of a prince in his own right. In America of the 1850's he probably enjoyed a greater degree and variety of material comfort and satisfaction than his like had known in any other society. However vulgar they may have seemed to the fastidious consumer of the day, or may seem to the connoisseur of the present, the power-tooled chairs, tables, and beds of a century ago, loaded as they often were with cheaply contrived ornament, represented to many new purchasers a first practical approach to household "refinement." For a multitude of average citizens the cheaper, factory-produced furnishings provided a deliverance from home-carpentered contrivances and an introduction to those varied comforts of home previously restricted to people of considerable means.

Emerson once remarked that he had never known a man as rich as all men should be. He applauded that prospect, so fresh and

528

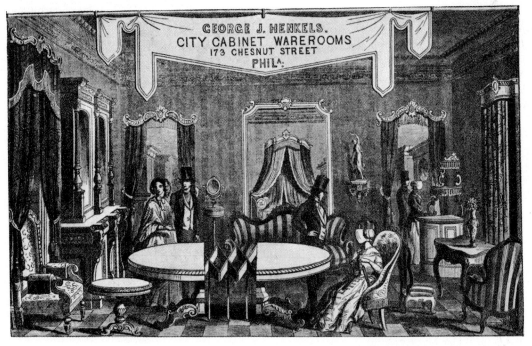

The Metropolitan Museum of Art

FACTORY-MADE FURNITURE OF THE 1850's. Advertisement from *Godey's Lady's Book*, 1850.

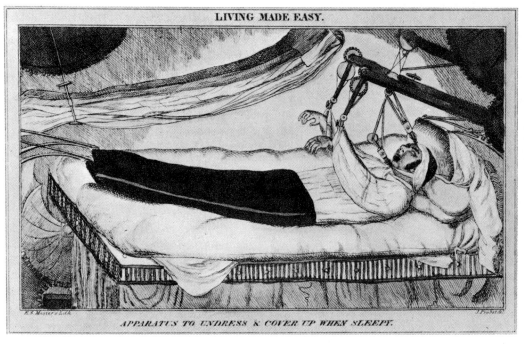

The American Antiquarian Society

LIVING MADE EASY, 1832. Lithograph by E. S. Mesier after a drawing by J. Probst.

NEW YORK CRYSTAL PALACE FOR THE EXHIBITION OF THE INDUSTRY OF ALL NATIONS. Lithograph by Nagel and Weingartner.

glittering in the day of the Crystal Palace, of all people enjoying the benefits that in the past had been reserved for the opulent. Thanks to improved technology, better means of communication and distribution, and more insistent advertising, greater quantities of inexpensive goods of a wider variety, and sometimes of superior quality, were be-

ing made, brought to market, and attractively displayed for sale before more people in mid-nineteenth century America than at any previous point in history.

At what point raising the standards of living became confused with exciting a taste for novelty and superfluity, was a question that already bothered some of Emerson's

contemporaries. The typical American's faith in some new gadget that would answer life's current difficulty was already a subject of caricature in the 1830's. After his tour of America Tocqueville reflected that the love of physical comfort, the near-passion for convenience, the confusion of contraptions with civilization, was characteristic of a new de- mocracy. Democracy held the promise of bet- ter things for everyone. ". . . to enlarge a dwelling, to be always making life more com- fortable and convenient, to avoid trouble, and to satisfy the smallest wants without ef- fort and almost without cost," Tocqueville wrote, were ideals that sometimes took the shape of heaven itself.

531

PATENT AMERICAN EXCAVATOR. From the *People's Journal*, 1854.

BIGGER BUSINESS

Quaint as they may seem measured against later developments, the industrial exhibits at the two Crystal Palaces called world-wide attention to the mechanical revolution that was so rapidly changing the course of human affairs. By these primitive beginnings man was already freeing himself from conditions of life that had remained fixed since the dawn of history. At a rate and to a degree unknown to any previous age he was gaining mastery of the materials that framed his existence. The exposition buildings themselves, made of ore and sand that had been scraped from the earth, melted, cast, and wrought into girders of iron and panels of glass, and then daringly flung in soaring domes and light, glittering arcades far over the stalls beneath—these buildings themselves were symbols of the new control man was assuming over the materials of nature and the audacity with which he transformed the elemental nature of those materials.

From the demonstrations at those first world fairs it was clear that the industrial nations would inherit the earth. The basis of the world's power was shifting from unimplemented human energy and brute strength to forces that could be generated in great quantities by power-driven apparatuses requiring the attention of relatively few skilled operators. At London an English firm exhibited an engine that possessed "the collective power of seven hundred horses"; another firm, a hydraulic press which had lifted a weight of over one thousand tons. Although a number of American exhibits won international applause, at neither fair could this country match the total achievements of England, especially in the heavy metal industries, and the world was entering an age of iron and steel used on a gigantic scale.

However, in the history of industrial development America's position was unique and fortunate. The political geography and the social climate of Europe had been more or less settled in the horse and carriage era. America, politically and socially, was only beginning to take final shape as the steamboat, the railroad, and the other factory-made tools of civilization gave a fresh direction and a farther reach to human effort. With such new appliances political boundaries could safely stretch to wider dimensions and common social ideals could spread with unprecedented freedom. With them, too—especially with the railroad, the administration of business, as of government, could be carried out on a larger scale to keep pace with the physical expansion of the nation.

So long as water remained the principal source of factory power, however, industrial plants clung to the banks of the faster running streams. Even the fuel-using industries persisted in the use of wood or charcoal long after England had turned to coal and, staying near to the retreating sources of wood, remained small rural enterprises. The total operations of such manufactures grew by the multiplication of small and scattered units at points where power of either sort was adequate. Tocqueville was "astonished," not by the "marvelous grandeur of some undertakings," but by the "innumerable multitude" of the smaller ones in America.

When coal came into general use in the 1840's American industry was practically reborn, most remarkably the primary metal manufactures whose scale of activity was gradually accepted as the barometer of industrial progress, if not, indeed, the measure of civilization itself. Even before the widespread introduction of coal, the use of metal had increased at a spectacular rate in America. During the first half of the last century the population increased fourfold, but the total consumption of iron increased more than twenty times over. Directly or indirectly each American at mid-century was using five times as much iron as his forebear had used fifty years earlier.

In spite of the fabulously growing domestic market, American manufacturers had, before 1840, already furnished locomotives to Russia, Austria, Germany, and even Great Britain. The railroad from St. Petersburg to Moscow was built by American contractors and 162 locomotives and nearly 2700 freight and passenger cars were supplied for the line by an American firm. Some years later a British railroad company bought a fifteen-thousand dollar steam shovel from America for its excavating. It was the first of these devices, so beloved by American sidewalk superintendents, to be seen in England.

The American Antiquarian Society

A COAL DELIVERY AT THE KENSINGTON IRON WORKS AND ROLLING MILLS, PHILADELPHIA, ABOUT 1845. Lithograph by Wagner and McGiugan after a drawing by William H. Rease. The plant obviously used water power for rolling the iron.

THE LAZELL, PERKINS, & COMPANY, IRON MANUFACTURERS, BRIDGEWATER, MASS., ABOUT 1860. Lithograph by Robertson, Seibert, and Shearman after a drawing by J. P. Newell. Coal is being delivered by rail at the extreme left.

The introduction of coal led to even more dramatic consequences. When coal could be hauled to the factory by railroad, the steam engine became at once a practicable source of industrial power. Freed from his dependence upon near-by woodlands, and watercourses and the limited power they were able to provide, the manufacturer could mass his operations into larger and more productive units at any selected point along the railroad tracks where labor could be attracted.

In the basic metal manufacturing industries the interplay of circumstances forced an ascending spiral of development. The railroad that brought coal to the iron furnaces encouraged improvements in smelting and other fundamental operations. Improvement in the techniques of iron manufacture, together with the availability of coal, stimulated the use of steam-powered machinery. The growing use of steam engines increased the demand for iron worked to more exacting specifications and in larger masses and, in turn, made its manufacture possible.

The need for more and better iron manufactured with the use of coal put a greater demand on railroads for more and better rails and rolling stock. The quantitative demands of the railroads themselves, as they spread in an enormous net over the continent, created a domestic market for iron and steel that no other nation could command. By 1860 the railroads alone absorbed about half the output of the country's iron mills and furnaces. The increasing volume of operations made it desirable to integrate the processes of manufacture in still larger units. Industrial organization was entering a new phase in which the problems of constantly increasing production could be efficiently centralized, if need be far from both the source of raw materials and the ultimate market for finished products.

Although such consolidated enterprises did not exist on a large scale until after the Civil War, the trend was already obvious. The Lazell, Perkins, & Company plant, shown in the accompanying illustration, was described in the 1860's as the largest iron works in New England. Its

The Harry Shaw Newman Gallery

A TRIP HAMMER AT THE NASHUA IRON COMPANY, NEW HAMPSHIRE, 1859. Lithograph by Endicott and Company after photographs by J. S. Miller.

twenty-eight buildings housed rolling mills, machine shops, forges, a foundry for brass as well as one for iron, smith shops, pattern shops, and storehouses. Five coal-burning steam engines supplemented its eleven water wheels. Everything from knives and forks and hoopskirts to boilers and engines found the way to its scrap heap, part of which is visible in the illustration, for decarbonization and conversion into new equipment ranging from small anchors to "monster guns" for the army.

The day of truly giant machinery as well as of giant industry came after the Civil War. Before 1860 some plants were equipped with large-size lathes, planers, and other tools, including trip hammers weighing up to seven and a half tons but so precisely adjusted that they could crack a walnut shell without harming the meat. Such hammers were at the time the most powerful appliances for working metal in America.

Virtually every phase of American industry, largely in the North to be sure, was given a sharp spur by the demands of the war. Even while it was engaged in the bloodiest conflict in history the North exported not only huge quantities of wheat and other foodstuffs, harvested by modern machinery and hauled to seaports by modern railroads, but manufactured products as well. The North, indeed, seemed to gain strength as it fought and emerged from the four years of hostilities with a new and arrogant faith in its prowess. Following Appomattox, northern industry went surging ahead to triumphs undreamed of in ante bellum years. To recall what had been achieved before the war in contrast to the developments that immediately followed it, observed one chronicler of the times, was like reviewing "ancient history."

Military demands for iron and steel products of higher and more uniform quality, handled in larger masses and worked to more exact specifications, had tremendously encouraged improvements in metalworking practices. Directly after the war American manufacturers undertook to make steel by the Bessemer process, a procedure which de-

MAKING STEEL BY THE BESSEMER PROCESS, 1886. Engraving from *Harper's Weekly*.

lighted onlookers with its brilliant shower
of hissing sparks as the air was blown
through the incandescent pig iron in the
converters, and which also within a few
years brought the price of steel tumbling
down. Production, meanwhile, soared up-
ward. Twenty years after the close of the
war, America was the greatest steel-manufac-
turing nation in the world. The metal that
in 1864 had been rare, costly, and restricted
to small appliances had become within
barely a score of years a basic commodity
used on a colossal scale. A large part went
into rails. The great volume of farm produce and manufactures from the West could
never have been carried to market on the
relatively soft iron rails that had earlier
served the purpose.

These were years, writes Professor Nevins,
when America became "immeasurably the
world's greatest single source of food. The
fertile prairies, netted by a railway system
which brought them next door to the European capitals, were forcing the yeoman
farmer of Yorkshire and the *junker* of Prus-

"THE ARRIVAL OF ENORMOUS QUANTITIES OF GRAIN AT . . . NEW YORK," 1877. Engraving from *Leslie's Weekly*.

"THE WORLD IS MY MARKET: MY CUSTOMERS ARE ALL MANKIND...." Engraving after a drawing by Gray Parker. From the *Daily Graphic*, 1877.

sia to the wall. American bread was baked for the table of the Berlin workman, American cheese was eaten by the French artisan, and American bacon used for the breakfast of the British clerk." These were years, too, when American shovels, buckets, axes, and similar implements were capturing such remote markets as Sydney and Melbourne. An Australian bushman, reported one trade journal in 1873, "would as soon think of felling a tree with a flint implement from the drift as with an axe of English pattern." Watches made by machinery at Elgin and Waltham were already successfully competing with hand-made Swiss models in such remote markets as Australia, Russia, and India. Russian peasants were learning to drive Chicago reapers, New Zealand farmers used plows from South Bend, and women of the world were mastering the complicated simplifications offered by New York sewing machines. By the time it celebrated its hundredth birthday at the great world's fair held in Philadelphia, in 1876, America had become one of the industrial powers of the world.

Even in the middle of an untimely business depression and amid scenes of political corruption that belied every principle to which it was pledged at its birth, the nation found reason to admire itself in the centennial mirror. What other people could reflect such remarkable progress in the material conditions of life? James Russell Lowell observed with bitter sarcasm that

Brother Jonathan could also challenge Europe to produce such examples of malpractice as were provided by Jay Cooke, Boss Tweed, and the Grant Administration. But interest centered in other things, as the popular print illustrated on pages 540-41 indicates. It had been a century of material progress unparalleled in history.

At the Exposition, Machinery Hall was the focus of attention. And at Machinery Hall nothing so aptly demonstrated America's industrial powers as that "treasure of industry," the prime-mover of all the thousands of machines at the Fair, the great seven-hundred-ton Corliss steam engine. It was the most powerful, and in many ways the most handsome, machine that had yet been built by man. Here was the fitting monument to industrial advance. Here was metal of highly refined quality, shaped to a mammoth size yet to precise scale, and capable of tremendous power. With cylinders bored to a diameter of more than a yard, gear wheels thirty feet in diameter—the largest cut gears ever made—and, among other things, thick piston rods of tireless speed and efficiency, the Corliss engine was capable of producing up to 2500 horsepower yet it ran with the quiet perfection and the authority of a pocket watch. The spectacle was enough, as one witness remarked, "to run anybody's idees up into majestic heights and run 'em round and round into lofty circles and spears of thought they hadn't never thought of runnin' into before."

PART OF THE UNITED STATES INDUSTRIAL EXPEDITION TO MEXICO, 1879. From *Leslie's Weekly*, after H. A. Ogden.
The Library of Congress

THE GIANT CORLISS ENGINE AT THE PHILADELPHIA CENTENNIAL EXHIBITION, 1876. Chromolithograph from *Treasures of Art, Industry and Manufacture Represented in the American Centennial Exhibition at Philadelphia*, Buffalo, N. Y., 1877.

THE CENTENNIAL MIRROR OR A REFLECTION ON ONE HUNDRED YEARS OF PROGRESS IN THE UNITED STATES. Published by the American Oleograph Co. on the occasion of the Phila-

MIRROR,

1876

AMERICAN OLEDGRAPH CO. MILWAUKEE

delphia exhibition of 1876.

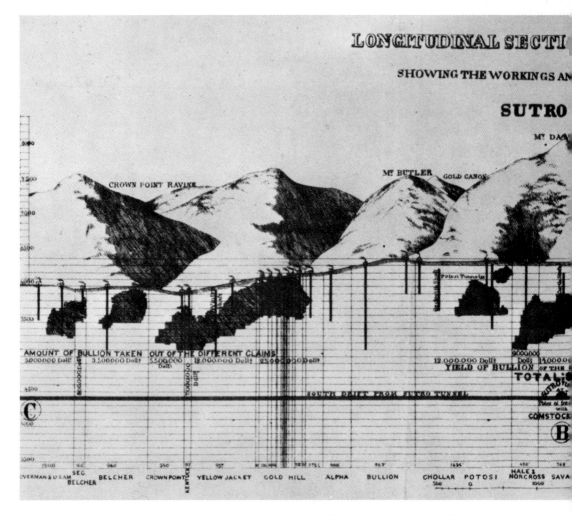

TOPOGRAPHICAL MAP SHOWING THE SUTRO TUNNEL AT VIRGINIA CITY, NEVADA. From the *Closing Argument of Adolph Sutro on the Bill before Congress to Aid the Sutro Tunnel*, Washington, D. C., 1872.

America's quick rise to industrial prominence in the years following the Civil War was underwritten by a wealth of natural resources that had barely been touched before the war. In the East of course, large areas of woodland had been cleared, the earth farmed, and the timber put to myriad uses; streams had been tapped for whatever energy their currents could supply to the lumbering water wheels of industry; and coal had been mined in some quantity to feed the iron furnaces. In California prospectors had picked fabulous wealth from the streams and mountainsides. But all this was like an impromptu rehearsal for the

great and systematic treasure hunt that got under way in the 1860's and '70's.

As we have seen, when Lincoln was elected President, the legion of farmers equipped with modern agricultural machinery had only begun the occupation of the immense and immensely fertile prairies of the West. Only gaze at the map of that great heartland of America, admonished Lincoln, and be "overwhelmed with the magnitude of the prospect presented." Beyond reach of plow and harvester, in the hills and mountains from Pennsylvania to California, lay a priceless inheritance of mineral wealth that remained almost unsuspected until the dec-

542

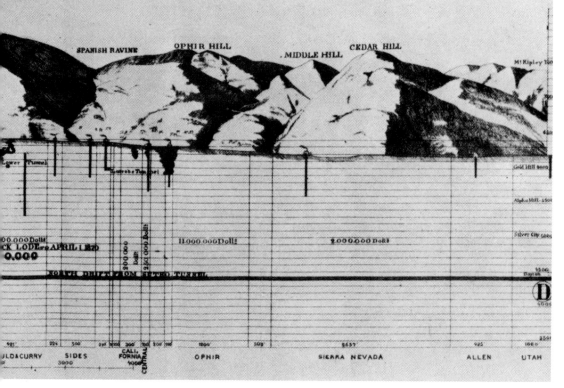

SPANISH RAVINE   OPHIR HILL   MIDDLE HILL   CEDAR HILL

The New-York Historical Society

ades following Appomattox—a large share of the world's coal, vast pools of oil, some of the greatest deposits of iron on the earth's crust, lead, copper, and silver, all in quantities beyond any reasonable expectation.

One of the most spectacular early assaults on that underground wealth was made along the eastern slopes of the Sierra Nevada Mountains near Lake Tahoe. Here, in the 1860's, one of the richest veins of silver on the globe attracted organized capital and engineering skill in a concerted manner and on a scale unprecedented in American mining. Only expensive machinery and techniques, far beyond the resources of an in-

dividual prospector, made possible the continuous and profitable exploitation of the famed Comstock Lode. Financed by more than a score of mining companies, Adolph Sutro's tunnel, almost four miles long, which intersected the lode at a depth of sixteen hundred feet, drained off the mines, and provided a practical way of carrying ore to the surface at a point near Carlson's River, was one of the great engineering feats of the last century; and for a score of years it paid extraordinary dividends.

What happened in Nevada was more or less typical of post-war developments throughout the country. At every promising

543

point large-scale, consolidated assaults were made against the holdings of nature. Within in a relatively few years great tracts of the earth were gutted of their coal and production of the mineral so precious to the newly rising factories trebled. The mining of iron ore in the Lake Superior region alone increased more than tenfold. Petroleum, which few people had heard of before the war, was by 1870 being pumped at the rate of five million barrels a year and being put to an increasing number of industrial uses.

The early history of the Pennsylvania oil fields probably illustrates most clearly and colorfully the general trend of these great extractive operations—the first, lucky "strike," the frenzied dash for wealth by speculators of every stripe, the intensive exploitation of likely fields, and the gradual emergence of a relatively few, heavily financed controlling interests whose power and ability dominated the industry.

The American Antiquarian Society
EXCITEMENT IN THE OIL FIELDS, 1865. Lithograph by Ehrgott, Forbriger Co. Cover for the "Petroleum Galop" by Oily Gammon, Esq.

PITHOLE AND BALLTOWN, 1865. Photograph by John A. Mather.   *The Drake Museum, Titusville, Pennsylvania*

Genuine Conne......e Coke

View of Bravo Works

View of Trotter Shaft

8000 OVENS, CAPACITY 8750 TONS DAILY

Process of Manufacturing Coke at the Works of the
H.C. FRICK COKE COMPANY,
CONNELLSVILLE COKE REGION PENNA
POST OFFICE PITTSBURGH PA

Mining Coke

Watering and Drawing Coke.

COKE FURNACES OF THE FRICK COMPANY, CONNELLSVILLE, PENNSYLVANIA. Lithograph by the National Bureau of Engraving.

In 1865 a general stampede to Pithole Creek, Pennsylvania, followed gushing reports from that area. Virtually overnight a town sprang up with fifteen thousand inhabitants, over fifty hotels, two banks, and the third largest post office in the state. Then, as the wells soon petered out, oildom's most booming town was quickly evacuated and it quickly reverted to an open wheat field. But more enduring discoveries were made elsewhere in the state and to process the flow of oil a great new refining industry grew up. Five years after the hollow excitement of Pithole, the Standard Oil Company of Ohio was formed with a capital of one million dollars and the great buildup of large operating units, concentrated capital, and centralized control was fairly begun.

That trend toward consolidation was the typical aspect of American business in the latter years of the nineteenth century. Organizations of vast influence exploited the natural resources of the land at a formidable rate and converted them into industrial wealth and power. When Henry Clay Frick bought the Connellsville coke fields in Pennsylvania he gained a virtual monopoly of a commodity indispensable to the new steel industry. When, in turn, Andrew Carnegie incorporated Frick's interests into his own growing steel company he took a long step toward consolidating an industry of almost imperial scope. With the further acquisition of other mineral fields, ore fleets, railroad lines, and mills, the Carnegie corporation came to control every stage in the production of steel from ore to finished article. It was the largest steel business in the world.

The functions of business carried on over such broad areas and in such a complex manner could never have been successfully integrated into a centralized structure without improved means of communication. The tempo of the whole process increased with every new improvement. Morse's telegraph had become one of "the life currents of business"—and a big business in its own right—in the post-Civil War years. Combined with the ubiquitous and speedy American press, it went far to synchronize and integrate business activity throughout the nation. Shortly after the war another new instrument was flashing numbers in the offices of brokers who were located far from the exchange. The stock "ticker," as it was dubbed, vastly widened the influence of the main centers of finance. Also shortly after the war, and after repeated, earlier failures, a cable was finally laid between Newfoundland and Valencia, 1950 miles across the Atlantic on the west coast of Ireland, and communication between America and the markets of Europe became practically instantaneous. It was a cabled message to J. P. Morgan in Germany which in 1901 enabled the financier to defeat the efforts of Edward H. Harriman and to maintain control of the Northern Pacific Railroad.

The telephone, the typewriter, and the other paraphernalia so dear to business enterprise, themselves the fruit of improved mass-production methods and for the most part American inventions, still further accelerated business traffic and added to the complexity of business life.

Quite aside from the facilities they provided, or rather because of them, the typewriter and the telephone undoubtedly increased the total volume of business operations out of all proportion to any resultant increase in effective production. But, as Thorstein Veblen pointed out, in business

AWAITING THE REPLY OVER THE TRANS-ATLANTIC CABLE, 1866. Painting by Robert Dudley. The tall man silhouetted against the window is Cyrus W. Field, who was mainly responsible for the successful completion of the cable.

The Metropolitan Museum of Art

as in war, any technological advantage gained by one competitor immediately becomes a necessity to all the rest, on pain of defeat, regardless of the ultimate cost. In the fiercely competitive strife of American business each new "necessary" gadget became obligatory on all business firms once it had been adopted by a rival, however much it may have complicated the basic operations of a firm—and however much it may have added to the nervous tensions and general discomfort of the mass of humans called upon to operate the new conveniences. Not to keep pace would be to lose some small advantage, or at least prestige, and thus to lose business. Within the scope of these contrivances for facilitating and abridging labor, Veblen concluded sadly, there was no alternative. Life was offered on no other terms. By every circumstance business grew automatically and inevitably bigger.

The American Telephone and Telegraph Co.
ALEXANDER GRAHAM BELL AT THE NEW YORK END OF THE FIRST TELEPHONE CONNECTION TO CHICAGO, 1892.

THE AUDIT DIVISION OF THE METROPOLITAN LIFE INSURANCE CO., NEW YORK, 1897. From the souvenir number of the *Weekly Bulletin* of the company.

A NATIONAL ADVERTISING SHOW AT MADISON SQUARE GARDEN, NEW YORK CITY, 1906. Photograph by Byron. The sign at the end of the auditorium reads: "If your business isn't worth advertising, advertise it for sale."

Regardless of all else, the purely quantitative accomplishments of American industry can hardly be overestimated. Within a quarter of a century after Lincoln's death America had become the leading industrial and manufacturing nation in the world. Large-scale mechanized enterprises were looting the earth of its natural treasures and turning them into a fast-flowing abundance of consumers' goods that revolutionized the traditional ways of ordinary living. "Two pounds of ironstone mined upon Lake Superior," exulted Andrew Carnegie, describing a typical instance in this growing miracle of production, "and transported nine hundred miles to Pittsburgh; one pound and one-half of coal, mined and manufactured into coke, and transported to Pittsburgh; one-half pound of lime, mined and transported to Pittsburgh; a small amount of manganese ore mined in Virginia and brought to Pittsburgh—and these four pounds of materials manufactured into one pound of steel, for which the consumer pays one cent." Compared with that complicated and productive operation, as the Beards pointed out, the deeds of the ancient pyramid builders were banal and practically useless.

For the builders of the new, economic pyramids all things seemed possible. The ancient belief that the want of material goods was a natural condition of human life had been reduced to a quaint superstition. And there was no visible limit to the growing output of the American industrial machine. There was, indeed, no simple way of stopping the machine from outracing the demands it had arisen to satisfy. The modern dilemma, already apparent in the earlier, primitive days of machine technology but now grown large and acute, was how to induce the mass of people to want more than they could be decently satisfied with, so that mines and factories could continue and increase their output.

The rise of large-scale commercial publicity in answer to that dilemma, during the latter decades of the century, opened a new era in American culture. Never again would the average citizen be able long to free his attention from the insistent claims of advertising matter in myriad forms. Visitors from abroad during the 1880's and '90's complained that this country was daubed from one end to the other "with huge white-paint notices of favorite articles of manufacture." Even more ubiquitous and inescapable was the colossal volume of promotional material that all but took over the columns of newspapers and magazines during those same years. The art was then only in its childhood but it had already become a separate big business involving enormous outlays of money, labor, and ingenuity. And it was already, for better or worse, influencing the American way of living to an incalculable degree.

The Library of Congress
MAKING USE OF THE PRESENT MODE OF ADVERTISING. Cartoon by Hamilton, from *Judge*, 1886.

THE TRIUMPHAL PROGRESS OF A RAILROAD "CHIEFTAN" THROUGH WESTERN AMERICA, 1885. From *Judge* magazine. The placard on the front of the locomotive refers to the notorious reply "The Public be Damned," attributed to William Vanderbilt when he was asked by reporters why he did not give more consideration to the public in operating his railroads.

"I am of the opinion," wrote Tocqueville in the 1830's, ". . . that the manufacturing aristocracy which is growing up under our eyes is one of the harshest that ever existed in the world; but at the same time it is one of the most confined and least dangerous. Nevertheless, the friends of democracy should keep their eyes anxiously fixed in this direction; for if ever a permanent inequality of conditions and aristocracy again penetrates into the world, it may be predicted that this is the gate by which they will enter."

A half-century later Lord Bryce felt that the confinement Tocqueville noted had vanished and the danger grown present and large—that out of the fierce competitive struggle for business new leaders of industry in control of large organizations had emerged whose powers had "developed with unexpected strength in unexpected ways, overshadowing individuals and even communities" and menacing the very freedom of American society.

The truly gigantic corporations of the next century were only dimly foreshadowed at the time of Bryce's first visit to America. Yet the centripetal movements of American business that had their beginnings before the Civil War were swirling in larger and swifter patterns. The railroads were already controlled by a relatively few "chieftains," as Bryce called them. "Nearly all the great lines are controlled and managed either by a small knot of persons or by a single man," he wrote. ". . . These railway kings are among the greatest men, perhaps I may say are the greatest men, in America. They have wealth . . . they have fame . . . they have power, more power—that is, more opportunity of making their personal will prevail—than perhaps anyone in political life, except the President and the Speaker, who after all hold theirs only for four years and two years,

"AND HE ASKS FOR MORE." Monopoly, astride its profits, asks for more tribute from the farmer, the gardener, the mechanic, the merchant, and the laborer. Lithograph by Louis Dalrymple. From *Puck*, May 7, 1890.

while the railroad monarch may keep his for life. When the master of one of the greatest Western lines travels toward the Pacific on his palace car, his journey is like a royal progress. Governors of States bow before him; legislatures receive him in solemn session; cities seek to propitiate him, for has he not the means of making or marring a city's fortune?"

In industry the advantages of consolidation were many. More inclusive operations under centralized control increased economy and efficiency. As factories grew more prolific the embarrassment of overproduction became intolerable. In a competitive market there could be no slowing up, for the basic condition of cheap, automatic, mass manufacture was "running full." To pause or to stop meant ruin, as Andrew Carnegie pointed out in explaining the genesis of the trust. To eliminate competition by purchase, merger, or economic war, and thus to gain control of production limits and price levels, was as logical as it was inevitable.

Under whatever name—pools, trusts, holding companies, or corporations—such consolidation was the pre-eminent feature of American economic life as the century turned. The United States Steel Corporation, formed in 1901 with a capital of one billion, four hundred million dollars, was only the most spectacular of a score of huge business structures which by then dominated a number of the great staple manufacturing industries of America, and which exercised what were widely termed monopolies over many of the basic commodities of life.

That the new industrial consolidations, each reaching for a national market, helped to knit the country closer together than ever was clear. That the scale of their operations made possible new economies and efficiencies in production was indubitable. That the nation continued to grow in strength and prosperity while the trusts flourished is history. The chief complaint against the system was that it created—or was the creation of—a class of strong individuals who not only took more than their fair share of profits but who, as Tocqueville and Bryce had previsioned, had accumulated more power than the people and the government in the general control of American life, but whose regard for the national wealth and the public welfare was not usually a main, or even an important, consideration. Owning 149 steel plants, 250,000 acres of coal land, 112 ships on the Great Lakes, and more than 1000 miles of railroad, the U. S. Steel Corporation could have supplied Alexander Hamilton's treasury out of petty cash.

To regulate trust operations in the interest of the public welfare the Sherman Act was passed by Congress in 1890. But busting the trusts proved the labor of Sisyphus. It provided more income for corporation lawyers for greater ingenuity in devising ever new ways of getting around the law.

For a while the act was all but a dead letter in the legal archives. Theodore Roosevelt took up a cudgel against the Standard Oil Company, among others, and succeeded in breaking it up to the satisfaction of the courts. But the stock of the Standard Oil companies was more valuable after the dissolution of the holding company than before. Whatever its evils and the necessity to control them, increasing bigness in business seemed inevitable. It was just as inevitable that government's part in the regulation of matters of common concern would grow bigger.

During her visit to the United States in the 1830's, Harriet Martineau was deeply impressed by the sight of a procession of "gentlemen . . . with sleek coats, glossy hats, gay watch-guards and doe-skin gloves!" marching down Broadway "with an easy air of gentility." The marchers were the journeyman mechanics of New York — "such dandy mechanics" as she had never seen.

In America, as elsewhere, she noted, there were, to be sure, troubles between employers and workmen. "But," she added, "the case of the men is so much more in their own hands there than where labour supera-

LONGSHOREMEN'S NOON, 1879. Painting by John George Brown.

The Corcoran Gallery of Art

bounds, that strikes are of a very short dura-
tion. The only remedy the employers have
the only safeguard against encroachments
from their men, is their power of obtaining
the services of foreigners, for a short time.
The difficulty of stopping business there is
very great; the injury of delay very heavy;
but the wages of labour are so good that
there is less cause for discontent on the part
of the workmen than elsewhere. All the
strikes I heard of were on the question of
hours, not wages."

A half-century after Miss Martineau's
observation the position of the American
workman had considerably changed. He no
longer sported a glossy hat, although he continued to expect the day when he would; the
idea that a "topper" was beyond the expectation of any sober and earnest wage earner
died hard in this land of plenty. Compared
to rates in Europe, wages were still high,
although they bore a diminishing ratio to
the cost of things as well as to the share of
the nation's wealth gathered in by the captains of trade and industry. Strikes, for more
wages as well as for shorter hours, were not

The Ship Ahoy Restaurant, Seabright, New Jersey
"TEDDY" ROOSEVELT ATTACKS THE STANDARD OIL
COMPANY'S MONOPOLY. Drawing by C. R. Macauley,
about 1906.

always brief and at times they had reached a
bloody intensity. But the danger of the workmen "encroaching" on their employers had
been reduced to a ludicrous improbability—
their case was considerably less "in their own
hands." "The great coal-mining and coal-
carrying companies, which employed their

STEELWORKERS AT NOONTIME, ABOUT 1890. Painting by Thomas Pollock Anshutz.

Collection of Victor Spark

tens of thousands," reflected Theodore Roosevelt in his *Autobiography*, "could easily dispense with the services of any particular miner. The miner, on the other hand, could not dispense with the companies. He needed a job; his wife and children would starve if he did not get one." And the "only remedy" of the employers had been applied so assiduously that most of the nations on earth had been combed for labor—labor which knew nothing of the traditional American standard of living and was always ready to undercut the demands of the native and naturalized workmen.

Such an army of wage earners could hardly be organized with the same speed and concerted purpose that the administrators of industry had shown in marshaling their own interests in the years after Appomattox. It was a motley horde, recruited and drafted from every possible source, speaking a babel of tongues—but often not English—and still divided by Old World hostilities, made up of skilled and unskilled workers all competing for places in a rapidly changing mechanized economy, and widely imbued with a feeling that to join a union was to betray the tradition that this was a land of equal opportunity. Unionism implied that America was no longer a classless society, that there were social and economic prejudices which made

it no longer certain that the free individual, by the strength of his own back and character, would rise to success and prosperity by some New World law of nature. Unions would seek to prevent men like Carnegie and Schwab from rising to the loftiest heights of personal achievement. And in the success of such Brobdingnags of industry a solid part of American society saw the true moral of democracy.

During the closing years of the century a gospel of wealth was preached from high places with earnest conviction. In the long run, argued Bishop Lawrence of Massachusetts, wealth came only to the man of morality and to the man of morality the secrets of wealth would be revealed. "Godliness," he concluded, "is in league with riches." In his infinite wisdom, it was elsewhere reported, God gave success and wealth to those best suited to exercise the powers they implied—presumably to Gould, Fisk, Vanderbilt, among other less notorious stewards of the public weal.

From the top of the heap Andrew Carnegie pointed out that "the millionaires who are in active control started as poor boys, and were trained in that sternest but most efficient of all schools—poverty. . . ." From the pulpit it was further observed that the poor were always with us, that they

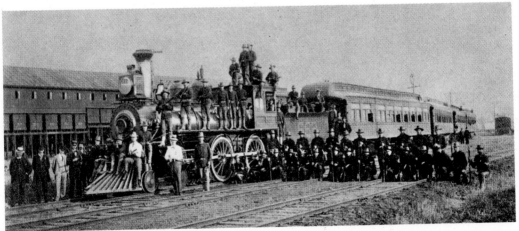

FEDERAL TROOPS AT THE PULLMAN STRIKE IN CHICAGO.

A CERTIFICATE OF MEMBERSHIP IN THE BROTHERHOOD OF LOCOMOTIVE FIREMEN, 1878. Lithograph by Hammerstein Bros. & Co. Indianapolis Lithographic Institute.

CELEBRATING THE PASSING OF THE NATIONAL EIGHT HOUR LAW FOR GOVERNMENT EMPLOYEES, 1868. Lithograph by Britton and Rey.

wore the badge of failure from their own shortcomings, and that they must in all conscience accept the leadership and charity, if any, of the nobles of industry. Unemployment itself, added the Governor of Massachusetts, was to all intents an act of God.

The advance of organized labor against such traditional and annointed habits of thinking is one of the most significant developments of recent American history, a development still too new and unfinished for clear appraisal. Only in comparatively recent years has the American labor movement won anything like general social approval. For years the strike, whatever the circumstances, was widely regarded as unpatriotic, justifiable in other nations, perhaps, but un-

American. (The august president of Harvard, Charles William Eliot, called the strikebreaker the true American hero.) The use of private detectives or of state-controlled police to breach employees' picket lines in the interest of management was condoned by public opinion and supported by the courts. In the Pullman strike of 1894 the federal government itself seemed to take a stand directly antagonistic to union labor by sending federal troops to subdue the strikers —and by issuing an injunction which, while aimed at Eugene V. Debs, in effect enjoined any private citizen from trying to persuade a railway employee to exercise his right to terminate his contract with his employer.

The struggle of labor against such heredi-

tary obstacles was continuous and sangui-
nary. Between 1881 and 1906 some thirty-
eight thousand strikes and lockouts took
place, involving almost ten million workmen
and precipitating an exceptional amount of
violence. As the century turned the economic conflict was far from resolved,
although organized labor had taken its first
long steps towards recognition. By 1900
thirty-six states had labor agencies of some
sort and the federal government itself
included a bureau of labor. The American
Federation of Labor, most important of the
large organizations, counted more than half
a million members and had trebled that
number five years later. "The Big Four" railroad brotherhoods had established satisfactory relations with their employers. In the
central bituminous coal fields the United
Mine Workers had won important victories.
Although most employers actively resisted
labor's demand for an eight-hour day—that
centuries-old utopian standard reported by
Sir Thomas More—at the Carnegie steel
plant at Braddock it was discovered with
some surprise that the men produced more
in eight hours than they could in twelve.

So far, however, the advancing unions
included only skilled laborers, and by no
means a majority of them. The unskilled
and semi-skilled remained largely unorgan-
ized and impotent, too often the victims of
conditions which no gilded aphorisms could
brighten and which no apologist could
reconcile with the boasts of triumphant
democracy. It was only one token of an
uncontrolled situation that the list of "gainfully employed" children under fifteen years
of age was steadily mounting as the new century dawned. "I shall never forget my first
visit to a glass factory at night," wrote John
Spargo in 1906. "It was a big wooden structure, so loosely built that it afforded little
protection from drafts, surrounded by a high
fence with several rows of barbed wire
stretched across the top. I went with the foreman of the factory, and he explained to me
the reason for the stockade-like fence. 'It
keeps the young imps inside once we've got

The Museum of the City of New York
A CARRYING-IN BOY IN A VIRGINIA GLASS FACTORY,
1911. Photograph by Lewis W. Hine from the Jacob
A. Riis Collection. "He works all night every other
week."

'em for the night shift,' he said. The young
imps were, of course, the boys employed,
about forty in number, at least ten of whom
were less than twelve-years of age. It was a
cheap bottle factory. . . . Cheapness and
child labor go together. . . . The hours of
labor for the night shift were from 5:30 P.M.
to 3:30 A.M. I stayed and watched the boys
at their work for several hours and, when
their tasks were done, saw them disappear
into the darkness and storm of the night.
That night, for the first time, I realized the
tragic significance of cheap bottles."

The poverty that drove youngsters to toil
like that was indeed, as Andrew Carnegie
pointed out, the sternest of all schools; but it
was not exactly a breeding ground for millionaires. Theodore Roosevelt, reflecting on
the widespread evidence of poverty in the
country, thought it constituted "a standing
menace," not merely to the prosperity of
America but "to our very existence."

THE WORLD OF TOMORROW

Thomas Jefferson once declared that he liked the dreams of the future better than the history of the past, in which statement he spoke for most of his countrymen. That preference was not simple escapism, for in America tomorrow meant always and certainly a day of bigger and more industrious undertakings. Compared with such confident expectations the records of the past and the realities of the present were trivial; normalcy was constant, energetic growth and improvement. As Lord Bryce aptly put it when he revisited America after an absence of twenty years, everybody, from the workman to the millionaire, had "a larger head of steam on than his father had."

As the nineteenth century waned and then gave way to the twentieth, that faith in progress burned brighter than ever before in the history of the country. Even "the standing menace" of poverty and unemployment that Theodore Roosevelt had lamented would surely disappear before the advances of an industrial civilization so richly endowed. Statisticians could already show on the curves of their graphs that, despite the great concentration of wealth in the hands of a few, by "tomorrow" the laborer would be working fewer hours, his pay would gradually rise, and the poor, if always with us, would be better off. So, at least, one of them proved in the *Atlantic Monthly* late in the century.

The brighter tomorrow promised for the twentieth century was given a dramatic rehearsal at the World's Fair that opened in Chicago in 1893. The Great Exposition was the herald of the Age of Electricity. Here for the first time the general public got an impressive notion of what electric service might do for it. Electric lights had already been installed in the streets of several cities, several thousand street cars were already traveling over more than two thousand miles of track in the nation, and in various other ways the new force had been applied

THE WORLD'S COLUMBIAN EXPOSITION AT NIGHT, CHICAGO, 1893. Photograph by W. H. Jackson from *The White City*, Chicago, 1893 (?).

The Metropolitan Museum of Art

to human service. But even among sophisticates there had been some bewilderment and skepticism at the prospect of a queer brightness enclosed in a glass bulb that obeyed the pressure of a button and of cars speeding through the streets without any visible means of propulsion. Mysteries were involved beyond ordinary understanding.

At Chicago, however, electricity was everywhere, for all to see and believe, performing tasks of every description. At night the fair itself was bathed in the "unearthly beauty" of electric lights. "Toward the east," wrote one awed visitor, "darkness is setting over the waters of the lake. Northward and to the west a heavy pall of smoke broods over the great midcontinental metropolis, and far to the south the lurid flames of a blast furnace are faintly visible on the dusky horizon. Suddenly a beam of light shoots like a falling star from the lofty dome of the Administration building, and a moment later its symmetrical outlines stand out in tracery of fire. At its base is a circling wheel of light, and a hundred torches further relieve the black abyss beyond. Meanwhile a thousand lamps, clustered around the central avenue, have turned the night into day."

To many this almost supernatural revelation was illuminating in every sense of the word. By daily practical demonstrations it became apparent even to the minds of very ordinary people that power—power that could be converted into light or motion or heat—could be dispatched through a thin copper wire wherever it was needed. "Sell the cook stove if necessary and come," Hamlin Garland enthusiastically wrote to his aged parents. "You *must* see this fair." They came, and they cried at the contrast of that world of promise to the realities of life on their Dakota farm.

The giant reciprocating steam engines which generated the power that turned the dynamos at the fair were themselves objects of awed curiosity. The Allis-Corliss engine used in the operation of two of the dynamos was probably the greatest stationary engine in the world.

Seven years later at the Paris Exposition, Henry Adams was guided through the mysteries of Electricity Hall by Samuel Langley, the pioneer in aeronautics. "To him," wrote Adams, "the dynamo itself was but an ingenious channel for conveying somewhere the heat latent in a few tons of poor coal

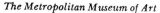

THE GREAT ALLIS-CORLISS ENGINE AT THE CHICAGO FAIR, 1893. Illustration from Hubert Howe Bancroft, *The Book of the Fair . . .*, Chicago, 1893.

The Metropolitan Museum of Art

hidden in a dirty engine-house carefully kept out of sight; but to Adams the dynamo became a symbol of infinity. As he grew accustomed to the great gallery of machines, he began to feel the forty-foot dynamos as a moral force, much as the early Christians felt the Cross. The planet itself seemed less impressive, in its old-fashioned, deliberate, annual or daily revolution, than this huge wheel, revolving within arm's-length at some vertiginous speed, and barely murmuring—scarcely humming an audible warning to stand a hair's-breadth further for respect of power—while it would not wake the baby lying close against its frame. Before the end, one began to pray to it; inherited instinct taught the natural expression of man before silent and infinite force. Among the thousand symbols of ultimate energy, the dynamo was not so human as some, but it was the most expressive."

Meanwhile, the invention and improvement of the turbine had made it possible to develop water power as well as steam power, on an unprecedented scale. As much potential power was daily flowing over Niagara as was contained in all the coal mined throughout the world during the same period. In 1895 the enormous cataract was harnessed, with the aid of gigantic turbines designed in Switzerland, for the production of electrical power.

By later standards it was a toddling step toward generating power in great volume. But, at the time, the transformation of Niagara's magnificent torrent into measurable units of available energy was like the transmutation of a fleeting, uncontrollable dream into a tangible, practical reality. H. G. Wells, who visited the falls in 1905, admired them, not for their sheer beauty as travelers usually do, but for their almost infinite serviceability as a power source. He looked forward to the happy day when all their "froth and hurry . . . all of it, dying into the hungry canals of intake, should rise again in light and power, in ordered and equipped and proud and beautiful humanity, in cities and palaces and the emanci-

pated souls and hearts of men."

In the past mills had been located at the place where power was generated, were it water or steam, within reach of shafts, gears, or belts. With electrical transmission factories could be placed almost at will and power carried to them over constantly increasing distances by the most tenuous devices. "By 1902," wrote Victor S. Clark, "a transmission line carrying 40,000 volts and more than 200 miles long was in constant and successful use between the mountains and San Francisco . . . the Niagara station was supplying electricity to consumers 185 miles away."

Power had become amazingly flexible, mobile, and delicately attuned to the largest or the smallest demand. It could be "piped" into big industrial plants in heavy loads or threaded into the home in small allotments suitable for individual needs. For a few cents an hour common man, at his job or in his home, came into an inheritance of energy which he could tap at will and which no absolute monarch of the past, for all his men and horses, could have commanded for his personal service. In a sense, one threw a switch or pushed a button and a Niagara Falls did the work.

For the sake of economy and in the interest of general public utility, separate companies evolved with the specific purpose of generating "juice" for home, hospital and factory, for city streets and, gradually, for remote farms. Although most of the companies were privately controlled, their continuous and efficient operation became a matter of vital interest for the public welfare—a matter of life and death for increasing millions of people, and subject to increasing governmental regulation. Perhaps nothing so heavily underlined the growing interdependence of people within our mechanical civilization as the occasional breakdown of a major power plant.

"Electricity," exulted one writer at the time of the Chicago fair, "is the half of an American . . . no nation has displayed such aptness in adapting [the new discovery] to

FLEXIBLE POWER.

practical use." That may have been, but to the world at large the most typical industrial achievement of America was the extraordinary methods of production that had developed into a recognizable system before the First World War, notably "Fordism." At Ford's plant, in those last rosy years of peace, the future pattern of mechanized mass production was set, a pattern which attracted industrialists the world over to witness and ponder.

As earlier stated it was Henry Ford who finally combined Whitney's and Evans's systems into a modern method of power-driven assembly-line manufacture. Ford, of course, went well beyond that. Taking advantage of the time and motion studies made in the interest of scientific shop management by the Philadelphia engineer, Frederick Winslow Taylor, Ford arranged the sequence of operations in his factory so that work was conveyed past files of specialized workmen in a non-stop flow; each workman had every second necessary to do his particular job,

"but not a single unnecessary second"; no workman had to stir from his post, or stoop for anything; every part, each a precise duplicate of countless others, was conveyed where it was needed for assembly in a vast tributary system of synchronized currents; wherever possible routine replaced human skill, machines replaced human strength. The American system of manufacture had reached a degree of refinement where even humans had carefully prescribed, automatic functions. Just as war broke out in Europe in the spring of 1914 the time required for the final assembly of a Model T, which had taken twelve and a half hours a year earlier, was reduced to ninety-three minutes. Ford dreamed of producing a car every minute and, in time, his factory did somewhat better than that.

When the war reached America in 1917 it created sudden challenges that the nation's industry, for all its aggressiveness and "know-how," could not answer. Ships were needed in unheard-of quantities; clothing

THE FINAL ASSEMBLY LINE AT THE FORD MOTOR COMPANY'S HIGHLAND PARK PLANT, 1913. Bodies were skidded down the wooden ramp and lowered onto the chassis as they moved along below.

The Ford Motor Company

and equipment, coal, steel, guns, ammunition,—materials of all sorts—wanted on a scale that beggared any past experience. "The supreme test of the nation has come," Wilson appealed in a White House pamphlet. "We must all speak, act, and serve together!" But America's economic enterprise, highly individualistic and competitive by long tradition, was not geared that way, however patriotic the intentions of its leading spirits. For a short while chaos reigned as rival organizations got in one another's way in their strenuous efforts to rise to the demands and possibilities of the moment. Three months after war was declared the War Industries Board was set up as a planning agency for the nation's entire economy. Under completely centralized control, with an acceptable common objective, and with the elimination of "competitive nonsense," industry produced at a prodigious rate.

Hog Island, near Philadelphia, as one example, was converted from a dismal, soggy, salt swamp into one of the great manufacturing cities of the world. "Giant cranes were unloading huge pieces of steel and logs from the freight cars," wrote one witness of the scene in 1918. ". . . Sirens were blowing. Those titanic human woodpeckers, the compressed air riveters, were splitting the ears with their welding. A half dozen scows were dredging the river and a dozen pile drivers were descending with giant whacks upon the logs at the water's edge."

The real history of America's part in the war, as Professors Morison and Commager observe, is not so much the story of Belleau Wood and St. Mihiel and Chateau-Thierry as of mobilizing industrial resources at home. America emerged from the war the most powerful industrial nation on earth. Meanwhile the civilian population, kept fully and purposefully employed, enjoyed a higher standard of living, in general, than it had ever known. It was a very impressive demonstration of what a planned economy could accomplish. And, as Wilson very elo-

BUILDING SHIPS AT HOG ISLAND, 1918.

Brown Bros.

Harper's Magazine
A FLAPPER. Drawing by John Held, Jr.

efficiency, literally to stick to his last; new ones were forbidden. Types of automobile tires were reduced from 287 to 9, buggy wheels from 232 to 4, and other items in proportion. After the war, that trend toward standardization was carried even further. As Secretary of Commerce, Herbert Hoover, after some nine hundred conferences with manufacturers, managed to reduce the variety in sizes and types of bricks from 66 to 4, of bed springs from 78 to 2, of milk bottles from 49 to 9, and so on down the line. Standardization of models reached a point, indeed, where critics from abroad claimed that the flappers of the 1920's, and their escorts, barring size and at a hundred feet, seemed to be as uniform as Ford cars.

Ford cars, in turn, were hardly more uniform than the facades of chain stores that sprang up throughout the country—grocery, cigar, drug, five-and-ten-cent stores, restaurants, and other sorts of centrally managed outlets which offered services and relatively inexpensive mass-produced goods of uniform quality. At chain hotels, wrote one traveler in the twenties, the rooms were so much alike that he could remember in what city he was only by posting a local newspaper on the wall.

Another thing learned from wartime experience was the technique of large-scale propaganda. The campaign to mobilize public opinion in support of the Allied cause

quently pointed out, America had gone to war to prove the efficacy of co-operation by men of good will and moral purpose.

One of the lessons learned from wartime experience was that in almost every industry commodities had been made in a profusion of sizes and shapes far beyond any special need or convenience such a variety might serve. By War Industries Board regulations the shoemaker was obliged, in the name of

YOUTHS (arriving in New York)—And to think that we've been kidded all our lives for being twins!

The New York Public Library
ANOTHER ASPECT OF STANDARDIZATION. Cartoon by Donald McKee from Life magazine.

THE FIVE AND TEN; A WOOLWORTH STORE IN ROCHESTER, N. Y. Photograph by Rowe, 1948.

had developed such effectiveness that, sped on its way by all the means of instant communication, it reached, not only every remote corner of the United States, but distant homes in faraway lands, encouraging a uniformity of outlook that lingered into the years of peace.

From such successful practices the high-pressure advertising of the 1920's—and later years—was born without a pain, except perhaps to the consumer. "The whole bag of psychology has been up-ended and shaken out," wrote Stuart Chase, summarizing that development, "to provide word patterns which can make people do things they had not planned to do, buy things they have no use for, believe things they never thought possible, see things which are not there, fear things which do not exist, hope for things which are unattainable." That much of the advertising was misleading, if not dishonest, was undeniable. But the new techniques of mass dissemination of information and misinformation created situations which were not anticipated by those who had guaranteed freedom of speech in our land.

THAT LIBERTY SHALL NOT PERISH FROM THE EARTH BUY LIBERTY BONDS

FOURTH LIBERTY LOAN

The Museum of the City of New York
ADVERTISING THE CAUSE OF DEMOCRACY, 1918. Lithograph by Joseph Pennell.

INSTALLING A WATER WHEEL AT FORT LOUDOUN.

According to the *Commerce Yearbook for 1928* America then controlled almost half of the world's total available power. Forty times as much energy was being consumed by the average American as by his forebear a century before, and most of that increase had come about in the few years that had elapsed since World War I. By 1944 the Tennessee Valley Authority (T.V.A.) system alone was producing almost half as much energy as the utilities of the entire country had produced in 1917. "These figures have deep human importance," writes David Lilienthal. ". . . A kilowatt hour of electricity is a modern slave, working tirelessly for men. Each kilowatt hour is estimated to be the equivalent of ten hours of human energy; the valley's twelve billion kilowatt hours [per year] can

be thought of as 120 billion man hours applied to the resources of a single region!"

The most distinctive characteristic of the modern age of mechanized power was the manner in which power was parceled out to the general public, on a purely impersonal basis, either from a central source or through small producing units like the internal combustion engine. The increase of the number of autos alone was phenomenal during the 1920's. At the close of the decade, one writer estimated, more than three quarters of the nation's prime-mover capacity was located under the hoods of pleasure cars. Adding to that the other sources of power that the average American citizen could tap, it was as though he held in command a large gang of alert, mechanical servants ever and willingly at his service.

The word service had taken on a new meaning in this modern mechanized world. The vastly extended use of machinery in everyday life had made its maintenance a large-scale business in itself. "Fifty years ago," Dr. Clark pointed out, "the itinerant tinker and the village blacksmith supplied this need for the average community. Today the most conspicuous aid of our mechanized society is the automobile service station. But even in this technical sense, service calls for less and less manual labor and now consists chiefly in supplying machine parts. . . . The highly skilled tool maker is still indispensable, but the common craftsman has been displaced. His service has disappeared, and the service of the supply shop has taken its place." In the actual building of the machines human intervention was being reduced to designing, testing, and assembling parts produced by automatic power-driven tools.

The Standard Oil Company of New Jersey
MECHANIC GREASING A CAR. Photograph by Bubley.

A SERVICE STATION IN CHEROKEE, OKLAHOMA, 1947. Photograph by Todd Webb.
The Standard Oil Company of New Jersey

The Standard Oil Company of New Jersey
AN INDUSTRIAL LABORATORY, 1949. Photograph by
Bubley. The Chemical Division of the Esso Research
Center at Linden, New Jersey. An oxidation unit
built to prepare oxygenated compounds.

Many of the early advances in American industrial techniques had been the handiwork of practical men, men who contrived new machinery out of their daily experience in the workshops and who improvised slapdash, if often inspired, expedients to master the workaday problems of production. Even as late as the 1870's, it is said, one of the important figures in the development of the Bessemer process, John Fritz, made most of his drawings for new machinery with chalk on the floor of the pattern room. Once a new machine was built he would say: "Now, boys ... let's start her up and see why she doesn't work."

By the time American production went into high gear, during and immediately after World War I, the rule-of-thumb superintendent had been largely replaced by the expert technician, instinct had given way to laboratory specifications, and ordinary human judgment had been superseded by scientific management. Staggering increases in efficiency and production were made. In the

A FULLY AUTOMATIC ASSEMBLY LINE: RIVET-SETTING IN A GENERAL ASSEMBLY UNIT. As carriers move from station to station giant jaws of the rivet-closing machines move up to the automobile frames and squeeze the cold rivets shut. A frame moves off this assembly line every eight seconds.

The A. O. Smith Corporation

ten years following the war the output per person engaged in manufacturing increased more than fifty per cent. Ford boasted that raw iron ore delivered on Monday morning could be marketed as a finished automobile by Wednesday noon, allowing fifteen hours for shipment.

It is difficult to place such recent developments of technology in historical perspective, not so much because they have involved new principles as because they have proceeded at such a bewildering, accelerating pace. The achievements of the 1920's, immense as they were compared with those of the century's early years, were dwarfed by those of the last two decades. Statisticians who chart the mounting curve of production are among the busiest people in our civilization.

In the long view much that has developed in the last quarter of a century is the inevitable growth of trends that reach far back into the American past. The fully mechanized assembly line, beginning with an "au-

tomatic inspector" and ending in unbelievable stacks of identical finished products made almost entirely by inanimate energy and machinery, is but the logical fulfilment of Whitney's century old dream "to substitute correct and effective operations of machinery for that skill of the artist which is acquired only by long experience."

Back in the 1830's William Ellery Channing had preached that the human being in industry must not himself be reduced to a machine, "made to be kept in action by a foreign force, to accomplish an unvarying succession of motions, to do a fixed amount of work, and then to fall to pieces at death. . . ." A century later the earlier need to supplement the nation's insufficient manpower with mechanical aids and shortcuts was developing into a technology that threatened to eliminate the man altogether. In 1940 Dr. Channing might have seen an automatic strip mill in which, on a floor almost a half-mile long, not a single workman was visible.

STACKS OF PAINTED AUTOMOBILE FRAMES FRESH FROM THE ASSEMBLY LINE, READY FOR LOADING IN THOUSANDS BY GIANT CRANES INTO FREIGHT CARS.

The A. O. Smith Corporation

FRACTIONATORS AT THE PHILLIPS GASOLINE PLANT, BORGER, TEXAS, 1942. Photograph by John Vachon for the Farm Security Administration.

Where the men were who were not being called upon to operate the new machinery was a question not seriously pressed in the 1920's. Many had transferred their activity to selling and servicing what the machines made. Others were absorbed by expanding industries that manufactured new products. But there were probably between two and three million unemployed, many of them displaced by machinery, even during the piping late days of that decade. However, the combination of advancing technology and unrestricted, competitive private enterprise would, it was assumed by those whose assumptions carried weight, still provide a "natural" solution for society's worst difficulties, as in the long past.

While Coolidge and Hoover kept government out of business with almost religious zeal, the nation's privately managed industries passed from one triumph of production to another. "We have not reached the goal," announced Hoover in 1928, "but given a chance to go forward with the policies of the last eight years, and we shall soon with the help of God be within sight of the day when poverty will be banished from the nation."

Five years later, in the trough of the Great Depression, nearly one third of the working force of the country was seeking work and not finding it and going hungry as a consequence. The moral beauty of free enterprise had not been widely questioned in America, although it had some keen critics. "Private profit a public advantage" was a pat phrase freely used by men of good will to excuse the need of any concerted social objective in their pursuit of success. But the formula completely broke down in the 1930's for innumerable reasons that are still being discovered. Any system that could bring a people to its knees, workless and hungry amid plenty, seriously needed re-examination.

Most Americans considered the Great Depression an aberration of natural law and history. Actually it had been increasingly clear for years that no industrialized country could permit unrestrained economic enterprise without disastrous social consequences. The false glamour of the 1920's obscured the

THE PARADOX OF PLENTY, DUBUQUE, IOWA, 1940. Photograph for the Farm Security Administration by John Vachon. An interested bypasser scans a sign of the National Association of Manufacturers.
The Library of Congress

Workers Balloting at a National Labor Relations Board Election for Union Representation at the River Rouge Ford Plant, 1941. Photograph by Arthur Siegel for the Farm Security Administration. Up to the end of January, 1941, the board dealt with almost thirty-three thousand cases involving nearly seven million wage earners.

point; but it became painfully evident in the following decade. For all its freedom of action, and despite its enormous potential, private enterprise of the traditional sort was impotent and bankrupt and the federal government inescapably became executor and receiver. As never before, in a multitude of ways, the government began to impinge upon the lives of citizens.

From now on there would be less planning by the captains of industry, benign and wise as they might be, and more planning by the chosen representatives of the people, inept and limited as they could be. That wholesale invasion by the state of areas in the past reserved for private business, observed Stuart Chase, was the most important social change of recent times. "There is as yet no name for this invasion," he wrote. "It is not socialism in the orthodox sense; it is not fascism defined as the last stand of big business; it is not the cooperative commonwealth. What is it? For the moment all we can do is call it 'X'."

Whatever it was it was not, as many believed, an innovation of the New Deal. It had always taken a considerable amount of government "meddling" — through land grants, tariffs, subsidies, special services such as postal delivery, public schools, highway construction and maintenance, etc.—to make a free-enterprise economy work effectively. The pace and degree of intervention had increased with breathless rapidity to meet the challenge of the times. But in theory and practice it was in harmony with the long-established American tradition that the state "must be permitted to pass such rules and regulations as may be necessary for promoting the general welfare of the people."

In the words of Professors Morison and Commager: "Historically the Franklin D. Roosevelt administration did for twentieth-century American capitalism what the Theodore Roosevelt and Wilson administrations had done for nineteenth-century business enterprise: it saved the system by ridding it of its grosser abuses and forcing it to accommodate itself to larger public interests. History may eventually record Franklin D. Roosevelt as the greatest American conservative since Alexander Hamilton."

573